THE GOLDEN THREAD

Bruce Meyer

THE GOLDEN THREAD

A Reader's Journey Through the Great Books

Harper*Flamingo*Canada

The Golden Thread:
A Reader's Journey Through the Great Books
Copyright © 2000 by Bruce Meyer.
All rights reserved. No part of this book may
be used or reproduced in any manner whatsoever without prior written permission except in
the case of brief quotations embodied in
reviews. For information address
HarperCollins Publishers Ltd,
55 Avenue Road, Suite 2900,
Toronto, Ontario, Canada M5R 3L2

www.harpercanada.com

HarperCollins books may be purchased for
educational, business, or sales promotional use.
For information please write:
Special Markets Department,
HarperCollins Canada,
55 Avenue Road, Suite 2900,
Toronto, Ontario, Canada M5R 3L2

First HarperFlamingo ed.
ISBN 0-00-200033-4
First HarperPerennialCanada ed.
ISBN 0-00-638494-3

Canadian Cataloguing in Publication Data

Meyer, Bruce, 1957–
The golden thread :
a reader's journey through the great books

Includes index.
ISBN 0-00-200033-4

1. Literature – History and criticism.
2. Books and reading.
I. Title.

PN45.M49 2000   809   C00-931209-9

00 01 02 03 04 RRD 5 4 3 2 1

Printed and bound in the United States
Set in Caslon

For Kerry, Katie,
Carolyn, Margaret and Homer

CONTENTS

THE THREAD,
THE LABYRINTH,
AND THE HERO

L O N G ago, so the story goes, there was a king of Crete named Minos whose wife did the unimaginable. She mated with a bull that had appeared out of the sea, a gift of the ocean god Poseidon. The result was an offspring with the body of a human and the head of a bull, a terrible creature of uncontrolled appetite named the Minotaur. Rather than kill the Minotaur and anger Poseidon, King Minos decided to hide his wife's shame in a palace from which the beast could not escape. In Book VIII of *Metamorphoses*, the Roman poet Ovid explained what happened next:

> Minos determined to rid his home of this shameful sight, by shutting the monster away in an enclosure of elaborate and involved design, where it could not be seen. Daedalus, an architect famous for his skill, constructed the maze, confusing the usual marks of direction, and leading the eye of the beholder astray by devious paths winding in different directions...so Daedalus constructed countless wandering paths and was himself scarcely able to find his way back to the entrance, so confusing was the maze.

Not long after the Minotaur had been confined to the maze known as the Labyrinth, King Minos defeated the Athenians in a sea battle and extracted a regular tribute from the vanquished city. The tribute was horrific. Athens would be razed to the ground unless, every nine years, its citizens sent seven boys and seven girls, the flower of their youth, to Crete, where they would be led into the Labyrinth and torn apart by the Minotaur.

Despairing that all was lost, the Athenians paid this terrible tribute several times, until a young man named Theseus volunteered himself. But Theseus was no ordinary individual. One version of the story suggests that he was the son of Poseidon (and, therefore, half-brother to the Minotaur). Another version suggests that he was the son of the king of Athens, Aegeus. Whatever his parentage, he had, at a tender age, killed two brigands who were terrorizing a local highway, and using his great strength, he had lifted a heavy stone beneath which he found a mighty sword. In other words, he had the qualifications necessary for a mythic hero. All he had to do was prove himself.

On his arrival in Crete, Theseus befriended and won the confidence of King Minos' daughter, Ariadne. He persuaded her to fashion for him a long golden thread that he would carry into the Labyrinth and unwind as he went, thus leaving a path that he could follow for his escape. He also smuggled in a dagger. Once inside the maze, he twisted and turned his way through the puzzle until he came face to face with the dreaded beast and killed it, liberating his native city from the burden of its tribute. And as he made his way out of the Labyrinth by following the golden thread, Theseus solved one of the key puzzles of the ancient world, presenting living proof that no question, no conundrum, is beyond the reach of interpretation and solution.

I always like to remind myself of this story when I am reading a work of literature for the first time. There is something challenging in every text, something that puzzles the mind and begs us to consider what the author is saying, how the author is saying it, why certain things are being said and others are not, and just what it all means. Reading literature is a matter of understanding what lies down those deep, twisting corridors, and of searching for some means of preparing ourselves for what could be encountered. Like Theseus, I look for the threads I can follow in a book to find my way through the labyrinths of comprehension. When I read, I want to see daylight at the other end; I don't want to set down a book I have just finished reading and blithely go on with my life, knowing that there was something important I missed. I despair when others go blindly into the labyrinth and hope that they will find their way out of a text—and if the text is something as challenging and complex as Dante's *Inferno* or James Joyce's *Ulysses*, I wish them luck. But I know that such a reader will, in the end, fall victim to something unexpected that lurks around the next turned page. And the victim? There are several.

The first is the reader, that poor soul devoured by a monster aptly named "I don't know." The reader has lost a glorious opportunity to grasp something that is not of the past but of the present, a statement about being human, a reminder of how we might find solutions to the labyrinths of daily life.

The second victim is the book itself, that great work of art that has lived for so long only to perish in our world of quick solutions and surface readings. It is nowhere near ready to expire into the oblivion of contemporary consciousness. In fact, most of the works that we call "the great books" speak to us in our contemporary situation so much and so often that we overlook just where certain ideas relating to justice, heroism, courage, faith, love, honor, terror, curiosity, and understanding come from. The assumption that our world is the result of ideas and events that have taken place only within the past two generations simply doesn't hold true, and the more we examine how literature functions as a continuum, the more we realize that our world is the product of generations of brilliant imaginations that, like us, simply wanted to figure things out.

And the third victim is the literature, that tradition that has been called "the greatest continuous conversation in history." I know of no highly regarded writer in our era who has not read most of the great books. For a writer, literature is not just "typewriting," as Truman Capote put it, but the extension of a series of ongoing ideas that speak directly to us. And when contemporary authors dust off an old story and reinvent it for their own purposes, they are not denying the tradition in which they are working, but adding their own perceptions to it and extending it so that the continuum will speak to future generations. Most writers realize that if the tradition is kept alive solely by the process of telling an old story as well as possible in the contemporary idiom, they are guaranteeing for their children the same imaginative, spiritual, and often political rights that they themselves have enjoyed. The stories, the golden thread of ideas, the imagination and all it contains are some of the few things that can be passed from generation to generation without the fear that something important will be lost or that the value of the inheritance will depreciate. But what keeps that inheritance alive?

Here is a simple truth: nothing prepares us better for reading than reading. Reading is a process not just of assimilating ideas but of learning the skills, the fundamental structures, and the repeated story lines that make further reading a richer, more enjoyable, and much more powerful experience. Countless authors through the ages have learned the craft of writing by reading the works of their predecessors, and in part their publications are commentaries on what they have read. But more to the point, each writer has felt an obligation to extend the tradition. Tradition in literature is not how a work becomes static over a period of time, but how it is constantly reinvented. The myth of Theseus is an example.

In its earliest form, it is a story that raises the question of what a hero does. In Theseus, we have an individual who is willing to sacrifice himself for his society; he believes in his heart that he is operating by a set of moral standards. He is willing to undertake a journey for what he believes, and on that journey he arms himself with his wits and his cunning more than with artificial weapons. He enters a world that promises certain death, a mazelike structure that would seem hellish even by modern standards, and there he confronts the most unimaginably awful creature and overcomes it. His actions, his battle, and his emergence from this deathlike world are a signal to others that great obstacles and challenges can be beaten, and his message is one of hope—that everything in the end will work out for the best. But what is most important about this simple story is the manner in which later authors retell it.

Homer uses the Theseus myth as the basis for *The Odyssey*. When Odysseus tries to return home from the Trojan War, he is blown off course. He undergoes a series of challenges—events that test not only his wits and his cunning but his will to survive. He goes down into the underworld and receives a vision of the future, and then returns to battle the labyrinthine sea until finally, after great struggles, he is able to return home, overcome his wife's suitors, and reestablish his kingdom.

Virgil tells exactly the same story in *The Aeneid*, but from a Trojan point of view. The medieval romance of *The Quest of the Holy Grail* adds a Christian twist to Virgil's "Roman" story, and Dante retells both Virgil and the medieval romances in his *Divine Comedy*. John Milton, Jonathan Swift, Voltaire, Samuel Johnson, Mary Shelley, Sigmund Freud, and of course James Joyce also get in on the act—all looking for a story that will reflect the human struggle to overcome great odds in the name of courage, honor, justice, and security, and all listening intently to what others before them have said. The amazing thing about repeated stories is that they test our own imaginations, not only by setting scenes and explaining situations that go beyond our wildest dreams, but by continually asking us to think of ourselves as the heroes and to accomplish, if even in a small way, the same tests of courage, honor, justice, and security when we encounter challenges in our own lives that frighten and dismay us.

But what is even more amazing is that all of us seem to carry this type of story inside us. The early twentieth-century poet Rainer Maria Rilke commented on this very issue in his *Letters to a Young Poet*, and concluded that we make our own stories and our own terrors because something in us needs testing and, perhaps, reassurance:

> We have no reason to harbour any mistrust against our world, for it is not against us. If it has terrors, they are *our* terrors; if it has abysses, these abysses belong to us; if there are dangers we must try to love them. And if we arrange our life in accordance with the principle which tells us that we must always trust in the difficult, then what now appears to us as the most alien will become our most intimate and trusted experience.

In other words, we learn from what we read, and what we read, if it doesn't kill us, makes us stronger. That, I think, is one of the profound benefits of literature: those who embark upon a quest to read what the broad panorama of literary texts has to offer seldom come away the lesser for the experience.

The great books that are represented in this volume are wonderful places to learn more about how our brains work, especially the way in which our imaginations are constantly referring to literature to solve our problems (even when we don't realize it). I wish that I could have included more books in this discussion. I look at those texts I have chosen and for every one of them there are twenty, thirty, or even forty more that I would have liked to include. I have selected these texts because, for me, they represent a thread that exists in literature, a series of connections that helps to explain what literature contains, and how a text expresses not only what an author says, but what we as readers need to hear.

I have attempted to show not merely how the books are connected, but how we can learn to craft our own threads by understanding the wealth of means by which the authors have created their works. At times, it has been necessary to explain some essential literary terminology, and I trust that these explanations will enlighten readers unfamiliar with some of the structural aspects of a text. A work of literature is as much a matter of how it goes about saying what it says as it is a question of what it says. Art is the balance between form and content, and I know of no author who has not recognized this truth in the composition process. Yet I also realize that the techniques themselves are part of the beauty of a text; they are the means by which writers have overcome the problems they have encountered in making their ideas and words reach into the imaginations of readers and listeners and seize upon something vital in the human spirit.

Imagine, for example, that you are in a palatial hall long ago in Greece. The moonlight off the Mediterranean is shining in through the windows, and off in the distance you can almost hear the sound of the waves upon the shingles. A cool breeze flickers the light from the braziers as the bard enters the hall. It has been a long evening and you are sleepy from the roasted lamb, the wine, and the conversation. The bard raises his lyre and begins to pluck the first strains of an epic poem, his voice clear and resonant against the night air. But you do not fall asleep, even though the rhythm of the words is lulling and the melody he sings is haunting. There are moments in what he is saying that your ear strains to listen for, benchmarks of phrases and images that make you pause and reflect on his words. And his tale, a story of a mariner struggling against the hypnotic waves, seems almost to exhaust his voice when suddenly he breaks off, having brought the hero through yet another travail, another test. He pauses. The melodic strains of his verses are continued by a band of minstrels, as dancers appear almost out of nowhere, stepping and twirling in time to the music. Off in the corner, the bard rests his voice and prepares himself to sing another episode, and you sit up on your lounge and imagine the next part of the story, because the tale is as familiar to you as your own dreams.

In that moment, from a time so long ago, you have just encountered elements of writing that seem incredibly familiar to you, the techniques of poetry and narrative verse that are still being practiced today. You have listened to episodes of a story that are told in just enough time to be sung by a human voice (a structure that is still used by novelists as they create chapters), and you have heard the language of description that fills our books, magazines, and newspapers that we devour each day. And if there is one thing that stays with you in this short journey between your own age and that evening so long ago when *The Odyssey* was performed in its original tongue, it is that the more things change, the more literature stays the same.

Throughout the centuries, writers have been trying to define just why literature mirrors our dreams for extemporality and eternity. The Bible suggests that man and woman were created in Eden into a state of timelessness, and that the fall was the entry into a world of death and toil governed by time. In the Judeo-Christian tradition, longing to escape time was equivalent to wishing for a return to paradise. In the Classical world, the longing for a timeless state was a nostalgia for the Golden Age, when humankind lived in harmony with nature. William Shakespeare thought he had the answer when, in *Sonnet 18*, he announced that the object of his affections would not fade like a summer rose because he, the poet, had encapsulated all of the beloved's finest attributes in fourteen lines of beautiful English verse:

> *But thy eternal summer shall not fade,*
> *Nor lose possession of that fair thou ow'st,*
> *Nor shall death brag thou wand'rest in his shade,*
> *When in eternal lines to time thou grow'st;*

So long as men can breathe, or eyes can see,
So long lives this, and this gives life to thee.

Shakespeare was on to something important here: inside a literary text, things never change. The story that was written long ago is the same story that someone can read a hundred, even a thousand, years from now. Writers have always recognized that a literary text—a poem, a story, a novel, or a play—is a repository where the author not only praises life and all its experiences, but also captures and freezes life for future generations to relive and reimagine.

In the ancient Mesopotamian *Epic of Gilgamesh*, the dying King Gilgamesh laments that he is a failure. He has failed to save his friend from death, he has failed in his quest for the flower of immortality, and his accomplishments in life seem to be fleeting. He wonders just what his purpose on earth has been. But at this juncture in the story, the chronicler/narrator breaks in and reminds Gilgamesh to look around at his surviving accomplishments—a city, its sturdy walls, the victories that he won over his enemies. And then the narrator interjects a small comment that seems to sum up what the poem—or any poem for that matter—is about: "Great is thy praise." The very act of praising something, of examining what makes it vital and real, and the process of conveying that information to readers so that they can reinvent the object or the moment exactly as it was: that is the purpose of literature. It is a form of sustained living.

The great authors know how to accomplish this. They understand what they are saying, how they are saying it, why they are saying it, and what it all means: the four essential questions that are part of the composition process. It should be the duty of a reader to approach the text with the same respect for the process as the writer, and with the same dedication, interest, and passion that the author has brought to the work. James Joyce may have had this idea in mind when he remarked that it had taken him ten years to write *Ulysses* and it should take a reader ten years to read it. I do not think the same should hold true for the Bible, a work of compilation and rearrangement that took shape over the course of centuries, although that possibility always exists. The point is that prepared readers enter the text with a golden thread—those four questions of what, how, why and the big what, the sum of all the parts of the reading process—to help them find their way in and out of the text, and to navigate a book's twists, turns, and dark passages. What emerges from this process, this reader's journey into the labyrinth of page after page and character after character, is the necessity of having a means of finding one's way in and out of the most impenetrable maze of ideas. These four questions allow readers to get the most from a text, and are the best way to honor a work that has so much to give. The purpose of this book, therefore, is not to provide a surrogate for reading the great books, but to create a compass by which they can be better understood. I want my readers to think like heroes, to be prepared for what they encounter, to use their wits and their cunning to find their own ways. This book is about how we can solve the labyrinth, and about how we should find the benchmarks that lead to daylight at the corridor's end.

And what of those benchmarks, those moments of familiarity that trigger recognition in the reader, that sense of "this is something I know, something I have seen before"? Literature is supposed to be familiar to us. The Danish philosopher and theologian Søren Kierkegaard remarked that the Bible always seemed familiar to him because every time he read it, he felt it was about him. As readers who have been raised in a world that is permeated by these texts—almost to the point where the texts have themselves become invisible—we are often apt to take our most important stories for granted. In fact, we so grossly underestimate the presence of literature in our lives that there is a movement among many contemporary critics and educators to dismiss the great books as works that have lost their relevance. I shudder to think, however, what modern Caribbean literature would be without Derek Walcott's splendid retelling of Homer's *The Odyssey* in a calypso manner, or what twentieth-century poetry would be without T.S. Eliot's attempt to recast *The Quest of the Holy Grail* as *The Waste Land*. Surely those critics and educators will reconsider their position, if only for the sake of future generations that will need to tell the story of a journey or a tale about how life might be restored to a parched kingdom. I believe that Homer, Dante, Virgil, and all the other great authors are still with us, and that they continue to mean the world to readers who eat, dream, make love, travel, despair, hope, fear, challenge, and persist in their pursuits of goals that always seem unattainable just before they are won. I believe that humanity will never lose its heroic ability to celebrate life, not only because that is what the great books have taught us, but also because that is the way human beings are. To recognize this truth is to grasp the first fine strands of the golden thread that can make a hero of anyone who is willing to follow his or her imagination.

ONCE UPON A TIME

The Bible

A T the center of the tradition of Western literature, one book stands alone: the Bible. No writer in that tradition can claim not to have read it or been influenced by it, even in some remote way. If Kierkegaard thought that the Bible was a story talking to him, and about him, it may have been because the Bible is not only pervasive in Western culture, but contains about ninety percent of what Western culture thinks, feels, believes, fears, loves, and desires. It is a compendium of stories that repeat themselves over and over in our moral and literary consciousness to the point that almost any story that works toward a just and happy ending is a reflection of what the Bible tells us.

At the same time, the English-language Bible, in its various translations and editions, is a work that has constantly signaled the best that the language can do. As well as a record of holiness and the articulation of divinity, it is a forum for the aspirations of what one hopes the language will express. The Bible is often called the good book because it is perceived as both a statement of what God thinks and a record of what humankind wants literature to do. Writing in 1828, Thomas Babington, Lord Macaulay, expressed the impact that this book had on the English language:

The English Bible [is] a book which, if everything else in our language should perish, would alone suffice to show the whole extent of its beauty and power.

But what does Macaulay mean by the "beauty and power" of the language? Perhaps he noticed the way in which the Bible provides us with not only a record of things we might say in literature, but also the way we can go about saying them.

The Bible is a guidebook for writers on how to make their works beautiful and powerful—a series of texts where the problems of writing have been solved in intriguing and persuasive ways. Thomas Carlyle, the nineteenth-century British historian and essayist, suggested that even the most impoverished of writers throughout the ages can be said to have learned from the Bible because it is the one book that most people are likely to own:

> In the poorest cottage are Books; is one Book wherein for several thousand years the spirit of man has found light, and nourishment and an interpreting response to whatever is deepest in him.

Carlyle realized that the Bible as a work of literature teaches us not only about the fascinating relationship between God and humans, but about the way people have tried to put that relationship down on paper. And as a response to that challenge, the writers and translators of the Bible have never failed to make the book a paragon of what literature and language can and should accomplish. In this sense, the Bible is a school for writers, and the smart ones learn their trade by reading and understanding it as a work of literature. Just about everyone, from the first English poet Caedmon of the seventh century to contemporary writers such as Toni Morrison, can lay claim to writing within the tradition that the Bible has fostered. Writers through the ages are less apt to be dazzled by content than a literary technique—give them a useful structure for saying something important, and they immediately pay attention and learn from the printed word. Among all other books, the Bible is the place where writers learn to be writers.

Yet the problem with the Bible is the very fact that it has meant so many things to so many people. As a testament of faith, it has shaped history. As a profession of the mysteries of God, it is the guide for belief that will inevitably reach far beyond our own time. But as a literary text, it has taught us how to express love, how to communicate ongoing truths, how to relate history, and how to contextualize our common desire for hope. As a work of literature, it has given us our notions of getaway vacations; the sentiments that we express on greeting cards; the pervasive societal concepts of history, lawfulness, and political order; our ability to determine a truth from a falsehood; and our notions of life and death and life after death. It is the most quoted, most copied, and most influential of all the texts that make up the great books—yet for all the impact it has on our world, it is also the one text that remains the most mysterious. It is primarily a book that speaks of love and salvation rather than hatred and punishment—witness the fact that in Western thought, our notions of hell are more the result of Virgil and Dante than of anything found in the Bible.

The amazing aspect of the Bible as a work of literature is that it gradually becomes more convincing as it moves from a position of imaginative surmise in its use of explanatory mythology to historiography or known fact, and then takes the process a step further by declaring that there are certain philosophical truths that have been borne out through a careful examination of the study of time and history. As a work of literature, it is a history of time that traces the experiences of two major characters—God and man—from the beginning of all things to the end of earthly time. In the case of man, the faces change from book to book and even verse to verse, but the theme remains the same. It tells the story of humankind's growing independence from the Creator as a kind of journey narrative, and it follows the relationship through an incredible series of events to a projected conclusion where they will be reunited. To create a tone of profound fact, it uses wisdom and the established and accepted truths about how the world operates and how human beings should behave. It uses prophecy, the process of looking ahead and predicting what might happen as a result of faith or imaginative vision, to offer a sense of certainty in what will be. The phrase "As it was in the beginning, is now and ever shall be," which enters into numerous Christian liturgies, is a reminder that there is a continuum of certainties operating in the universe, and that God has a plan for everything. The Bible's overwhelming tone of certainty is surprising when we consider it: it comes not so much from fact but from a language that is poetic, serious, open-ended, and charged with multiple meanings in its words, images, and ideas. What is even more amazing is that the Bible is a storybook. When the Bible speaks in stories, the reader is asked to interpret what they mean, and these parables and narratives always present the reader with a range of possible interpretations.

But where the Bible really establishes its power is in the way it appeals to our imaginations. For the most part, it contains narratives not about actualities, but about miraculous ideas that speak directly to our imagination. And although our modern minds tell us that we shouldn't believe everything we read, the Bible presents a compendium of various types of stories that are so powerful, they are worthy of belief. The traditional name for these stories is *myths*, a term that in recent times has come to suggest anything ranging from a fanciful idea to a complete falsehood. In literary terms, however, the concept of myth evolved by critics such as Claude Lévi-Strauss, Joseph Campbell, and Northrop Frye suggests any system of beliefs that has its foundation in the imagination or the literary text. But more than merely a narrative of fantastic events and characters that is subject to skepticism, a myth is really our means of expressing, through the imagination, what we cannot or dare not say with logic. Myths work in our minds in terms of images (the mental pictures conjured by words); we associate one mental picture with another until we have built up a vast, even slightly implausible, explanation of something. Myths are rarely logical, yet they seem to say a great deal about the way our minds work. And when we cannot come up with fact or scientific laws to explain a person, an event, or why we do things in a certain way, our imaginations take over and create an answer for us. The Bible reflects a number of different approaches to the definition of mythology, and all of them appeal to our imaginations, perhaps because they reflect the way our imaginations work. Our minds desperately want to make sense of what we see and what we experience, but when logic, science, and fact fall short or simply aren't available, the mind goes to work and invents an appreciable alternative. That is what mythology is: information that fills the vacuum of fact.

The first type of mythology a reader encounters in the Bible is *explanatory* mythology, where the structure of the universe is presented. This type of mythology shows us that everything we know is governed by a sense of order, and we are relieved because it suggests that the operative principle behind the universe is not chaos, but a plan. The explanatory mythology that we encounter in

Genesis tells the reader who is in charge of everything, how the universe was made, and how it is supposed to operate. It is an owner's manual for the cosmos. And right from the very start, God is in charge, operating according to a blueprint:

> In the beginning God created the heaven and the earth. And the earth was without form and void; and darkness *was* upon the face of the deep. And the Spirit of God moved upon the face of the waters. And God said, Let there be light; and there was light. And God saw the light, that it *was* good: and God divided the light from the darkness.

What the opening passage of Genesis tells us is that the order in the universe is artistic, operating by a sense of taste and judgment, and that the plan behind all creation is working to make things for the best. But more than merely explaining the work of a cosmic artist, this passage communicates an obvious sense of security, a feeling that order will always take precedence over chaos. This is important to the Bible, because one of its chief statements is that everything will, in the end, work out for the best; yet there is no question as to whether the world could have been made differently. In an empirical tone, it tells us that this is the way things are. Explanatory mythology seldom endeavors to ask why something was made or whether it could have been made differently. God is satisfied with it, and that seems to be enough. Like an artist hard at work on a composition, God keeps standing back from his work to make sure it is the best he can do (Gen. 1:18):

> And to rule over the day and over the night, and to divide the light from the darkness: and God saw that *it was* good.

God seems to experience the same moment of consideration that authors experience when they draft and redraft a single word or phrase in a moment of creativity. The other suggestion is that the universe is a work of art comprised of myriad creative decisions, and like a literary text is a labyrinth of possibilities.

What underlies the "creative" opening of the Bible is the notion of *inspiration*, the act where God animates inanimate objects. The word *inspiration* is derived from the Latin word *spirare*, meaning "breath." The notion of inspiration is a poetic one, and it is a concept that lies at the very heart of literary creation. If something takes on a life of its own, it is because its creator, its author, has made it so well that it becomes a living thing. By breathing into a creation, one animates it with a life force. In Genesis 2:7, God breathes into the inanimate dust that is Adam, and the consequence of this act, something akin to mouth-to-mouth resuscitation, is that Adam "became a living soul." From this story of humankind's creation comes the notion of *poetic inspiration*, the idea that the poet receives a spiritual gift from the great beyond. As a piece of explanatory mythology, inspiration suggests that the whole universe is animated and infused with life because it is both figuratively and physically the vessel containing a fragment of a greater life, the breath of God. The concept of breath as the root of poetic inspiration is a popular idea among the great poets and writers of the ages. In *Lycidas*, for example, John Milton mourns the death of his friend Edward King, who had his breath stolen from him through drowning. Explanatory mythology is the imagination's way of explaining why things are as they are, how they came into being, and what purpose they serve in the divine plan.

Jacopo Bassano. The Animals Entering the Ark. It appears that Noah is desperately trying to keep track of both the animals and the weather as the storm clouds of the great cataclysm gather in the sky. Behind him, his family try to separate the sheep from the goats.

But explanatory mythology is only part of what the Bible offers us. If explanatory mythology answers the question *why*, the second type of mythology that the Bible presents, *instructional* mythology, answers the question *how*. Instructional mythology creates a series of guides or directions for how certain tasks can be accomplished. God's commandments to Noah for building the ark (Gen. 6:14–19) read like the instructions for assembling a garden shed or connecting a new stereo system. In the spirit of *Popular Mechanics*, instructional mythology brings out the do-it-yourselfer in biblical characters, and is meant to provide the divinely inspired blueprints for certain necessary tasks. Beneath these orders and commands is the emphatic suggestion that if such steps are followed directly, everything will work out according to plan. In this sense, the characters in the Bible are instruments of a god who is a stage manager. Those who do his bidding and follow his instructions are rewarded. In the study of *rhetoric*, the art of persuasion through language, instructional or functional mythology is known as

process analysis. In process rhetoric, the details of a procedure are laid out step by step, much like a set of instructions.

Humankind's ability to follow instructions is crucial in the Bible because God has a plan and wants everything to work out properly. Milton makes a great deal of the concept of a divine plan in *Paradise Lost*, where the fall of Adam and Eve and the suffering it brings results in a newer, better life achieved through faith, salvation, and Christ's sacrifice—the game plan for *Paradise Regained*. Those who don't follow God's instructions, such as the dwellers in the wicked cities of Sodom and Gomorrah, are simply swept away; the God of the Old Testament really doesn't have time for slow learners or for disobedient students, a small matter that the New Testament seeks to rectify. Instructional or functional mythology may not seem like a major issue in the overall scope of the Bible, but it is a fundamental building block in the elaborate structure that leads to *moral* or *legal* mythology, the third type of mythology in the good book.

Moral or legal mythology is really a set of do's and don'ts. It

*Jan van Eyck.
Adam. There is
little that is
heroic about van
Eyck's Adam. He
is slightly emaci-
ated, rather
sickly and very
typical of a
middle-aged
male; yet he is
also concerned
for his dignity
and his inno-
cence.*

*Jan van Eyck.
Eve. Van Eyck's
Eve seems to
embody some of
the Medieval
ideals of beauty.
Certainly her
rotund belly and
full breasts
suggest an allur-
ing fecundity,
the sort that
would make a
man give up
paradise and
eternal life to
enjoy.*

seeks to outline taboos and boundaries of correct behavior, and offers readers a code of conduct not only in the relationship between humankind and God, but in the sphere of interpersonal dynamics. When Noah's sons discover him naked and drunk (Gen. 9:22–23), "their faces *were* backward, and they saw not their father's nakedness." Quickly, they cover Noah, and are "blessed" because they have taken responsibility for looking out for another's dignity. Similarly, when Adam and Eve are cast out of the garden in Genesis 3:7, they question their own nakedness and put on fig leaves because they are concerned for their dignity as well. In the Old Testament, failing to protect one's dignity is a serious taboo, and personal dignity a very important issue. Medieval romance, building on the idea of the Bible as a law book for proper behavior, presents an elaborate code of conduct, the result of which is that only the morally lawful, such as the perfect knight Sir Galahad, achieve the important goal of the quest. Those, such as Sir Lancelot, who succumb to moral misdemeanors fail to receive the ultimate reward of the story—the Holy Grail.

The most fundamental taboo in the Bible is God's injunction against eating the fruit of the tree of knowledge (Gen. 2:17). Adam and Eve, to the detriment of humankind, trigger the fall by failing to live up to the moral code that God has placed before them. Clearly, the consequences of breaking a taboo are severe: the law is the law. In Exodus, however, where Moses receives the Ten Commandments directly from God, moral or legal mythology becomes a major force. God finally puts his policies in writing (verbal agreements and handshake covenants in the Bible work only on rare occasions), and when Moses descends from Mount Sinai with the laws, they are "carved in stone" and become the rules by which an entire society must function.

What the presence of moral or legal mythology means for literature is that the text is more than merely a vehicle for a story; it becomes a source of lawful authority and a code that governs not only the imagination but also the conduct of daily life. The presence of moral or legal mythology in a book also stipulates, for the reader, that the text is something that must be upheld as truthful. The work suddenly becomes more than an imaginative statement: it is the core truth of a society, a source of authority, and a sacred

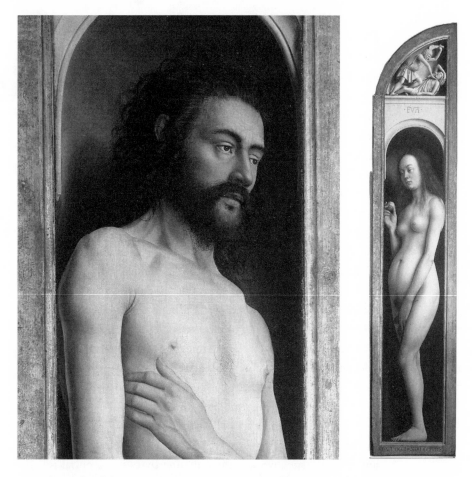

text. A work of the imagination gains considerable power when it crosses that normally solid boundary between illusion and reality. Readers are often confused when they encounter texts that blur this boundary because it often leads to a literal reading of a work. After all, once the "truth" is established it is supposed to be upheld without question and accepted as faith until a plausible challenge and re-evaluation can be presented. Saint Augustine, for one, was concerned about how to distinguish between fiction and reality. The fine line between the two is a critical distinction that is noted only by those who can separate form, content, and context. Even when this distinction is in place, the written word still has the power of authority, and the old adage "if it is written, it must be so" is a difficult obstacle to navigate. Setting jokes and satire on that fine line between fiction and reality, or between fiction and a sacred text, as Salman Rushdie discovered, can lead to all sorts of complications. Western literature, however, from very early on, has attempted to articulate the distinction between the two, and many authors delight in blurring the boundaries.

The fourth type of mythology that the Bible offers us—*historical* mythology—further complicates our perception of the boundary between truth and fiction because it operates in the realm of facts. As Stalin often remarked, "History belongs to those who write it." In the case of the Bible, history is presented from the perspective of a specific group, and the vision it offers is theirs alone. One might expect such a history to be slanted almost to the point of propaganda, but the history in the Bible gives us a picture of both the highs and the lows of the Israelites. It mixes suffering with joy in such a way to suggest that God will never desert his people, even in their times of trouble, and that one should always hold out hope for better times because there is a beneficent order behind the universe. But for the foes of God's people, the biblical account is a different matter. When the enemies of Israel are struck down, we seldom hear their side of the story because they exist outside the moral codes and laws that govern the people of Israel. The idea of 360 degree reportage is a modern concept. To our ears, the history told in the Bible may seem one-sided, yet the authors of the texts can be forgiven. After all, it was their own story they were telling, and their perspective was the only one that was essential for the progress of the narrative.

Historical mythology is the process of chronicle. The Bible is one of the oldest history books. It documents the growth and development of a people from the moment their founder, Abraham, chooses to leave Ur of the Chaldees. Where it is unable to use historical data, the Bible falls back on the same structures that it uses to fill the absence of science—the imaginative answer. This can be seen in the fifth chapter of Genesis, for instance, where a whole list of characters (including the famous Methuselah, who lives for almost a millennium), whether real or fictional, are named for narrative expediency so the authors can get on with the story they are trying to tell. This account of the generations is also a useful device to show the passage of time and to collapse a number of texts into a single chapter. In narrative terms, the Bible moves quickly when it wants to and is highly selective in the events it presents.

The Bible also undergoes some distinct narrative transformations from chapter to chapter and book to book that work on the reader in subtle and persuasive ways. The imaginative structures of the Bible constantly remind the reader that his or her life runs a course similar to that of the universe—exactly the idea Kierkegaard recognized when he said that the Bible was about him. Ecclesiastes 3:1 tells us that "To every *thing* there is a season, and a time to every purpose under the heaven": human life is not just a cog in the machine of the universe, but a reflection in miniature of the grand scale. The individual, in this sense, is a microcosm, a smaller version of the macrocosm, the larger picture.

In other words, the story of the universe is the story of an individual life. Each person leaves the unknown at the time of his or her birth and returns to it at the time of death. As Sigmund Freud points out in *Civilization and Its Discontents*, life can be perceived as an extended narrative that separates two experiences of the unknown—the experience before birth and the experience after death—and our culture and our religion, the great store of human narratives, are responses that protect our fragile psyches during this interlude between unknowns. Indeed, the space between these two unknowns is spanned by the human ability to make a narrative from experience. The story that we tell ourselves about ourselves is a pattern that our literature constantly reflects. It is a story that has a beginning, a middle, and an end—where, we hope, everything will work out for the best and leave us with either a reward or the satisfaction of knowing that there has been some important purpose to life.

As Aristotle points out in his *Poetics*, a literary story must have a beginning, a middle, and an end. In the case of the Bible, Genesis, the story of how humankind began on the earth, is the most recognizable of all the narratives. And Genesis, because it is the beginning of all beginnings, has become synonymous with our personal starts in the world. As a story, it has shaped the way we think of childhood, innocence, horticulture, and ecology, and it is the source for our ideas of the perfect places to dream—those getaway vacations that we hope will take us back to something we lost long, long ago.

Every human being has a past, a personal "once upon a time" that is marked by a faint memory of a beginning. The question that arises from a speculation about origins usually focuses on how existence comes into being, and how a plausible explanation can trace all instances of effect to one great cause. In his third-century autobiography *Confessions* (a book he originally intended as a preface to the Bible), Saint Augustine wonders where he came from and suspects that there may have been some other life before this one. Perhaps, says Saint Augustine, it was a life where the individual existed in a state of divine grace or a proximity to God that is closer to humankind's natural state of being than what is possible to ascertain in daily existence. Saint Augustine senses that there may have been some entirely different story to his past than what he understands, but he can only speculate. His imagination cannot fathom what it could be:

> I do not know where I came from when I was born into this life which leads to death—should I say this death which leads to life? This much is hidden from me.

The question is an age-old one: what happened before I began? It is a troubling question, and one that logic has never been able to satisfy when everything is new and untarnished by time or

experience. But that point at which memories begin, either in the larger human story told in the Bible or in the personal stories of our own lives, is a moment that is always associated with paradise, a place of innocence, divinity, and the presence of a caring and benevolent overseer.

First memories, as both Saint Augustine and John Locke point out, are the most important because they set the tone and the standards against which everything else in experience will be measured. In the biblical story of humankind, Eden is the matrix, the measure, and the standard. Indeed, the concept of paradise that most of us carry in our imagination is the idea of the garden described in Genesis 2:8–9:

> And the Lord God planted a garden eastward in Eden; and there he put the man whom he had formed.
>
> And out of the ground made the Lord God to grow every tree that is pleasant to the sight, and good for food: the tree of life also in the midst of the garden, and the tree of knowledge of good and evil.

The fact that humankind's history begins in a garden has had a profound impact on the way we imagine nature. To the ecologist, nature in its pristine, unblemished form is the true work of God, a throwback to paradise before humans came and spoiled the natural world by reordering it. To the office worker in a northern climate on a cold, rainy late November evening—buoyed by glossy travel brochures of beaches and blue skies—paradise is a place with palm trees and a distinct absence of deadlines and responsibility. These concepts of paradise, ideas that we normally associate with Eden, are fictitious afterthought creations, the ripple effects that often come from stories that lie at the core of the imagination. Such notions signal that there might be an alternative to this reality if only we can escape the boundaries of time and death.

Eden has many associations and connotations. In one sense, it is a place without time where everything remains unaltered by the pressures of the world, a place without entropy or death. In the first chapter of Genesis, man is given dominion over the flora and fauna of the entire world. There is no mention specifically of a garden:

Unknown. The Garden of Paradise. The notion of the hortus conclusus, *the walled garden that acts as a metaphorical paradise, is depicted here. Each flower has a symbolic purpose so that the painting is meant to act as an allegory. Man, in the lower right, discourses with the divine angel.*

And God said, Behold I have given you every herb bearing seed, which *is* upon the face of all the earth, and every tree in which *is* the fruit of a tree yielding seed; to you it shall be for meat. And to every beast of the earth, and to every fowl of the air, and to every thing that creepeth upon the earth, wherein *there is* life, *I have given* every green herb for meat: and it was so.

In the second chapter of Genesis, however, the situation is much more specific. Adam and Eve are placed in a garden "planted eastward in Eden," and told to "dress it and to keep it," a suggestion not merely of humankind's sovereignty over nature but of stewardship.

Eden, as described in Genesis 2:9–14, is a mineral-rich garden with good soil that is watered by a great river with four tributaries, the Pison, the Gihon, the Hiddekel, and the Euphrates—a situation that suggests a location somewhere in the current-day Middle East. The specific location, however, is not the point of the description because the exact spot is impossible to ascertain owing to the breadth of geography that the garden encompasses. Most important is that Eden is a source of life; at the center of the garden, with its four headwaters, is a fountain—a wellspring and a source of sustaining energy for the unfallen world. A longing for that wellspring of life, that center of beginnings, is reflected in our constant need to control and shape nature to our own ends, a need that finds its worst expression in the way we treat our environment, and its most common and gentle expression in our desire to make gardens.

Just about anyone who has engaged, either seriously or casually, in Western-style gardening, beyond the mundane petunia in the window box, is making a conscious, or perhaps unconscious, attempt at restoring a little bit of that lost paradise. The cloisters of medieval cathedrals and monasteries were attempts to build model Edens, places of retreat and contemplation that would give the illusion of being as extemporal as the original Eden. These enclosed gardens, or *hortus conclusus*, were protected places cut off from the rest of the world, where the practical aspects of herb and vegetable growing could be undertaken while the mind could simultaneously become closer to God through contemplation and imagination. A garden is the standard setting in Western literature for anything that is ideal. The medieval French romance poem, *Le Roman de la*

Rose, locates the Rose, the symbol of ideal beauty and eternal love, at the center of a garden. The Dreamer hero in the poem is forced to undertake a quest in order to prove his worth to the Rose, just so he might steal a single, perfect kiss. The sexual and sensual associations of the garden always work themselves into the picture. In his poem on the joys of bachelorhood, *The Garden*, Andrew Marvell contemplates what Eden must have been like:

> *Here at the fountain's sliding foot,*
> *Or at some fruit-tree's mossy root,*
> *Casting the body's vest aside,*
> *My soul into the boughs does glide:*
> *There like a bird it sits, and sings,*
> *Then whets, and combs its silver wings;*
> *And, till prepared for longer flight,*
> *Waves its plumes in the various light.*

The modern university or college quadrangle is a slightly more secular attempt to reflect the idea of paradise, though it is based on the medieval idea of the walled garden. The cloister of Salisbury Cathedral, for example, still has a large cedar of Lebanon at its center, just as the original paradise had the tree of life at its heart.

Other medieval garden arrangements placed a fountain at the heart of the design and featured either four small streams or four stone pathways leading from the center to the walls. But, alas, once paradise is lost, as Milton points out in the first lines of his epic poem *Paradise Lost*, nothing short of divine intervention, at an enormous cost, can bring humankind back to that proximity with God:

> *Of Man's First Disobedience, and the Fruit*
> *Of that Forbidden Tree, whose mortal taste*
> *Brought Death into the World, and all our woe,*
> *With loss of Eden, till one greater Man*
> *Restore us, and regain the blissful Seat,*
> *Sing Heav'nly Muse...*

The human imagination, however, has an answer for everything. Where divine intervention fails or seems to take its sweet time restoring humankind to that holy state of grace and bliss, social action takes over, and from this desire to find a better place comes the notion of utopia, the idea that the perfect place really doesn't exist except as an imaginative concept.

There are six discernible utopias. *Eden*, the first utopia, is the model for all the succeeding descriptions of the perfect place to live. *Arcadia*, the Classical world's answer to Eden or the Promised Land, is a place without death where a shepherd society lives blissfully with its flocks. The *Land of Cockaigne*, a medieval invention, partly in response to the horrors of plague and famine, is akin to the modern Club Med, a hedonistic place where everything is miraculously provided in gluttonous quantities. The *Perfect Moral Commonwealth* is the Puritan reaction to the Land of Cockaigne, a place where the entire society works by a strict theological or moral code; this type of society was attempted by the pilgrims at Plymouth, Massachusetts, in the seventeenth century. The *Rational Republic*, or world according to science, is where the laws that govern the physical world are applied to the societal realm. The final utopia is the *New Jerusalem*, that jeweler's delight of "kingdom come," a heaven on earth where humankind has stepped beyond time and death and lives again in close proximity to God.

Within the Bible there are several sub-Edens that must also be considered because they express a constant desire to reconstruct that perfect place. The Promised Land of Exodus is a "land of milk and honey," a place God has promised to the children of Israel. During the Israelites' forty years of wandering in the desert, it becomes a moral goal as well as a geographical location. When the Promised Land is finally attained, its social center, its heart, is manifested in the city of Jerusalem, and at the heart of Jerusalem is the temple. When Jerusalem falls, the concept of the holy city is transformed yet again into a vision or a promise. The oft-recited Psalm 137 expresses the longing to return to the heart of the Promised Land and to flee the captivity of Babylon:

If I forget thee, O Jerusalem, let my right hand forget *her cunning*. If I do not remember thee, let my tongue cleave to the roof of my mouth; if I prefer not Jerusalem above my chief joy.

The restored Jerusalem, especially the one found in Maccabees, is a foreshadowing (a preview of coming attractions) of the New Jerusalem, where the kingdom of God will be restored to humankind at the end of time. The idea of Jerusalem is much like the "ever-retreating horizon" or the "longed-for homeland" that we see in such Classical works as Homer's *Odyssey* or Virgil's *Aeneid*; but unlike its Classical parallels, Jerusalem is an idea that is constantly being constructed, destroyed, and reconstructed. This cycle of creation, destruction, and recreation—or a beginning, a fall, and a redemption—reflects a key pattern in Western literature that the Bible has made emphatic: the pattern of comedy.

We tend to think of comedy as anything, whether crude or sophisticated, that makes us laugh. On a very simple level, the modern definition of comedy is anything that is funny, or able to satisfy our need for a happy ending. Tragedy, on the other hand, is anything that leaves us emptied through a dashing of our expectations and a denial of our desire to see things work out properly. It is a shame that these terms have become so abused by contemporary language, because they mean a great deal more than we give them credit for. The word *comedy* is derived from the Greek word *komus*, meaning "revels." In the traditional sense, the idea of the revels was a celebration, usually with music and dance (a kind of show) that was performed to celebrate an important union such as a wedding. Prospero in Shakespeare's *The Tempest* celebrates the union between Ferdinand and Miranda with a command performance by the three goddesses Juno, Iris, and Ceres. When the performance is over, he declares (IV.i.148), "Our revels now are ended." The betrothal between Ferdinand and Miranda is set. Ferdinand has proven his love for Prospero's daughter, and the celebration marks the completion of a process not unlike the one that the Dreamer hero of *Le Roman de la Rose* undergoes. In the Bible, the revels take place when God and Man are finally brought back together again at the end of time, a moment in Revelations when the fall is undone and the divine relationship between God and humanity is restored. In this sense, the Bible is a "comic" book because it suggests that sooner or later a happy ending is possible through a grand-scale marriage of man and God, and that the wrongs of the fall will be put right.

When Adam and Eve fall from paradise in the third chapter of Genesis, several things happen as a result. First, God puts enmity between human beings and snakes because of the serpent's role in tempting Eve and Adam to eat of the fruit of the tree of knowledge. Next, the human misery of childbirth suffered by women is "greatly" multiplied (Gen. 3:16), and Adam, who hitherto was an equal partner in paradise with Eve, is instructed by God henceforth to keep an eye on his wife and "rule over her." The loss of sexual equality is a blow to humanity because it means that one-half of the male/female equation is supposed to have the upper hand. The third consequence is that humankind is forbidden to eat any more special fruit, either of the tree of knowledge of good and evil or of the tree of life. Adam was told that if he ate of the tree of knowledge of good and evil, he would "surely die" (Gen. 2:17), and so, as the fourth consequence, death enters the world. God then tells Adam and Eve that all the ground of the world is "cursed" (Gen. 3:17) and that it will not readily yield the life-giving plants that they had enjoyed in paradise. They must "eat of" the ground "all the days of" their life, and the ground is going to be a tough place to

Lucus Cranach the Elder. Adam and Eve. In this Renaissance vision of what paradise might have been like, the animals co-exist with humankind in a peacable kingdom. Eve seems confident that she is making the right decision about fruit, but Adam appears less certain as he scratches his head.

earn a living because it will be covered with all sorts of nuisances such as "thorns and thistles." God reminds Adam that he is dust, "and unto dust" he shall return. When paradise is closed to humanity, God adds that he is doing this to protect the tree of life (Gen. 3:24) and to preserve, for a later date, that spark of divinity and energy that enabled not only the creation of Adam and Eve but the creation of the entire world. The suggestion is that we are allowed only little glimpses of the life of that imagination that brought the universe into being, and in these little glimpses we perceive something that could possibly sustain a greater life for humankind than we currently know.

Later apocryphal or "add-on" versions of the story suggest that when Adam and Eve are driven out of paradise and the gate is locked behind them (with flaming cherubim standing guard at the entrance to the lost garden), time enters the world. Seventeenth-century poet Henry Vaughan suggests in his fascinating and evocative poem *Corruption* that the fall not only put the earth's axis into its current twenty-eight degree tilt, but brought about the course of the seasons, the measured span of a single human life, and that grand foe, death.

As Vaughan puts it in his poem, the sense of nostalgia for that lost, perfect world is an overwhelming passion that we must carry with us all of our days, the final consequence of the loss:

Sure, It was so. Man in those early days
  Was not all stone, and Earth.
He shined a little, and by those weak Rays
  Had some glimpse of his birth.
He saw Heaven o'er his head, and knew from whence
  He came (condemned,) hither,
And, as first Love draws strongest, so from hence
  His mind sure progressed thither.
Things here were strange unto him: Sweat, and till
  All was thorn, or weed,
Nor did those last, but (like himself,) died still
  As soon as they did Seed,
They seemed to quarrel with him; for that Act
  That felled him, foiled them all,
He drew the Curse upon the world, and Cracked
  The whole frame with his fall.
This made him long for home, as loath to stay
  With murmurers, and foes;
He sighed for Eden, and would often say
  Ah! What bright days were those!

Vaughan is one of numerous poets who have sought to embellish and understand why humankind fell and what the consequences of Adam and Eve's actions were. In terms of explanatory mythology, the fall of man is a myth that tells us why life is so miserable. Anyone who has walked through a snow blizzard must surely have asked not only "Why me?" but "Why is this happening?" and "What did the human species do to deserve the sting of winter ice and the pain and grief of an all-too-short life?" The anonymous medieval poet who wrote *Adam lay yboundin* summed up the misery of the world by concluding that the fall took place so God could allow us to find heavenly grace (how else might we have found it?) through the glory of his son's sacrifice and the wonderful presence of the Virgin Mary:

Adam lay yboundin, boundin in a bond,
Foure thousand winter thought he not to long.
And al was for an appil, an appil that he took,
As clerkes findin wretin in here book.
Ne hadde the appil take ben, the appil taken ben,
Ne hadde never our Lady a ben hevene quen.
Blessed be the time that appil take was,
Therefore we mown singin Deo Gratias.

In other words, the misery of humankind is all part of a divine plan and we should be grateful for it. Medieval logic aside, this is small consolation, and what readers for thousands of years have been left with in the wake of the story of the fall is an overwhelming sense of remorse and nostalgia. The original home was a much better place, and one way or another we are determined to get back there. Apocryphal information aside, the Bible is very elliptical in the specific details it gives us about the fall and what actually happened. Writers such as Dante and Milton draw upon a large body of post-biblical stories in order to explicate more fully the story of this disastrous event.

What humankind is left with is the feeling that things, at some point in time, were much better than they are now. The Anglo-Saxon poets of the late Dark Ages in England were particularly good at painting the world as a very unpleasant place to live. One comes away from such famous Anglo-Saxon poems as *The Wanderer* and *The Seafarer* with the sense that the earth is a comfortless place locked in a perpetual winter, where everything is covered with dank hoar-frost. In both poems, the speakers—what in literature is called the *persona*—suffer from the profound sense that they have come into the world too late, and that the glorious past is now completely over. They feel cut off from the center of events, as if they are outcasts and exiles living in a world that is wasted, fallen, and beyond redemption. In *The Wanderer*, the speaker laments:

A wise man may grasp how ghastly it shall be
when all this world's wealth standeth waste,
even now, in many places, over the earth

walls stand, wind-beaten,
hung with hoar-frost; ruined habitations.
The wine-halls crumble; their wielders lie
bereft of bliss, the band all fallen
proud by the wall...

The Maker of men hath so marred this dwelling
that human laughter is not heard about it
and idle stand these old giant-works.

One major consolation redeems the world from being a total, despairing waste, however, and that consolation is God's grace (the idea that there is some good behind all this misery), the one remnant of Eden that remains after the fall. *The Wanderer* ends with a small hymn to divine grace:

So spoke the sage in his heart: he sat apart in thought.
Good is he who keeps faith: nor should care too fast
be out of a man's breast before he first know the cure:
a warrior fights on bravely. Well it is for him who seeks forgiveness,
the Heavenly Father's solace, in whom all our fastness stands.

Here, the Bible's message to trust in God seems to have stuck; yet we cannot help realizing that the voice of lamentation in the human range of tones is a very powerful and sad register. What pervades any notion of the fall and our realization that we exist in a hostile nature is the *elegiac*.

Elegy is more than just a lament for someone who is dead, though that is the meaning that the term most often conveys, rather bathetically. Elegy is also a realization that the world is not what it used to be, that something has gone seriously wrong with the universe, and that some imaginative consolation must be found to save the moment from utter despair. Elegy is also one of the key points where the Judeo-Christian way of looking at life and literature crosses paths directly with the pagan Classical mentality. The notion of the elegiac, that the world was a good place that has become broken, is what fuels the impetus toward utopias. Rather than simply mourning the loss of perfection in nature, humankind picks itself up, dusts itself off, and sets about the task of trying to rebuild the glorious past; what cannot be rebuilt serves as a vision of perfection, a constant reminder that life can be made better. At the same time, a reminder of a much better past carries with it a suggestion that our world exists in a state of grief, that we have lost something important that should be mourned. In this respect, any mention of Eden or of the Golden Age carries with it a strong sense of the elegiac. The story of Eden at the opening of the Bible serves as a signal that grief, not joy, is what should be expected of the world.

In Classical literature, the Golden Age was a period when there was no death, no illness, and humankind enjoyed a state of happy perfection. Nature in this realm was timeless and provided everything human beings needed to be sustained. As Ovid notes in *Metamorphoses*—that rather racy history of time that details the folly-bound relationship between humankind and the gods of the Classical world—the Golden Age was

> when men of their own accord, without threat of punishment, without laws, maintained good faith and did what was right. There were no penalties to be afraid of, no bronze tablets were erected, carrying threats of legal action, no crowd of wrong-doers, anxious for mercy, trembled before the face of their judge: indeed, there were no judges, men lived securely without them...The peoples of the world, untroubled by fears, enjoyed a leisurely and peaceful existence, and had no use for soldiers. The earth itself, without any compulsion, untouched by hoe, unfur-rowed by any share, produced all things spontaneously and men were content with foods that grew without cultivation.

According to Ovid, what brought about the end of the Golden Age was a change in divine management when Jupiter (Zeus) overthrew his predecessor, Cronus. The Classical mentality, however, was not willing to relinquish the concept of the ideal place, and so it created Arcadia, the shepherd's land where the beautiful pastoral world of lush, green, rolling hills was lulled by the music of bleating lambs and the soft strains of plainsong accompanied by lyres—an image that conjures up English country picnics with a hamper spread upon a car rug.

Arcadia, particularly in poetry, is a world where nature is supposed to cooperate with human beings. However, when a young shepherd dies, cut off in the prime of his youth, something terrible has gone wrong with the entire system of nature. The other shepherds gather to grieve and lament, and their songs—their elegies—mourn the premature passing of one who was meant to live and be fruitful. What the Classical or pagan world tells us is that Arcadia can never be restored and that the young shepherd can never come back to life. The Christian tradition of the Bible's New Testament offers an alternative to grief: resurrection. It says that although a death may take place, it is the foundation for a rebirth and for everlasting life. The Bible wants to be elegiac, but it is not. Where the Classical world becomes tragic because there is no imaginative way to overcome death, the Christian tradition is comic: it tells us that even though death may occur, the course of human events will still conclude happily. The elegy, in the Classical sense and as a recurring literary form, observes an absence in nature, a distance between humankind and its natural state, because it implies that the end of all nature is death.

Milton's *Lycidas* suggests that the sudden incursion of death into the otherwise balanced and harmonious world triggered a "fall" that made nature uncooperative. Milton addresses the boughs of the laurel tree, that symbol of poetic inspiration and the idyllic, Arcadian lifestyle, in the opening lines of the poem:

Bitter constraint, and sad occasion dear,
Compels me to disturb your season due;
For Lycidas is dead, dead ere his prime,
Young Lycidas, and hath not left his peer.
Who would not sing for Lycidas? He knew
Himself to sing, and build the lofty rhyme.

The point of the elegy is to allow the persona to work his or her way toward some sort of solace. Thomas Gray's famous *Elegy Written in a Country Churchyard* contains this somber observation, reminiscent of the pessimistic wisdom of Ecclesiastes: "The paths of glory lead but to the grave." Gray, however, concludes his poem with "The Epitaph," or famous last words:

> *Large was his bounty, and his soul sincere,*
> *Heaven did a recompense as largely send:*
> *He gave to Misery all he had, a tear,*
> *He gained from Heaven ('twas all he wished) a friend.*

> *No farther seek his merits to disclose,*
> *Or draw his frailties from their dread abode,*
> *(There they alike in trembling hope repose)*
> *The bosom of his Father and his God.*

Milton offers a similar note of consolation at the conclusion of *Lycidas*:

> *So Lycidas, sunk low but mounted high,*
> *Through the dear might of him that walked the waves.*
> *Where other groves, and other streams along,*
> *With nectar pure his oozy locks he laves,*
> *And hears the unexpressive nuptial song,*
> *In the blest kingdoms meek of joy and love.*

In other words, death in the Judeo-Christian way of looking at the world is not something to be lamented—it is a process that takes humankind closer to God and returns the soul to its original Edenic state. Death is a natural consequence of the fall, and should be accepted as the will of God because it is all part of a divine plan. Where the Classical world mourns the fall of nature, the Judeo-Christian world simply suffers and takes death in its stride. This is a key difference between the two worlds of Western literature: in the Classical world, there is tragedy, but in the Judeo-Christian world, where God is in charge, tragedy cannot exist. This is the essential point that the Roman writer Boethius makes in *The Consolation of Philosophy*, and it is the issue that underlies Job's trials in the Bible: as long as God is in charge, things aren't entirely bad.

The Bible recognizes that the prevailing force in the universe is the grace of God, and that God always likes the story to work out well in the end. Like every good reader (and the Bible tells us that God is constantly reading the world and keeping track of everyone's record of good and evil), he loves happy endings. His own story, the story of time, is therefore going to end happily. In the end, as Revelations tells us, the good are going to be saved and reunited with God through his son, Christ, in a marriage ceremony. When this happens, Saint John of Patmos writes, not only will there be rejoicing at the redemption that has taken place, but there will be the consummation of a longed-for union—a marriage—and the completion of a comedy.

The idea of a "marriage" or union between God and humanity forms the basis for the Western tradition of love poetry. The Song of Solomon, perhaps the most beautiful and sexy of all the books in the Bible, is actually a script in which the two principal characters, a man and a woman, move about a city, presumably Jerusalem at the heart of the world, and seek each other with a desperate passion. What their search amounts to is a chase in which one never finds the other, but each says many fine things about the beloved. And it is a frantic search (Song of Sol. 3:2–3):

> I will rise now, and go about the city in the streets, and in the broad ways I will seek him whom my soul loveth: I sought him but I found him not. The watchmen that go about the city found me: *to whom I said*, Saw ye him whom my soul loveth?

What ensues is a description of the beloved that moves from head to waist and from toe to mid-section, a description that discreetly and erotically leaves the more intimate parts of the body to the reader's imagination. Medieval love poetry followed this same pattern, and the need to utter praises of the beloved, to offer the world some sort of description, no matter how simple, forms the basis for the rhetoric of love in poems as diverse as Robert Burns' *My Love Is Like a Red, Red Rose* ("My love is like a red, red rose/ That's newly sprung in June,/ My love is like a melody/ That's sweetly played in tune") and the simple rhyme "Roses are red, Violets are blue."

For all its urgency and its beauty, for all its sensuality and eroticism, the Song of Solomon is over before the relationship between the two lovers, the female voice of the bride and the male voice of the bridegroom, is consummated. What is important about the Song of Solomon, however, is that it foreshadows the union between humanity (the bride) and Christ (the bridegroom) that will take place at the end of time. In effect, the book of the Bible that is Western literature's basis for love poetry is the key to the happy ending in the whole work, the moment when the true comedy is cemented with a union and a celebration. In this sense, love really does make the world go round.

Most important, however, is the way the Bible tells the story of time. It begins with the start of a "beautiful friendship" and follows that relationship through a whole series of ups and downs. The one character who remains a constant and a catalyst throughout the scope of human experience is God. The Bible, it can justly be said, is the story of the world from God's perspective. It is not so much the word *of* God—after all, it is a heavily edited, composite anthology of a very diverse range of stories—but more the word *about* God. It is time as seen through God's eye. He sees all and is omniscient and continuous because he exists outside of time. God is beyond the reach of the imagination, of course, but what the Bible tells us is that God is reachable *through* the imagination, and the imagination, like heaven or Eden, is limitless, boundless, and beyond time.

I am reminded of a joke made by the Canadian philosopher Marshall McLuhan when he said, "Man's got to dream or what's a metaphor?" Perhaps the only barriers that lie between us and the Edenic bliss that Adam and Eve knew, once upon a time, are the limitations of our own capacity to dream. Certainly, our literary texts offer us ways to expand those horizons—and as the central stories of Classical literature tell us, life is a journey outward and back again from a place we call home.

2

THERE'S NO PLACE
LIKE HOME

Homer's *The Odyssey*

LTHOUGH he did not do it too often in his career, John Keats can be said to have offered same-day service on his poems. Such was the case behind the composition of his first significant sonnet, *On First Looking into Chapman's Homer*. Keats' former schoolteacher, a man named Charles Cowden Clarke, invited the young poet to his home for an evening of literary conversation. Early in the evening, Clarke showed Keats a copy of George Chapman's 1611 translation of *The Iliad* and *The Odyssey*, a work that had been brought into the English language in the same year as the King James Version of the Bible. Chapman's translation of Homer's epics had been acclaimed by a number of authors before Keats came along. The usually taciturn eighteenth-century poet Alexander Pope called the translation "a daring, fiery spirit." The truth of the matter was that the "fieriness" in the work was more the product of Homer's imagination than of Chapman's skills as a translator. Nonetheless, the young Keats and his mentor immediately read the whole work cover to cover during that October night in 1816. And at dawn, Keats went home full of inspiration and poetic zeal.

To Clarke's surprise, and to the envy of modern postal systems everywhere, a copy of Keats' poem *On First Looking into Chapman's Homer* arrived in the ten o'clock mail later that morning. In the poem, Keats dreamed of the places to which he had been transported by Homer's poetic imagination:

Much have I travelled in the realms of gold,
  And many goodly states and kingdoms seen;
  Round many western islands have I been
Which bards in fealty to Apollo hold.
Oft of one wide expanse had I been told
  That deep-browed Homer ruled as his demesne;
  Yet did I never breathe its pure serene
Till I heard Chapman speak out loud and bold:
Then felt I like some watcher of the skies
  When a new planet swims into his ken;
Or like stout Cortez when with eagle eyes
  He stared at the Pacific—and all his men
Looked at each other with a wild surmise—
  Silent, upon a peak in Darien.

Keats borrows his first lines from Homer's famous opening lines of *The Odyssey*:

The hero of the tale which I beg the Muse to help me tell is that resourceful man who roamed the wide world after he had sacked the holy citadel of Troy. He saw the cities of many peoples and he learned their ways. He suffered many hardships on the high seas in his struggles to preserve his life and his comrades home.

What Keats has caught in the opening lines of his sonnet is the popular assocation that *The Odyssey* always evokes: that it is purely a poem about travel. In his epic of the aftermath of an international war that drained the life out of a continent and a civilization, Homer writes about a man, Odysseus, and his struggle to get home. But *The Odyssey* is not just the idea of a journey, of traveling in "realms of gold" and seeing "many goodly states and kingdoms"; it is also the way that "demesne"—a realm or feudal possession— shapes the person who owns it. *The Odyssey*, for all its splendid descriptions of travel and of strange sights in a strange world, is not about the journey but about the destination. It is the story not only of a man who longs for home, but of the home that has shaped the way the man sees the world.

Home is not just where the heart is in *The Odyssey*. It is also the center of perception, the force that shapes the soul of an individual and dictates the rules for how one should behave in the world. After all, just about any place, even a grotty cave inhabited by a one-eyed giant with a bad attitude, can be a home. In Book IX of *The Odyssey*, when Odysseus enters the cave of Polyphemus the Cyclops, he is challenged by the perceptually one-dimensional giant as to who Odysseus is and just what he is doing in the cave. Odysseus, with all the cockiness that his character expresses throughout the work, proudly makes his identity known:

I am Odysseus, Laertes' son. The whole world talks of my strat-
agems, and my fame has reached the heavens. My home is
under the clear skies of Ithaca. Our landmark is the wooded
peak of windswept Neriton. For neighbours we have many
peopled isles with no great space between them, Dulichium and
Same and wooded Zacynthus. But Ithaca, the farthest out to
sea, lies slanting to the west, whereas the others face the dawn
and rising sun. It is a rough land, but a fit nurse of me. And I,
for one, know of no sweeter sight for man's eyes than his own
country. The divine Calypso certainly did her best to keep me
yonder in her cavern home because she wished to be my wife,
and with the same object Circe, the Aeaen witch detained me in
her castle; but never for a moment did they win my heart. So
true it is that his motherland and his parents are what a man
holds sweetest, even though he may have settled far away from
his people in some rich home in foreign lands.

It seems like a long answer, but the underlying message is quite clear: home is what defines the individual.

In his rambling response to the Cyclops—more a *curriculum vitae* than the quick answer Polyphemus wanted—Odysseus not only gives a little summary of Ithaca's geographical location in rela-tion to other notable islands, but presents some details as to the topography and economic geography of his homeland. His speech shows that he is proud of where he has come from and that he recognizes that there is nothing sweeter to a person's eyes than the sight of his or her own country. It is the sort of feeling we can have when, returning from a long journey or vacation, we are suddenly confronted by a lengthy line-up at the customs wicket: we should be annoyed at the delay and the inconvenience, but the prospect of being home mitigates our impatience.

The land of birth is always a "fit nurse" because it gives us a sense of who we are. Still, it is startling to realize that at the root of Odysseus' remarks to the Cyclops lies the very essence of nineteenth-century nationalism: a force that created and shaped the map of contemporary Europe, and that evoked sentiments as profound as the lyrics to dozens of national anthems and the words to almost every patriotic poem written in the last two hundred years. A case in point is Part XX of W.B. Yeats' poetic sequence *Words for Music Perhaps*, the evocative *I Am of Ireland*:

'I am of Ireland,
And the Holy Land of Ireland,
And time runs on,' cried she.
'Come out of charity,
Come dance with me in Ireland.'

One man, one man alone
In that outlandish gear,
One solitary man
Of all that rambled there
Had turned his stately head.
'That is a long way off,
And time runs on,' he said,
'And night grows rough.'

Like Homer, Yeats recognized that if one was going to either return home or reinvent the principles that make a home worth having, then pride, love of country, and an understanding of just what that country means were necessary prerequisites for attaining the reality of a homeland.

Defining a homeland, as both Homer and Yeats understood, meant articulating what qualities of a particular place speak to an individual and set that individual apart from other people in other countries. For Yeats, as for many "national" poets who expressed the ethos of their countries, defining an identity was a thankless job. The last thing people like to be reminded of is their own peculiar habits—yet these eccentricities lie at the core of nationality.

In the case of Homer's Odysseus, the journey to those "cities of many peoples" is the school where he learns what he is by experiencing what he is not. Like every good epic hero, Odysseus announces his pedigree to those he visits before he says anything else—the same sort of pedigree that one sees in the opening lines of the fifth chapter of Genesis. The listing of a pedigree is important because it lets the reader know that the individual in question, the central character, is someone to be reckoned with, that he or she comes from a long line of notable characters and, like modern royalty, is a person of significance. But in Odysseus' response to the Cyclops, what is most important is where he is *from*, a place unlike any other place in the world. That is the peculiar nature of one's national identity: it is *not* like anything one will see anywhere else. It is special.

But more than simply a poem about how nationalism got its start, *The Odyssey* is about an individual who is attempting to

escape the travails that have separated him from his own identity. It is not only about going the distance, but of realizing what the distance means. When Odysseus and his crew visit the land of the Lotus-eaters, the sailors consume moly, a hallucinogenic plant that makes them forget all about home. Moly is the most dangerous and illicit of substances because it makes an individual "think no more of home." What keeps Odysseus sane is what almost drives him insane: longing for Ithaca. All of Odysseus' emotional suffering, whether on Circe's idyllic island or during the singing of *The Iliad* at King Alcinous' palace in Book VII, implies that the farther one goes from home, the greater one's desire to return.

The key to what makes a home a home is the notion of hospitality. *The Odyssey* is really a book of etiquette, an Emily Post–style guide to the do's and don'ts of entertaining guests. In Books VI and VII, the "Nausicaa" and "The Palace of Alcinous" sections, when Odysseus finds himself naked and near death on a foreign beach shortly after yet another shipwreck, he is taken to the palace and accorded the sort of welcome that modern-day readers would save for only their closest relatives. He is bathed, clothed, rested, and fed before he is asked any specific questions about who he is. Odysseus is not treated as a castaway so much as he is treated as a guest. In fact, the degree of hospitality seems almost linked to the neediness of the individual. And the rewards can be great, as Odysseus suggests after the initial kindness Nausicaa shows him on the beach:

> You are the first person I have met after all I have been through, and I do not know a soul in this city or this land. I beg you to direct me to the town and to give me some rag to put around myself, if only the wrapper you may have brought for your linen when you came. And in return, may the gods grant you your heart's desire; may they give you a husband and a home, and the harmony that is so much to be desired, since there is nothing nobler or more admirable than when two people who see eye to eye keep house as man and wife, confounding their enemies and delighting their friends, as they themselves know better than anyone.

Dosso Dossi. Circe and Her Lovers in a Landscape. The temptress who wields the power of metamorphosis over Odysseus' men is transformed here into a woodland Sibyl, pointing to a tablet and surrounded by venerous beasts. She seems more an outgrowth of nature than one who would alter it for her own purposes.

The same treatment is shown to Odysseus' son, Telemachus, when he shows up unexpectedly at the home of another Trojan War veteran, Nestor. Before Telemachus is allowed to ask any questions about the whereabouts of his father, Nestor invites him in and treats him royally. Indeed, news and information in *The Odyssey* are passed from one source to another as "dinner conversation," only after the visitor has been made welcome. In that temple of the Greek world, the home, important information is meant to be conveyed as part of a social ceremony. For this reason, the incursion of the suitors into Odysseus' own home while he is away, and their advances toward Penelope, who is not conclusively proven to be a widow, is the absolute sacrilege. Likewise, when Odysseus forgets his manners in the cave of the Cyclops, he is disobeying the unspoken pact that exists between a host and a visitor. He is not minding his manners. Manners are the key to survival in the Homeric world because they suggest that even in a world that has survived a conflict the magnitude of the Trojan War, there is still some modicum of order, a code of conduct that preserves the fine line between peace and anarchy.

The ritual of hospitality also contributed to the manner in which *The Odyssey*—that is, the poem itself—first appeared. In Book VIII, "The Phaecian Games," we learn that poems such as Homer's first master work, *The Iliad*, were performed on ceremonial occasions for large groups of diners or listeners. Indeed, Alcinous, always the jovial and generous presence, announces that the recitation of that poem about the Trojan War will open the games:

I invite you that are sceptred kings to my palace with a view to entertaining our visitor indoors. I shall accept no refusal. And let our glorious bard, Demodocus, be summoned. For no other singer has his heavenly gift of delighting our ears whatever theme he chooses for his song.

Few passages in literature are packed with as much information about the nature of a text as these sentences. Homer is telling us that poems such as *The Iliad* and *The Odyssey* were originally not written texts, but memorized stories that were sung to musical accompaniment. Extended narrative poems such as these soon became known as *epics*, and they were the rage in the Classical world. Unfortunately, we tend to misuse the word *epic* today to mean anything that is large and overwhelming, a tome or an enormous challenge.

The ancient Greeks put poetry in two categories: the *lyric* and the *choric*. Choric poetry was meant to contain the expressions of a group—hence the idea of a *chorus* (which will be discussed in chapter 3). Lyric poetry, on the other hand, was meant to express the ideas and emotions of a single individual, with the voice behind the poem personalizing the information by connecting it directly to experience. Our modern idea of the pop singer comes from this tradition, although its route stems not directly from epic performance, but from the troubadour tradition of the eleventh century. The idea of lyric poetry, of the voice behind the poem being able to say, "This is what I know," and reacting to the events with pathos, empathy, and subjective emotion, meant that the performance of an epic poem such as *The Iliad* or *The Odyssey* was an event with incredible immediacy.

What is important about the Homeric epic is that it was originally meant to be sung. In fact, the modern concept of the *lyric*, both as words to a song or as a short poem, owes its origin to the fact that poetry was originally sung to the accompaniment of music. (The lyre was a small, hand-held harp—the sort of harp that contemporary readers now associate with angels.)

Imagine the entire *Odyssey* being performed after a formal, elegant banquet. The poet/performer would enter the hall. He would be accompanied by a group of musicians or he would be carrying his own instrument, a small harp or lyre. There might be some dancers as well, who would perform at intervals when the poet rested his voice. A silence would fall in the hall. After strumming a few opening chords on the lyre, the poet would begin his "song." The audience would listen to the words and the story, of course, but also to how the story was told—the meter and rhythm of the language, the clever linguistic moments that the poet would build into the telling to make the language memorable and enjoyable, and the order in which familiar events were told or foretold. The listeners would revel in the power of language to create an entire world. But what made that power so persuasive and so entertaining was the poet's skill with that language. In order to keep the audience engaged during the lengthy recitation, poets like Homer were obliged to build various *devices* or literary tricks into the text that would help the reader to stay awake and follow the narrative.

The first of these devices was a turn of phrase, a figure of speech known as the *Homeric epithet*. The term *epithet*, alas, is another one of those words that the modern world misuses. In the contemporary sense, an epithet is a swear word, usually used as an adjective to dress up an insult. In the literary sense, however, an epithet was a means of enlivening the recitation and performance of a long verbal piece. The epithet was a verbal turn of phrase whereby a commonplace image was suddenly aligned with two other images that played against each other. A prime example of the Homeric epithet is the phrase "the wine-dark sea." Like a metaphor, the Homeric epithet works in a tripartite fashion, only backwards. The reader hears "sea" and then associates the sea with darkness, with foreboding or danger. There is also the association between the sea and wine, where the sea's waves, coupled with the regular rhythms of the poetic line, become mesmerizing and lulling. Then there is the wine-darkness of the sea, an image that suggests a full-bodied Merlot, something beyond the colour of red (where sailors take either warning or delight). James Joyce, in his retelling of *The Odyssey*, the 1922 epic novel *Ulysses*, parodies the Homeric epithet with his phrase "the snot-green sea."

Another way that Homer keeps his audience with him during the lengthy recitation of the entire epic—a performance that would likely have taken place at one sitting—is through the structure of the poem's narrative. No rule states that an author has to start his story at the beginning and follow it through chronologically to the end. In fact, the very predictability of this approach can be dreary to a listener or reader. What Homer discovered was that he could start his story *in medias res*, or in the middle of the action, and by dropping his reader into the midst of the story, he could make the sense of "You are there!" all the more powerful. *The Odyssey* opens at a point in the timeline of the narrative that is equivalent with Book VIII. In other words, we leap right into the action.

Homer throws us another curve ball with his opening. He begins not with the story of Odysseus, but with the story of Telemachus looking for his father. The "Telemachad," as it has been called, may be a fragment of another epic journey poem that Homer has tacked onto the front of his master work. Books I–IV describe how the son, having had enough of the suitors who are pursuing his mother, escapes Ithaca to seek his father. Along the way, he is assisted by Athena in the guise of Mentor—a term for an older, wiser adviser that has entered our vocabulary directly from *The Odyssey*. The "Telemachad" functions in much the same way that "shorts" used to work in movie houses: it warms up the audience for the main feature. Homer then presents us with that shift of scene that has become known in contemporary storytelling as the great "meanwhile."

Meanwhile, off in some other part of the seas, Odysseus is washed ashore, naked, starving, and in desperate need of hospitality. He enters *The Odyssey* in much the same way that Adam enters the Bible. When he becomes the guest of King Alcinous, he is obligated to tell who he is, how he got there, and what he has been doing for the past ten years since the end of the Trojan War. Odysseus obliges by telling his story beginning in Book VIII, and this is where the real *Odyssey*, the story of the travels of Odysseus, begins. At this point, Homer falls back on another literary device: a means of backtracking in time known as the *digression*.

Digressions in literature are one of the truly fun aspects of storytelling because they permit the author to delay the progress of the narrative by filling in background information, by offering asides and insights that, though not essentially part of the main story, are interesting in their own right. Digressions give the author the chance to tell a story within a story. They provide necessary background information that makes the reader feel more a part of the proceedings once the narrative starts to move ahead again, and they assist the reader in understanding the "causes" behind the "effects" that the story describes. In other words, they allow the author to offer the reader some key hints as to why certain events take place as the narrative unfolds. In casual conversation, digressions can be the signal flag of a bore and the opportune moment for one to duck out of a story because they announce, "This tale is going to be longer than you anticipated and the telling more complicated than you ever imagined." The eighteenth-century English novelist

Laurence Sterne playfully constructs an entire novel, *Tristram Shandy*, on the principle of the digression. In the opening chapter of the first volume, the protagonist Shandy announces his birth, but first he feels obliged to bring the reader up to speed on his uncle Toby. After an incredible series of digressions, explanations, narrative wanderings, and off-topic discourses, the novel concludes and the young Shandy's life never progresses past his birth.

Digressions come in many forms. They can take the form of a Shakespearean "aside" or address to the audience that is out of context with the dialogue, and can contain necessary background information. They can also be direct, chronological retellings of what happened between points A and Z during a certain period of time. Homer, however, has yet another trick up his sleeve. He sends his hero to the Underworld because, in literature, the land of the dead is a veritable C N N, with accurate, almost up-to-the-minute reports of what is happening in the world above.

The dead, called the Shades, know everything of the past and the future. Their only problem is that they have no idea what is happening to themselves that precise moment in the Underworld. Homer makes apt use of the journey to the Underworld—a literary device known as a *nekusis*—in Book XI of *The Odyssey* to bring his hero up to date with key information about the real world, both past and future. He also uses the *nekusis* to answer any outstanding questions that may be in the listener's mind about what happened to key characters from his other epic poem, *The Iliad*, between the conclusion of that work and the beginning of *The Odyssey*.

What such journeys suggest is that certain individuals, because of their cunning or their ability to deal with grand pressures on a grand scale, are eligible for a trip to the nether regions. This journey within a journey gives the hero the cachet of one who has been to the worst place imaginable and returned to talk about it. And the world below provides the epic hero with the opportunity to learn not only about the world from which he is cut off, but also about his own future. A *nekusis* often presents the reader with information that foreshadows key events in the narrative. Having thus heard important information from a semi-reliable source (in the case of *The Odyssey*, the always-reliable blind prophet Tiresias and the dead Achilles), the reader is able to exclaim, when the events do come to pass in the narrative, "I *knew* that was going to happen!"

Only special characters in literature get to visit the dead. In the apocryphal mythology of the New Testament, Christ is said to have gone down into the underworld on Holy Saturday, the day of Lachrymosa (or tears), and kicked open the gates of hell to release the souls of righteous individuals, such as the Old Testament characters and prophets, who were born outside of the reach of Christian grace. Virgil borrows the idea of the *nekusis* in *The Aeneid*, and his description of the Underworld has entered post–New Testament Christian thought and become, as we shall see in chapter 4, the basis for most people's image of this terrible place. Dante, in tribute to Virgil, picks up on *The Aeneid*'s legalistic hell in *The Inferno* and places all his enemies in various states of torment, each according to his or her own psychosis.

If digressions are an important part of the success of an epic, the performance of the piece is equally key. An epic poem must be structured in such a way that it does not tire the voice of the performer. The entire performance, if delivered at a single sitting, might take from ten hours to sixteen. When read aloud on the Irish RTE and the Canadian CBC radio networks, James Joyce's *Ulysses*, for example, took twenty-two hours. The average length of time a normal human being can sustain a projected voice of continuous speech for performance purposes, as most university lecturers will attest, is about an hour and forty minutes. After that, even the most trained voices are apt to run into problems of hoarseness and dryness. To solve this problem, Homer focused the narrative structure of *The Odyssey* around very specific moments and events. These, in literature, are called *episodes*.

The word *episode* in its contemporary sense reflects much of the original meaning: it is another installment in the story. An episode is a compact unit of a sub-story within a larger story, a moment that the author has selected for detailed examination. It usually contains a narrative and thematic incident that crystalizes a key point in the development of events. The episode was useful in the epic because it not only allowed the performer to describe a specific incident and then rest his voice, have a drink, or go to the bathroom during a brief interlude (a moment in the performance that usually entailed music, dancing, or singing), but also provided the listeners with a chance to rest their minds and absorb what they had just heard. The interlude is still celebrated today for exactly these reasons: the performance of multi-act operas or plays usually breaks conveniently so that everyone can run to the bar or the facilities.

The idea of the focused event that makes for an episode has given us the contemporary concept of the chapter, a means of isolating and selecting a sequence of key events that forms a unified sub-story within the larger narrative. Chapters in novels, or in non-fiction works such as this, allow the reader the privilege of moving through a much broader narrative at a more leisurely pace. They serve to break up the story into digestible portions, and they are the reason why extended narratives such as the modern novel are so popular—chapters break a much larger narrative down into portions that make for an entertaining evening or an absorbing bus ride. The chapter, not surprisingly, also gave rise to that most modern of literary genres, the short story. Like a chapter, a short story can be digested at one sitting and deals with a focussed theme or depiction of an event. All these literary developments entered the world because Homer wanted to spare the voices of the bards who were reciting his work. What is amazing is that the epic form, invented so long ago, should reach into the twenty-first century and continue to shape the entertainment and reading habits of millions of people.

We exist in a print-based world, but the world in which the Homeric epic was born was memory-based. In its heyday, *The Odyssey* would have been recited from memory, and the work that we now see on the printed page would have been part of the oral tradition. We tend to think that a literary text is something that exists on the page and is reanimated by the reader for that instant of recognition when the work is read. But poetry was something that was originally recited, passing not from page to page, but from reciter to listener. We still think of poetry as something "we learn by heart," but the prospect of memorizing a text as large as *The Odyssey*, let alone the handful of grade school poems that most of us have, is daunting. It is hard for us to imagine that up until the twentieth century, literature was created in the spirit of the oral tradition. A case in point is William Wordsworth's famous poem

Lines Composed a Few Miles above Tintern Abbey. Wordsworth had no manuscript for the poem. During a foot journey from Wales northward to his home in England's Lake District, he composed the entire poem in his head, all 159 lines of it.

Few poets in the twentieth century have endeavored to create their work not only *from* memory but *in* the memory—the Georgian tramp poet W.H. Davies is perhaps the one, rare exception—yet the whole art is shaped around various sonic techniques and verbal designs that are meant to appeal to the nervous system, that "hard drive" of our bodies where physical memory is encoded. Meter, rhyme, assonance, and alliteration—the stuff of traditional poetry—are all appeals to our physiology. The steady, marching rhythm of the original ancient Greek version of *The Odyssey* was meant not only to mimic the waves or to suggest the continuous forward motion of the epic events, but to ingrain the phrases, the ideas, and the images on the memories of the poem's listeners, for whom the recitation was a sensual, bodily experience.

Poets such as the Phaecian performer Demodocus from Book VIII would have many such epics in their oral repertoires—a feat of memory that seems beyond comprehension to most modern readers. The suggestion is that Demodocus has a special gift from the gods, the gift of inward vision or poetic sight, because he is blind:

> The equerry now came up, leading their favorite bard whom the Muse loved above all others, though she had mingled good and evil in her gifts, robbing him of his eyes but lending sweetness to his song.

The image of the blind poet becomes a recurring motif in Western literature. It suggests that such individuals have an inward eye, the ability to see and understand a greater landscape within themselves as a form of compensation from the gods for their physical challenge. Milton, of course, is the modern embodiment of this idea. His sonnet on his blindness, *When I Consider How My Light Is Spent*, in which he laments the loss of his sight but sees in it the hope for some greater purpose, has become one of the great statements on this theme:

When I consider how my light is spent
Ere half my days, in this dark world and wide,
And that one talent which is death to hide,
Lodged with me useless, though my soul more bent
To serve there with my Maker, and present
My true account, lest He returning chide;
"Doth God exact day-labor, light denied?"
I fondly ask; but Patience to prevent
That murmur, soon replies, "God doth not need
Either man's work or His own gifts; who best
Bear his mild yoke, they serve Him best. His state
Is kingly. Thousands at His bidding speed
And post o'er land and ocean without rest:
They also serve who only stand and wait."

Milton perceives his blindness not so much as a gift from the Muses as Homer would reason, but as a "yoke" that he must bear as a Christian. He returns to the issue of the blindness of poets in Book III of *Paradise Lost*, where his discussion is partly a tribute to Homer's epic treatment of the inward eye, and partly an excuse to show that *The Odyssey* is operating as an influential model for his own poem:

With other notes than to th' Orphean Lyre
I sung of Chaos and Eternal Night,
Taught by the heav'nly Muse to venture down
The dark descent, and up to reascend,
Though hard and rare: thee I revisit safe,
And feel thy sovran vital Lamp; but thou
Revisit'st not these eyes, that roll in vain
To find thy piercing ray, and find no dawn....

...Cease I to wander where the Muses haunt
Clear spring, or shady Grove, or Sunny Hill,
Smit with the love of sacred Song...

One can almost feel Milton's sense of isolation and the darkness that filled his little house just north of London in the village of

Chalfont St. Giles. There, he dictated to his daughters *Paradise Lost*, a poem he composed entirely in his head. For Milton, like Homer's Demodocus, the inward light—the light of inspiration that seems to come from somewhere other than the physical world—is what inspires his song:

> *So much the rather thou Celestial Light*
> *Shine inward, and the mind through all her powers*
> *Irradiate, there plant eyes, all mist from thence*
> *Purge and disperse, that I may see and tell*
> *Of things invisible to mortal sight.*

The blind poet not only sees the things of this world, but sees beyond physical reality and offers some understanding of why events happen as they do. The individual who sees beyond the visible world is called the *vatic*, a word that many will recognize as the root of that famous Holy See, the Vatican.

The vatic poet is part prophet. In ancient literature, particularly in Sophocles' Theban plays (the subject of chapter 3), blind characters are able to see what folly-bound humans cannot. They offer advice that, though rarely heeded, is the gospel truth. It is no accident, therefore, that when Odysseus descends to Hades in Book XI of *The Odyssey*, one of the people he meets among the Shades is the androgynous prophet Tiresias. It is Tiresias in *The Odyssey* who presents the most foreshadowing information—in fact, he gives the entire story away just so that anyone who has to leave early won't feel cheated. But beyond setting up the suspense for what will follow in Homer's poem, Tiresias offers a glimpse of the sequel. He tells Odysseus that his adventures will not be over just because he returns home and reestablishes his rule over Ithaca. He warns that the protagonist of *The Odyssey* will suffer from itchy feet as he enters his senior years:

> You must take a well-cut oar and go on till you reach a people
> who know nothing of the sea and never use salt with their
> food, so that our crimson-painted ships and the long oars that
> serve those ships for wings are quite beyond their ken. And this
> will be your cue—a very clear one, which you cannot miss.
> When you fall in with some other traveler who speaks of the
> "winnowing-fan" you are carrying on your shoulder, the time
> will come for you to plant your shapely oar in the earth and
> offer Lord Poseidon the rich sacrifice of a ram, a bull, and a
> breeding-boar... As for your own end, Death will come to you
> out of the sea, Death in his gentlest guise. When he takes you,
> you will be worn out after an easy old age and surrounded by a
> prosperous people. This is the truth that I have told you.

This advertisement for a lost epic known as *The Telegony*, or the further voyages of Odysseus, is the basis for a famous poem by Alfred Tennyson, *Ulysses*. In that poem, the aged Odysseus decides that

> *'Tis not too late to seek a newer world.*
> *Push off, and sitting well in order smite*
> *The sounding furrows; for my purpose holds*
> *To sail beyond the sunset, and the baths*
> *Of all the western stars, until I die.*

It may be that the gulfs will wash us down;
It may be we shall touch the Happy Isles,
And see the great Achilles, whom we knew.
Though much is taken, much abides; and though
We are not now that strength which in old days
Moved earth and heaven, that which we are, we are—
One equal temper of heroic hearts,
Made weak by time and fate, but strong in will
To strive, to seek, to find, and not to yield.

Brave words. But what makes the Tiresian prophecy so engaging is the idea that the same boundless energy that animates *The Odyssey* and the character of Odysseus will not be limited to the journey home. Homer is saying that there is more to come, entertainment for future evenings of revels and ritual. There is also the indomitable spirit of the individual.

What we cannot forget in all this discussion is that Classical epics such as *The Odyssey* were operating on the pleasure principle. The poem was meant to be entertaining, and even today it reads like a novel, or at least like the sort of book one should take along on a beach vacation. As performance pieces in their own time, the Homeric epics (and some critics believe they were the product of a school of poets, rather than a single author) were extremely popular. Depending on the occasion, the host would request a specific poem to be performed. As we've observed, the recitation that takes place in honor of the Phaecian games in Book VIII of *The Odyssey* is *The Iliad*:

When they had satisfied their appetite and thirst, the bard was inspired by the Muse to sing of famous men. He chose a passage from a lay well known by then throughout the world, the Quarrel of Odysseus and Achilles, telling how these two had fallen out at a rich ceremonial banquet and dismayed the rest by the violence of their language.

Odysseus' reaction to hearing the passages from *The Iliad* performed is one of extreme nostalgia:

It caused Odysseus to lift his purple mantle with his sturdy hands and draw it down over his head to hide his comely face, for he was ashamed to be caught weeping by the Phaecians. But in the intervals of the worthy minstrel's song, he wiped the tears away and removing the cloak from his head reached for his two-handled cup and made libations to the gods. Yet whenever Demodocus started to sing again, encouraged by the Phaecian lords, who were enjoying the tale, Odysseus once more hid his face and wept.

Like Keats, who was only the reader of a Homeric epic, the central character of the poem (known as the *protagonist*) is himself moved by the words. This is one of the few examples that we have in early literature where the text is *self-conscious*, and where the author is informing us as to how such pieces of literature should be presented to an audience. For listeners who might have heard *The Odyssey* recited in its own time, the scene must surely have made them feel as if Odysseus himself were in the room. The only problem, however, is that Odysseus could not possibly have been in the room: *The Odyssey* and *The Iliad* were composed at least five hundred years after the events they describe.

Peter Paul Rubens. The Judgement of Paris. The "cocky" Trojan prince is depicted here as he is presented with the no-win situation of having to determine the most beautiful among the goddesses. The ramifications of his choice led to the Trojan War's fateful outcome, and, indirectly, to the founding of Rome.

The Bronze Age, the era that embraces the period up to and including the Trojan War, lasted from 2000 BC to 1200 BC. It was a time of relative stability in the western Mediterranean. What brought it crashing down, however, was a huge international conflict that aligned the Danaans (the Greeks) against the people who would become their traditional mortal enemies: the Trojans, who inhabited what is modern-day Turkey. The whole event was triggered by a cocky Trojan prince named Paris, who kidnapped Helen, the wife of a Greek king named Menelaus. When Paris took the abducted Helen home to Troy, his father, King Priam, realized that he had an economic and political trump card in his hand against his trading rivals to the west and refused to give her up. Suddenly, as during the Cold War that took place following our last world war, east lined up against west and the world was divided down the middle. To answer the insult that had been leveled at the Greeks as a people, all the small kingdoms, including Odysseus' Ithaca, came to the rescue of Helen and launched an invasion of Asia Minor. It was a situation not unlike the ententes and alliances that led to the start of the First World War. With national and even racial pride on the line, both sides fought for ten years, wasting all their economic and political resources until a resolution was won.

That resolution came when the cunning Odysseus devised the stratagem of the Trojan horse—a present for the enemy that lies at the heart of the old cliché, "Avoid Greeks bearing gifts." Hidden inside the hollow wooden horse were Greek troops led by Odysseus, who, once inside the sacred city of Troy, leapt out, opened the gates, and massacred the unsuspecting Trojans. For his cunning and his effort, Odysseus was accorded by history—and by Homer—the label of "sacker of Troy." It is a label that will come back to haunt him as a literary character when his story is related by the Roman poets Virgil and Ovid in later works: the Romans in *The Aeneid* perceive themselves as the inheritors of Troy, and look upon the Greeks as their mortal enemies.

The actual Trojan War lasted from 1194 BC to 1184 BC. During this ten-year period, the entire western Mediterranean civilization came to a standstill. The international economy that had taken

generations to build suddenly faltered, then collapsed. Political dynasties in the home countries, as *The Odyssey* suggests, were left in the hands of plunderers and poor administrators. Homer's prequel to *The Odyssey*, *The Iliad*, deals with only a brief period near the end of the Trojan War, chronicling the quarrels and unrest that were splitting the Greek alliance and fragmenting the tired army at the very point of victory. Unlike *The Aeneid*, *The Iliad* does not deal with the bloody sack of Troy—something restrained and reserved in Homer avoids the gruesome, graphic details of violence. Instead, Homer's poem ends with the heroic but seemingly senseless battle in which Achilles kills Hector before the walls of the city. In this final scene, Homer is emphasizing that war is folly, a futile pursuit that ultimately destroys the very best individuals in a society. In the wake of the war, there is no Marshall Plan. There is only a universal vacuum, an empty, elegiac world where the individual struggles not only to return home but to survive.

If a single individual really composed the entire poem, if a man named Homer really did exist, he likely saw the world of *The Odyssey* not from the point of view of Odysseus, the Greek "sacker of Troy," but from the perspective of a Trojan. All historical evidence suggesting that there was a real Homer points to the fact that he hailed from the losing side of the war. For all the semi-facts

and speculation, it is hard to separate the legend from the author. Modern scholars have surmised that he was from Asia Minor, from a place called Chios, rather than from a host of Greek cities that claimed him as their own. Tradition has it that he, like the poet who recites *The Iliad*, was blind. Another tradition has him dwelling in the city of Smyrna, a notion that T.S. Eliot borrows for the third part of *The Waste Land*, where Homer is transformed into the homosexual Greek merchant Mr. Eugenides.

Whoever Homer was, he had a profound and thorough knowledge of the Mediterranean, its geography and its history. The geographic detail of *The Odyssey*, an account so exact in its descriptions of landmarks that modern interpreters of the work have been able to navigate by it, suggests that he was as well traveled and as well versed in the "cities of many peoples" as his ill-fated protagonist.

Homer was unquestionably skilled at drawing on real events and places, but above all he was a master in the realm of the imagination. Aristotle in his *Poetics* pays Homer perhaps the greatest tribute that can be accorded an author of imaginative writing:

> Above all, Homer has taught other poets how to tell untruths as they ought to be told, that is, by the use of fallacy. If one thing exists because another thing exists, or happens because this other happens, people think that, if the consequent exists or happens, the antecedent will also exist; but this is not the case. Thus if a proposition were untrue, but there was something else which must be true or must happen if the proposition were true, then it is this something else that we should lay down as a fact; for the mind, knowing it to be true, may fallaciously infer the truth of the original proposition.

Aristotle is attempting to explain in this rather knotted sequence of reasoning that Homer was a master of fiction, but more so a master of the fantastic. Fear in literature, the act of allowing not only the protagonist but the audience or reader to experience that excitement, is the result of a whole series of cause-and-effect relationships that the author is constructing. If something goes bump in the night and we are not certain what it is, then surely, says the imagination, something strange and awful must have made the

Jean Auguste Dominique Ingres. The Apotheosis of Homer. In this rather stiff and stylized canvas, Ingres draws a direct association between the power of the poet's vatic imagination and the approval of heaven. At the painting's lower left can be seen Newton, Descartes and other notables of the Enlightenment, a not too subtle suggestion on Ingres' part that science and imaginative writing share the same roots.

noise. Homer achieves this not only through his incredible sense of detail, but through his ability to locate all the actions of his narrative in a world that is inhabited by spiritual forces. This kind of world is called the *animate universe*, and it is the imaginative realm in which Classical poetry and drama are set.

To understand the concept of the animate universe, we have first to reexamine the world of the Bible. In the Bible, there is only one God, rather than a whole pantheon of opposing and disagreeable deities such as we have in *The Iliad* or *The Odyssey*. God is in his heaven, and aside from the odd miracle, such as a pillar of fire or a great flood, he tends to leave the world alone. Einstein's comment, "I am convinced that he does not play dice with the universe," is a perspective situated in the Judeo-Christian universe, where God watches the world and humankind from a safe distance. But such is not the case in the Classical or pagan imagination. In the Classical universe, the gods play active roles in the affairs of humans. They bet on individual characters who happen to strike their fancy and they play dice with the fates of men and women. To make matters worse, each god has a whole contingent of sub-deities who are active on earth. The Sacred Cattle of the Sun are the property of Apollo, for example, and when Odysseus' men serve themselves a barbecue, they incur the wrath of the sun god. Polyphemus the Cyclops is the son of Poseidon, the god of the sea, the same nemesis who continually blows Odysseus off course. The message is that if you put a foot wrong in the animate universe, if you step on the wrong rock or eat the wrong animal, someone in the heavens is going to take offense. No wonder it takes so long to get home.

The principle of the animate universe of the Classical or pagan world, as opposed to the *inanimate universe* of the Judeo-Christian cosmos (where God has simply said, "All this is yours, do with it as you may"), means that figures such as Odysseus experience nothing akin to divine grace. With every action a risk and every locale a hazard, the Classical world is a dangerous place. In fact, it is a place where tragedy is possible. The tragedy of Sophocles' Theban plays, for instance, comes about because the cosmic structure does not possess mercy. The metier of the world is suffering. And if nature and the heavens are without mercy, then humans naturally follow suit. On the other hand, there can be no tragedy in the Judeo-Christian world because everything is within God's grace and part of a divine plan. Terrible things happen to Job, of course. God does play dice with *his* fate. But God knows that he is going to win the bet with Satan because he has that extra edge—foreknowledge. The Book of Job, the one biblical text that comes closest to being a philosophical dialogue from Classical literature, ends happily, comically, because everything is restored to Job—everything, that is, except the servants and the children who somehow get dashed in the process.

Most Classical characters are not as fortunate as Job. In fact, in the context of the animate and tragic universe in which *The Odyssey* is set, the survival and return of Odysseus is nothing short of a miracle. His very existence, in spite of all that the heavens and nature set against him, is a testament to the resilience of humankind. To twentieth- and twenty-first-century readers, who have survived some unspeakable hardships of history, Odysseus becomes a metaphor because he is able to use his intelligence, his cunning, and his wisdom to carry him through the most difficult of situations. Odysseus is the ultimate psycho-warrior.

Odysseus' survival and triumph also signal to readers in all ages that the life of one person can affect the destiny of an entire nation. Ithaca needs Odysseus to return, and his single-minded determination to get home is what saves his people from political anarchy. What Homer indirectly creates through the story of *The Odyssey* is a comic literary structure that later authors will replay time and time again when they set out to tell the stories of how their nations survived. Thanks to Homer, this structure and its ten essential attibutes have become almost a universal formula, a system for shaping an *epic* story.

The rule in literary studies is that if we want to understand the psychology of a nation, what that country's people hold dearest to their hearts and their imaginations, we need look no further than its epics. The first essential attribute of an epic, therefore, is that it deals with the destiny not just of an individual, but of a nation. Think of some of the great epic poems that have been written in Western literature: the medieval French *Chanson de Roland* (where a band of brave knights fight to the death, à la Verdun of 1916, to prevent the invasion of France by the Moors); Edmund Spenser's great English epic of the struggles of Protestantism over Catholicism, *The Faerie Queene*; or Camoëns' epic of the growth of the Portuguese nation through the art of navigation, *The Lusiads*. These poems encapsulate and define the spirits of their peoples, and go a long way toward articulating what those nations most want to preserve from their collective experience. The heroes of these poems, whether Odysseus, the Red Crosse Knight, or the beleaguered Roland, make decisions that affect the course of history and, as heroes, become national *exempla*, role models for all future citizens. Nowhere is the epic hero's role as an exemplum more in evidence than in Virgil's epic to end all epics, *The Aeneid*. In *The Aeneid*, as we shall see in chapter 4, the single-minded determination of a sole character can reshape the destiny not only of an empire but of the world.

In terms of its scope, an epic is usually set in the context of the broader world, and this feature is the second attribute of the form. The epic creates a picture of an entire world—accordingly, the setting of any epic is vast. In *The Odyssey*, Homer sets the standard by making his canvas the known world of the Mediterranean, and thereby reaches to the limits of both geographical knowledge and the imagination. George Lucas' *Star Wars* films suggest that in the contemporary world, our knowledge is as far-reaching as the very limits of the galaxy.

The third important attribute arises from the limitlessness of an epic's setting. Because the epic ranges so freely across the map of the imagination, it can draw upon the limits of what is possible, not only in the physical world, but in the realm of the supernatural. In almost every epic, especially the ancient ones, the supernatural plays a major role. *The Odyssey* is set in a polytheistic animate universe where the gods and their sub-deities become actively involved in the events. The Bible, especially the New Testament, comes close to the epic because it deals with the life and influence of a single character (Christ), who undergoes a *nekusis* (the Harrowing of Hell), and whose actions have far-reaching consequences. Christ is the only major supernatural human character in the Bible—he is the son of God—yet his supernatural attributes are not demonstrated as powers but as miracles, and the miracles of the New Testament reflect Christ's empathy rather than antipathy toward humankind.

Like the Bible, an epic relates its narrative in an *elevated* (a highly poeticized and stylized) language and treats the events with considerable seriousness—the fourth attribute of the epic. In some respects, particularly in the early attempts by Homer and his followers, this type of poem approached the same level of linguistic seriousness that is found in sacred texts. To achieve this linguistic seriousness, epic poets rely on the grand eloquence of simple yet direct language, and it can be said that stylistically *The Odyssey* is written with a grand simplicity. This same sort of simplicity and directness is the hallmark of the inheritor of the epic tradition, the modern novel.

One of the qualities shared by great novelists of the modern era, such as Tolstoy, Faulkner, or Mann, is their ability to relate their narratives with the distance and intelligence that comes from an expert use of the objective perspective. Epic poems always convey a sublime sense of *objectivity*—the fifth essential element of the epic form—because poets such as Homer believed they could gain greater audience engagement and imaginative connection by not taking the side of the protagonist. The reader or listener of an epic senses that the story is presented from arm's length, and that the author is dispassionately intelligent enough to remain unbiased and non-partisan in the relation of the events.

Perhaps this sense of non-partisanship evolves because epics are rarely, if ever, written in their own times. The epic form draws much of its success and its intelligent objectivity from the work of historians, who have already gone where the poet's imagination treads, and have sorted out all the questions and hazy bits that might surround a particular event. The listener benefits from this distance as well. Epics are the by-products of time, and rely on the fact that the stories they tell have been around long enough for readers or listeners to know what is going to happen. In this respect, the central question one uses to approach the epic is not "What is going to happen?" but "How is the author going to entertain me with the telling?" This sixth attribute of the epic suggests that the form's focus is not the events, but the art of relating the events. In this sense, these poems are schools that teach us what literature can do best.

The very nature of chronicle that lies at the heart of the epic leads to the seventh attribute. Epics usually consist of great historical or mythical deeds that require enormous valor, superhuman strength, courage, or endurance. If the epic speaks for what is best in humankind, that is because it takes as its subject matter events that are in themselves notable and memorable. Perhaps in a few hundred years, someone will sit down and write an epic about Winston Churchill and the Second World War. If so, he or she will write with the benefit of history, and the knowledge that an individual's will and determination can be reflected in the spirit of an entire nation.

If an epic about Churchill were to be written, it would, like *The Odyssey*, rely not simply on history for its textual information, but on other stories and works of literature. The eighth attribute of the epic is that it is *intertextual*—it borrows ideas from other works and refers, in subtle ways, to other texts. Perhaps the most intertextual long poem ever written, a poem that approaches the epic in its scope and proportions, is T.S. Eliot's *The Waste Land*. In that poem, Eliot tells the story of a declining culture and explains, through an intermittent narrative voice and a chorus of other speakers who chime in throughout the text, how that culture might be saved. If intertextuality smacks of theft to some more scrupulous readers, we have to remember that it was T.S. Eliot who explained the contemporary notion of intertextuality rather glibly with the statement, "An immature poet imitates and a mature poet steals." *The Waste Land*, of course, is not an epic, but contemporary readers view it as an "epic" event in twentieth-century literature. Closer to the mark, at least on the basis of intertextuality, are Ezra Pound's *Cantos* (an implosion of cultural information) and his intriguing short epic *Hugh Selwyn Mauberley*, which tells the story of a poet, not unlike himself, in the years following the First World War. The one modern work that is definitely an epic in all its respects, a novel that is closely modeled on *The Odyssey*, is James

Joyce's *Ulysses*, a tour de force that is the subject of the final chapter of this book.

Intertextuality in literature means that an author not only draws upon a vast array of sources and information to express his or her story, but also relies extensively upon the resources of the reader. In *The Odyssey*, Homer takes it for granted that his listeners will have a thorough practicing knowledge of the religion of the time (the worship of the Olympian gods) and a sound familiarity with history and sacred texts relating to the Greek experience.

The religious aspects of the epic are what connects it to the spiritual concerns of the society for which it speaks. Not only is the poem as serious as a sacred text, but it is also, presumably, written with divine assistance. Those blind poets, those vatics, realized that the scope of the subject, the tone, and the imagery were beyond the expression of mere mortals. The very outsized nature of the epic suggests that it is a work of superhuman vision and expression. Rather than take the blame or accept the praise for achieving something divine, epic poets through the ages have claimed that the poem has been channeled from above. The ninth attribute of the epic is its constant appeal to forces beyond the physical realm to assist the poet with the telling of the story. This appeal for divine help is called the *invocation*.

The word *invocation* comes from the Latin *voca*, meaning "to call." An invocation is, in its strictest sense, the act of calling upon a spiritual presence, the helping hand of divine assistance. It is often signaled by an appeal to the Muses (those female spirits of the arts who live atop Mount Helicon in the Classical world), as in the opening lines of *Paradise Lost* where Milton pleads, "Sing Heav'nly Muse." The invocation can also be announced in a text with the word "O," as in the opening lines of the Prologue to Shakespeare's play *Henry V*:

O for a Muse of fire, that would ascend
The brightest heaven of invention;
A kingdom for a stage, princes to act
And monarchs to behold the swelling scene!

Whenever this "O" turns up in a text, we must assume that a voice from beyond is speaking through the poet at the poet's request. What the writer is doing is calling upstairs: for if more is known in heaven than can be dreamed of in all our books, the capable and authentic epic poets go right to the source.

The idea of the text being a joint creation of the poet and a divine being has its most startling manifestation in Virgil's *Aeneid*, because whenever Virgil reaches a rough spot in the narrative, a point where his voice is overcome by emotion, he calls upon the Muses to help him out. These moments of extreme emotion almost derail the storyteller from his story. It is the Muse who brings the poet back to equilibrium and who restores order, that most important of Roman virtues. For Homer, however, always the cocky and confident storyteller, especially in the guise of Odysseus, the invocation is found only at the very beginning of his work. Once the epic poet invokes the Muse, the reader or listener is to assume that the whole work is a process of some divine and wonderful imagination that lies far beyond both the text and the world at hand.

The tenth and final attribute of the Homeric epic, as we have already discussed, is the sequence in which the events of the story are presented. It is Homer who invents the concept of starting the story *in medias res*, and who devises the useful idea of digressions to make the story even more engaging. This process of scrambling the chronology has two important effects: it both collapses narrative time and lengthens the process of the real-time storytelling. The hosts of those stylized banquets where the Homeric epics were first performed must surely have felt that they were getting a lot of bang for their buck.

As Aristotle observed in the *Poetics*, partly to define the nature of the epic and partly to pay tribute to Homer, the epic avoids "monotony" because it allows the storyteller to be in many places at once. In literature, this is called *omniscience*, and it is the backbone of what we today refer to as the *third-person narrative*, where all the characters are referred to as "he" or "she." Omniscience is clearly an objective stance because a narrator can be in two or more places at once if he or she is standing outside the story. If the narrator were to tell the story from inside the events, as an eye-witness or a participant, for example, then the storyteller would be chronicling the events from the perspective of the *first-person narrative*: or "I saw this" and "I did that." Omniscience is extremely useful to the epic, not only because it lends an objectivity to the relation of events, but because it places the narrator far enough outside the action to allow him or her to shuffle the sequence of time. This allows events in the narrative to appear to transcend time or work outside of time. Perhaps Keats had this in mind when he wrote the opening lines of *On First Looking into Chapman's Homer*, when he talks about traveling "the realms of gold."

In the end, *The Odyssey* is about the splendor of the world and how one can experience it through the imagination. Later commentators, such as Freud, suggest that *The Odyssey* is a metaphor for the process of waking and returning to consciousness. As Odysseus traverses the "wine-dark sea," there is a sense that he is trapped in the nether world of the imagination, the nightmare. The more he struggles, it seems, the deeper he sinks into that darkness; yet he knows that there is some sort of light shining at the end of the tunnel, and that he must reach it. That light is home.

The Nobel Prize–winning poet Derek Walcott, in his 1993 stage play *The Odyssey* (an early performance of which took place in an open-air theater on a hilltop in St. Lucia, within sight of Walcott's own home), concludes his blues-calypso rendition of Homer's story with a song that encapsulates the sentiments of the original Greek epic:

I sang of that man against whom the sea still rages,
Who escaped its terrors, that despair could not destroy,

Since that first blind singer, others will sing down the ages
Of the heart in its harbour, then long years after Troy, after Troy.

And a house, happy house for good, from a swallow's omen,
Let the trees clap their hands, and the surf whisper amen.

For a rock, a rock, a rock, a rock-steady woman
Let the waves clap their hands and the surf whisper amen.

For that peace which, in their mercy, the gods allow men.

Home is what shapes the way we see the world. It gives us our values, our truths, because it is the place where we feel we belong. Virgil's *Aeneid* (a work written as a literary response to *The Odyssey*), a story about a people looking for a new home, is really about the protection of personal values, the need for a sense of security, and what happens to those who threaten that security. Home, as has been said, is where the heart is. But what lies beyond it? The tug between the desire to explore and know the world and the longing to be where one is defined and at home remains an unresolved issue. As long as there is a tension between wanderlust and what one can trust, as long as human beings suffer from homesickness, *The Odyssey* will repeat itself in every story of a great journey, and will always hold a special place in the imagination.

The scope, structure, and techniques of Homer's epic must have had an enormous impact on Keats because in 1818 he sat down and wrote another sonnet about Chapman's *Homer*, a poem called *To Homer*. In it, Keats observes that the epic is all about how one sees things, especially if one is a blind, vatic poet and storyteller: "There is a triple sight in blindness keen." Perhaps Keats is remarking on the fact that epic poets see the world not only through the inward eye, but through the desire to order and shape vast amounts of information and incredible expanses of time into a single, coherent vision. As we know, the Classical world lacked a sense of divine grace. What it presented instead was the idea of hope, the belief that against the odds, humankind would somehow succeed. Through the ages, writers have sought to articulate the concept of hope, whether it is what one must abandon at the gates of hell in Dante's vision, or the idea that "man will not merely endure, he will prevail," as William Faulkner articulated in his Nobel Prize address. Epics are about hope, even if they end tragically, because they show us the way to what Abraham Lincoln called "the better angels of our nature." They remind us that we are human, that we have both collective and personal desires, and that in the great scope of human struggle there is something we must protect, something that is worth all the fight and all the effort. Or, as Keats put it, "on the shores of darkness there is light."

3

THE WHOLE
SAD STORY

Sophocles' Theban Plays

EVERYTHING seemed calm and peaceful at sea that April night. The water was like glass and reflected the light of the constellations in the cold, dark depths. The strains of lilting dance music wafted from the liner as it made its maiden voyage toward New York. But then, out of nowhere... The ship was supposed to be unsinkable. How could this be happening? For those on board the S.S. *Titanic* that night of April 15, 1912, the unthinkable *had* happened. There were various responses: heroism, fear, horror, and tremendous grief. One passenger remarked that as the great liner slid beneath the icy waves and the cries of the dying evaporated into the starry sky, she felt a tremendous sense of emptiness. One moment, the world had been complete, almost perfect. The next minute, everything that they had staked their lives on for that voyage was gone.

When the newspapers printed their reports of the disaster in the weeks following the sinking, when the tally of 1,513 lost souls had been counted, the event was deemed an act of fate, a tragedy of the highest proportions. Thomas Hardy, the English poet and novelist, responded to the unparalleled loss of life at sea with his poem *The Convergence of the Twain*:

> *In a solitude of the sea*
> *Deep from human vanity,*
> *And the Pride of Life that planned her, stilly couches she.*

What Hardy is echoing very precisely in the opening lines of his poem is not merely the loss of an ocean liner that did not have enough lifeboats, but the very nature of tragedy.

In its traditional sense and the way it works within the literary continuum, tragedy is the result of human vanity, of the blind confidence that leads to a realization as cold as the North Atlantic, a realization that there is no hope. Yet for all that can be said about tragedy as a literary form, it remains one of the most abused and misused terms in the modern world. To the ancients, it was a serious matter, a means of showing human beings the chinks in the armor of the human personality. In the modern world, however, it has been misidentified with events such as the sinking of the *Titanic*. Yet that catastrophe lacked several of the key elements of tragedy: there was no *spectacle* (except for those in the lifeboats), no *thought* (elevated philosophical pronouncements delivered at the moment of catastrophe), no *diction* (the elevated poetic language that explains the situation as it happens), and until James Cameron and Céline Dion came along, no *song* associated with the event.

Tragedy, as it has come down to us through the ages, is the result of a type of pride known as *hubris*, a blindness to the fact that Fate has a strange way of intervening in human events to make the worst of any given situation. Hubris flies in the face of fate. It was hubris that made the designers of the *Titanic* declare that the ship was unsinkable. It is the process by which an individual or a group turns away from the reality at hand and chooses instead to deal in the false comfort of illusions. It is the avoidance of truth that weakens the human position, that leaves those caught up in the sin of omission vulnerable to the power of invisible forces in the universe that would crush man utterly.

The literary concept of tragedy comes from three great defining plays that were written in the fourth century BC by a democratically minded Athenian playwright named Sophocles. What Sophocles presents in his three plays about the ill-fated hero Oedipus (*Oedipus the King*, *Oedipus at Colonus*, and *Antigone*) is the story of a man who grows up an orphan, returns home to kill his father, marry his mother, become king, and put his foot in his mouth. But it gets worse. He blinds himself after his mother's suicide, wanders away to a sacred grove in another city, and waits to die. There, because of a local law, he is refused sanctuary, and rather than trouble anyone further, he goes off quietly, and dies an unwanted exile and prophet no one will heed. The whole mess gets even more complicated because of the children. The two sons he has left at home fight over his lost kingdom. When they murder each other, the king gives one brother all honorable rites of burial, but orders the other left unburied, as an example to traitors. Oedipus' daughter Antigone rebels against this tyrannical law, buries her brother, and then is put to death for performing the requisite honor to the dead.

To the modern reader, the violence, the pity-evoking suffering, and the horror that comes from watching other human beings tormented profoundly seem beyond reason, and yet somehow so familiar. How could anyone make sense of the terrible events that so many experienced in the twentieth century? Yet that suffering happened, and no one can explain it to us in terms that we might find reasonable.

Tragedy is the one form of literature that is bound to leave us with questions, and when we cannot answer them satisfactorily, we are left with more questions. Romeo and Juliet are dead. Oedipus is destroyed. Lear's heart is broken. Coriolanus falls. How could such things happen? How could events get so out of hand that the innocent become the victims of a few hasty words and a few bad decisions? Does fate play upon the weak spots in a character? Are these characters the victims of destinies foretold by the gods, or are they their own worst enemies, unwittingly putting unreasonable conditions and semantic imperatives on their own lives that they must live by?

The word *tragedy*, as it exists in the contemporary sense, tends to mean anything that causes us grief because it is sad and unfortunate. It is derived from two ancient Greek words, *tragos* meaning "goat," and *oide* meaning "song." So what does a "goat song" have to do with suffering and grief? To understand the connection, we have to think back to the shepherd's world of Arcadia, the Classical world's notion of the Golden Age. The world was more or less perfect until the death of the young shepherd signaled that something had gone grievously out of kilter within the balance of nature. To lament the passing of this young shepherd, to offer him a proper elegy, the shepherds, it was surmised, sang a herding song in his memory, a goat song. That song spoke not simply of the need to find consolation, but of the grief that everyone shared. It described the loss of someone irreplaceable, a void that had entered the universe, and the utter helplessness that everyone felt in the face of death. Hence tragedy became the vehicle for expressing the emptiness and suffering that the presence of death brings. As we know, the Classical or pagan world view did not feature the built-in concept of mercy and divine goodness. In the pagan pantheon, there was as much discord in heaven as there was on earth, and the gods used people as pawns in their own struggles. (The Christian view, in contrast, saw humans as God's flock to be tended and nurtured.) Consolation, the ability to perceive that there is good in all events, no matter how bad they might be, was absent in the pagan perception. When life goes wrong for a character, there is no promise of salvation or hope; there is only absolute negation. Tragedy, and all the emotions it carried with it, became the only response of the bereaved survivors, a means of expressing their suffering and channeling it into something that others might understand.

The Christian universe, on the other hand, makes tragedy impossible because a loving God has a plan in which everything will work out for the best. Even though Christ dies, he rises from the dead. The resurrection is a signal to everyone that physical death is not the end of life, and if life is to continue—as Saint Paul argues and Christ promises—one need only possess the fortification of faith to answer death with life and to turn tragedy into comedy. God always promises a happy, comic ending, even if that ending is logically and physically against the rules of nature. Tragedy, by contrast, capitulates to nature. It says, "This is the end," and it leaves no escape clause, no consolation, and no hope.

The literary notion of tragedy was originally defined by Aristotle in his *Poetics*, in response to his reading of Sophocles' Theban plays. Aristotle says that tragedy has six key attributes: plot, character, spectacle, diction, thought, and song. The first of these, *plot*, is the most important of the six because the audience gets caught up in the events to the exclusion of logic and reality. Plot is essentially a question of what happens in a work of literature. The narrative line, the story, is what most audience members tune in to first when they go to the theater.

A story can have various types of plots. The first of these—the linear plot—is the simplest to follow because it moves chronologically from point A to point Z without jumping around in the process. Linear plots are essential to the Classical idea of drama because, in the process of going from point A to point Z without leaving any points out, they entail what Aristotle saw as the essential ingredient in drama: the unity of time and place. In this unity, all the events happen in one setting. The players do not have to change costumes, and the stagehands do not have to change sets. The action begins and ends in one place, is continuous, and is presented in real time as often as possible, rather than in selective or collapsed time.

Among the other types of plots are *digressional plots* and *reversed plots*. In a digressional plot, a character has a flashback, and a scene from the past is presented or explained at length. Digressions, however, are always messy when presented on stage. Shakespeare never used them because the shift in time schemes is apt to confuse an audience. More recent dramatists such as Thornton Wilder have used digressions to great effect. The contemporary British dramatist Harold Pinter used the reversed plot, the process of telling a story backwards, in his play *Betrayal*. But linear plots help dramatists maintain the spectacle of the presentation, and to focus the audience's attention on *what* is happening more than *how* the events are presented.

In Sophocles' plays, what catches the audience's attention, however, is the protagonist of the drama, the character on whom the entire weight of suffering seems to fall. Aristotle says that the second attribute of tragedy is *character*, and as sad as it sounds, the point of tragedy is to watch another human being suffer. The audience for a tragedy is aware as it enters the theater that there is no hope for the protagonist—the hero or heroine is not going to escape the fate that awaits him or her. But that is exactly what brings people out in droves. They are not drawn by sadistic cruelty, but by a kind of hopeful curiosity, and the pain of having that aspiration dashed. And tragic heroes never fail to remind us of just how far our hopes can fall when things go wrong.

Of course, these characters bring it on themselves. They have a *tragic flaw*, something in their personality that makes them overlook the possibility that fate will intervene and ruin their lives. Tragedy picks on the weaknesses in the human character and exploits them to create the spectacle of someone suffering greatly.

From the audience's safe distance, it appears that the human mind simply has a fascination with pain, perhaps because suffering presents a problem to the reader or audience member. The big question is not "What is happening?" but "Why is this happening?" Perhaps we all have an inner need to find both explanation and consolation for the bad things that happen. In many ways, tragedy is the curiosity to find cause in the effects that we witness. The point is to learn something: the characters learn from their mistakes, if they survive them, and the audience learns what leads people into their worst nightmares.

This concept of hoping against inevitability, of willingly giving over our attention for several hours in the belief that this time it all might be different for a tragic hero, is called *poetic justice*. In simple terms, poetic justice is the natural human hope that everything will work out well in the end, that the wicked will be punished for their sins, and the good will be rewarded or at least allowed some consolation for their suffering. If poetic justice is our desire to see a comic resolution to the events we are witnessing, then tragedy is the process whereby any hope for a positive outcome is dashed. We see the character go down in utter defeat, and we suffer with that character because he reflects ourselves. Each of us sees on the stage or the page a human being who, when confronted by a dilemma, reacts to the situation in the only way he or she knows how. Every protagonist is a mirror image of the self, and the more human and fallible a character seems, the more likely he or she is to elicit an emotional response in the audience when disaster strikes.

Underlying all this is the question of identification or empathy. Suffering is something everyone understands, though few want to experience it themselves. Tragedy, therefore, is a vicarious experience where the worst that can happen to a human being is played out upon another at a safe distance on the stage; yet the suffering that the audience members share is real. For example, the torment experienced by audiences who went to see Shakespeare's *King Lear* performed in London in the mid-eighteenth century got to be so bad that one theater owner rewrote the ending of the play. Rather than have poor Lear stumble out with the hanged Cordelia in his arms and cry "And my poor fool is hanged" as he falls stricken to the floor, the theater owner, ever fearful of lawsuits from the parents of young ladies with delicate hearts, turned the tragedy into a comedy. Up jumps Lear from the floor as he announces to the audience, "I feel much better now," while Cordelia revives and says, "My neck will feel better soon." The production then ends with a song-and-dance number, a revel straight out of the comic formula—all to spare the theatergoers the pain of seeing the hero and his world dashed to pieces.

This incredible capacity to provoke suffering on behalf of another human being, especially a fictitious one, is one of the great mysteries of tragedy. It is the mystery that troubles Saint Augustine in Book III of *Confessions*:

> Why is it that men enjoy feeling sad at the sight of tragedy and suffering on the stage, although they would be most unhappy if they had to endure the same fate themselves? Yet they watch the plays because they hope to be made to feel sad, and the feeling of sorrow is what they enjoy. What miserable delirium this is! The more a man is subject to such suffering himself, the more easily he is moved by it in the theatre. Yet when he suffers himself, we call it misery: when he suffers out of sympathy with others we call it pity. But what sort of pity can we really feel for an imaginary scene on the stage?

Saint Augustine, as we shall see in chapter 7, sought a philosophical remedy for the dilemma presented by stage tragedy. He believed that only a critical vision, the ability to discern between what is real and what is not, could intervene in this process of identification that takes place between an audience member and the tragic hero. Readers or audience members, he reasoned, identify with a protagonist because he or she is the center of attention, and in the case of a tragedy, that character is suffering under some extremely unfortunate circumstance. In *The Odyssey*, for example, Odysseus explains that he has "had a long spell of evil luck," yet the listener continues to focus attention on him, hoping for the best. Everyone wants the tired wanderer to get home. When he does reach Ithaca and restores his fortunes, everyone is relieved. Had he not, there would have been an enormous outpouring of grief, a response that Aristotle calls a tragic *catharsis*. In a catharsis, the audience's emotions build until they reach the breaking point, when the tears begin to flow. Pity is evoked, and all hope seems irredeemably lost.

The process of bearing witness also lies at the heart of tragedy. The initial reaction on the part of a reader or theatergoer is to turn away. But something in the human makeup causes us to want to look, and that something is the third attribute of tragedy, *spectacle*. Until Arthur Miller came along in the twentieth century with *Death of a Salesman* and brought the weight of suffering to the working middle class, tragedy was the domain of the high-born. Like epic heroes, tragic heroes are outsized characters who play an enormous role in the shape and direction of their societies. When they fall, they bring the world down with them. In the case of *Oedipus the King*, the downfall of Oedipus unleashes not only political instability in his native city of Thebes, but a blood-cycle of tyranny, murder, and anarchy that takes two sequels (*Oedipus at Colonus* and *Antigone*) to resolve. Even then, the world that is left is a vacuum, an empty place that lacks the dignity, the elegance, and the greatness that it once had.

Tragedy, in the Sophoclean sense, rests upon the shoulders of the major players. Royal or presidential motorcades draw huge crowds of onlookers because the great ones attract and hold our attention. They are celebrities. As we shall see in chapter II when we examine how Giorgio Vasari questions what it is about the famous that fascinates us, there is something in all of us that wants to be famous. We psychologically wager our hopes and dreams on celebrities to represent us, yet when they fall or fall short, we shudder at their failure.

Spectacle is the interrelation of the events, the context, and the characters. It comes about when the viewers watch an elaborate process of both plot and performance unfold before their eyes, a process where the events hurtle toward fearsome inevitability. In *Oedipus the King*, an attendant remarks on the suffering that is taking place on the stage when Oedipus finally learns the truth of his identity:

He shouts for someone to unbar the doors.
And show all Thebes the father's murderer,
The mother's—shame forbids the unholy word.
Incontinently he will fly the country
To rid his house of the curse upon his own lips;
But scarcely has the strength, poor sufferer,
And none to guide him. He cannot bear the pain.
As you shall see. The doors are opening.
Yes, you shall see a sorry spectacle
That loathing cannot choose but pity...

Enter Oedipus blind.

No one, it seems, except the audience and the occasional attendant or blind prophet, has the slightest idea that a series of fatal errors is being committed, and that the protagonist cannot escape the destiny that awaits. But when the matter comes to a boil, when the characters no longer live under false assumptions, they are overwhelmed by the truth, and the truth tears them apart.

The tragic hero reacts not only physically to the course of events (Oedipus, for example, puts out his eyes with his wife/mother's brooch), but also intellectually. Oedipus has to tell everyone how he feels as the drama progresses and offer some sort of philosophical slant on the matter. When he is about to learn the terrible truth of his identity, he reacts with intellect rather than emotion:

I am the child of Fortune,
The giver of good, and I shall not be shamed.
She is my mother; my sisters are the Seasons;
My rising and my falling march with theirs.
Born thus, I ask to be no other man
Than what I am, and will know who I am.

The impact of this philosophical reaction is felt not only in the hearts and minds of the audience, but in the intellect and inner life of the character. Like a crowd gathered at the scene of an auto accident, the audience feels pity and helplessness; yet everyone stands around watching, wanting to know what will happen next.

The spectacle of tragedy hinges upon whether the actions being portrayed are worth watching. Few things attract our attention like the grief of others. Aristotle says in his work *Poetics* that the spectacle of suffering holds an audience's attention because it presents a process where events go from good to bad, and from bad to worse. This process of disintegration goes through several stages. In *Oedipus the King*, Oedipus is leading the good life. For fifteen years, he lives happily with his wife, Jocasta, who bears him four children: his daughters Antigone and Ismene, and his sons Eteocles and Polynices. But suddenly, a nagging question comes back to haunt him: who is Oedipus? The question of personal identity—"know thyself"—is at the heart of the Classical Greek personality. For a man, especially a king, not to understand his own background was akin to being blind—blind to self-knowledge. Shockingly, that question is answered for him: he is the murderer of his father, the incestuous husband of his mother, and a figure destined to be haunted by a fate that he cannot escape.

Aristotle calls this surprise the *reversal*. Everything is turned upside down in a matter of minutes because Oedipus has made his *discovery*. This, in turn, leads to the *calamity*, the unavoidable consequences of knowing the truth. Aristotle explains that tragedy is different from comedy because events go straight downhill after the reversal and at no point improve:

> The change in fortune will be, not from misery to prosperity,
> but the reverse, from prosperity to misery, and it will be due,
> not to depravity, but to some great error either in such a man as
> I have described or in one better, but not worse.

The audience's reaction to this sequence of events is pity, about the only good thing that happens in a theater during tragedy.

Because tragedy focuses on the issue of suffering, authors must present their work with a high level of seriousness and sensitivity. They accomplish this task through language. The fourth attribute of tragedy is *diction*, the way in which the language of the work conveys the action. Diction in literature is more than merely the manner of speaking: it is the care that authors take in their choice

of words, the precision with which they use them, and the impact that language has on the reader or audience.

In language, there are various levels of diction, as demonstrated by the difference between professional vocabularies and street language. We hire professionals such as lawyers and doctors, with their specialized vocabularies, to undertake many of the duties in our daily lives, such as accounting, jurisprudence, and medicine. Professional vocabularies are one of the reasons why medical and legal dramas are so popular with television audiences. People tune in to courtrooms and emergency room situations to hear the world translated into a unique manner of speaking. The trend of cowboy shows on North American television in the late fifties and early sixties ran its course because, eventually, the audience knew not only what the characters were going to say but how they were going to say it. The moguls of television-land learned their lesson quickly, however, and the language of the legal and medical systems has provided enough interest to amuse generations of audiences. Less compelling by far, of course, is a four-word vocabulary, sprinkled with expletives, that someone uses to express a whole range of emotions and thoughts. Language both shapes and limits the expression of ideas; the more words an individual has, the more he or she can articulate subtle concepts. Indeed, a strong vocabulary is a means of guaranteeing individual freedom because it allows a person to be specific about an idea, to express and categorize desires and abstract concepts, and to engage an idea with lucidity and honesty.

The language of tragedy, especially that of Sophoclean tragedy, is the language of the epic. It is poetry, but a poetry that is clear, direct, and eloquent in its power and simplicity. Unlike the beautiful yet complex language of the Song of Solomon, the diction of tragedy conveys more than it engages, and tends to avoid complex poetic figures of speech. We must remember that when Sophocles wrote the Theban plays, they were performed in large, open-air amphitheaters without the benefit of sound systems. The message had to be loud and clear.

Language was one of the three tools that dramatists had at their disposal to create character. The other two tools were action and a device that the Greeks invented for becoming a character—the

Gustave Moreau. Oedipus and the Sphinx. Here, the tragic protagonist achieves his moment of heroism by answering the questions of the sphinx. The serene, almost beautiful face of the sphinx is deceptive; it has the body of a bobcat, the wings of an eagle, and the power to destroy. Oedipus' tragedy comes not from confronting an external beast, but from his inability to master his inner darknesses and mysteries.

persona. In Classical Greek theater, acting was based on demonstrating a character not merely through gestures or voice but through the use of masks. These masks were called personas. The actor would speak through the mask and give voice to the figure he was portraying. Today, the masks often appear as decorations—the masks of comedy and tragedy—to remind people of the tradition at the root of contemporary theater. In literature, the persona has become the name for the voice within any piece of writing, the speaker of a poem or prose work. Even a factual newspaper article about the workings of local government or the damage caused by a fire is assumed to have a speaker behind it, a presence in writing that signals the continuous connection between the printed word and the oral tradition.

Language also allows us inside the mind of the protagonist. In tragedy, we are allowed to see not just what the characters are doing, but what they are thinking. The very fact that the protagonist and the other main characters respond both emotionally and intellectually to events makes them real to the reader or the audience member. What we are witnessing is the downfall of someone we can understand, someone like ourselves. Dramatists such as Sophocles achieve this through the use of the fifth attribute of tragedy, *thought*. Thought is more than merely showing us what characters are thinking: it is the process of helping us to understand how we are supposed to react, both emotionally and intellectually, to the spectacle of tragedy. In a Classical tragedy, we learn about what is going on and how we are supposed to respond through the presence of the *Chorus*.

The Chorus is the mouthpiece of both the action and the audience's reaction. In the contemporary idiom, we tend to think of a chorus as a group of clean-cut singers who stand behind an orchestra, or the refrain of a popular song. What has come down to us is the notion that the Chorus has something to do with singing, an assumption that is not far off its original purpose. The earliest Choruses were groups of singers and dancers who would provide the entertainment during interludes in the action of a sacred ritual or a recitation. By the time Sophocles inherited the notion in the fourth century BC, the Chorus may have seemed like a cumbersome idea. What, as a dramatist, was he to do with a group of people on the stage who were there to provide an edifying diversion for the audience? Sophocles and his contemporaries solved the problem by making the Chorus the ambassadors of the play. In an age before program notes, a time when audiences were not quite sure how to read what they saw, the Chorus became the interpreters of the action.

In *Oedipus the King*, for example, the play concludes with a statement from the Chorus about what everyone has just witnessed:

Sons and daughters of Thebes, behold: this was Oedipus,
Greatest of men; he held the key to the deepest mysteries;
Was envied by all his fellow-men for his great prosperity;
Behold, what a full tide of misfortune swept over his head.
Then learn that mortal man must always look to his ending.

A Classical Persona. The idea of donning a mask in the theater to create a character indirectly gave birth to the notion of voice in all contemporary writing. Note the mouth frozen in an expression of surprise, awe, and terror at a tragic spectacle.

83

And none can be called happy until that day when he carries
His happiness down to the grave in peace.

Pretty grim stuff. But the message the playwright wants to leave
with the audience is loud and clear: happiness cannot be trusted.
By having the Chorus articulate this, by putting a group of people
on the stage whose sole purpose is to react to the tragedy and
express what the audience is thinking, the dramatist can send
people home with a sense that their suspicions are confirmed. The
mitigating presence of the Chorus must have been some small
consolation to the theatergoers.

The pronouncement from the Chorus at the end of *Oedipus the
King* demonstrates what Aristotle calls the sixth attribute of
tragedy: *song*. The entire trio of the Theban plays is written in
poetry, and poetry is the closest that language comes to approxi-
mating song. But Aristotle's idea is more complex. Clearly, there is
little to sing about in a tragedy, little that is either happy or sad,
because tragedy, in its most definite sense, goes beyond sadness
into bleakness. But the role of the Chorus is to provide the play
with song—not to break the action with interludes, but to heighten
it with reactions. As is the case with modern blues performances,
it is the privilege of the audience to react. When a singer such as
Muddy Waters suddenly cries out, "My woman done me wrong,"
someone in the audience always yells back, "Tell me about it!" In
essence, that is what the Chorus does: it responds. But the blues,
as a modern form of entertainment and cultural expression, is also
a form of mass catharsis, a means of articulating in an objective
forum very subjective experiences such as loss of love, grief, and
jealousy. Song is a means of ordering and making objective an
overwhelmingly subjective experience. The Chorus has the same
effect that poetry had on Wilfred Owen and Ivor Gurney, those
neurasthenic poets of the First World War: it brought into the
open and put into an objective format the traumatic emotions they
felt from having witnessed a horrible spectacle.

Wilfred Owen said of his writings about the war that "the Poetry
is in the pity." The pity in Sophocles' Theban plays stems from the
fact that the suffering cannot be avoided. This sense of inevitability, the headlong rush of the narrative toward doom, occurs

because these plays, like *The Odyssey*, are set in an animate universe where love, mercy, and providential grace are either absent or ignored. In *Antigone*, for example, Antigone argues with her accuser, Creon, and helplessly defends the concepts of honor to the dead and familial love. She attacks Creon's cold, legalistic way of looking at the world, an unbending perspective that is totally without pity. Nonetheless, she is put to death for disobeying the law and burying the body of her slain brother. In the Classical perspective, all the pity in the world cannot mitigate the presence of fate. The Chorus in *Oedipus the King* realizes just how powerful a presence fate has, and mourns:

> *All the generations of mortal man add up to nothing!*
> *Show me the man whose happiness was anything more than illusion*
> *Followed by disillusion.*
> *Here is the instance, here is Oedipus, here is the reason*
> *Why I call no mortal creature happy...*
>
> *Time sees all; and now he has found you, when you least*
>   *expected it;*
> *Has found you and judged that marriage-mockery, bride-*
>   *groom-son!*
> *This is your elegy:*
> *I wish I had never seen you, offspring of Laius,*
> *Yesterday my morning of light, now my night of endless darkness!*

This weight of fate upon an individual is both hard to bear and hard to watch. Oedipus exclaims, "What fate has come unto me?"

In the Classical world, fate is not merely inevitability; it is the pattern of life that the gods have laid out for each individual. Underneath the recognition that each person must play out his or her part and suffer the good with the bad is the fear that the good *brings* the bad. The suspicion is that the higher one reaches, the farther one has to fall. This scale of highs and lows in a human life is given the name *fortune*. Fortune is the pattern in an individual's life that can be charted to include the best of times and the worst of times. The question is not how one enjoys the good, but how one copes with the bad. Fortune is often perceived as a set of scales, where everything must balance out, a concept that later Christian mythology translates into the idea of an individual's personal account book of good acts and sins. As we shall see in Boethius' *The Consolation of Philosophy*, fortune is often depicted as a great wheel that takes its passengers on a carnival ride of rises and falls. But to a much greater degree, the idea of an individual's fortune is expressed as a tide, where life is a matter of ebbs and flows.

Shakespeare was a great admirer of Sophocles, and he borrows the idea of fortune as a tide for a famous speech by Brutus in Act IV, Scene iii of *Julius Caesar*:

> *There is a tide in the affairs of men*
> *Which, taken at the flood, leads on to fortune;*
> *Omitted, all the voyage of their life*
> *Is bound in shallows and in miseries.*
> *On such a full sea are we now afloat*
> *And we must take the current when it serves*
> *Or lose our ventures.*

In modern terms, this is the notion of *carpe diem*, of seizing not only the day, but the opportunities that the moment presents. What is underlying Brutus' speech—a notion that Shakespeare has cribbed from Sophocles—is the idea that fortune is a natural and cyclical phenomenon.

In *Oedipus at Colonus*, the Chorus observes rather philosophically that fortune is a kind of wheel, an idea that still exists in North America, if bathetically, as the theme for a popular game show:

> *More and more misfortune follows*
> *From the blind man's indignation.*
> *Or the hand of Fate directs it.*
> *Who can say God's purpose falters?*
> *Time is awake, the Wheel is turning,*
> *Lifting up and overthrowing.*

The image of fortune as a wheel—a kind of *schadenfreude* or a cycle of good things and bad things that others suffer—was very popular during the Middle Ages, especially after the plague, when everything seemed dark and the notion of a merciful Providence seemed more and more remote. Shakespeare, who knew how and when to steal a good idea, puts this very concept into the mouth of Kent in Act II of *King Lear*, the most Sophoclean of his plays:

> *Fortune, good night;*
> *Smile once more; turn thy wheel.*

The assumption is that there is a force in nature called fortune, and that it takes an active role in shaping the destiny of human beings.

Tragedy, fate, and fatalism are all about one's perspective. If one is able to see the larger design of the universe, then bad events are not so bad. But if one is blind to the big picture, then tragedy can strike. Sophocles spotted this, and he makes blindness a key motif throughout the Theban plays. In fact, none of the characters seem to know where they are going or what they are doing or saying in these dramas, except for those who are already blind. The Greeks loved a good paradox.

Whenever the Classical playwrights needed someone to see clearly in their dramas or epics, they always called in a blind person. As we shall see in chapter 13, Shakespeare uses the same paradox to create a verbal motif in *King Lear*, where Lear looks at the world through images of blindness and uses language that works completely in negative terms. Sophocles was not inventing anything new; in fact, he was drawing on a rather popular concept in the Classical Greek world that suggested blindness was closely tied to prophecy; that a blind person could see things that others could not. In *The Odyssey*, Odysseus, not coincidentally, meets Tiresias in the underworld. Later, when Sophocles needs someone who can read the world with a strong inner eye, it is Tiresias he calls upon.

There are several stories as to how Tiresias lost his sight and came by his compensation of prophetic vision. In the first version, he was asked to judge a debate between the gods on the following question: "Who has more fun with sex, men or women?" Like just about everyone associated with tragedy, Tiresias made a bad choice: "Women," he answered. For this foolhardy response, he was blinded by Hera and given female genitalia as a punishment.

In the second story, Tiresias saw Athena bathing one day and was blinded for being a Peeping Tom. She then felt sorry for him and gave him the gift of "second sight," the ability to see remote or future events. Another story, this one told by Ovid in *Metamorphoses*, is that Tiresias saw two snakes mating, struck them with his staff, and was simultaneously blinded and turned into a woman. In *The Waste Land*, T.S. Eliot seems to refer to Tiresias' androgyny in the description of the sterile love affair between the secretary and her lover in "The Fire Sermon":

(And I Tiresias have foresuffered all
Enacted on this same divan or bed;
I who have sat by Thebes below the wall
And walked among the lowest of the dead.)

The idea of "foresuffering," of knowing what is going to happen and the truth that lies behind events, is what Eliot has taken from Sophocles; the problem with prophets, however, is that they are seldom heeded. The prophetess Cassandra, for example, walks the walls of Troy in *The Iliad* and in Shakespeare's *Troilus and Cressida* and goes mad because she sees the future but no one will listen.

The burden of second sight means that one can see the truth when others cannot. In *Oedipus the King*, Tiresias complains about his situation: "When wisdom brings no profit, to be wise is to suffer." Whenever a serious matter needs to be sorted out in either *Oedipus the King* or *Antigone*, Tiresias is called upon, and as events in Thebes would have it, he is never off duty. In *Oedipus at Colonus*, however, Tiresias never appears, and he disappears from *Oedipus the King* once Oedipus has blinded himself—the suggestion is not just that Thebes is not big enough for two blind men, but that Tiresias' presence becomes unnecessary once Oedipus sees the truth for himself. Oedipus puts out his eyes to avoid seeing any more of "the sorry spectacle / That loathing cannot choose but pity," and declares that he has had enough: "Teach me no other lesson." There is much, however, still to learn.

Part of tragedy's purpose is didactic. Tragedy teaches the audience or the reader the value of things by removing them from the stage. The Greeks valued family, home, and the honor of lineage above all other considerations, and Sophocles tears down those institutions one by one throughout the sequence of the Theban plays. He dispenses with family in *Oedipus the King* in a rather dastardly fashion, and then destroys the concept of home in *Oedipus at Colonus*, a play that gives us the motif of the wanderer, a piteous figure who will underscore a number of important literary characters including Mary Shelley's Daemon in *Frankenstein*. In *Antigone*, a play that is one of the sources for Shakespeare's *Romeo and Juliet*, Sophocles attempts to negate the one human resource that might battle and conquer tragedy: love. And when all is said and done, the survivors of the great struggle in the tragic universe are left with nothing but emptiness and memories of what once was.

The tragic universe is a horrible place, yet the purpose of tragedy is to show the reader, if only through the rather rough ride of negation, what should be valued in life. In *Antigone*, Antigone declares to Creon, in a moment of defiance that defines her character, "My way is to share my love, not share my hate." She sets love against the power of the law and mortal men. For her, there is a redeeming element in the universe, and she is willing to die for it. Sophocles asks his audience, "What do you value?" When those values are challenged, corrupted, or completely ignored, then everyone must witness the consequences.

But even though the world is a cold, cruel place, a "darkling plain" as Matthew Arnold called it in his poem *Dover Beach*, there is still something worth believing in, as Sophocles knew. In *Dover Beach*, Arnold offers his view of what Sophocles understood:

> *Sophocles long ago*
> *Heard it on the Aegean, and it brought*
> *Into his mind the turbid ebb and flow*
> *Of human misery; we*
> *Find also in the sound a thought,*
> *Hearing it by this distant northern sea.*

The "grating roar" of "pebbles which the waves draw back and fling" upon the shore of that Victorian seaside town brings "the eternal note of sadness in." But tragedy, the bleak prospect of all in the human condition that can defeat us, is not without its antidote.

The force that stands against the darkness on the "darkling plain" is there in *Antigone*. It is love:

Ah, love, let us be true
To one another! for the world, which seems
To lie before us like a land of dreams,
So various, so beautiful, so new,
Hath really neither joy, nor love, nor light,
Nor certitude, nor peace, nor help for pain;
And we are here as on a darkling plain
Swept with confused alarms of struggle and flight
Where ignorant armies clash by night.

In the back of Sophocles' mind, there must have been the question of how tragedy could be avoided. Certainly, the way to avoid tragedy, in his view, was to speak cautiously, think clearly, and keep one's vision in focus.

A few centuries after Sophocles, the Romans would come up with the maxim that Arnold may have had in mind when he wrote *Dover Beach* as a wedding night present for his wife: *amor vincit omnia* or "love conquers all." The Romans, in their profound sense of destiny and confidence, would look at the world with a feeling of mission. If you love something with enough determination and enough dedication, great things can be possible. They knew the universe was a dangerous, tragic place, yet their chief literary character, a survivor of a world that had been utterly destroyed, set off with his small band of outcasts and built the city that would rule the world. The Romans simply believed that one should get on with life rather than suffer. This did not stop some of their greatest dramatists, such as Seneca, from writing some outstanding tragedies; but the Romans lived with the belief that there were two things stronger than tragedy: destiny and human will. What Aeneas, the hero of *The Aeneid*, demonstrates is that if one looks at the world with a clear and focused vision, then tragedy can be overcome.

His inheritors a thousand years later in the Italian Renaissance, writers such as Vasari and Machiavelli, took the belief a step further. They said it is possible to plan ahead, that vision and fortune can be shaped to one's own purposes. Science itself would prove a great weapon, when properly controlled, against the presence of tragedy. The sad part is that it takes suffering to understand how suffering can be overcome. Nonetheless, in the recognition that there are antidotes to tragedy lies the heart of the modern world—the concept that humans need not be victims of their own folly, and that tragedy is something the world can, by degrees, learn to avoid.

4

A CAPITAL IDEA

Virgil's *The Aeneid*

W HEN it was time to locate their capital city, the founding fathers of the United States of America thought long and hard about some of the options that were open to them. They believed that heaven itself had ordained their future, and that greatness lay in store for them, no matter what hardships they might endure. This belief had its origins in the prophecies of Roman greatness that are told to Aeneas during his visit to the underworld in Book VI of *The Aeneid*:

> See, my son! It will be through this inauguration that Rome shall become illustrious, and extend her authority to the breadth of the earth and her spirit to the height of Olympus. She shall build her single wall round seven citadels, and she shall be blessed in her manhood's increase...

As the American politicians looked around the capital city of their burgeoning republic, the message was loud and clear: America was the new Rome. What is most interesting, however, is that the founding fathers of America went out of their way to make that message as self-evident as the truths they enshrined in the Declaration of Independence. The way they presented that concept to the world was through their choice of the real estate that would cradle their own Rome.

Visitors to Washington, right up to the end of the Civil War, complained that the city was a hot, humid, mosquito-infested flood plain, a bowl-shaped geography where the air did not circulate in the stifling, mid-Atlantic summers. Whatever had the founding fathers been thinking? But it wasn't just any old piece of swamp land. It had some special features. Those astute gentlemen who had brought the great ideas of the Enlightenment to practical fruition in the new world had one particular reason for placing Washington, D.C., where it is today: the site was surrounded by seven hills. And a city with seven hills, as they had been told by a seventeen-hundred-year-old epic poem about a displaced band of "the hungry and the homeless," was a city destined to become the greatest seat of power in the world. They had been schooled on *The Aeneid*, and, inspired by it, they wanted to refound the city that had inspired the creation of Rome: Troy.

In Book I of Virgil's *The Aeneid*, the displaced Aeneas laments the loss of his native city, but he sees that it is his destiny to rebuild Troy in a new location in Italy:

> We have forced our way through adventures of every kind, risk-ing all again and again; but the way is the way to Latium, where Destiny offers us rest and a home, and where Imperial Troy may have the right to live again. Hold hard, therefore. Preserve yourselves for better days.

Virgil's message to readers is: hardship is inevitable. What one does with hardship is the test of character that makes the difference between tragedy and success. What Aeneas suffers from during his epic journey toward that "ever-retreating horizon" is the "sorrow, deep within him" over the loss of his home. As we saw in chapter 2, *The Odyssey* evolved from the desire to return home, and *The Aeneid* is the expression of that same desire. However, it is different in that the goal is not for the hero to relocate himself in his identity but for him to discover and establish a new identity greater than anyone imagined. Rome, the ultimate end of all the struggles and travails of Aeneas, is not Troy. What is lost can never be regained, especially in the animate universe of Classical fatalism. Instead, what *The Aeneid* says is that virtues, one's belief in home, family, truthfulness, loyalty, freedom, and destiny, are ideals that can be carried from place to place, abstract concepts that never lose their meaning or their value, the cornerstones of brave new worlds. When the found-ing fathers of the United States of America decided that such truths could be the basis for a new nation, they had their copies of *The Aeneid* open in front of them.

In Book III, "Aeneas' Travels," Virgil makes the message even more adamant when yet another prophecy for the vagabond band of Trojan refugees is given:

For you, your rest is won. You have no expanse of sea to plough, no land of Italy, seeming always to recede before you, as your quest. You may look at your copy of the river Xanthus, and at a Troy built by your own hands, with fairer prospects, I hope, and no more fear of danger from the Greeks. And if I ever reach Tiber's estuary, stand beside it on its fields, and see those city-walls which have been promised to my people, then one day in Italy we shall create by our mutual sympathy kindred cities having close ties with Epirus, a Western Land sharing one founder, Dardanus, and one same history with you; and you and we shall be equally a Troy. May this be a duty for our descendants to inherit!

The notion that the seat of political greatness in the world is something that can be inherited is a concept that originated with the fall of Troy. Troy, to the ancient world and especially the world of the Homeric epics, was a holy city.

The myth of Troynovant was based on the idea that the original city of Troy, that bastion that had withstood the onslaught of the Greek siege for a decade, was remarkable not only for the strength of its walls, as Homer tells us in *The Iliad*, but for its seven towers on seven hills. When Romulus, the successor to the great Trojan survivor, Aeneas, decided to found the city that prophecy had decreed would not only exceed Troy and its glories but eventually rule the world, he chose a site on the Tiber River that was surrounded by seven hills. There he founded Rome. The belief throughout history was that after Rome fell, the mantle of Troy was up for grabs. Anyone with a strong sense of destiny and a piece of real estate that featured seven hills could lay claim to world-class status. Think of some of the major cities that have played a role in the modern world. London, Paris, and Moscow all have one thing in common: they possess seven distinct hills that ring their outskirts.

It may seem strange to connect this ancient text with modern real estate, but *The Aeneid* is one of those books that has been all things to all people throughout its presence in Western literature. It has been a textbook for kings and a how-to book for moral leadership. It is a story about the relationship between a father and his son, and about the need for family togetherness, whether that family is viewed as a singular domestic unit or as a national group. Like the Bible, *The Aeneid* is a book that few today read cover to cover. It has the cachet of being a book of mystery, perhaps for the factual and descriptive density of its text, its overwhelming sense of referentiality, and the implosiveness of a narrative that literally sucks the entire scope of Classical thought into its vortex. In fact, it seemed so mysterious that it was used as a tool for augury up until the late nineteenth century. Charles I of England used it as an oracle book, an *I Ching*, and the ill-fated monarch is said to have consulted it shortly before the Battle of Naseby. Virgil's dense text, with its mythological and historical references that meant a great deal to Romans but very little to its modern readers, makes for difficult going, yet for all the ways in which it seems so off-putting to the contemporary mind, it is a text that has infiltrated the world in ways that seem almost incredible.

Like *The Odyssey*, *The Aeneid* is a story about the importance of home, but it speaks to the group rather than to the individual about what home really means. As a text that leaves no holds barred in terms of its descriptions of violence and carnage, it foreshadows the graphic depictions of blood-letting that many found so *nouveau* in sixties cinema. Even the more recent trend toward Tarantino-esque violence in films of the 1990s harks back to this sensibility. *The Aeneid* is a book that challenges the sensibilities and examines violence, its impact, and its aftermath with a startling frankness. When coupled with the Roman notion of justice—the idea that an individual must pay for his or her crimes both physically and psychologically—that graphic quality makes for a horrifying spectacle of punishment. It also gives Freud the foundations for his notion that it is individual psychoses that are the most terrifying element in the unconscious. And when Dante decides to tour the universe and descend into the realms of the afterlife, it is Virgil he takes as his guide for his trek through the Malabowges and circles of that hopeless place—indeed, it is from *The Aeneid*, and not the Bible, that the Western idea of hell is taken.

In the two thousand years that *The Aeneid* has been read, it has had a strange impact on literary culture. Up until the twentieth century, it was mandatory reading for every school boy in Europe, because the message that comes through loud and clear is, "You want to grow up to be just like Aeneas, don't you?" What resulted from its consistent pedagogical use was that leaders not only tried to model themselves on Aeneas: they were measured against him for either their moral triumphs or their shortcomings. The northern Renaissance humanist scholar Desiderius Erasmus turned to *The Aeneid* when he composed *On the Education of a Christian Prince*, his answer to that scurrilous Italian guidebook on leadership, Machiavelli's *The Prince* (which is the subject of chapter 12). Erasmus' teachings on leadership, which were supremely influenced by what Virgil had to say about the nature of those in charge of society, were read up until the late nineteenth century, when the young George V of England laid claim to being the last European monarch to have had the book on his curriculum for statesmanship.

What Virgil was trying to create was a textbook for the ideal Roman, and to his mind, every Roman ought to be equipped to be a leader. What he ended up creating for Western literature and culture was a paragon, an unbeatable role model in the guise of a young, displaced Trojan officer who simply wanted a place to rest his travel-weary band of exiles. Every time a nation has had to establish or reestablish itself, it turns to *The Aeneid* as both a textbook and as an oracle—the text provides both a good story about refugees and a set of rules for how to reestablish order in a world that has dissolved into chaos.

Throughout the ages, writers and political theorists—Machiavelli, Erasmus, and even the authors of medieval romance—have used *The Aeneid* as a model for their handbooks and blueprints for ideal leadership. There is a strange feeling many readers have when they encounter medieval romance, and the stunningly perfect character of Sir Galahad, for example, that they have seen this person, this moral paragon on two legs, somewhere before—and their suspicions are correct. As we shall see in chapter 8, the authors of such works as *The Quest of the Holy Grail* thought that they were rewriting *The Aeneid* in a Christian context. In doing so, however, they drew more on the character of Aeneas and his single-minded dedication to his cause of establishing the nation that would become Rome than on the attributes of Jesus Christ. So thoroughly did those medieval authors use Virgil's work as a model in terms of narrative structure, character, and moral behavior, in fact, that their whole genre was dubbed "romance," or a story in the Roman manner. *The Aeneid* became a model for all future works of literature that attempted storytelling on a grand scale, and the template for a whole new genre that emerged during the late Middle Ages, the familiar form that is known in many languages as the "roman" and that in English is called the *novel*. The dime-store notion of the hero who overcomes his tribulations and saves the day is not as far from Virgil's work as we might think. Every time we encounter a young knight in a romance or a morally correct protagonist who perseveres to the bitter end, we are reminded of the romance notion of Sir Galahad, and, indirectly, of Aeneas.

It's no stretch, then, to point to *The Aeneid* as the source for the wave of idealistic charisma that swept John F. Kennedy into office in 1960. The familiar *Life* magazine photos of the young leader, clad in shorts, playing with his son on the beach at Hyannisport, echoed the scene in Book II of *The Aeneid*, when the hero escapes the burning ruins of Troy holding his young son by the hand and carrying his elderly father on his back. There is something in the Western character that makes us want to believe that social stability, political vision, and public morality begin with the powerful iconography of the father and the son, even if it is merely the product of a well-timed photo op. *The Aeneid*'s impact surfaced again when William Jefferson Clinton, who evolved a whole Kennedy simile as part of his election campaign, came close to impeachment because of his antics with a White House intern and a cigar. Clinton's flaw was not just his dalliance; it was the fact that he failed to deliver the promise of Aeneas, the concept in which leaders put the nation first and their own private concerns second. The same American public that was willing to forgive Clinton for his trysts (just as Aeneas is excused for his tryst with the heart-broken Dido) felt disappointed at the lengths he went to to explain away his actions. In Virgilian terms, he should have simply owned up and gotten on with the business of leadership.

Who would think that our contemporary ideas of leadership in business and politics could be traced to a story that justified the Roman conquest of the known world almost two thousand years ago? In truth, Virgil's epic, of all the major works of the Classical world, survived the Dark Ages and the Middle Ages both because it was considered a dense and important text that had explained the psychological makeup of the city that ruled the world, and because, especially to Christian interpreters, it was perceived as the work of a righteous pagan who had foretold the coming of Christ. The strange connection of Virgil to Christianity comes through a poem of his, the fourth "eclogue" or pastoral poem, a verse to which later translators applied the title *The Golden Age Returns*.

The *Eclogues* were completed around 37 BC, after Virgil had been forced to flee his farm near Mantua during the civil war that led to the ascension of Caesar Augustus—the man who gave the Aeneas-like refugee sanctuary and support in Naples until the political hostilities had been settled. The *Eclogues* largely reflect Virgil's longing for a state of peace and for the sanctuary of having his own home on his own land, a theme that would become central to *The Aeneid*, which he would begin shortly after 30 BC. As a poet, Virgil was fascinated by rural life. His poor health as a young man forced his retirement from city life to the countryside, where he became an astute observer of agricultural practices. These he recorded in two types of poems, the *Georgics*, a series of didactic studies of how farm life is conducted, and the *Eclogues*, the celebration of what it is to live close to nature, to be influenced by the natural cycles of growth and decay, and to desire some sort of alteration in the plan of things.

To Virgil in *The Aeneid*, and especially in the *Georgics*, the control of nature, and ultimately the joy that comes from being part of nature, stemmed from the way the art of farming was practiced, the governed peace that resulted from humans ruling the environment. To have humankind preside over nature in an artistic and administrative fashion seemed a logical extension of the Roman idea of governing and shaping the world according to Roman virtues. The underlying principle is that the world *is* something one can control and shape toward one's ends—a notion that was not lost on such Italian-minded Renaissance thinkers as Machiavelli, who looked to Virgil as both guide and inspiration.

The *Eclogues*, however, took a much more benign approach to the relationship between humans and nature. In these poems, the world is a beneficent place, a Land of Cockaigne that provides for people without hardship or struggle. It is in the *Fourth Eclogue* that Virgil expresses what this ideal world would be like. He says it will be a new era of peace, harmony, justice, and bounty that will be brought into fruition, very soon, by the birth of a child. Christian readers took one look at the text of the poem and declared that it was about the coming of Christ:

With him, the Iron Race shall end and Golden Man inherit all the world. Smile on the Baby's birth, immaculate Lucina; your own Apollo is enthroned at last...

He will foregather with the gods; he will see the great men of the past consorting with them, and be himself observed by these, guiding a world to which his father's virtues have brought peace...

Enter—for the hour is close at hand—on your illustrious career, dear child of the gods, great increment of Jove. Look at the world, rocked by the weight of its overhanging dome; look at the lands, the far-flung seas and the unfathomable sky. See how the whole creation rejoices in the age that is to be!

Not only was this child to be an incarnation of Apollo, in many respects a pagan parallel to Christ, but he was to be the son of the supreme God and the first-born of a new golden age. The world that results from this birth is perceived by Virgil as a kind of paradise, a place as close to the biblical Eden as any Classical fatalist could imagine. Although there is no suggestion that the new age would be an age of grace, Christians nonetheless bought into the idea that Virgil was miraculously enlightened in his thinking, and they revered him not only for his *Fourth Eclogue* but for his entire body of work. There was something very non-pagan about what he had to say. He created an epic hero who was not an immoral, philandering scoundrel like the Greek Odysseus, while also predicting the first step toward the establishment of the kingdom of heaven on earth. In a world that lacked credible literary models that fit in with the demands of Christianity, Virgil was as close to the ideal writer as anything the Classical world had produced. In an era when so much Classical learning vanished into the abyss of scholarly neglect and public ignorance, Virgil's works were considered worthy of preservation. *The Aeneid*, in particular, became the one book every educated person had to read.

A great deal happens in *The Aeneid*. Like *The Odyssey*, it opens *in medias res*, dropping the reader right into the heart of the story. A small band of Trojans, led by a young prince from the fallen city, is wandering around the Mediterranean in search of a place to resettle and eke out an existence that might, in some small part, mirror the greatness that was once Troy. In Book I, "The Trojans Reach Carthage," Virgil sets the tone for the entire work. The travel-weary Aeneas is introduced to the Carthaginian queen, Dido, and their tragic love relationship is set in place. Book I does much to establish the key principle that readers in both Roman and medieval times found so important: the virtue of emotional balance and control over rampant, passionate emotions.

Virgil's epic is really a story about how to maintain one's emotional balance. It presents a distrustful view of anything that is not completely level-headed. In this respect, *The Aeneid* is the one work that captures the essence of the Roman world view: keep everything in balance, honor the gods, and let leadership see things through to a just conclusion. *The Aeneid*, as it was seen from the perspective of the Middle Ages and in the wake of the fall of Rome, is a warning as much as it is a guide to those who assume the mantle of leadership. As long as capable, sound-minded people are in charge, the world, the *pax Romana*, is safe and secure. It is also for this reason that Machiavelli found *The Aeneid* so important to the notion of leadership that he explores in *The Prince*. Machiavelli believed that dispassionate, intelligent leadership was the only thing that could save Italy from the divisiveness and hardship of the times. For his model, he turned to the core story at the heart of the Roman and Italian mentality, so much so that the cynical Machiavelli almost perceives Virgil's legendary, mythic Aeneas as

a flesh-and-blood creation. Certainly, the spirit of Aeneas underlies Machiavelli's thinking when he claims in chapter 6 of *The
Prince* that the successful leader must be an armed prophet: "That
is why all armed prophets have conquered, and unarmed prophets
have come to grief." In the spirit of these lines are the opening
words of Book I of *The Aeneid*: "This is a tale of arms and the
man," or the alternative translation that has come down through
the ages, "I sing of the arms and the man."

The other major idea that Virgil establishes in Book I of *The
Aeneid* is that this is to be a story of suffering and hardship but not
a tragedy. The Virgilian perception of the ancient world clearly
differs from the Sophoclean concept of fate, where man is a victim
of the universe. In Virgil's view, an adherence to a principle or a
goal and a dedication to family, the gods, and one's people can
determine the outcome of an individual life. In other words, the
morality of an individual is the battleground for the epic struggle.
The hero must fight an inward battle to overcome his own instincts
and emotions in order to achieve his goal. Suddenly, what we see
in *The Aeneid* is the realization that humankind exists to struggle
both with nature and with its own nature; the inner battle can be
won only if the hero is as strong and smart inwardly as he is
outwardly. Virgil never lets the reader know what exactly is going
on inside Aeneas. There are no internal monologues, no Hamlet-
style soliloquies that provide insight into the hero's psychology or
inward life. Yet the single-mindedness of Aeneas' actions throughout the epic, and the constant temptations that he either overcomes
or preaches against, suggest that he is exercising a considerable
power of choice in what he does.

There is also an element of free will in Virgil's universe. Unlike the
Sophoclean universe, the world of Virgil's works offers some hope.
Granted, the universe is a dangerous and tragic place. However, the
gods give Aeneas a destiny, not a fate. Destiny means that there are
two possibilities in store for a character. If the character plays his
cards right and keeps faith with what the gods have foretold for him,
then everything will work out in the end. On the other hand, a character has the choice of ignoring his destiny, and in Aeneas' case,
there are many temptations that he must resist, the most significant

among these being the Carthaginian queen, Dido, who offers him an easy life but not the life that is prophesied for him. If there are weaknesses in the epic hero, they are sins of omission rather than sins of commission. What this amounts to is a very Roman idea: remain obedient to the gods and in the end you will win.

In Book I, as Aeneas visits a temple in a grove of trees in Carthage, he encounters a vision of the nature of the world that he has known, and he comes to understand just what his place is in the grand scheme of things:

> ...he saw pictured there the Trojan War, with all the battles round Ilium in their correct order, for their fame had already spread over the world. Agamemnon and Menelaus were there, and Priam; there, too, was Achilles, merciless alike to all three. Aeneas stood still, the tears came, and he said:"O Achates, where in the world is there a country, or any place in it, unreached by our suffering? Look; there is Priam. Even here high merit has its due; there is pity for a world's distress, and a sympathy for short-lived humanity."

As he gazes on the scene, Aeneas is filled with pity and nostalgia, but pity and nostalgia are backward-looking emotions, and in the Virgilian world one must always look forward. The past cannot be changed, but the future is something that is always there, on the horizon, waiting to be reached. When Dido offers Aeneas and his band a refuge because of her "fierce love" for him, he declines, because his destiny, what the gods have promised, dictates that he must move forward to the new Troy. He can get there only if he blinkers himself to all other options.

At this point in the narrative, Virgil offers the reader a digression. Book II tells the story of the Trojan horse and the sack of Troy, which neither *The Iliad* nor *The Odyssey* depicts. It is a horrific vision of frenzy, carnage, and despair, and it is told by the most reliable eye-witness possible, Aeneas. He opens the chapter by warning the reader about what he is going to say:

> Majesty, too terrible for speech is the pain which you are asking me to revive, I am to tell how the Greeks erased the greatness

which was Troy and the Trojan Empire ever to be mourned. I witnessed that tragedy for myself, and I took a great part in those events. No one could tell the tale and refrain from tears, not even if he were a Myrmidon or a Dolopian, or some soldier of the unpitying Ulysses.

But tell the tale he does. The story is one that constantly mixes the facts of the past with the future, almost to the point that time becomes less and less an issue as the narrative unfolds. For Roman readers, the fact that so much of the present was foretold in the past must have made *The Aeneid* a page-turner, and it must have left them with a sense that they were living in a continuing story, a narrative that embraced not only distant events and settings but immediate knowledge, places, and figures. What Virgil wanted his epic to do was to connect the past to the present—something that good historical writers ever since have been trying to do. That sense of immediacy is part of the power of *The Aeneid*, and its numerous prophecies are like instants where the author turns and speaks directly to the reader.

The horrific spectacle of the Greeks loose in the city of Troy must have been frightening enough to Roman readers of the epic, but Virgil goes one step further and strikes at the core of the family-oriented Roman psyche. The most powerful image of the entire epic is the tableau from Book II where, in the burning city of Troy, Aeneas carries his father, Anchises, on his back and pulls his son, Iulus, by the hand:

But now through the town the roar of the fire came louder to our ears, and the rolling blaze brought its hot blast closer. "Well then, dear Father," I said, "come now, you must let them lift you onto my back. I will hold my shoulders ready for you; this labour of love will be no weight to me. Whatever chances await us, one common peril and one salvation shall be ours. Iulus must walk beside me, and my wife shall follow at a safe distance in our footsteps..." So saying, I bent down and cloaked my neck and shoulders with a red-brown lion's skin. Then I took up my load.

As in the story of Orpheus and Eurydice, Aeneas attempts to retrieve his beloved from the perils of the underworld, but when he turns and looks back, he cannot find his wife in the confusion. In one of the story's most terrible moments, Virgil evokes a sense of tragic pity when Aeneas' wife, Creusa, suddenly disappears in the slaughter:

> Then, in the severe stress of my anxiety and haste, some unkind power robbed me of my wits. For after leaving the streets I knew, I lost direction, and I was running over trackless country when—oh, terrible!—my wife, Creusa—did she stop running because some bitter fate meant to steal her from me, or did she perhaps stray from the path or just sink down in weariness? We cannot know; but we never saw her again. I had never looked back for her when she was lost, or given her a thought till we came to the hillock consecrated to the ancient worship of Ceres... I was mad with horror; I upbraided every deity, and cursed the whole human race. In all Troy's overthrow nothing which had happened was so heartrending to me as was this loss.

Aeneas goes back to Troy and retraces his steps, but his wife is nowhere to be found. He witnesses Odysseus (in *The Aeneid* he is called by his Roman name, Ulysses) presiding over the piles of plunder taken from the city and its temples, the fires raging out of control, and the long line of frightened survivors, mostly women and children, awaiting their fates at the hands of the conquerors.

Beneath the catharsis-producing events of the loss of Creusa, Virgil is hiding one of the important themes of *The Aeneid*: the danger of extreme emotions. Aeneas' loss occurs during a moment of anxiety and haste. When he discovers Creusa is gone, he is "mad" with grief. Throughout the epic, moments when either Aeneas or other characters lose control are viewed disdainfully by Virgil, because part of the issue of maintaining balance is the way in which people keep their eyes on their ultimate goal. Seeing the larger picture, in Virgil, is the result of clarity of thought. When that clarity is lost, even for a moment, the whole universe is left in peril. The hero, therefore, is someone who never lets down his guard and never wavers from his vision. However demanding this may seem to a modern reader, it is an important attribute of how a hero or leader is perceived, not only in the literary sense but also in a political one. A leader/hero is not supposed to have weak moments. He is supposed to be infallible. So persuasive and pervasive is Virgil's perception of the hero that the entire genre of romance literature comes down to the way in which its ultimate hero, Sir Galahad of *The Quest of the Holy Grail*, remains constantly steady and true to his cause and calling.

As pitiable as it may seem, however, the death of Creusa in Book II, "The Sack of Troy," serves another key purpose in *The Aeneid*, for she is the first of many spectral presences who appear to Aeneas to offer him a prophecy of the future. When Aeneas searches the streets of the fallen city in vain for his lost wife, she appears to him as a ghost (in much the same way that Hamlet's father appears to him on the battlements of Elsinore Castle) to offer him news of the future and to restore some measure of balance to his grief-stricken mind:

Sweet husband, why do you allow yourself to yield to a pointless grief? What has happened is part of the divine plan... You have to plough through a great waste of ocean to a distant exile. And you shall come to the Western Land where the gentle current of Lydian Tiber flows between rich meadows where men are strong. There happiness and a kingdom are in store for you, with a queen for you to marry.

The reassurance, connected as it is to a utopian vision and to nationalistic sentiments, places the grief Aeneas is suffering in the context of the larger picture. What Creusa also does is prepare the way for Book III, where Aeneas continues the narration of his travels, a story that for at least one book resembles *The Odyssey*.

To a greater extent, Creusa's death sets in motion the emotional pendulum of *The Aeneid*'s chapters. One of the key things a reader should notice about a work of literature is the way it is structured from book to book and from chapter to chapter.

Virgil constructs *The Aeneid*, for dramatic purposes, around the issue of *tone*, the emotional register of the language and the ideas. As he moves the reader through the narrative, he shifts the tone and its narrative content from control to frenzy, then back to control and then to frenzy once again, a movement that suggests the world is a place that is constantly seeking a restoration of balance.

Book IV, which tells the story of the love affair between the widowed Aeneas and Dido, ends tragically when, as Aeneas sails away with his followers to pursue his destiny in Italy, she commits suicide atop the harbor tower. The suggestion is that Dido is foolish when she gives all for love "in the mad heat of a sudden passion," and that she lets her emotions get the better of her. Love, in the Virgilian world, is based on devotion and understanding, not on hormones and pheromones. In reaction to her death, Aeneas seems cold, almost cardboard, in his insensitivity, yet Virgil suggests that personal love is a minor consideration in the grand scheme of things. Love for one's country and for the destiny that rests upon the shoulders of an individual are far more important.

Such a sentiment finds its way even into the most modern of love stories—or as Bogart suggests in *Casablanca*, the problems of the world's little people don't really add up to much in the grand scheme of things. If love is, indeed, "the same old story, a fight for love and glory, a case of do or die," it may be because *The Aeneid* has taught our culture that personal happiness is secondary to the greater good. What threatens that cause is the loss of clarity that comes from letting the emotions overwhelm the intellect. Aeneas' heart says one thing while his head says another. He is a leader because his intellect is his commanding virtue.

"Destiny will find a way for you," Aeneas is promised in yet another prophecy in Book III. But no matter how often the higher forces of the universe promise him the glories of the future, he is constantly confronted by suffering, and it is usually a suffering that is triggered by those who cannot control their baser instincts. As he reaches the shores of Italy, he is delivered yet another blow: his father, Anchises, dies. Again, the hero must confront his loss and his grief:

O bitterness! I lost my father, lost Anchises, my solace in every
adventure and every care. Yes, here in my weary plight, you,
best of fathers, forsook me, after I had brought you so far and
through so many dire perils in vain... This blow was my last
anguish. For I had reached the destination of my voyage.

Aeneas' answer to the death of his father is to hold funeral games
in his honor. To the Roman mind, the public spectacle of games
allowed a death to be ritualized in a gesture of celebration. Games
also represented a kind of sanity of the spirit, a demonstration of
the notion that if one is to have a strong mind, one should also
have a strong body. The funeral games act not only as an entertaining diversion in the text for the sports-minded Roman readers
but as a demonstration that games, actions conducted according to
rules, could reflect the possibility of order and sanity in the world.
The games are also a demonstration of the soldierly arts: sailing,
boxing, running, riding, and archery, and an opportunity for the
displaced Trojans to practice and prepare indirectly for the war
they must inevitably fight against the indigenous inhabitants of
Italy. Virgil comments:

> Whatever is to befall, it is always our power of endurance which
> must give us control over our fortune.

This relationship between sports and military training, and the
collective identity reflected in physical achievement, supports the
notion of team spirit that lies at the heart of nationalism. The
Trojans are warned that "When you come to Latium you will have
to defeat in war a hardy nation, wild in its ways," the same sort of
speech a coach gives his football club on the eve of a big game. But
beyond merely being a chapter about unity and preparation, Book
V is a marvelous piece of press-box journalism. In describing the
games with the play-by-play energy and enthusiasm of a modern
sports broadcast, Virgil created one of the first pieces of sports
writing and set the standard for every piece of sports reporting that
would follow, from *Casey at the Bat* to *Sports Illustrated*.

As the games draw to a conclusion, yet another prophecy is
issued to Aeneas: he will have to descend to the underworld in

order to receive the vision of the future (yet another prophecy) that will tell him how to establish his nation in the new land. Book VI of *The Aeneid*, however, goes beyond all expectations as a *nekusis* in an epic narrative, for it is from "The Visit to the Underworld" that the Western notion of hell—a place of endless psychoses and perpetual, legalistic punishment—is drawn.

Virgil's sense of the fantastic is frightening. He is writing not just to the needs of his narrative but to the souls and fears of his readers. If *The Aeneid* is a kind of narrative labyrinth, a psychological, dream-like world akin to *The Odyssey* in which someone is attempting to recover or reestablish the consciousness of his own identity, Aeneas is perpetually wandering in a timeless landscape of promises and prophecies. The underworld that Aeneas encounters in his *nekusis* is far different from the dark realm of the Shades that Odysseus found during his descent. Virgil's shade-world is a highly structured place, a landscape that is mapped and divided into locales that are assigned to specific purposes.

Entrance to the underworld in *The Aeneid* is gained by a kind of ticket-of-leave, the golden bough:

> Yet permission for descending to the earth's hidden world is never granted to any who has not first gathered the golden-haired produce from its tree, for beautiful Proserpine has directed that this must be brought to her as a special offering. Each time the bough is torn from its place another never fails to appear, golden like the first, and its stem grows leaves also of gold. So therefore you must lift up your eyes and seek to discern this bough, find it as it is required of you, and pick it boldly. Then, if it is indeed you whom the Fates are calling, it will come willingly and easily; if not, by no strength will you master it, nor even hack it away with a hard blade of steel.

There is a tremendous sense of preordination in this statement. The fact that the bough is given only to those who are decreed worthy by the Fates suggests that there is a divine plan to the universe. Those who are meant to experience the powers and wonders of the afterlife are permitted to do so by the gods. What preordination meant to the Classical world was that one's fate is inescapable; to medieval Christians, however, Virgil's sense of preordination must have appeared to be an inspired understanding of the comic plan God has for humankind, and a clear message that God wanted Aeneas to succeed so Rome would eventually become the foremost seat of the Christian world. Such connections between the pagan Classical world and the medieval world reassured readers that they were part of a much broader continuum. They took a great deal of relief from *The Aeneid*'s theory of a continuous history, a history that connected the Holy Roman Empire or the Papal See to events that were shaped not simply by Providence but by Olympus. This strange paradox, the urge to excuse the plans of pagan gods for Christian theology, made the reapplication of Virgil's afterworld all the easier to understand in the Christian context. The Christians of the Dark and Middle Ages needed an imaginative structure for hell and heaven. Saint Paul mentions hell, but he never gives precise details about its landscape, its torments, and its terrifying specters. Had it not been

Claude Lorrain. The Trojan Women Setting Fire to Their Fleet. Beneath this rather stylish eighteenth-century seascape there lurks the message of madness. The Trojan women, after years of wandering, went mad and set fire to Aeneas' ships. The fleet, however, was saved by a rainstorm because destiny in the Classical world was a much stronger force than mere folly or madness.

for Virgil, those tableaux of damnation that adorn countless cathedral portals throughout Europe would have seemed more of an idle threat than a promise of the judgment of a legalistic God who keeps accounts on the good and bad deeds of each Christian.

The sense of hopelessness that Dante catches in his descriptions of hell in the *Inferno*, for example, is attributable to Virgil, whose underworld is a place of darkness, "with the shadows round them and night's loneliness above them." Like Dante's hell, Virgil's has a number of important features that act as benchmarks on the *nekusis*. There is an entrance hall, which, though it does not bear the despairing message of "Abandon all hope ye who enter here," is frightening nonetheless. The entrance hall is a structure not unlike the jaws of Jonah's whale from the Bible—and with this signal, of course, later Christian readers came to associate hell with the Leviathan in the great schema of post-biblical mythology.

Virgil describes the portal to the underworld:

In front of the very Entrance Hall, in the very Jaws of Hades, Grief and Resentful Care have laid their beds. Shapes terrible of aspect have their dwelling there, pallid Diseases, Old Age forlorn, Fear, Hunger, the Counsellor of Evil, ugly Poverty, Death and Pain.

By giving almost human attributes to such abstract constructs as Pain, Fear, and Poverty, Virgil is implementing a figure of speech known as *personification*. What personification allows an author to do is transform his landscape from a physical one of identifiable objects into an intellectual one filled with ideas rather than people, places, or things. What the reader is meant to see is not just a human-shaped figure who represents death but a presence that contains all of the awesome and awful notions one associates with dying.

By moving the narrative and setting beyond the physical and into the intellectual, Virgil is hinting that Aeneas' visit to the underworld is a kind of double-narrative structure that is meant both to be read and to be interpreted. This phenomenon is called *allegory*, an extended metaphor where what one sees is meant to suggest multiple interpretations. Allegorical landscapes are like books. They are meant to be read, and they usually appear in a work of literature for didactic purposes—in other words, both the protagonist and the reader must learn from what they read. The author of an allegory is saying to the reader, "Yes, the protagonist is in a physical underworld, but he is also in the middle of an idea and I want you to interpret what you see intellectually as well as spatially." Poor Aeneas. He thinks he is in a place, but the place is also a set of ideas that he must use his intelligence to navigate and to interpret.

When authors engage in allegory—as do Richard Langland in his dream-vision poem *Piers Plowman*, Edmund Spenser in *The Faerie Queene*, Geoffrey Chaucer in *The House of Fame*, the anonymous author of *The Quest of the Holy Grail*—the landscapes described become less and less physical and more and more cerebral, to the point where the story is suddenly set in a world that bears little resemblance to this one. Allegorical landscapes often appear in dream-vision writings, in which the protagonist is a sleeper who suddenly wakes to find himself in another world, a world filled with meanings that he must understand and fears that he must confront. Even Charles Dickens gets into the allegorical act. In his famous novella *A Christmas Carol*, he has Ebenezer Scrooge literally sleep through a series of visitations by the ghosts of Christmases past, present, and future, and each of them takes him on a journey through time and space that defies the laws of the physical world. The allegorical landscape, the imaginative realm that seems to exist inside the mind, is what Freud sought to understand, because everything in an allegory is there to tell us something.

Allegorical landscapes such as the one found in *The Aeneid* can be frightening if one enters them without the proper interpretive preparation or without that golden bough that protects the traveler. Beyond the monstrous entrance hall of hell, for example, Virgil creates a terrible vision of misery and suffering. The first stage in the journey would be enough to turn away most mortals, but Aeneas is dedicated enough to his purpose not only to see what is before him but to see through it—the proper stance one should take with an allegory:

Gustave Doré. Charon. The frightening spectre of the boatman of the underworld who ferries the souls of the damned across the River Styx would be enough to scare even the most stout-hearted away, yet Aeneas seems to take it all in stride as a kind of learning experience.

There in the mud and murk seethes the Abyss, enormous and engulfing, choking forth all its sludge into Cocytus. Here there is a warden of the crossing, who watches over the river-water. He is the dreaded Charon: a ragged figure, filthy, repulsive, with white hair copious and unkempt covering his chin, eyes which are stark points of flame, and a dirty garment knotted and hanging from his shoulders... The souls stood begging to be the first to make the crossing, and stretched their arms out in longing for the farther shore... It is forbidden to convey them past the banks of dread and over the snarling current before their bones have found rest in a due burial place...

Aeneas' reaction to the scene borders on a tragic catharsis: he pities them. His reaction is reminiscent of the lines T.S. Eliot offers in *The Waste Land*: "So many, I had not thought death had undone so many." For all its terror, the afterworld has been visited before by other heroes, and Charon, the boatman, is used to seeing them. He tells Aeneas to stop and explain himself:

Whoever you are who stride in arms towards my river, come, say why you approach. Check your pace; speak now, from where you are. This is the land of the Shades, of Sleep and of Drowsy Night. It is sin to carry any who still live on board the boat of the Styx. I even regretted that I ever admitted Hercules to the lake when he came here, and Theseus too and Pirithous, though they were Sons of Gods and of unvanquished might.

A trip to the underworld is a requisite duty of an epic hero, and Virgil uses this trip to establish Aeneas in a lineage of heroic individuals (the Underworld is, in many respects, the metaphorical equivalent of the labyrinth). By placing his protagonist in the world below, Virgil is saying that his man is equal to anything that has gone before. Here, says the author of an epic, is someone who is greater than the torments of the world, an individual who possesses a special attribute or attributes setting him apart from the rest of humanity.

Once across the river Cocytus, Aeneas encounters the realm of

purgatory. Like the Christian purgatory, it is a limbo for distressed souls who have received the benefits of a decent burial but who cannot let go of their psychoses. Virgil's last stop before hell is a cold, dark place of troubles and fixations. It is here that Aeneas encounters the shade of Dido:

Among them was Phoenician Dido, who was roaming in the broad wood with her wound still fresh upon her. Troy's hero found himself near to her and as soon as he recognized her dimly through the shadows, like one who early in the month sees or thinks that he sees the moon rising through the clouds, his tears fell and he spoke to her in the sweet accents of love.... But in her the anger blazed and grimly she glared, holding her gaze averted and fixed on the ground; she was no more moved by what Aeneas had begun to say than if she had been hard flint or a standing block of Parian marble.

As the authors of medieval romances such as *The Quest of the Holy Grail* were quick to point out, woods, especially dark, dense ones, are metaphorical waste lands, labyrinths of endless questions that can be navigated only by clear thought. Dante will recognize in the

Inferno that suicides are condemned to a wood, a labyrinth built from fixations and anxieties from which there is no escape. The suggestion on the part of Virgil and later authors is that woods represent eternal conundrums where one cannot "see the forest for the trees."

Like Dante's afterworld, Virgil's is a place that is devised around categories and classifications. In purgatory, for example, can be found the souls of wailing infants, "weeping at the very entrance way... for the dark day had stolen their mothers' breasts and plunged them into death before their time," or the shades "of those who had been condemned to die by false accusation." For Virgil, purgatory is a place where souls struggle to understand their fates, where there is no means of finding an explanation for what has happened, and where the torments of the upper world are carried on, without relief, in the realm below. Purgatory is not a place of punishment as much as it is a place to file those who are confronted by overwhelming absurdities. They all seem to be waiting for an answer that will never come. Those consigned there live on the edge of catharsis, that moment when the individual, like Aeneas at the moment of his wife's death, is overcome by an extreme of emotion and plunged into senseless inaction.

The next major attraction in Book VI is the visit to hell itself. It is a terrible place, full of frightening architecture and tormented souls undergoing the punishment of the gods. It is a fiery spot, presided over by its tyrant king, Rhadamanthus of Cnossos, a forerunner of the devil. His "rule is most pitiless," a suggestion on Virgil's part that hell is a place for despots and those who would follow them:

> ...this was Tartarean Phlegethon, the Burning River of Hell.
> Opposite stood a gigantic gate with columns of solid adamant,
> such that no human force, nor even warring Gods of Heaven,
> could uproot them. An iron tower also rose high into the air....
> From within groans were clearly heard. There was a sound of
> savage flogging and clanking or ron chains being dragged, Aeneas
> stopped, listening in terror to the noise and the shouting...

The hell of *The Aeneid* is a place of punishment where the gods hold men and women accountable for the actions of their natural lives. What this means in the scope of Western literature is that suddenly the life of an individual is an account book, a ledger where the good is held in balance against the bad and where the misdeeds of the natural world are transformed into the torments of the next. In Virgil's view, "each of us finds the world of death fitted to himself":

> Here dwell those who hated their brothers while life was theirs or struck a parent or entangled a dependent in deceit, or, having found riches, gloated over them alone, setting none aside for their kindred, and of these there are many indeed; and then others who were killed for adultery or took part in an unrighteous war, shamelessly betraying their liege-lords; all these imprisoned within, awaiting their penalty.

True to his Roman outlook, Virgil can imagine no greater crimes than those committed against family values. But there is one clear message that is articulated among all the sufferers: "Be warned, learn righteousness; and learn to scorn no god." Suddenly, the fatalistic, nihilistic universe of Sophoclean tragedy is mitigated by the force of morality. There is a recognition on Virgil's part that life is something that one must lead well, according to a set of moral and ethical rules. He is not the first to acknowledge this, but in Virgil's vision of the afterlife, the threat of retribution for actions against nature or the gods and humans is seen as a persuasive force for establishing both peace of mind and peace on earth for humankind. No wonder medieval readers appreciated his outlook; it is almost identical to the message of Christianity. What is also amazing is that this connection between moral retribution and family values is still played out today in the arguments of many fundamentalist Christian, right-wing groups, which seek to criticize what they see as moral lapses in society with threats of a hell that is found not in the Bible but in *The Aeneid*, the supreme text of family-value politics.

Humans, in Virgil's view, a view that is expressed quite clearly in Book VI, are moral creatures by nature. Their souls contain a small piece of the divine. The moral life, he argues, honors in people what is truly the best that nature gives to them. To disobey the laws of morality is to sin against heaven, and heaven, in Virgil's view, is ultimately a good place. In a rare moment of philosophical speculation, Virgil expresses what he sees as the nature of humankind:

> From Spirit and Mind are created men and the beasts; and from which ocean beneath its marbled surface brings into being, all have their lives. The strength in their seeds is the strength of fire and their origin is of Heaven; in so far as they are not hampered by the body's evil, nor their perceptions dazed by their members which are of the earth, and the parts of them which are embued by death.

To Virgil, the baser instincts can pull an individual down into the depths. For him, the highest aspect of human nature is the soul, and it is up to the individual, as demonstrated through Aeneas, to school and train his soul to maintain the highest principles. The internal life is suddenly more important than the external life. If the individual fails in his moral schooling, purgatory or hell is waiting just over the edge to correct any faults in the afterworld. What is most startling about this moral schema for the universe is that it implies the gods want each individual soul to experience some improvement as a consequence of life; ultimately, the goal of humankind is to mirror the goodness of heaven, and heaven itself may be a place not of capricious, mean-spirited deities but of peace, harmony, and security.

The final stop on Aeneas' tour of the underworld is heaven, the "pleasant green places in the Fortunate Woods" (as opposed to the dark, suicidal ones), where the souls of the good, the righteous, and the pure are allowed to dwell in a sylvan landscape that is not far off the vision of the Golden Age that Virgil offers in the *Fourth Eclogue*. The light is brilliant, the stars and the sun are always visible, and the "bright spirits" take exercise through games or rhythmic dancing, singing, and feasting. It is the home of Orpheus, the lost, lamented poet who accompanies the activities of the blessed on his lyre. When Aeneas asks him about the social conditions in heaven, Orpheus gives him an account:

> No one has a fixed home. We live in shady woods and lie here on soft river-banks, or dwell in meadows which the streamlets keep ever fresh.

Heaven is also the vantage point from which the future can be seen. In a scene that Milton borrows for the conclusion of *Paradise Lost*, the shade of Anchises takes Aeneas to a mountain top and in a gentle, fatherly gesture, shows his son the future history of Rome, a vision that will be lavishly painted upon the shield that is presented to the protagonist in Book VIII, the arms for the man that Virgil promised in the epic's opening lines.

Aeneas' travels in the afterworld are more than just a moral allegory on the good and bad aspects of the conduct of life. The underworld scenes allow Virgil to remove time from the middle of his narrative, to show the connection between the past, the present, and the future, both on a grand scale and on an individual, human scale. What Virgil is trying to suggest is something that the Bible tells us: each of us is a smaller, compact version of the larger scope of things and a reflection of the universe in which we live. This reinforces the moral exemplum of Aeneas, as well as the idea that history is contained in each present moment of existence, a moment in which the individual must do honor to his family, his nation, and the gods. This is the meaning of the balance that the overall structure of *The Aeneid* attempts to convey, and *The Aeneid* is a guide to how one can achieve that balance, if only on a fundamentally domestic level. No matter how much the pendulum of the individual chapters may swing between the oppositions of madness and sanity, one thing is clear: the moral path of life is the only option. From the very bottom of society to its very top, whether yeoman or leader, morality must be the course of conduct. *The Aeneid*, as Virgil had planned it, was ultimately to show that the course to peace, harmony, and security lay through a determined, strong, and moral leadership and a determined, strong, and moral nation that dutifully obeyed. This, Virgil believes, is the antidote to tragedy, and in the tradition of previous epics such as *The*

Odyssey, Virgil foresaw a happy ending, a rest at the end of the sufferings.

This vision is what saves *The Aeneid* from lapsing into tragedy at its most emotionally trying moments. The promise of a world to come constantly reminds both Aeneas and the reader that everything will work out in the end—a fact not borne out by the book itself, as Virgil died at Brindisi in 19 BC while only a chapter more than halfway through the projected plan for twenty-four books. Unfortunately, *The Aeneid* ends just as Aeneas is about to reign victorious over his nemesis, Turnus, the ruthless king of the Latins. Had the narrative not been cut short by the death of Virgil, the pendulum motion of the tone and plot of the epic would likely have continued. The underlying truth of *The Aeneid* is that life is a struggle, but a struggle that, in the end, is well worth the effort. What emerges from the narrative, however, is a different picture. Life, in reality, is the story of continuous time, and Virgil recognizes that.

In Book VIII, "The Site of the Future Rome," Aeneas receives as a gift from the gods an enormous shield on which is painted the history of the Rome to come, a saga that stretches from Aeneas' struggles right through to the reign of Augustus. Virgil's final words in Book VIII reveal just how important it is for Rome to be the product of leadership, for Aeneas lifts "onto his shoulder the glory and destiny of his heirs," and carries the burden of the past, present, and future with pride and confidence. Like the prophetic Sibylline books, which were housed in the temples of the Roman forum and disappeared during the reign of the emperor Nero, the idea of destiny is that it is more of a continuum without end than a comedy that works to resolve all the issues and challenges with one happy marriage. Like the golden thread that Theseus used to find his way out of the labyrinth, *The Aeneid* has become one of the key tools of navigation for the Western literary imagination. Even more than the Bible, it suggests that humankind's place in the grand scope of things is a matter of imaginative perseverance, a never-ending, always evolving state of affairs to which each new author adds his or her contribution. The point to the story is that Rome was not built in a day, and readers of the work, especially those founding American fathers, realize that happiness is more a process of pursuit than a single destination. As a textbook for management that influenced everyone from Renaissance monarchs to Machiavelli and Otto von Bismarck, its simple message is to plan ahead and work consistently toward a goal. What readers have learned from Virgil, and perhaps the overarching message of the entire work, is that the freedom and destiny of a nation can be maintained only if its leaders are schooled in the arts of vigilance and morality. From that position *The Aeneid* has reached far beyond anything Virgil might have foreseen for his work—a work he wanted to have destroyed on his death because he thought it fell far short of what he intended it to say.

The notions of working "as hard as a Trojan" and "preserving oneself for better days" lie at the core of *The Aeneid*. These are what lay behind the confidence that Rome possessed when it spread its power over eighty percent of the known world, and they are the notions that would inspire generations of leaders to pursue great, expansive visions. But what is more surprising is that an out-of-work civil servant in Quattrocento Italy would dream of restoring his conquered and divided people to greatness through the realization that fate, tragedy, and hardship are matters that can be overcome. Machiavelli believed, as a direct result of being schooled on Virgil, that destiny is something that can be shaped if one is focused and true to an agenda or a vision. The nineteenth-century notion of *realpolitik* that so haunted the twentieth century can be traced to Machiavelli's prescriptions for statecraft; but underlying those notions is something far older, far more pervasive, and far more ingrained. Virgil's epic, however, represents only one side of the Roman literary imagination—the ordered, clear-thinking approach to solving the problems that storytelling and the imagination allow us. The other side of the Roman mind is even more complex. Works such as Ovid's *Metamorphoses* suggest that the nature of the world is one of chaos, albeit a chaos that is gradually working its way toward a state of order. In Ovid's view, courage, honor, clear-mindedness—all those Virgilian virtues—are fine in their own right, but they seldom save anyone from the negative and chaotic pressures of the universe.

But for what it is worth—and it is worth a great deal—*The Aeneid* is a story of consistency and how much that matters in the grand scheme of things. It is the story of a man who, with his elderly father on his back and his small son by the hand, escaped what amounted to the end of the world. His experiences have taught Western readers that reality is something that can, with the assistance of morality, dedication, honor, courage, resolve, and fortune, be commanded, shaped, and recreated toward one's own ends—a notion that eventually gave us the great ideas of the Renaissance.

5

STAYING OUT
OF HARM'S WAY

Ovid's *Metamorphoses*

ONCE upon a time, there was a powerful and wealthy Mandarin who had a beautiful daughter, Koong-shee. When it came time for her to be educated, her father hired a brilliant, though impoverished, young scholar named Chang. Each day the scholar and the young woman would meet beneath the spreading and shady boughs of an old willow tree at the center of the Mandarin's property. As their lessons progressed, the two suddenly realized that they were in love. When her father discovered Koong-shee's love for Chang, he imprisoned her behind a heavy fence and banished the scholar from his lands.

But just as love finds a way, so did the scholar. He helped Koong-shee escape, and together they fled to an island where they might live together. However, the cruel Mandarin, who vowed merciless revenge upon them both for the way they had betrayed his trust, pursued them without rest. The pursuit continued unabated until the two lovers were almost dead from exhaustion. When it seemed as if the Mandarin would catch the two lovers, they fled across the open waters in a house boat, but the Mandarin vowed that, with all his power, they would never be able to put ashore anywhere in the world. With their hope for a happy life together dashed and the tiny boat leaking badly, the scholar and the young woman inspired pity in the gods and were transformed into two bluebirds who, with the open sky before them, were able at last to find happiness.

The story of the Blue Willow china pattern is a typical transformation legend, based on an old Chinese tale of repressed love and the terror that is felt when authority attempts to crush human passions. It describes the possibilities for metamorphoses that lie just beyond the boundaries of either society or nature, and it calls upon the power of the imagination to provide a poetically just means of resolution for a hopeless situation. If such stories seem implausible it is because the Western mind has come to separate fancy or imaginative stories from reality. Yet these stories still speak to us. They tell us that the impossible is possible. In the tradition of the Western imagination, where poetic justice is founded on the principle of endless optimism, the notion of fantasy, the idea of breaking the bounds of nature to achieve a solution to a problem, is a hope that is always held out to the imagination as an alternative to the cold factuality at the root of tragedy. In other words, such stories allow us to ask, "What if?" and then witness the results.

Transformation stories or *metamorphoses* answer a distinct longing in the human heart to see some sort of poetic justice emerge from desperate situations, to see happiness, or at least mercy, result from events that would otherwise end in tragedy. In the hands of Classical authors such as Ovid, who wrote a long poem about mythical transformations titled *Metamorphoses*, these stories suggest that there is an out for special characters when they are confronted by the stark inevitability of the fatalistic pagan universe. Such incredible moments, when terrified maidens are transformed

into trees or suffering lovers into birds to escape the clutches of powers beyond their control, fly in the face of tragedy. In the story of Echo and Narcissus in Book III of *Metamorphoses*, where a nymph falls in love with a beautiful young man who is in love only with himself, the transformation that takes place is an alternative to death:

> Now grief is sapping my strength; little of life remains for me—I am cut off in the flower of my youth. I have no quarrel with death, for in death I shall forget my pain: but I wish that the object of my love might outlive me: as it is, both of us will perish together, when this one life is destroyed.

Metamorphoses are a form of second life, another chance at a different kind of existence. They offer the imagination respite from terror, pain, and grief, and, in turn, transform the universe from a tragic structure into a potentially comic one. They are a display of pity from the gods, and thus are akin to the tragic catharses that audiences experience in their reaction to tragedy. Just as audience members want to do something to alter or correct the situation, the gods, with their metamorphoses, are trying to set right what has gone wrong in the natural order of things.

Metamorphoses cannot happen to everyone: they are the mercy that comes through dire peril, the release from suffering that comes only at the expense of dreadful suffering. They are a warning to humans that the gods are capricious and that fate, whatever it may be, is ultimately terrible. Underlying Ovid's anthology of stories about the relationship between the gods and man, there is the troubling Sophoclean notion that the universe is a dangerous place for mortals. The best anyone can hope for is to stay out of harm's way, because folly, despair, and plain bad luck are the *modus operandi* behind human existence. In Ovid's hands, however, the fatalism of Sophoclean tragedy is mitigated by the fact that the gods, at least sometimes, realize just how horrible they are being to humans and, in bizarre gestures of compensation or consolation, relieve the unlucky mortals of their suffering by transforming them into plants, animals, or natural phenomena such as echoes.

As explanatory mythology, Ovid's *Metamorphoses* suggests that

The Blue Willow China Pattern. The story of the two lovers who struggle to emerge from a repressive world is almost a universal motif, the stuff of Romeo and Juliet *and its descendants, such as* West Side Story.

nature is a product not merely of divine creation but of the correc-
tive measures that come from miscreation, a series of inventive
apologies or attempts at justice that compensate for lucklessness
when mortals are in the wrong place at the wrong time. Wherever
humankind looks, there is a reminder in almost every bird, flower,
tree, or natural phenomenon that the gods are just as capricious as
the meanest of human spirits, and as capable of bad behavior as the
worst of mortals. In Ovid, all of nature is a reminder that there is
no single, mediating, benevolent spirit behind creation as there is
in the Bible. This is the animate universe of Sophoclean tragedy,
where one dare not put a foot wrong and where even the honorable
and the careful are likely to end up in harm's way. The gods in this
realm do not plan an individual's fate so much as they correct or
modify it. They are victims of the same sorts of passions and
desires that operate in the mortal universe. Misrule, misfortune,
and misadventure are to be expected in both the natural and supernatural order of things. The whole universe, it would seem, is one
giant web of folly and irresponsibility.

Of all of the essential authors of Classical literature, Ovid is the
most paradoxical. On one hand, he is telling a series of bawdy,
lurid, and horrific tales about the nature of the gods—stories that
still seem scandalous, even pornographic, to today's readers. The
gods cannot be trusted. At the same time, these stories of transformation suggest that in moments of extreme grief, agony, terror,
violation, or suffering, there is still some attempt by some universal power to save the sufferer or improve a miserable situation by
altering the laws of nature to the point where tragedy is mitigated,
even slightly. Underneath Ovid's terrifying view of the relationship
between humans and gods there is a desire to see order established
in nature—an order that humankind must persevere to create—
and a secret wish that, when tragic inevitability rears its ugly,
Sophoclean head, poetic justice is possible in some way.

Ovid's treatment of the Roman stories of explanatory mythology—how the phenomenon of the echo came into being, for
instance, or why kingfishers nest in a certain way—suggests that
there is a distinct longing in the human heart for poetic justice.
Even if poetic justice is not possible, there is a moment in Ovid's
stories when the laws of nature are suddenly bent to accommodate

the notion of mercy. To contemporary readers, this process of seeing beyond nature, of imagining what can become of things rather than merely looking at the way things are, is the basis for science fiction and fantasy writing. Fantasy locates the reader in a realm where nature exists but its laws are not written in stone. Magic is possible. Shakespeare recognized this in some of his best comedies—*A Midsummer Night's Dream* and *The Tempest*—where he puts at the disposal of the characters a set of circumstances that would not be possible within the predictable and stable limits of nature.

Sometimes the changes are not magical but horrific, of course. In this way, Ovid provides a foundation for what will, almost nineteen hundred years after the penning of *Metamorphoses*, become known as Gothic literature, the genre commonly called horror. As we shall see in chapter 16, Ovid is one of the presiding spirits behind the vision of Mary Shelley. In the nineteenth century, the idea of stretching the physical limits of things triggered the sub-genre of Gothic literature—a sub-genre based on the notion that life can be restored to the inanimate, and that the transforming forces of nature can be harnessed for immoral purposes. It is not every day that dead body-parts sit up and learn to read *Paradise Lost*, as is the case in *Frankenstein*, yet in Ovid's world, where the imagination rules and misrules, people can be miraculously transformed. When the rules of nature are bent for an implausible escape, an iota of fleeting happiness, or a resolution to a seemingly unresolvable situation, we are not only pleased, but delighted. Everyone, from the Brothers Grimm to Walt Disney, who sees that possibilities can lie in overwhelming impossibilities owes a debt of gratitude to Ovid and his book of transformations, *Metamorphoses*.

The generations of readers who have reveled in both the scandal and the fancy of Ovid's stories have been far more generous to him than his own contemporaries. Ovid was as different from the scholarly and serious-minded Virgil, for example, as one could possibly be. Like many modern literary scenes, the writers' milieu of ancient Rome was a broad spectrum of voices that embraced the academic writers on one extreme and the bohemian set on the other. Ovid fell in with a scandalous school of poetic bad boys that included the Roman erotic poet Catullus.

Ovid was born in Sulmo in 43 BC and was trained to join the extensive civil service of the Roman Empire. However, as his education neared completion, he fell in with a group of poets who were known for their bawdy love lyrics. As Ovid's own literary career progressed, he became known for his writings about the affairs of the heart. He penned a series of short love poems known as the *Amores*, about the difficulties of love and how one should go about understanding the passions. Ovid's ribald observations about the complexities of the passions influenced a young Florentine named Dante Alighieri some twelve hundred years later, as the author of *The Divine Comedy* struggled with his own poetic perspective on love in a little book called *La Vita Nuova*—a work that itself (as we shall see in chapter 10) later influenced the sonnet tradition practiced by Shakespeare. Ovid followed the *Amores* with an even more scandalous poetic study of how to conduct a love affair, the *Ars Amatoria* or *The Art of Love*. When his observations proved to be slightly too astute for the Romans and their family values, Ovid wrote a sequel called the *Remedia Amores* (in the contemporary idiom, *Extra Help*) on how to end a love affair. Needless to say, for a literary culture that officially embraced the straight-laced Virgil as its creative paragon, Ovid's poetry was immediately viewed as morally questionable—and was therefore something that everyone *had* to read to remain *au courant* in the Roman social scene.

By the time *Metamorphoses* had been written, circa 8 BC, Ovid had a reputation as a literary *enfant terrible*. For reasons that remain unknown, he was banished—perhaps for corrupting public morality—to the port city of Tomis on the Black Sea, a place as far from the fashionable gossip and banquets as one could go in the Roman Empire. Robert Graves, in his novel *I Claudius*, suggests that Ovid's banishment may have been the result of his part in a large sex scandal that involved members of the emperor Augustus' extended family. Whatever the case, Ovid was the first of many notable authors to write from the position of an exile, grieving and longing for a home to which he could never return. Later Italian writers such as Dante or even Machiavelli would look to Ovid's frankness, his brazen attitude toward strict social and political mores, and find in him a model for their own flippancy, candor, and earthiness. It is also *Metamorphoses*, a series of poems intended to be recited aloud rather than read privately or sung ceremonially, that sets the tone of playful irreverence that later generations would find so appealing in the voice of Italian literature.

Like *The Aeneid*, Ovid's *Metamorphoses* is an implosive work that attempts to chronicle the difficult, ongoing relationship between humans and gods. There is no single protagonist in this collection of interwoven stories. The narratives flow from one myth into another almost as a stream of consciousness. As a poem, it is not an epic, though its scope is epic in that it tells the story of the human race and attempts, like the Bible, to present a history of time. In a structure not unlike that of *The Aeneid*, *Metamorphoses* presents a series of chapters that more or less tell the story of how order is established from chaos. Cyclical in nature, it begins with the overthrow of the Titans by the mischievous Olympians, depicts the interaction of the Olympians and humankind, and then becomes a second-rate version of *The Aeneid* by attempting to chronicle the rise of Rome.

Ovid chooses the same ambitious scope that is found in the Bible, though the Bible is much more personable because of the continuous relationship between the well-developed character of God and the intriguing collection of sub-protagonists who worship him. Where the Bible tells the story of a fall away from God and humankind's gradual journey back to him through a comic series of catastrophes and redemptions, Ovid depicts a broad cycle in which order gives way to chaos and the ultimate struggle of man is to overcome the disorder that exists in heaven to reestablish a peaceable kingdom here on earth. In this broad structure, order and chaos are constantly at odds. Like the emotional pendulum of *The Aeneid*, *Metamorphoses* leads the reader to the brink of sanity and security and then recoils into terror, frenzy, and disorder. The message is that the world is not a safe place; history is a series of overthrows (a perspective not unlike Marx's nineteenth-century view of history as a series of endless struggles).

In the opening paragraph of the book, Ovid says that all change comes from "heavenly powers," and change is the order of the universe. This suggestion that everything is in a state of flux and recreation, not merely creation, is responsible for natural and human activity, carries with it the counternotion of time as an unbroken thread. What Ovid is really saying is that the stability of the Augustan world is possible only because of the vigilance of those in charge—a very Virgilian idea:

> My purpose is to tell of bodies which have been transformed into shapes of a different kind. You heavenly powers, since you were responsible for those changes, as for all else, look favourably on my attempts, and spin an unbroken thread of verse, from the earliest beginnings of the world, down to my own times.

In essence, Ovid is saying that the state of flux that made the world what it is, the cycles of creation and recreation that are at work not only in nature but in the heavens, is still at work in his own time. This notion of perpetual change, and thus the potential for perpetual imbalance and disorder, must have seemed disconcerting to Virgilian-minded Roman readers, who sought peace, order, and good government from the authority that Augustus had brought to society following the disorder of the civil wars. Yet for all the uncertainty, Ovid seems to be conveying that the path to order lies through chaos, and that chaos, disorder, and discord, whether in heaven or on earth, are a means to an end. The fact that the heavenly powers alter the things of nature to their will suggests that heaven itself is a place of change, and that the uncertainties of heaven are reflected in the uncertainties of the world.

This is a very fatalistic view of the world, one that is in keeping with the Sophoclean view of the universe as a tragic place, yet in Ovid's hands, there is the suggestion that the "thread of time" that links the beginning of things to the present world is leading mankind toward some sense of permanence, harmony, and stability. Time, in this sense, is progress, and progress implies improvement. Though the world is a dangerous place, as Ovid tells us, it is gradually getting better. This idea of the improvement of the world through time is what rescued Ovid's writings from the scrap-heap upon which so much Classical literature was cast by the coming of Christendom. After all, the Bible carries the same message: things are getting better.

In the pagan version of Genesis, order is made out of chaos, a "shapeless mass" of "nothing but a weight of lifeless matter." Book I of *Metamorphoses* tells a creation story not unlike that found in Genesis I. Into the new order, humans are created:

> It was at this point that man was born: either the Creator, who was responsible for this better world, made him from divine seed, or else Prometheus, son of Iapetus, took the new-made earth which, only recently separated from the lofty aether, still retained some elements related to those of heaven and, mixing it with rainwater, fashioned it into the image of the all-governing gods.

Ovid's man contains an element of the divine spark, a small scintillation rather than an inspiration, but still an element of some greater life force wherein exists the possibility of better things to come. Like the biblical Adam, Ovid's first man is fashioned in the image of something heavenly, a comparison that certainly was not lost on eager medieval commentators, who sought to find redeeming features in pagan literature.

Like Adam, Ovid's first humans are also born into a Golden Age, an Arcadian-style existence free from threats. Ovid suggests that this first world was a place that had no need for laws because the natural or first order of the world was soundly in place and no one threatened anyone else:

> In the beginning was the Golden Age, when men of their own accord, without threat of punishment, without laws, maintained good faith and did what was right. There were no penalties to be afraid of, no bronze tablets were erected, carrying threats of legal action, no crowd of wrong-doers, anxious for mercy, trembled before the face of their judge... Never yet had a pine tree, cut down from its home on the mountains, been launched on ocean's waves, to visit foreign lands: men knew only their own shores... The peoples of the world, untroubled by any fears, enjoyed a leisurely and peaceful existence, and had no use for soldiers. The world itself, without compulsion, untouched by the hoe, unfurrowed by any share, produced all things spontaneously...

But change is the way of the world. The Golden Age was forced to give way to the power of entropy. Book I tells of a war in heaven (not unlike the war that Milton will allude to in *Paradise Lost*), in which the outcome of the struggle was the ouster of the Titans and the ascendancy of the Olympians. This divine upheaval is followed by the story of Deucalion and his wife Pyhrra, who survive a cataclysmic flood and reseed the human species by tossing rocks over their shoulders. The suggestion is that heaven, as in the Bible, has the power to destroy the world, and the rule of law must be maintained under threat of annihilation from above.

The creation of humankind, the Edenic state of the Golden Age, the flood and the recreation of humans by Deucalion serve to establish the themes of entropy—the progressive breakdown of order in both human affairs and in nature—and of constant change. This theme of change, or the concept of *mutability*, is perhaps one of the most important contributions Ovid makes to literature. Mutability is the theme that the English Renaissance and the later Metaphysical poets such as Henry Vaughan and

George Herbert draw from *Metamorphoses*. Mutability, as depicted in Edmund Spenser's "Two Cantos of Mutabilitie" from Book VII of *The Faerie Queene*, is the force that appears to govern nature:

> *For she the face of earthly things so changed,*
> *That all which Nature had established first*
> *In good estate, and in meet order ranged,*
> *She did pervert, and all their statutes burst:*
> *And all the worlds faire frame (which none yet durst*
> *Of Gods or men to alter or misguide)*
> *She altered quite, and made them all accurst*
> *That God had blest; and did at first provide*
> *In that still happy state for ever to abide.*

The fact that change can even be more powerful than heavenly creation suggests that there is no stability in nature. Nature, as a divine creation, exists only so long as it remains unaltered. The suggestion underlying Ovid's *Metamorphoses*, and one of the chief reasons why it has continued to be viewed as an important work of the imagination, is that the fixed laws of nature can be "burst," as Spenser says, and that beyond the limitations of things, there exists yet another realm. Is this the realm of the imagination? Is this the other option to death? In Act V, Scene i of *Hamlet*, where Shakespeare's protagonist looks upon the skull of the court jester, Yorick, he realizes that mutability is the way of the world:

> ... as thus: Alexander died, Alexander was buried, Alexander returneth to dust; the dust is earth; of earth we make loam; and why not loam whereto he was converted might they not stop a beer barrel?
> *Imperious Caesar, dead and turned to clay,*
> *Might stop a hole to keep the wind away.*
> *O, that that earth which kept the world in awe*
> *Should patch a wall t'expel the winter flaw!*

Joachim Antonisz Wtwael. The Battle Between the Gods and the Titans. Wtwael takes his vision from Ovid's Metamorphoses, *but the dynamics of the painting are fueled by the sort of passion that Milton attempted to express in his notion of the war in heaven in* Paradise Lost.

Metamorphosis, the power of sudden transformation as an escape from terror, despair, and tragic inevitability, offers the imaginative possibility of escape, although such escapes are mixed blessings.

Those brooding Renaissance minds that allowed melancholy to triumph over reason, sometimes to the point of utter despair, saw in Ovid's ideas of transformation the power of the imagination to present an alternative to death—the outside chance of a comic presence in a tragic, fatalistic universe. While so many of the stories of transformation that Ovid relates appear to have the connotations of mercy, the reality remains that the world of *Metamorphoses* is a nasty place only seldom mitigated by the power of the imagination. What is to be expected is tragedy rather than change, mutability rather than stability. When the gods offer change, it is merely a stop-gap measure between catastrophe and anarchy.

Midway through the narrative of Book I, Ovid breaks off from his discussion of cosmological mythology and enters into the meat of what *Metamorphoses* is about: the impact that the gods have on the human species and the changes that contact with the divine wreaks upon individuals. It is in Book I that Ovid tells the first, and perhaps the most famous, story of a metamorphosis, the legend of Apollo and Daphne. This story shows that what mortals abandon in their moments of terror at the hands of the gods are the very things which made them attractive to the immortals in the first place. Daphne's beauty is the cause of her catastrophe. In fact, Ovid seems to suggest that uniqueness in a human being is as much a flaw as it is an attribute, a burden that is more a curse than a blessing. As the innocent maiden is being raped by the sun god, she cries out in her agony to the supreme ruler of the Classical pantheon:

"O father," she cried, "help me! If your rivers really have divine powers, work some transformation, and destroy this beauty which makes me please all too well!" Her prayer was scarcely ended when a deep languor took hold on her limbs, her soft breast was enclosed in thin bark, her hair grew into leaves, her arms into branches, and her feet that were lately so swift were held fast by sluggish roots, while her face became the treetop. Nothing of her was left, except her shining loveliness.

Underlying each transformation in Ovid there is a terrible sense of irony; in Daphne's case, the beauty that she sought to lose is the only thing about her that remains from her original state. Ovid also seems to be suggesting that the gods are driven by terrible passions, that humankind is a plaything of the immortals, or as Kent expresses it in Shakespeare's *King Lear*, "As flies to wanton boys are we to th' gods; / They kill us for their sport."

Book I's themes of creation, overthrow, order, and disorder are underscored by Book II, in which the mischief and folly of the gods in heaven become the key issues. In this book, the gods cheat each other. They are not paragons of virtue but exempla of disorder; they steal from each other and betray each other almost as if they were the worst of all possible humans. What this problematic behavior engenders in the overall structure of *Metamorphoses* is an uncertainty principle—a randomness much akin to the chaos theories of contemporary advanced mathematics but on a much grander scale. This sense of uncertainty is carried into the question of sexual identity and gender in Book III of *Metamorphoses*, in which Ovid delves into the issue of androgyny, particularly in the story of Bacchus, the Roman god of frenzy, extreme passion, and wine. What seems to emerge from Books II and III is a dislocation of perceptions, the sense that nothing—not personal identity, gender, or stability in the pantheon—can be taken for granted.

But Ovid is far from finished with his dislocation principle: in Book IV he challenges the stability of human relationships and tells a series of tales about love relationships that have gone terribly wrong. In fact, he shifts course entirely in Books IV to VI, from simple order and disorder to passion and terror. To establish this new theme, Ovid revamps the structure of his tales, abandoning the linear narrative, the straight-line sequence of cause-and-effect events that stretches from the beginning of the world to the point where human beings and their tribulations assume the focus. Beginning in Book IV, the process of telling stories suddenly takes a dark and complex turn. Book IV is a series of stories within stories that are told by the spinster daughters of a king named Minyas as they sit weaving at their looms. The metaphor at work in this structure is that all stories are somehow connected to each other, either as direct consequences of events or as a series of free associations triggered through the telling of a particular tale.

The daughters of Minyas recount stories about the terrors of love. In presenting these stories as a series of old wives' tales, Ovid is suggesting that what one should fear most about the world is the very thing one hopes to trust the most: love. Love in this context does not make the world go round so much as it makes the world recoil with horror. Figures such as Pyramus and Thisbe, Hermaphroditus and Salmacis, and Cadmus and his wife act as warnings about what can happen when love is either fated or is blinded to the dangers that constantly lurk in this animate universe. And if the universe is inhabited by fates that seek to disarm and destroy human relationships, even at moments when they appear poised to succeed, it is because love offers no greater sense of certainty than anything else and is just as capable of being a flashpoint for tragedy.

Ovid's depiction of the story of Pyramus and Thisbe, two lovers who attempt to reach each other through the barriers that society presents, is a case in point. Later, Shakespeare attempts to recreate this tragic story. But the play of the Mechanicals in *A Midsummer Night's Dream* is a parodic examination of what can happen if no possibility of a comic resolution exists. Ultimately, the Mechanicals' play is a dismal failure because Shakespeare has set the world of *A Midsummer Night's Dream* in the realm of the imagination, and in the imagination, poetic justice and comic outcome take precedence over dashed hopes and cathartic outpourings. Comedy mocks the seriousness of tragedy by constantly reminding the reader that everything must work out in the end because the human heart seeks resolution and reconciliation ahead of grief. But the tragic theme of thwarted love is something Ovid understands. It is also something that Shakespeare understood, for he takes the story of young lovers thwarted in the pursuit of their desires and transforms it into *Romeo and Juliet*.

Book IV of *Metamorphoses* also makes another small but important contribution to the literary continuum: the *framing device*. Every narrative has an implied speaker. When multiple narratives had to be told, authors such as Boccaccio in *The Decameron* and Chaucer in *The Canterbury Tales* used multiple narrators. They set a scene that contextualizes the telling of multiple stories, a context that allows the stories to act not only as responses to and commentaries on each other, but as resonances that provide variations on a particular theme.

Needless to say, the daughters of Minyas are terrified of love. For them, love is something that, while potentially heroic, is frightening. The final story in Book IV, the story of the rescue of Andromeda by the chivalrous Perseus, is straight out of dime-store romance novels: Perseus is the knight in shining armor who rescues the damsel in distress. For all their terror, however, the stories of Book IV pale in comparison to the horrific, almost Gothic tales that are presented in Books V and VI.

These books deal with the theme of rape. There is no love in Book V. There is crime, injustice, inhumanity, and cruelty. The stories of the rape of Proserpine and the brutalization of Philomela by her brother-in-law, Tereus, are reminders that the misdeeds of the gods take on unspeakable dimensions when reflected in the action of human beings.

One of the most powerful and the most piteous stories in all of Classical mythology is the story of Philomela and her sister, Procne, from Book VI. As a statement of explanatory mythology, it tells the story of the origins of the swallow and the nightingale. As a literary motif, it carries the weight of being both a symbol of beauty and a metaphor for tragedy. The story Ovid tells describes a close relationship between two sisters. When Procne is married to a foreign king, Tereus, and relocated to a distant land, her sister longs to see her. Granting her wish for a visit, Tereus comes to fetch Philomela in his boat. On the way back, however, Tereus rapes Philomela and shuts her up in a tower, silencing her by cutting out her tongue. Despairing her fate, Philomela spends her time weaving the story of her rape, abduction, and brutalization at the hands of her brother-in-law into a tapestry, which she then smuggles to her sister. On discovering the meaning of the handicraft, Procne frees her sister and serves her own son, Itys, to Tereus for dinner. When Tereus asks where his son is, Procne responds, "The boy you are asking for is here, inside you." Then Philomela leaps forward, thrusts the boy's bloody head into Tereus' lap, and flees. In a fit of blind fury—the unleashed passions that Virgil feared and warned against in *The Aeneid*—Tereus pursues the two sisters:

Drawing his sword he was rushing in pursuit of Pandion's daughters, when it almost seemed the girls' bodies were hovering in the air, raised up on wings: in fact, they were hovering on wings. One of them flew off to the woods, the other flew under the eaves of the roof: traces of the murder were still visible on her breast, her feathers were still crimson with blood. The king, made swift by grief and longing for revenge, was also turned into a bird.

The metamorphoses of Philomela into a nightingale, Procne into a swallow, and Tereus into a hoopoe suggest that extremes of emotion are what catches the attention of the gods.

The story of Philomela and Procne that so moved Ovid in *Metamorphoses* has become an important literary motif, a representation of the sterility of sex when it is driven only by lust. In *The Waste Land*, T.S. Eliot summons the story in Part II, "A Game of Chess," where a typist services a man upon a divan in a loveless act of sex:

> *Above the antique mantel was displayed*
> *As though a window gave upon the sylvan scene*
> *The change of Philomel, by the barbarous king*
> *So rudely forced; yet there the nightingale*
> *Filled all the desert with inviolable voice*
> *And still she cried, and still the world pursues,*
> *"Jug Jug" to dirty ears.*

Joseph Severn. John Keats. The pensive young medical student is seen here musing on eternity. It was Keats who gave us the modern notion of the nightingale as a symbol for eternity, replacing the old, plaintive idea of a voice suffering in the darkness.

In Part III, "The Fire Sermon," the nightingale again sings her sterile, bathetic song, a great reduction of the song of the "immortal bird" that Keats hears on Hampstead Heath in *Ode to a Nightingale*:

> *Twit twit twit*
> *Jug jug jug jug jug jug*
> *So rudely forc'd.*
> *Tereu.*

Eliot's Philomela is dissipated, worn out, a symbol of a culture that no longer puts up a fight but simply submits to the indignities of the rapacious. Eliot comments on this ennui, this exhaustion of both the heart and the spirit that seems the malaise of the modern world:

When lovely woman stoops to folly and
Paces about the room again, alone,
She smoothes her hair with automatic hand,
And puts a record on the gramophone.

What lies at the root of the modern malaise is a loss of the energy that fueled the Western imagination to seek alternatives to what lay before it, no matter how bright or horrible. It is this transforming energy that fires Ovid in his vision. The power of the imagination to seek some alternative to violence and destruction seems to be at the root of the transformations of Philomela and Procne.

Ovid returns to this idea—that grief or rage can transform individuals into birds—in the story in Book IX of Ceyx and Alcyone. The tale is really the other side of the Philomela and Procne legend, for it tells of grief in the face of devotion and undying love. When a king named Ceyx is drowned while attempting to return to his beloved wife, Alcyone, the gods appear to take pity on the two by turning them into kingfishers. Ovid uses the legend to explain the folk belief that kingfishers build their nests on the water during the quiet, tranquil days of late summer—a very un-Audubon fabrication that would upset even the most amateur ornithologist. Yet the story explains not only the origin of the kingfisher, a bird that symbolizes grandeur and resurrection, but also the concept of the "halcyon days" or quiet moments of repose when domestic bliss and tranquillity reflect a greater and more pleasant order in nature.

In the end, Ovid is suggesting that the outer bounds of human passions have the power to transform those who experience them. Even in contemporary literature, authors still recognize the power of extreme emotions to cause a transformation of sorts. In Toni Morrison's *Jazz*, for example, one narrator turns into another when he or she can no longer cope emotionally with the telling of the story. These overpowering moments are exactly the reason why Virgil calls on the Muse for assistance when his narrative becomes emotionally charged: there are limitations to the storytelling process, and the best way to refresh a narrative that becomes choked and cathartically unbearable is to shift the process of telling to a different voice.

So powerful are the stories in Books IV to VI, in fact, that Ovid himself is overcome. It is for this reason that he shifts the focus of his work, beginning in Book VII, to heroes. Books VII to IX examine not only the successful heroes, but also those who are dismal failures at their callings, those who leave problems, messes, and clean-up jobs in their wakes. In Book VII, the heroes, such as Jason, the protagonist of the story of the Golden Fleece, succeed in their quests, but by Book VIII, Ovid allows the theme of entropy and mutability again to creep into the picture, and his great men appear not to be up to their tasks.

Book VIII is also where Ovid chooses to place the story of the labyrinth. The labyrinth is one of the oddest creations in the literary imagination. It is a metaphor for the pagan world, a conundrum that was built upon fear of the unknown and the desire to placate the forces of nature, as well as a complex intellectual puzzle waiting to be solved by a clever mind. As a metaphor, the labyrinth is suggestive of wastefulness, wantonness, and dark, impenetrable knowledge of shamefulness and wrong. In medieval romance, the

Waste Forest will be presented as a metaphorical labyrinth, a place where the questing knights roam until they are able to discover their moral selves. Ovid's labyrinth is a crafted, secretive maze of wrong turns, the ultimate web of deceit:

> In his absence the monstrous child which the queen had borne, to the disgrace of the king's family, had grown up, and the strange hybrid creature had revealed his wife's disgusting love affair to everyone. Minos determined to rid his home of this shameful sight, by shutting the monster away in an enclosure of elaborate and evolved design, where it could not be seen. Dedalus, an architect famous for his skill, constructed the maze, confusing the usual marks of direction, and leading the eye of the beholder astray by devious paths winding in different directions...so Dedalus constructed countless wandering paths and was himself scarcely able to find his way back to the entrance, so confusing was the maze.

The fact that it is full of turnings, traps, and cul de sacs makes the labyrinth very like a complex story or an imaginative construct, similar to a dream or a nightmare, in which there is a great deal of information that can terrify but no one to make sense of it.

In a more contemporary sense, the labyrinth, especially in the hands of James Joyce, has come to represent a culture that is awaiting either artistic articulation or critical interpretation. For Joyce (as we shall see in chapter 18), the labyrinth, the complex story, was early twentieth-century Ireland. In his novel *A Portrait of the Artist as a Young Man*, Joyce names his protagonist Stephen Dedalus. When the young man attempts to escape the "traps and snares" of his soul-stifling culture, he resorts to a kind of flight—exile—like the mythical Daedalus. Stephen Dedalus' challenge is, in many ways, a heroic one: he is trying to find both the way out of his culture and the means to understanding his culture's needs, secrets, and intricacies.

If the labyrinth is an overwhelming question, then it is a question that demands an overwhelming answer. Such answers in mythology and literature are usually provided by individuals of heroic proportions. As Virgil suggested in his depiction of Aeneas, the purpose of the hero is not just to fight great physical battles but to overcome enormous intellectual challenges. The labyrinth, then, is meant to show readers that even the most complex problems have their solutions. The figure who solves the riddle of the labyrinth is Theseus:

> For, thanks to the help of the princess Ariadne, Theseus rewound the thread he had laid, retraced his steps, and found the elusive gateway as none of his predecessors had managed to do.

Yet Theseus is really a failed hero. He departs triumphantly from Crete with Ariadne by his side, but soon abandons her and makes a mess of his own life. What Ovid is suggesting is that heroic enterprises cannot go on forever, and heroes simply fade away like old soldiers as the narrative outstrips their usefulness as characters. For Ovid, the heroic quickly becomes yesterday's news. The focus of Book VIII is not Theseus' heroism but Daedalus' creativity. For Ovid, the real heroes of his story are the ones who present the

questions rather than the solutions, and he playfully delights in leaving a great many loose ends in his narrative thread.

The idea of loose ends, of the messes and aftermaths that heroic enterprises leave in their wakes, is at the heart of Book IX. In it, Ovid tells the stories of individuals such as Nessus who try to model themselves after some of the more capable heroes of *Metamorphoses* but fail miserably. Yet as if sensing that stories of heroes can become boring if they are told and retold—after all, one hero seems almost the same as the next—Ovid returns in Books X and XI to the issue of love. He is now interested not in the terrors of love, however, but in the idea of control and possession, how co-dependence turns into willfulness and how characters react in the face of overwhelming loss.

Book X tells the tragic story of Orpheus and Eurydice, a tale in which passion again is the cause of folly and downfall. Ovid's view is that it serves them right for letting love get out of hand; he seems to believe that love is as much an art as anything else, and one should practice it with dispassion and objectivity. Orpheus' quest to retrieve his beloved Eurydice from the clutches of the underworld is really a warning about the need to practice self-control, even when victory seems easily within one's grasp. Ovid relishes describing, with a sense of almost erotic tension, the ascent of the couple to the world above after Eurydice is given leave of the Shades:

Up the sloping path, through the mute silence they made their way, up the steep dark track, wrapped in impenetrable gloom, till they had almost reached the surface of the earth. Here, anxious in case his wife's strength should be failing and eager to see her, the lover looked behind him, and straightaway Eurydice slipped back into the depths. Orpheus stretched out his arms, straining to clasp her and be clasped; but the hapless man touched nothing but yielding air. Eurydice, dying now a second time, uttered no complaint against her husband. What was there to complain of, but that she had been loved? With a last farewell which scarcely reached his ears, she fell back into the same place from which she had come.

Antoine Louis Barye. Theseus Fighting the Centaur Bianor. In this depiction of another adventure of Theseus, he again takes on a strange half-beast, half-human creature by the might of physical strength rather than just cunning and intelligence.

Ovid follows this touching story of lost love with the suggestion that Orpheus' grief caused him to become homosexual, "the first to introduce this custom among the people of Thrace." In the end, Orpheus, who suffered grief because he could not control his passions for his lost wife, is the victim of unbridled rage. The powerful and beautiful music of his poetic song angers a group of wild women known as the Maenads, and in an act of blind rage they tear the bard apart, limb from limb:

> He stretched out his hands toward his assailants, but now, for the first time, his words had no effect, and he failed to move them in any way by his voice. Dead to all reverence, they tore him apart and, through those lips to which the rocks had listened, which wild beasts had understood, his last breath slipped away and vanished in the wind.

Perhaps this is the greatest fear of all from Ovid's personal perspective—the poet who is wordless in the face of anarchy and destructiveness. It seems to suggest that order in the world is possible as long as the lines of communication are open to beauty, music, and the sanity that underlies the civilizing powers of literary creation. It is a view that Freud takes up as his banner explanation for the existence of civilization in *Civilization and Its Discontents*, in which he argues that culture, religion, and literature are the defensive mechanisms that protect the human species from barbarism.

What is unique about Ovid is that he views human affections in broad terms, and suggests that a metamorphosis or a change in shape or attitude is merely a kind of transference of purpose, a defiance of the laws of nature that occurs when human beings unleash a ferocity that is unnatural. Whatever the outcome of such changes, however, the point still remains that one should avoid situations where a metamorphosis is possible, and the way to do that, as he suggests in his playful, backhanded way, is to maintain self-control at all times. The problem with this idea, though, was that many readers through the ages failed to understand that Ovid looked at the world, and at human relationships, from alternative and unexpected perspectives. For this reason, he has been labeled scandalous by a number of literal- and puritanical-minded critics. Nevertheless, the one message that is quite clear throughout his work is that the passions, whether practiced by humans or gods, are tricky matters, a morass of fear, terror, and unfortunate events that is ultimately a threat to humanity and the idea of progress.

Perhaps to mitigate the conundrum of change, Ovid again changes the course of his work in Book XII, leaving the fanciful stories of transformations and launching into the serious business of history. In Ovid's view, history *is* change, and if entropy and metamorphoses are the rules by which the universe operates, then the course of human events must function by the same rules. But rather than acknowledge that history is largely the product of destiny (the management guidelines of the gods, and a perspective that Virgil and even Homer understood), Ovid presents the idea that human beings, their weaknesses, and their follies are largely responsible for the way things are. Though this appears to be a misanthropic view, Ovid's retelling of the events that Virgil chronicled in *The Aeneid*—the Trojan War, the fall of Troy, the founding of Rome, and the eventual rise of the Caesars to power—is actually a portrait of the human race stumbling its way toward better days and an eventual escape from the tyranny of cyclical time.

The problems that confront humanity, Ovid believes, are stupidity, irrationality, and fortune. Though there is little that individuals can do with regard to fate, he believes that rational thought and relaxed good judgment are key ingredients in human progress. To illustrate his point, he opens Book XII by telling the story of the debate between the cunning Ulysses and the slow-minded Ajax for the rights to the armor of the fallen Achilles. In what amounts to a delightful parody of the art of rhetoric, Ulysses manages to enrage Ajax to the point where Ajax demonstrates how angry he is by killing himself. The armor, of course, goes to Ulysses, who wins the debate by default. In the process of relating this laughable legend of how extremes of anger can backfire, Ovid presents the rules for debating a point. The first rule is never speak first, and always allow one's opponent to present his or her argument. A refutation or response need not establish any points, but can merely consist of a critique of the first argument—something that Ulysses does with aplomb. The second point of debating is that one must always stick to the point. As his emotions get the better of him,

Ajax goes completely off topic and loses himself in his argument. He falls into the logical fallacy of the "red herring," the fact which does not matter in the course of the debate. Ajax's final failing is that he is a poor loser. The rule of rhetoric, as suggested by the great minds of the Classical art of persuasion through language such as Aristotle, Cicero, and Saint Augustine, is that one should maintain reserve during and after a debate.

What lies at the root of this parable is the notion that one should use one's restraint not only to keep the emotions in check but to win the day. This emphasis on using knowledge in place of passion, and on practicing a form of continuous cognizance, is perhaps one of the key messages of *Metamorphoses*. The apotheosis of this Roman perception of how one should respond to the world is demonstrated in the character of Julius Caesar, the hero of Book XII, who brings order to the world and a sane conclusion to the perpetual cycles of chaos and disintegration. In the end, what will triumph in the world is rationalism, the ability to see *beyond* the imagination. Yet it is evident that the path to this safe and successful destiny for humankind lies *through* the imagination. The transformations that Ovid chronicles are part of the human experience, a necessary means to an end, just as suffering and grief seem to pave the road to a new life in a new form.

Beneath all this suffering, there is a sense that human relations are always motivated by a desire of some kind. Understanding the nature of desire, whether it be lust, covetousness, grief over loss, or patriotic zeal, is really what *Metamorphoses* is about. As a work of literature, it has spoken to everyone from Shakespeare to Freud because it attempts to find a connection between events and their causes, the same study of cause and effect that motivates the science of psychology. And even when the causes and effects seem to take on horrific dimensions, there is still, in the animate universe of *Metamorphoses*, that one thing the Classical mind could not do without: hope.

When Alcyone learns that her husband Ceyx has drowned while trying to return to her, she is overcome with grief and transformed into a kingfisher. In a moment of tenderness, the final imaginative metamorphosis of the entire work, Alcyone flies to her husband's body and embraces him:

Changed into a sorrowing bird, she skimmed the surface of the waves. As she flew, a plaintive sound, like the lament of someone stricken with grief, came harshly from the slender beak that was her mouth. When she reached the silent, lifeless corpse, she embraced the dear limbs with her new wings, and all in vain kissed the cold lips with her hard beak. The people doubted whether Ceyx felt her, or whether it was the motion of the sea that made him seem to raise his head: but surely he had felt her! At last the gods had pity on them, and both were changed into birds. Their love endured, even after they had shared this fate, and their marriage vows were not dissolved when they acquired wings.

Like the Chinese legend of the Blue Willow, the stories of Ovid point us along a sometimes difficult route toward an important verity. Here the Roman maxim *amor vincit omnia,* or "love conquers all," seems to apply. The presence of love and devotion—not as possessiveness but as the foundation of an equal partnership between two dedicated souls, and as the force that drives the imagination to dream of things beyond the limitations of this world—contains the power to defy the laws of nature. It signals to the world what, in the words of the English poet Philip Larkin, is the true meaning of human relations: "What will survive of us is love."

6

FORTUNE
AND MEN'S EYES

Boethius' *The Consolation of Philosophy*

There is nothing quite like sitting all by oneself on a sunny summer morning in an empty Gothic cathedral such as the one in Rochester, England. The air inside is cool and soft on the face. The clear white light of the early day streams through the pale frosted windows in shafts that almost appear to be heavenly fingers. In the silence within the great mass of stone walls and rising, vaulted arches, it is possible to hear the birds outside—the swallows twittering in the leaded eaves, the sparrows and the starlings nesting in the stoic carvings, and the coo of doves or pigeons tucked in overhangs and niches. To the front, around the high altar, there is dark mysteriousness, almost as if a spirit moves within it.

On one of the pillars to the south of the holy table, a patch of the whitewash has been removed from the wall to reveal the muted but still active colours of a medieval fresco. If you examine it closely, you can see that the fresco depicts a statuesque, gowned woman wearing a crown. She is standing beside a device that looks like a Ferris wheel, and in the buckets of the mechanism sit small male figures, some clutching swords, others holding maces, and all wearing crowns. The elegant woman appears to turn the wheel, and some of the kings look as if they are donning their crowns at the outset of their reigns. They seem almost certain that fortune has smiled on them, and the painter has taken some pains to show a look of calm confidence and easy trust on their faces. On the other side of the wheel, however, the ride is far from smooth. The buckets are overturning, and as a passenger is spilled headfirst to the ground below, he loses his crown. This is how the Middle Ages perceived the question of fate. The fresco depicts the motif known

Fresco of the Wheel of Fortune. This fresco, in the chancel of Rochester Cathedral, shows the mythical wheel and the impact that Fortuna has on the course of human events.

as the wheel of Fortune, and it is turned by the hand of fate itself, Dame Fortune.

The idea of fortune as a personification and not merely an invisible force in the universe has come to us through the work of a Roman nobleman, translator, and civil servant of the late fourth century AD: Boethius. In a work that likely inspired that fateful fresco, Boethius envisioned Fortune, that Classical nemesis of humans, as a cruel mistress who set all individuals upon a great wheel—the wheel of Fortune—that she slowly turned with the dispassion and indifference of a pagan god:

> *With domineering hand she moves the turning wheel,*
> *Like currents in a treacherous bay swept to and fro:*
> *Her ruthless will has just deposed once faithful kings*

While trustless still, from low she lifts a conquered head;
No cries of misery she hears, no tears she heeds,
But steely hearted laughs at groans her deeds have wrung.
Such is the game she plays, and so she tests her strength;
Of mighty power she makes parade when one short hour
Sees happiness from utter desolation grow.

Fate, to the Classical mind, was an endless cycle of highs and lows, where the joy of the upswing could blind a man or a woman to the bitter reality of a downfall that might lie ahead. In a moment of role-playing in her dialogue with her pupil (Boethius), Dame Philosophy, the antithesis of Dame Fortune, explains the all-too-tricky nature of fate:

> Inconstancy is my very essence; it is the game I never cease to play as I turn my wheel in its ever changing circle, filled with joy as I bring the top to the bottom and the bottom to the top. Yes, rise up on my wheel if you like, but don't count it an injury when by the same token you begin to fall, as the rules of the game will require.

A game? Is life merely the sport of the gods as Ovid suggests in *Metamorphoses*? Surely there is some other meaning to existence. Surely some intelligent being, some divine manager, is working toward some larger plan. Otherwise, what is the point of living? As this question became more perplexing to the Western imagination, the need to answer it became more urgent. The problem with living in an animate universe is that it leaves no room for certainty. At the same time, in Boethius' world the model of Aeneas represented the idea that stability and certainty were virtues one could possibly believe in and attain.

As people grew tired of pitiless pantheons, the gap between Sophoclean terror and the simple human desire to believe in the chance of happiness was an issue that needed to be addressed. Christianity stepped into this gap by offering the possibility that the universe was comic rather than tragic, that a single loving and understanding God was in charge and that he would guarantee an individual's happiness, if not in this life then at least in the next, for the simple price of faith. The problem facing those who still lived in the Classical mentality, and the problem that the early Christians faced, was that they could not reconcile the world of the old imagination with the possibilities of the new.

It is strange to think that the way out of the pagan universe came from two minds that were both confronting overwhelming questions. The first, Boethius, was facing a very dark future. The second, Saint Augustine (as we shall see in chapter 7), was suffering a nervous breakdown. Yet when these men looked into the heart of the Classical, animate universe, seeking answers to the overwhelming crises of their lives and challenging the most basic imaginative assumptions of their world, their strength of intellect pulled them through to a new understanding of the relationship between God and humanity that transformed Western literature. Deep down, both Boethius and Saint Augustine wanted to live in a universe that offered comfort and security from the forces of despair.

While awaiting his execution in a prison cell in Padua (to this day the charges remain unclear), Boethius penned a work that provided the imaginative foundation for the medieval world and for later thinkers such as Machiavelli. Prisoners such as Elizabeth I and Sir Walter Raleigh, who had a lot of time on their hands and who faced equally bleak prospects, opened the pages of Boethius' *The Consolation of Philosophy* and spent their long hours of incarceration not only reading what that Roman prisoner had to say about his misfortune, but translating the work into the familiarity of their own idiom. The book seems to have spoken powerfully and clearly to them of what it means to face a future that is seemingly hopeless. It also advised them how an individual could confront his or her personal destiny with the courage to perceive the beauty and glory of a divine and loving hand in all events, and to find some meaning in the hopeless mess of life.

Through an imaginary dialogue with a personification named Dame Philosophy, Boethius comes to the conclusion that fate is only as bad as we perceive it to be, that our understanding of what happens to us is more the result of the perception we bring to our situation than it is a matter of being the victim of supernatural forces. He reasons that fate is something *we* control through our intellect, and not a folly dished out by the gods. And with the writing of *The Consolation of Philosophy*, one of the cornerstones of the animate, pagan universe suddenly crumbled beneath the realization that, ultimately, there is no tragedy as long as one trusts in the God of the Bible.

In his age, Anicius Manlius Severinus Boethius was perhaps the best person one could consult on the nature of tragedy. He understood the form thoroughly as a result of his efforts at translating from Greek to Latin the works of Sophocles and Aristotle, in particular Aristotle's *Poetics*. At an early age, Boethius was adopted into a noble family that held a prominent place in the administration of a Greek province, and there, absorbed as he was in two cultures, he began extending his broader understanding of the Roman cultural continuum to the Hellenistic and Bronze Age worlds that had fed the roots of the empire. With his contemporary and friend Cassiodorus, another ill-fated civil servant/scholar who also undertook translation as a means of broadening the Roman scope of ideas, Boethius is responsible for the scholastic tradition, a practice that valued the copying of texts as a crucial part of the learning process. This idea—that learning comes not just from talking or from experience but from the process of reading and critiquing a written text—had a profound impact on the Middle Ages, where the scriptorium and the scribe were, in many cases, all that stood between the continuum of Western thought and the darkness that always follows the loss of significant knowledge. In this light, Boethius can also be seen as one of the cornerstones of the Renaissance; almost eight hundred years after the Roman's brutal execution in a Padua prison cell, an Italian cleric by the name of Francesco Petrarca, a figure we know today as Petrarch, would take up the study of variorums in handwritten versions of Latin texts and trigger a movement known as Humanism that would change the face of Western learning.

As a writer, Boethius appealed to readers of the Dark and Middle Ages not only because he was an early Christian, but because he was able to transform and explain the fatalism of the Classical world by marrying it to the Christian ideal of an orderly universe with a benign God. The idea that there is one caring, controlling God in heaven directly challenged the notion of fortune. Boethius perceived life as a struggle, but ultimately a struggle with a purpose. And the purpose of everything could be discovered in one of two ways: either by waiting for events to unfold, or by questioning life in a very Socratic manner in an attempt to understand how an individual's fate relates to larger issues. Just as Socrates had declared that "the unexamined life is not worth living," so Boethius concluded that the unexamined individual destiny is an emotional cul de sac where grief is the only response to events. Dame Philosophy, in her dialogue with the prisoner Boethius, explains how crucial it is for a person to recognize that life is a battleground not just on the physical plain, but on the mental one:

> You are engaged in a bitter but spirited struggle against fortune of every kind, to avoid falling victim to her when she is adverse or being corrupted by her when she is favourable. Hold to the middle way with unshakeable strength. Whatever falls short or goes beyond, despises happiness but receives no reward for its toil. It is in your own hands what fortune you wish to shape for yourself, for the only function of adversity apart from discipline and correction, is punishment.

In the Classical definition of the term, fortune includes both the bad events that happen to a person and also the good. Broadly defined, fortune is the course of one's life, the highs and the lows. Boethius' contention is that good fortune often blinds an individual to the inevitable challenges and downfalls that occur as part of the cycles that are inherent in life. The good, he argues, can be misleading because during good times, we expect the benefits to last forever. Beneath the revels, he notes, there is a larger message: nothing stays the same. (This perspective also appears in the Book of Ecclesiastes.) To maintain our sanity and equilibrium, we must see through events and understand that there is a divine plan in the universe. We must take the good with the bad, he stipulates. Rudyard Kipling, in his famous poem *If*—, argues the same position as fatherly advice to his son:

If you can meet with Triumph and Disaster
And treat those two impostors just the same.

What lies at the root of Boethius' argument, however, is a much deeper message: do not trust what you see. Reality and experience must be questioned, and if they are open to constant scrutiny—as some of the great Greek Sophists whom Boethius translated suggested in their dialogues—then they are also open to interpretation. What this means is that it is possible not only to *understand* events but to *read* them, either as they occur or before they happen. In other words, reality is something that one can shape through the power of the mind.

As Book I of *The Consolation of Philosophy* opens, the persona of the work is sitting in his prison cell, lamenting his misfortunes. Although he is examining his situation, he is not thinking clearly. True to the warnings of Virgil, the prisoner is overcome by emotion and clearly lost in his own grief:

I who once composed with eager zest
Am driven by grief to shelter in sad songs;
All torn the Muses' cheeks who spell the words
For elegies that wet my face with tears.

No terror could discourage them at least
From coming with me on my way.
They were the glory of my happy youth
And still they comfort me in hapless age.
Old age came suddenly by suffering sped,
And grief then bade her government begin:
My hair untimely white upon my head,
And I a worn out bone-bag hung with flesh.

In a depiction of aging that is reminiscent of W.B. Yeats' comment in *Sailing to Byzantium* that "An aged man is but a paltry thing / A tattered coat upon a stick," Boethius suggests that overwhelming grief, terror, and fear can have a negative physiological effect on an individual. Something in the prisoner's Roman makeup is pleading for the kind of Virgilian sanity that uses objectivity and emotional detachment as a defence against misfortune. But that is not possible. Instead, the Muses (those Classical spirits of the imagination who conveyed divine inspiration to the lips of the epic poets) are now taunting the incarcerated soul with the full fury of unbridled emotionalism, thus separating him from dispassionate understanding—his true nature and intellectual home. What makes his predicament seem all the worse is that he has a profound memory of having once been secure, happy, and successful. How could he have fallen so far? Boethius laments:

First fickle Fortune gave me wealth short-lived,
Then in a moment all but ruined me.
Since Fortune changed her trustless countenance,
Small welcome to the days prolonging life.
Foolish the friends who called me happy then
Whose fall shows how my foothold was unsure.

The reason for the fall, he concludes, is that good fortune is as much an illusion as misfortune; in Kipling's words, both are "impostors" and should be treated with distrust. So what, therefore, is happiness if one must distrust the good events in life as much as one mistrusts the bad? The answer is simple. Happiness, says Boethius, is clarity of thought.

F
G
P... ....
Fortune.
From an
eighteenth-
century engrav-
ing. The
association of
Pan, a spirit of
nature, and
Fortune seems to
imply that the
world itself is a
dangerous place
and that all
creation is
fraught with
Ovidian
uncertainty.

Suddenly, in the depths of his despair, Boethius finds his prison cell crowded with the presence of a woman of "awe-inspiring appearance," a protean figure who keeps changing size:

> It was difficult to be sure of her height, for sometimes she was
> of average human size, while at other times she seemed to touch
> the very sky with the top of her head, and when she lifted
> herself even higher, she pierced it and was lost to human sight.
> Her clothes were made of imperishable material, of the finest
> thread woven with the most delicate skill. (Later she told me
> that she had made them with her own hands.)...On the bottom
> hem could be read the embroidered Greek letter Pi, and on the
> top hem the Greek letter Theta.

The Greek letters represent the two types of philosophy that Boethius had inherited: practical philosophy (represented by the letter Pi) and speculative philosophy (represented by the letter Theta). The changing shape of this personified figure, whom he introduces as Dame Philosophy, suggests that she has moments of enormous, overwhelming presence and importance, and other moments of more human and limited scope and impact. The first thing she does is send the Muses packing. In a fit of pique, she refers to the daughters of Mount Helicon as "these hysterical sluts," and declares that "they have no medicine to ease his pains." Lyricism, especially the elegy, expresses grief, but often has a difficult time presenting any alternative. When elegies fail, it is usually because they perceive neither justice nor compensation for any of the pain and loss they examine. The Muses, who sing the worst possible kind of the elegy (the elegy for the self), are only aggravating the prisoner's grief by reminding him that the unmitigated imagination has the power to blur the distinction between reality and illusion—something that powerful works of the literary imagination do. In a very fundamental sense, poetry is a trigger for the emotions because the compact language, the moving and engaging subject matter, the swiftness of its discourse, and its tendency to see the world through metaphorical logic rather than linear or discursive logic all serve to heighten the imagination. Odysseus, for example, was moved to tears by *The Iliad* not only because he had lived the events, but because the events were being communicated in the powerful medium of poetry. Boethius, taking a cue from Plato, who thought that poets should be banned in *The Republic*, realizes that poetry simply gets in the way of clear thinking. And so, Dame Philosophy dismisses the Muses. If human beings are to find the consolation, the recompense of understanding that comes from reasoning their way out of suffering, they must discover it through the cold light of dispassionate logic. Like Plato before him, Boethius chooses to present the road to reason through a series of questions and answers that form the script of a conversational inquiry.

Philosophy, we are told, is both a defense against suffering and a means of understanding it. Dame Philosophy informs Boethius that through the process of reasoning one is not just looking at a problem from an unemotional point of view, but declaring and defending a moral position. The purpose of philosophy, therefore, is to discover what is moral in a question or a situation and to allow reason rather than emotion to articulate it. When philosophers of the past have fallen victim to the whims of emotionally charged groups, such as in the case of Socrates, it is because emotionalism makes no distinction between right and wrong—it simply reacts, without reason. Dame Philosophy explains this connection:

> The sole cause of their tragic sufferings was their obvious and complete contempt of the pursuits of immoral men which my teaching had instilled in them.

If a society is to be considered moral, then, it must be governed by individuals who are able to make that important distinction between what they feel and what they think. Boethius makes a direct reference to the ideas of Plato in *The Republic*, where that Greek philosopher argues a society cannot hope to be just or moral until it is run by kings who are philosophers:

> You took your cue from him and said that the reason why it is necessary for philosophers to take part in government was to prevent the reins of government falling into the hands of wicked and unprincipled men to the ruin and destruction of the good.

The world, therefore, is not engaged in the tragic folly of the relationship between the gods and humankind so much as it is engaged in a much larger battle: the struggle between good and evil.

Boethius, we should remember, was living in a watershed moment in the Western imagination. On the one hand, he was a Roman and proud of the literary tradition of his pagan past. He saw it as a means of defending against the "barbarian" or outsider values that foreign Caesars had imposed upon the conservative and traditionally minded Romans. At the same time, however, he was also a Christian who was still struggling with some of the key formative issues of a theology that was daily being reshaped. In this Christian perspective, there was a new rule to the universe: God is good. God was not merely a heavenly administrator who could be bought off with the sacrifice of a ram or a bull at a local temple. He was omnipotent and completely in command. He had a plan for the universe and, in the end, everything was going to work out well for those who had faith in him and respected his laws. There was only one problem with this perception, and it is the key problem that Boethius is struggling with in *The Consolation of Philosophy*: if God is good and he has a plan, then why do bad things happen to good people? The question was more than just the old Platonic one—that society would be good if its leaders could be made moral. For Boethius, it went much deeper. The world would be made just and good only when individuals could be made just and good, he believed, and the best place to start was with his own self. He had to discover the good in life through the power of his intellect.

Indirectly, what Boethius created in his attempt to understand why bad things happen to good people was the contemporary notion of the *antagonist*. In Classical literature, the "bad guy" principle was not a major factor. There was the concept of *nemesis*, the forces in the universe that work against protagonists and prevent them from easily achieving their ends. In *The Odyssey*, for example, Odysseus incurs the wrath of the sea god Poseidon by blinding the god's son, Polyphemus (the Cyclops). Because Odysseus has insulted the god, Poseidon constantly prevents him from returning home by drowning his compatriots, blowing him off course, and delaying the journey back to Ithaca. Some of the major themes of the now-lost sequel to *The Odyssey*, *The Telegony*, were apparently reconciliation, forgiveness, and the process of making amends, for as the prophecies of *The Odyssey* suggest, Odysseus will make peace with his tormentor and go on to further adventures.

The idea of nemesis, however, is not so much a question of a god or a character being "bad" as it is a matter of vengeance or retribution. Nemesis is tied to the legalities of life, to justice, punishment, and the evening of unsettled scores. What Boethius perceived as a force in the universe was not a matter of justice—after all, in the Christian universe, God reserves his judgment for a much later date. Boethius saw that in a world that is working according to the divine plan of a loving God, there are those who turn away from him and act against the rules of nature and morality:

It may be part of human weakness to have evil wishes, but nothing short of monstrous that God should look on while every criminal is allowed to achieve his purpose against the innocent. If this is so, it was hardly without reason that one of your household asked where evil comes from if there is a god, and where good comes from if there isn't.

The antagonist is evil because he or she is operating by a different set of rules from the righteous and God-fearing. When such bad individuals inflict suffering on good individuals, the fault is not God's: the blame falls on the antagonist. If the world seems, at times, to be a wicked place where the bad are triumphing, it is not because of a failing on God's part; it is because the righteous have not exercised enough reason to understand that in the end the wicked cannot triumph. God will provide the comic resolution, the poetic justice, and the happiness that has long been sought:

And it is because you don't know the end and purpose of things that you think the wicked and the criminal have power and happiness. And because you have forgotten the means by which the world is governed you believe these ups and downs of fortune happen haphazardly. These are grave causes and they lead not only to illness but even death.

The message, then, is to trust in God and reason, and see what happens.

The problem with this idea of faith, however, is that the appearance of evil is continuous. Is it present in the world as a reminder of what good is—a dialectical notion that appealed to later philosophers such as Hegel—or is it there because God is not paying enough attention to mitigate the tragedy and suffering that evil causes? This question troubles the prisoner's mind:

> But the greatest cause of my sadness is really this—the fact that in spite of a good helmsman to guide the world, evil can still exist and even pass unpunished. This fact alone you must surely think of considerable wonder. But there is something even more bewildering. When wickedness rules and flourishes, not only does virtue go unrewarded, it is even trodden under-foot by the wicked and punished in the place of crime. That this can happen in the realm of an omniscient and omnipotent God who wills only good, is beyond perplexity and complaint.

Dame Philosophy responds that in the end, either through another turn of the wheel of Fortune or through divine judgment, justice is always done. She assures her pupil that "sin never goes unpunished or virtue unrewarded, and that what happens to be good is always happy and that what happens to be bad is always misfortune." The wicked, it would seem, are riding the same wheel as everyone else.

While the Sophoclean world held no promise of happiness, the Boethian universe embraces not only the possibility of it, but the presence of it. Dame Philosophy suggests in Book IV that happiness is our true nature, and that humankind, much like the wandering Odysseus, has been blown off course by all manner of distractions. She reassures her incarcerated pupil, "I will show you the path that will bring you back home. I will give your mind wings on which to lift itself; all disquiet shall be driven away and you will be able to return safely to your homeland." If people are to find happiness, she tells him, it is as easy as wanting to go home.

To accentuate the idea of reason as the road to happiness, Boethius adds to the middle of the text a narrative poem about the single-mindedness of Odysseus. This is one of several poems that find their way into *The Consolation of Philosophy*, and Boethius includes them because, like reason, narrative poetry always moves forward. Like a discourse, a narrative begins with a goal in mind, and in the process serves to illustrate important points. The Odysseus poem makes the point that a human life is a journey that begins with God and ends with God. Along the way, the individual is tugged and pulled by the pressures of the world, and ultimately must find his or her way back to the source of all happiness. In the case of those who are evil, Boethius believes that "the wicked are happier if they suffer punishment than if they are unrestrained by any just retribution." This paradox suggests that free will comes down to a choice between loyalty to God and morality, and the pursuit of evil. Punishment is a means of alleviating the burden of wickedness, not just for those who are victims of evil but for those who are perpetrators. Dame Philosophy explains:

> ...the wicked are more wretched when unjustly absolved from punishment than when they receive a just retribution. The logical conclusion of this is that they are burdened with heavier punishment precisely when they are believed to escape it.

In other words, in a universe that is ruled by good, there is absolutely no room and no tolerance for evil. Everything in the end will fall to the good, whether it be earthly reward or a place in the kingdom of heaven.

What this means in the overall shape of the universe is that there can no longer be any tragedy. Because everything—all human actions and divine justice—comes down to a resolution that God has planned from the very beginning of time, the presiding outcome of the universe must be comic. The variations in fortune that one experiences along the way are merely small detours on the road to happiness. The real tragedy in the universe, Boethius believes, comes when individuals cannot see the larger issue because of the suffering that they experience during their lifetime. In fact, tragedy is not only an overthrow of reason, a trigger for the catharsis that Aristotle sees as the chief result of experiencing the suffering of others, but a deflection from humanity's true nature, happiness:

Isn't this what tragedy commemorates with its tears and tumult—the overthrow of happy realms by the random strokes of Fortune?

He argues that tragedy is not the recognition of good but the realization that good has been lost. Change—the type of change in fortune and position that lies at the root of Classical tragedy—is part of the nature of the universe. When it arrives, we will not be surprised by it if we are reading our happiness through the process of reason, and if we understand that change is inevitably part of the scheme of things. Happiness is something that we should appreciate while we have it, though it is not something we can count on. If the way of the world is change, then change is something that we should expect, welcome, and turn to our own purposes.

This notion of reading misfortune, and learning to shape it to ends other than suffering, lies at the heart of *The Story of an Hour*, a brilliant short story by the nineteenth-century American writer Kate Chopin. In this brief narrative, Chopin tells of a woman, Mrs. Mallard, who receives news that her husband has been killed in a railroad disaster. She immediately falls apart and retires to her room to come to grips with her grief. During her seclusion, however, Mrs. Mallard comes to realize that the loss of her husband is, perhaps, the luckiest break of her life, and that she is now "free." Having read her situation and convinced herself of the joys that lie ahead, she leaves her room and starts down the stairs to meet the assembled mourners. Suddenly someone turns the key in the front door. It is her husband. Chopin concludes the story with the paradoxical statement that Mrs. Mallard died of "a joy that kills." True to the Aristotelian notion of tragedy, the entire narrative takes place within the space of an hour, and Chopin demonstrates just how startling the process of reversal can be for an individual.

Tragedy, in the Boethian sense, is the realization of the loss of a state of happiness. What this suggests, as Dame Philosophy points out, is that happiness is something we rarely appreciate or even recognize until it is gone. Tragedy can take a variety of shapes, however. In fact, it is almost unfair to suggest that there is a standard formula for it, even though whenever we witness a narrative that reminds us of what we can lose or what we have lost, the results are the same: we inevitably feel an overwhelming sense that life is brief, and that the things we value can slip through our fingers in an instant.

There are several types of tragedy in literature: downfall, rise and fall, instantaneous loss, and failed aspiration. The Book of Job, a profound influence on Boethius' arguments for faith, reason, and calm in the face of catastrophe, is the story of a downfall, of a man who loses everything except his trust in God. Boethius notes in Book II that "In all adversity of fortune, the most wretched kind is once to have been happy." The antidote for this kind of tragedy is patience. It's a matter of waiting out unfortunate events and being steadfast to one's principles in the hope that the wheel will turn again and allow fortune, in the words of *King Lear*'s Kent, to "smile once more." In any downfall, the affected person inevitably hopes for a return of those things that he or she has lost. Job has his fortunes restored by God, and his catastrophe ends more or less satisfactorily. But when matters cannot be set right, tragedy occurs. The suggestion in most downfall stories is that once events begin, there is no possible way to stop them. The universe has stacked the odds against an individual, and his or her ruin is not complete until everything has been taken away. Such is the case in Shakespeare's *Coriolanus*, where the protagonist is unable to stop an avalanche of catastrophe, no matter how noble he tries to remain.

The second type of tragedy is the rise and fall, where the audience watches the ascent of an individual only to witness his or her aspirations being dashed in the end. *Macbeth* follows such a pattern and is a problematic tragedy. Macbeth is a murderer, a usurper, and an opportunist who effects a rise to power and success based on all the wrong reasons. When his life starts to fall apart, the audience is inclined to say, "It serves him right," yet because he is the protagonist of the play and the central focus of the narrative, the audience places its aspirations on his success and survival. When Birnam Wood comes to Dunsinane Castle and all the supernatural prophecies come true, Macbeth's answer to his downfall is defiance, the same sort of confidence that put him on the throne of Scotland in the first place. But justice is served in the end and the paradox of the play is that the audience is forced into the difficult situation of

Unknown. Geoffrey Chaucer. The plump, almost pious burgher depicted here is a far cry from the Chaucer who appears in The Canterbury Tales *as the jovial, bumbling and self-mocking pilgrim who tells the childish Tale of Sir Toby. Chaucer's translation of Boethius suggests that consolation was a large part of the medieval way of looking at the world, and that even in the face of catastrophe, such as the one he describes in* Troilus and Cresseida, *something useful can be learned.*

siding either with justice and goodness or with the protagonist. When Macduff appears with the "usurper's cursed head," there is a catharsis of sorts, but it is tempered by the fact that, after all the bloodshed, a nation will have a rightful ruler and order will be restored.

The third type of tragedy is that of loss. The death of innocent individuals, such as in Shakespeare's *Romeo and Juliet*, is, perhaps, the most powerful incarnation of this type of tragedy because it takes the simple human desire for what is seemingly attainable and natural in life and dashes it on the rocks of stupidity, indifference, and overwhelming social constraints. When the prince offers his concluding remarks at the close of *Romeo and Juliet*, he explains that there "never was a story of more woe." Like the matter-of-factness of the Chorus in Sophoclean tragedy, the prince's remarks strike us as horribly self-evident. It seems a strangely obvious thing to say following the spectacle of a double suicide; yet there is little else that can be said. Tragedy leaves us grasping for frail explanations and consolations, and as Goethe said, "When ideas fail, words take over."

The fourth type of tragedy is that of failed aspiration, the sort of story F. Scott Fitzgerald tells in *The Great Gatsby*, where the legacy of almost attaining a goal and falling short reminds the reader that the possibility of failure always exists. As Saint Augustine suggests in *Confessions* (as we shall see in the next chapter), the worst possible position we can find ourselves in occurs when we are unable to distinguish between reality and illusion. Throughout *The Consolation of Philosophy*, Boethius stresses that this is the kind of vacuum of false assumptions into which tragedy is always ready to rush. As was realized by later interpreters and translators of Boethius, such as Geoffrey Chaucer in his poem *The House of Fame*, success and fame are merely a matter of rumor—and we should not trust rumor. Success, fame, wealth, and happiness, in the Boethian world, are just as deceptive to the unwary as misfortune, calamity, and catastrophe. Even one's goals should be open to question. If the ends do not justify the means, or if the ends are themselves ill-defined or questionable, then a character's actions are just as liable to fail as if he or she had pursued bad ends. The idea of striving for something and falling short against incredible odds is, of course,

the basis for Cervantes' *Don Quixote*, where the tragicomic knight-errant ultimately fails in his world of illusions.

According to Boethius, if illusions, the root of tragedy, can be controlled by reason, then fortune, the spirit that fuels illusion, can be mastered by the recognition of what lies behind the universe. In the Classical universe, the gods ordained the fate or destiny of every individual from the moment of birth onward. This notion suggested personal inevitability, a thumbprint of snares and traps that could be avoided temporarily but not permanently. The Christian idea, as Boethius articulates it in *The Consolation of Philosophy*, is much broader in its scope. Even if the plan is never revealed to an individual through prophetic means, events are running their course, or, in the words of the famous *Desiderata*, "the universe is unfolding as it should." Boethius argues that there is a grander scheme that must be recognized. Heaven is in order, even if earth does not seem to reflect that. Boethius says that Providence takes two forms—grace, or divine intervention, and fate, or destiny—each of which balances the other.

Grace lies behind all events and human actions. It is the spirit of a loving and forgiving God whose goodness humans can perceive only through reason. Boethius states that because of grace, all fortune is good: a problematic position, especially since bad things happen to good people. Yet he insists that we inhabit a comic universe, where there is a divine plan, where all events lead to order, and where tragedy cannot exist because everything is part of a much larger purpose. Providence—as Dame Philosophy explains—is not just heaven: it is the plan that will lead to heaven on earth:

> Providence is the divine reason itself. It is set at the head of all things and disposes all things. Fate, on the other hand, is the planned order inherent in things subject to change through the medium of which Providence binds everything in its own allotted place. Providence includes all things at the same time, however diverse or infinite, while Fate controls the motion of different individual things in different places and in different times. So this unfolding of the plan in time when brought together as a unified whole in the foresight of God's mind is Providence; and the same unified whole when dissolved and unfolded in the course of time is Fate.
>
> They are different, but the one depends on the other.

This notion that both Providence and fate come from God, and that all fortune is ultimately good because it is the work of God, is one of the key psychological drivers behind romance ideals of patience, virtue, and faith, the defining characteristics of Sir Galahad and Sir Percival in the Arthurian legends. But Boethius tackles a much larger issue in this discussion, and that is the way in which the Christian literary imagination perceives time. According to the literary notion of Providence, the fusion of imagination with reason—the very manner of the telling that Boethius implements in *The Consolation of Philosophy*—can not only clarify one's momentary sense of fear during a tough situation, but also stretch one's vision far into the future. So pervasive and insistent is this idea of playing along with God's game plan for humankind that many of the characters in romance—the knights-errant in particular—seem lost in a wilderness of time. For them, deliverance and redemption will come only after a long and arduous wait. Taken *ad extremis*, the Boethian notion of time as the linchpin of God's plan demands a high degree of sustained reasoning. It is the amalgam of Virgilian cogniscence and Christian patience, and to live up to such high expectations, one must be of incredible moral and intellectual strength—the very ingredients for the chivalric code of medieval romance. In the world of medieval romance (as we shall see in chapter 8), the strongest knights are those with the strongest intellects.

Reason, Boethius believes, is the key to order, not only in an individual's mind but in the world. His very Roman desire for order, fused with his sense of discourse and his Christian beliefs, compels him to find some force that will allay the power of emotional suffering. The path to this force, he realizes, is through the mind. "The only way," says Boethius, "to check [the emotions] is with a really lively intellectual fire." The recompense that the strength of reason provides for the victim of fortune is consolation: the understanding that comes from standing back and studying one's situation, and contextualizing the events in a rational framework. Consolation cannot change what has happened, but it can change one's perception of the events. When all that has happened is set against the broader context of a universe where justice will ultimately win out, and where all events are part of a divine plan based on morality and goodness, things are not as bad as they seem. The greatest weapon we have in our struggle against the world is the mind:

...nothing is miserable except when you think it so, and vice versa, all luck is good luck to the man who bears it with equanimity. No one is so happy that he would not want to change his lot if he gives in to impatience. Such is the bitter-sweetness of human happiness. To him that enjoys it, it may seem full of delight, but he cannot prevent it slipping away when it will. It is evident, therefore, how miserable the happiness of human life is; it does not remain long with those who are patient, and doesn't satisfy those who are troubled....Why then do you mortal men seek after happiness outside yourselves when it lies within?

The message of *The Consolation of Philosophy* has been taken up by almost everyone from Samuel Johnson to Ingmar Bergman.

Happiness, as Thomas Jefferson so eloquently put it, is a "pursuit" of sorts. But the question remains as to where one should pursue it. Is it an inward struggle or an outward struggle?

Shakespeare, in the most discursive and rhetorical form in poetry, the sonnet, questions the power of fortune to turn a successful man into an outcast in his well-known *Sonnet 29*:

> *When, in disgrace with Fortune and men's eyes,*
> *I all alone beweep my outcast state,*
> *And trouble deaf heaven with my bootless cries,*
> *And look upon myself and curse my fate,*
> *Wishing me like to one more rich in hope,*
> *Featured like him, like him with friends possessed,*
> *Desiring this man's art, and that man's scope,*
> *With what I most enjoy contented least;*
> *Yet in these thoughts myself almost despising,*
> *Haply I think on thee, and then my state*
> *Like to the lark at break of day arising*
> *From sullen earth, sings hymns at heaven's gate;*
> > *For thy sweet love rememb'red such wealth brings*
> > *That then I scorn to change my state with kings.*

After a very Boethian struggle, Shakespeare realizes, through the power of reason and reflective discourse, that what is most important in the world is that Platonic virtue, friendship, a human attribute that is held in the highest regard by Plato's philosopher kings. As in Book IV of Jonathan Swift's *Gulliver's Travels*, where the horselike creatures called the Houyhnhnms practice a rational existence, Boethius believes that human happiness is attainable only through the power of reason, and through such virtues as friendship, peaceful reflection, and moral living that are the result of the balanced and rational mind. In one of the most eloquent passages of *The Consolation of Philosophy*, Dame Philosophy assures the prisoner that fortune has nothing to do with happiness:

> If happiness is the highest good of rational nature and anything that can be taken away is not the highest good—since it is

surpassed by what can't be taken away—Fortune by her very mutability can't hope to lead to happiness.

Happiness, therefore, is the attainment of that old goal from the Greek philosophy that Boethius translated into Latin as a young man: know thyself.

What Boethius brings to the literary continuum is the understanding that context must be separated from content if one is to appreciate fully the meaning of the situation at hand. It was a North African bishop, Saint Augustine, who gave to Western literature the ability to discern between content and context, and to read the world objectively as if it were a text. Boethius' sense of dispassion and his plea for an objectivity that reaches beyond the miasma of emotions may seem slightly cold-natured to modern readers. Yet it was dispassion—that very desire to find serenity in the acceptance of the things one cannot change, the courage to change the things one can, and the wisdom to know the difference—that fueled the spirit of the Middle Ages and indirectly allowed the thread of literature to continue, unbroken, through the worst of times and the most difficult moments of misfortune.

7

TRUE
CONFESSIONS

Saint Augustine's Confessions

O N a clear day in the late spring of 1336, a young Italian who was about to take his vows and become a cleric went mountain climbing with his brother:

Today I climbed the highest mountain in this region, which is not improperly called Ventosum (Windy). The only motive for my ascent was the wish to see what so great a height had to offer.

A strange thing happens to him on the ascent, and he notes, "I started thinking in terms of time rather than space." As he scales the physical heights, he begins to measure himself against the history of the world, and to see personal experience as a reflection of a much broader scope of events and ideas. When he reaches the summit, he describes the view—all that he can see about him with his naked eye, the great distance, the features of the landscape, the horizons. Suddenly, something tells him to open a small book that he has carried with him to the summit and to read whatever passage falls open before his eye:

While my thoughts were divided thus, now turning my attention to thoughts of some worldly object before me, now uplifting my soul, as I had done my body, to higher planes, it occurred to me to look at St. Augustine's *Confessions*, a gift of your love that I always keep with me in memory of the author and the giver.

The young cleric's eye falls on a passage in *Confessions* that suddenly seems to sum up the moment:

As God is my witness and my brother too, the first words that my eyes fell upon were: 'And men go about admiring the high mountains and the mighty waves of the sea and the wide sweep of rivers and the sound of the ocean and the movement of the stars, but they themselves they abandon.'

Overcome by the sudden recognition that what he sees in the text speaks directly to what he sees in the world, and "having seen enough of the mountain, I turned an inward eye upon myself." And that was the moment the Renaissance began.

What that young Italian cleric—Petrarch—realized at that moment atop Mount Ventoux was that the voices of the past were relevant answers to the problems and challenges of the present day. No matter how much time and space was put between the Classical and the contemporary worlds, truth remained truth and the great authors of the past were never out of context with daily life. From that moment, Petrarch dedicated himself to his great passion: reading the literature of the Classical world. He traveled throughout Italy in search of the most complete versions of works, memorizing vast amounts of material, copying reams of pages and comparing one text to another in search of something called *authorial intent*, the truth of a text that is found in its complete, original version. Just as Boethius had copied and translated Greek texts into Latin so that they might be passed on to future generations, so Petrarch brought the Classical world to life again, and the information contained in those books—many of which had been lost for centuries—inspired a whole new way of looking at the world. In Petrarch's view, and in the view of those who followed his pursuit of learning, the human being was the measure of all things, and the individual was a microcosm of the wonder of the universe. One need only look into oneself, as Saint Augustine suggested, to understand so much of humanity and nature.

Of all the works in the literary continuum, Saint Augustine's *Confessions* is the one that most represents a watershed in that it changed the way we think of the individual as either a character or an author. It is one of the first autobiographies, a work where he takes a critical look at his own life and questions his actions, his motives, and his understanding, not for personal glorification but in the service of faith. When he began *Confessions*, Saint Augustine intended it as a preface to a much larger work where he would provide an exegesis, chapter by chapter, on the Bible. *Confessions* was his attempt to link his own personal story, his microcosm, to the macrocosm of the Bible, thereby showing the reader the parallel between the individual's search for God and humankind's journey toward the New Jerusalem. In order to do this, he chose a literary form that has come down to us as the *confession*. The term, which originally meant the "act of speaking together"—in this case, the dialogue between an individual and God—has been rather twisted over the years and now means anything from a lurid relation of personal misbehavior to a true crime story, with all the shocking details left in to titillate the reader.

What emerges from Saint Augustine's autobiography is only half of a dialogue. We do not hear what God has to say, although presumably the other half of the conversation continued through prayers and meditations. Saint Augustine, however, shares only fragments of this other character with his reader. In Book X, when Saint Augustine asks what his God is, the reply is given not by God himself, but through nature:

> But what is my God? I put my question to the earth. It answered, 'I am not God', and all things declared the same. I asked the sea and the chasms of the deep and the living things that creep in them, but they answered, 'We are not your God. Seek what is above us.' I spoke to the winds that blow, and the whole air and all that lives in it replied. 'Anaximenes is wrong. I am not God.' I asked the sky, the sun, the moon, and the stars, but they told me, 'Neither are we the God whom you seek.' I spoke to all the things that are about me, all that can be admitted by the door of the senses, and I said, 'Since you are not my God, tell me about him. Tell me something of my God.' Clear and loud they answered, 'God is he who made us.' I asked these questions simply by gazing at these things, and their beauty was all the answer they gave.

This half-dialogue, this one-sided conversation, however, is the process of an individual questioning himself by questioning the course of his life. Just as the universe has a beginning, a middle, and a promised end, so too does the individual. And if the world provides any answers at all, they come from within the heart, the mind, and the soul of each person. The way to find these answers, as Saint Augustine discovered, is to question one's own life, to examine it critically, and to frame it in the objective context of a piece of literature, where it can be observed and understood.

The act of confession, of recording on paper thoughts that are intended to be heard only by God, may seem strange—the reader is literally eavesdropping on a conversation. Yet the author intends us to listen in, and to use the model that the work establishes as a template for our own process of self-discovery. When Saint Augustine puts his thoughts on the page, it is not for God's benefit. God, after all, knows everything, and nothing can be hidden from him. Instead, the beneficiary of the confession is Saint Augustine, and anyone else who cares to listen. At the opening of Book V, he explains the process behind the act of confession:

> If a man confesses to you, he does not reveal his inmost thoughts to you as though you did not know them. For the heart may shut itself away, but it cannot hide from your sight. Man's heart may be hard but it cannot resist the touch of your hand. Whenever you will, your mercy or your punishment can make it relent, and just as none can hide away from the sun, *none can escape your burning heat.*

Confession is both a critique of life and an opportunity to praise God for the gift of that life. When he completes his examination of what confession is and what it entails, Saint Augustine explains the role of praise:

> Let my soul praise you that it may show its love; and let it make avowal of your mercies, so that for these it may praise you. No part of your creation ever ceases to resound in praise of you. Man turns his lips to you in prayer and his spirit praises you. Animals too and lifeless things as well praise you through the lips of all who give them thoughts. For our souls lean for support upon the things which you have created, so that we may

be lifted up to you from our weakness and use them to help us on our way to you who made them all so wonderfully. And in you we are remade and find true strength.

Praise is the act of acknowledging and celebrating the source for life. When it is set in the context of a confession, praise becomes an inquiry into how one can improve oneself and one's understanding of the world. Underlying Saint Augustine's book, in other words, is the simple desire of someone who wants to be a better human being.

What Saint Augustine is struggling against—his antagonist—is his own, weak self. The obstacle that he must overcome in his quest to be nearer to God is the old biblical problem of sin. In the Christian mythos as stated in Genesis, sin entered the world with the fall of Adam and Eve. Christ's crucifixion, as depicted in the New Testament, is supposed to relieve the burden of sin, and his sacrifice is set as an exemplum before each individual. As Saint Augustine sees it, Christians have a duty to model themselves after Christ, just as Romans, in Virgil's view, have a duty to model themselves after Aeneas. Life is a struggle to move closer to God by understanding just what sin is and how one should overcome it, not only in the legal or physical realms, but on the moral and intellectual planes as well. The human condition is a difficult one. Every human being is born into sin, in Saint Augustine's opinion, and the only way out is to study and assess one's life from birth onward, and to critique it to the point where one can understand the means to a new life that is unshakably within God's grace.

In one of the first instances in literature where the world is seen from the perspective of a child, Saint Augustine begins the narrative of his life and his struggle to overcome his sin with his earliest memories. In Book I, he strains to recall his experiences as an infant.

Hugo Van der Goes. The Fall of Man. In this fifteenth-century version of the fall of Man, the serpent appears very feminine. Legend has it that God punished all serpents for their role in the fall by removing their arms and legs. The fruit of knowledge, often depicted as a quince, is here portrayed as a traditional apple. For authors such as Saint Augustine, the fall of man was a metaphorical watershed. Man's condition, they realized, was to suffer, but only until some means to redemption could be found.

Who can recall to me the sins I committed as a baby? For in your sight no man is free from sin, not even a child who has lived only one day on earth. Who can show me what my sins were? Some small baby in whom I can see all that I do not remember about myself?...We root out these faults and discard

them as we grow up, and this is proof enough that they are faults, because I have never seen a man purposely throw out the good when he clears away the bad. It can hardly be right for a child, even at that age, to cry for everything, including things which would harm him; to work himself into a tantrum against people older than himself and not required to obey him...

For Saint Augustine, to be born is to enter into the fallen world of human sinfulness. How, then, can people pull themselves out of that condition of sinfulness and recognize that something greater lies beyond this reality of confusion and despair? He believes there are several key tools that are automatically at a human being's disposal—the "arms for the man" who must fight the moral and intellectual battle. These weapons are language, memory, and reason.

Think back to your earliest memory. How old were you when that event occurred? Four? Three? Two or one, perhaps? Most people's earliest memories date from about the age of three or four. A few lucky people will be able to remember life at the age of two and the struggle they experienced as their brain became acclimatized to the complexities of the language and the world. For most of us, the key to our memory process is that moment when we had the power of language to codify and articulate what we experienced. The stunning aspect of Saint Augustine's mind is that his earliest memory pre-dates language. He can remember what it was to learn to speak:

> I can remember that time, and later on I realized how I had learnt to speak. It was not my elders who showed me the words by some set system of instruction, in the way that they taught me to read not long afterwards; but, instead, I taught myself by using the intelligence which you, my God, gave to me. For when I tried to express my meaning by crying out and making various sounds and movements, so that my wishes could be obeyed, I found that I could not convey all that I meant or make myself understood by everyone whom I wished to understand me. So my memory prompted me. I noticed that people would name some object and then turn towards whatever it was that

they had named. I watched them and understood that the sound they made when they wanted to indicate that particular thing was the name which they gave to it, and their actions clearly showed what they meant, for there is a kind of universal language, consisting of expressions of the face and eyes, gestures and tones of voice, which can show whether a person means to ask for something and get it, or refuse it and have nothing to do with it. So, by hearing words arranged in various phrases and constantly repeated, I gradually pieced together what they stood for, and when my tongue had mastered the pronunciation, I began to express my wishes by means of them. In this way I made my wants known to my family and they made theirs known to me, and I took a further step into the stormy life of human society....

What is amazing about this passage is that its author not only describes how he acquired language, but explains the importance of that language as a conduit between him and the world. The other incredible aspect of Saint Augustine's mind, as this passage also reveals, is the way he constantly examines the simple actions in life that others might take for granted, and dissects them into smaller, understandable portions. This compulsion to subdivide larger issues into smaller compartments of ideas lies at the heart of one of Saint Augustine's key contributions to literature: the ability to discern between reality and illusion and to comprehend an artistic experience objectively. In this respect, he is one of the founders of literary criticism and art appreciation.

Using the themes of language and memory as the basis for his recollections about his own education, Saint Augustine lays the foundations for an important argument about the difference between reality and illusion. He recalls that his early interest in language was based more on the study of grammar and rhetoric— the operative structures of communication—than on literature:

For these elementary lessons were far more valuable than those which followed, because the subjects were practical. They gave me the power, which I still have, of reading whatever is set before me and writing whatever I wish to write. But in the later lessons I was obliged to memorize the wanderings of a hero named Aeneas, while in the meantime I failed to remember my own erratic ways. I learned to lament the death of Dido, who killed herself for love, while all the time in the midst of these things, I was dying, separated from you, my God and my Life, and I shed no tears for my own plight.

Literature, he believes, is a questionable matter because it presents the reader with an imaginative spectacle that, if not fully understood, can easily blur the distinction between reality and illusion. He believes that one should trust in the structures of language before delving into and being consumed by the content of communication:

Tell me that reading and writing are by far the better study. This must be true, for I would rather forget the wanderings of Aeneas and all that goes with them, than how to read and write. It is true that curtains are hung over the entrances to the schools where literature is taught, but they are not so much symbols in honour of mystery as veils concealing error.

In this statement, Saint Augustine is driving at the core purpose of literary criticism and the art of writing. No writers wish to create a mystery with their words. Their fundamental desire is to communicate with the reader, to share an idea or express a thought that can be challenged. Likewise, the purpose of literary criticism is not to mask a text in conundrums, statements, or jargon, but to illuminate and contextualize a writer's works, to show just how that writer is speaking, what he or she is speaking of, and on what strengths and backgrounds the writer is drawing. There is no mystery to literature, at least not to the great works. Granted, there are questions, but more often than not we can answer them by examining and probing the text itself with the illuminating power of an informed background of reading. Saint Augustine is stating that language, in its greatest moments, is built upon clarity: In *Confessions*, he is pleading for the clarity that comes from recognizing just what is being presented to the reader of a text or the audience of a drama.

Nowhere is this more evident than in Book III, where he criticizes the relationship between reality and illusion that confronts a theatergoer:

> I was much attracted by the theater, because the plays reflected my own unhappy plight and were tinder to my fire. Why is it that men enjoy feeling sad at the sight of tragedy and suffering on stage, although they would be most unhappy if they had to endure the same fate themselves. Yet they watch the plays because they hope to be made to feel sad, and the feeling of sorrow is what they enjoy. What miserable delirium is this!

What seems to unsettle Saint Augustine the most is his recognition that theater presents an illusion. Part of this recognition stems from what Aristotle had to say about tragedy—that it is based on spectacle and the human desire to focus attention on suffering. Always the realist, however, Saint Augustine separates the illusion from the theatergoer's catharsis, and concludes that people are all too willing to respond emotionally to fictional narratives. In short, he observes that an audience feels real emotions for false events; yet the same people, when outside the theater, are indifferent to the real suffering around them:

> But what sort of pity can we really feel for an imaginary scene on the stage? The audience is not called upon to offer help but to feel sorrow, and the more they are pained the more they applaud the author. Whether this human agony is based on fact or is simply imaginary, if it is acted so badly that the audience is not moved to sorrow, they leave the theater in a disgruntled and critical mood; whereas, if they are made to feel pain, they stay to the end watching happily.

Saint Augustine believes that people need to feel real emotion for real things, and to understand that plays and poems are artificial creations. What he demands is the awareness of the audience, the recognition that art is *not* reality. This detachment makes objectivity possible and literalism impossible. In other words, Saint Augustine says that we should look at art critically to understand just what we are seeing and to avoid being manipulated by it. Objectivity makes possible a completely different way for people to see drama or read a work of fiction because it allows them to understand what an author is saying through *the way* he or she is saying it.

As a professor of rhetoric, Saint Augustine was aware of the dangers inherent in language, chiefly the problem that occurs when readers or listeners confuse content with structure. Rhetoric—the art of persuasion through language, and the tricks and fallacies of logic that speakers use to convey their messages—could be used as a mask for meaning. If language amounts to a series of charades and deceptions, he argues, then the truth and morality it carries are the first victims in this crime. What he wants is honesty in language, or, failing that, the ability of individuals to see through the deceptions to find their own critical understanding of the truth. In brief, he asks that people understand not only what is being said, but how it is being said:

Rembrandt. Aristotle with a bust of Homer. Rembrandt seems to believe that the great authors learn from each other, and that their dialogue is a kind of thread that connects one thinker to another. As Aristotle learned the principles of literary criticism from studying Homer, so Augustine learned how to critique life by studying the approaches and ideas of Ambrose.

> I have known men of another sort, who look on truth with suspicions and are unwilling to accept it if it is presented in fine, rounded phrases. But in your wonderful, secret way, my God, you had already taught me that a statement is not necessarily true because it is wrapped in fine language or false because it is awkwardly expressed.... In just the same way, wisdom and folly can be clothed alike in plain words or the finest flowers of speech.

If an individual is able to make the distinction between form and content, not only from a moral point of view but from an artistic and interpretive one, then literary criticism takes on an entirely new perspective.

Nowhere is this belief more evident in *Confessions* than when Saint Augustine discusses the impact his greatest teacher, Saint Ambrose, had on his approach to reading. By illuminating the difference between structure and content, and by questioning the relationship of the text to larger concerns such as the order of the universe and the plan of Providence, Saint Ambrose revealed to his pupil a whole new level of understanding:

And when he lifted the veil of mystery and disclosed the spiritual meaning of texts which, taken literally, appeared to contain the most unlikely doctrines, I was not aggrieved by what he said...

As for the passages which had previously struck me as absurd, now that I heard reasonable explanations of many of them I regarded them as of the nature of profound mysteries; and it seemed to me all the more right that the authority of Scripture should be respected and accepted with the purest faith, because while all can read it with ease, it also has a deeper meaning in which its great secrets are locked away. Its plain language and simple style make it accessible to everyone, and yet it absorbs the attention of the learned.

Essentially, what Saint Ambrose taught Saint Augustine was the principle of looking at a text as an authorial statement that exists as a balance between form and content. We tend to take for granted that art, and particularly literature, communicates in this manner, and we exercise our critical abilities to allow us to read on more than one level at once. But this approach to interpretation was something entirely new, and Saint Augustine, as both a teacher and a student of the art of rhetoric, was very attracted to its possibilities.

He takes this relationship a step further when he perceives God as a paradox of the container and the contained. God is in all things as an animating and inspiring force—"the life of my life," as he calls it. Yet at the same time, God is the container that holds all things, embracing the universe both within it and outside it:

> You fill all things, but do you fill them with your whole self? Or is it that the whole of creation is too small to hold you and therefore holds only a part of you? And is this same part of you present in all things at once, or do different things contain different parts of you, greater or smaller according to their size? Does this mean that one part of you is greater and another smaller? Or are you present entirely everywhere at once, and no single thing contains the whole of you?

Saint Augustine, we must remember, grew up in a time and a place that perceived life through the dying traces of the pagan, or animate, universe. In that universe, God could not be an idea or an intellectual concept: God had to be something tangible, and if that something could not be defined precisely, one could always fall back on personification, the very process that Ovid used in *Metamorphoses*. But Saint Augustine suspected early in his life that God was a puzzle, perhaps a paradox, in which contradictory elements and ideas played off each other. Recognizing this paradox must have taken an immense amount of creative thinking, and it is a tribute to Saint Augustine's breadth of vision and philosophical energy that such a revolutionary perspective could even be considered.

God was more than just a life force and more than just a Platonic paradox, however. God was the goal of a quest that Saint

Augustine had set himself on. His vision of the Almighty was an attempt to reach beyond the confines and the terrors of the animate universe where people were victims of tragic circumstances and where fate determined an individual's destiny. Saint Augustine wanted to know God in an *inanimate* universe, and to succeed, he would have to undergo a struggle of heroic dimensions. His quest to understand God shaped the structure of *Confessions* indirectly and generated a range of literary genres that are still practiced to this day. They have had a profound effect on the way authors express their experience via the written word.

As a literary text, *Confessions* is an autobiography that tells the story of the growth of an individual personality from birth through to the moment when that personality's perspective on the universe is more or less complete. Saint Augustine begins by discussing his childhood, his education, and his early struggles to find a system of beliefs that would encompass his expansive view of the world. By using his own life to demonstrate how one should come to intellectual and imaginative terms with the universe, and by telling that story in his own words, he creates a model that will be followed by writers through the ages.

As we shall see in the discussion of Vasari, the standard structure of a saint's life—a type of literature known as hagiography or *acta sanctori* (the record of holiness)—follows a pattern where the achievement of the saint is chronicled and communicated through the events of his or her life. Usually, these lives begin with a study of what the saint's childhood was like, how he or she received an education, how the saint was changed or awakened by important events, and how he or she affected the lives of others by acts of holiness or miracles. An important example of hagiography is *The Golden Legend* by Jacobus de Voragine, one of the most pervasive texts in medieval literature. As a literary source for hagiography, its influence can been seen in everything from Chaucer's *Canterbury Tales* to the poetry of Keats and Dryden. When Renaissance writers searched for a structure that they could use to chronicle secular lives, they looked no further than the literature of the saints and the patterns established by Saint Augustine.

Perhaps the greatest contribution that Saint Augustine made to Western literature was the way he chronicled the growth of consciousness and understanding in an individual. *Confessions* triggered a whole sub-genre of literature in which the protagonist experiences the natural development of ideas and outlook that result from a growing mind. This type of literature, called the *Bildungsroman*, or novel about the moral and psychological development of an individual mind, usually chronicles the educational process by which a person comes to terms with the world. Although many authors have attempted the bildungsroman, one of the greatest examples of the form in Western literature is James Joyce's *A Portrait of the Artist as a Young Man*, the subject of chapter 18. In that work, Joyce describes the life of Stephen Dedalus, and shows how the growing consciousness of the protagonist mirrors the emerging cultural consciousness of the Irish people. Just as Stephen stretches his mind to accommodate the language of European culture, so Saint Augustine struggles to embrace the vastness of language as a structure for conveying truth and morality.

What is unique about Saint Augustine's idea of his own life is that he sees his inner world, and his potential to be nearer to God, as a metaphor for the outer world, and the process by which humankind might grow closer to the Creator. The key to his own and humanity's growth, Saint Augustine believes, is memory, that repository of past experience whose details can be replayed, scrutinized, and understood:

> All this goes on inside me, in the vast cloisters of my memory. In it are the sky, the earth, and the sea, ready at my summons, together with everything that I have ever perceived in them by my senses, except the things which I have forgotten. In it I meet myself as well, and the state of my mind at the time. In my memory, too, are all the events that I remember, whether they are things that have happened to me or things that I have heard from others. From the same source I can picture to myself all kinds of different images based either upon my own experience or upon what I find credible because it tallies with my own experience. I can fit them into the general picture of the past; from them I can make a surmise of actions and events and hopes for the future; and I can contemplate them all over again as if they were actually present.

Saint Augustine examines his own life from as much of an "arm's-length" stance as possible, but he realizes that even the grand possibilities of the human memory—intellect and imagination—are not quite up to the task of comprehending God:

> The power of the memory is prodigious, my God. It is a vast, immeasurable sanctuary. Who can plumb its depths? And yet it is a faculty of my soul. Although it is part of my nature, I cannot understand all that I am. This means, then, that the mind is too narrow to contain itself entirely. But where is that part of it which it does not itself contain? Is it somewhere outside itself and not within it? How, then, can it be part of it, if it is not contained in it?

Recognizing the paradoxical structure of the mind, Saint Augustine suddenly realizes that the human soul is a microcosm of God himself, the great paradox of the container and the contained. And although he acknowledges that he can never totally understand himself or the workings of his own nature, even as he can never come to a complete understanding of God, Saint Augustine is wise enough to perceive what the mind is capable of doing. Yet because the mind appears to work in a dimension completely different from the physical constraints of nature, he argues, it has a certain freedom that allows it to penetrate matters that are otherwise veiled to either the naked eye or the other senses:

> Material things are there by means of their images; knowledge is there of itself; emotions are there in the form of ideas or impressions of some kind, for the memory retains them even while the mind does not experience them, although whatever is in the memory must also be in the mind. My mind has the freedom of them all. I can glide from one to the other. I can probe deep into them and never find the end of them. This is the power of memory! This is the great force of life in living man, mortal though he is!

In other words, the way to God is to use the one faculty in the human makeup that is most Godlike: the memory. But like

Aeneas, Saint Augustine is never satisfied with what he finds in the immediate reach of his athletic mind. Instead, he seeks something that is always beyond his grasp, beyond the "ever-retreating horizon." In a gesture that seems to defy even the methodology of logic and reasoning, he suggests that the limits to the human imagination and memory imply that God is larger than anything a single human being can comprehend:

> So I must go beyond memory too, if I am to reach God who made me different from the beasts that walk the earth and wiser than the birds that fly in the air. I must pass beyond memory to find you, my true Good, my sure Sweetness.

This process of exceeding logic and reason to reach for something larger than mere comprehension can explain or contain is known in literature as *anagogy*. Søren Kierkegaard experiences this leap of faith when he, too, exhausts his mental capabilities in his search to understand God. The nature of anagogy will be taken up in chapter 8, where it is identified as an essential quality for successful knights in their quest for physical, moral, and spiritual perfection. As a result of what Saint Augustine perceives in *Confessions*, therefore, the search for God is a matter not of a physical quest but of a mental struggle. The inner world, the world of memory, of intellect, of reason, and even of imagination, is suddenly imbued with a profound sense of the divine. The mind, Saint Augustine believes, has the gift of discernment, the ability to tell the difference between truth and falsehood and between reality and illusion.

In distinguishing the real from the unreal, *Confessions* does not simply offer a metaphysical examination of the nature of reality. Instead, we are given the story of an individual who, through the power of his intellect, changed the way the Western imagination perceived the universe. As a student, Saint Augustine became attracted to a vogue philosophy of the day called Manichaeism, a paganization of some of the fundamental ideas of the Bible, and a philosophy, had it not been for Saint Augustine, that might have reduced Christianity to just another passing pagan cult. The movement, which was nearing the status of a religion by the time Saint Augustine encountered Saint Ambrose's persuasive arguments against it, suggested that the world was composed of a struggle between good and evil. But rather than examine the question in intellectual or intangible terms, Manichaeism looked to the physical world as the battleground between the forces of light and darkness. As a philosophy, it was the last gasp of the animate universe. It held, for instance, that a person who eats chicken should eat only the white meat and avoid the drumsticks because the light bits were good and the dark bits were evil. Sunlight was preferable to shade, light colours to dark, and so on, to the point where people had to be careful where they sat and what they ate. The Manichees believed that diet played a key role in the struggle, and that human excrement was the body's attempt to get rid of its evil.

Food? Excrement? Shade? Saint Augustine wondered just what these things had to do with a loving, forgiving, and wise God; yet the arguments on behalf of Manichaeism were so persuasive and powerful that they consumed his mind. He was even more troubled, however, by the course of his life, which he believed had been sinful and morally inadequate. He had been leading the high life in Rome and Milan. He had a mistress and a son by her, and his social exploits, though not chronicled in detail in *Confessions*, appear to have been legendary. Something deep inside him felt that there had to be another way of looking at the universe. How was it possible for other believers to come before God and embrace the Christian ideas of a world that was neither animate nor tragic?

My inner self was a house divided against itself. In the heat of the fierce conflict which I had stirred up against my soul in our common abode, my heart, I turned upon Alypius. My looks betrayed the commotion in my mind as I exclaimed, "What is the matter with us? What is the meaning of this story? These men have not had our schooling, yet they stand up and storm the gates of heaven while we, for all our learning, lie here groveling in this world of flesh and blood!"

Above all things, Saint Augustine desired the unification of his vision and his understanding, and directed the anger that he felt at his internal division on himself. The inward eye that would so engage Petrarch at the top of Mount Ventoux a thousand years later was suddenly turned, in all its critical force, on his own soul. Saint Augustine writes, "I was dying a death that would bring me life."

One can sense the turmoil that he must have experienced as he sat in a friend's garden one day and engaged in a tremendous intellectual and imaginative struggle to see the world in another way. In an event that is as close to a nervous breakdown as anything depicted in literature, Saint Augustine lost control of his body. His limbs thrashing, he moaned aloud and rocked back and forth:

> During this agony of indecision I performed many bodily actions, things which a man cannot always do, even if he wills to do them....I tore my hair and hammered my forehead with my fists; I locked my fingers and hugged my knees; and I did all this because I made an act of will to do it....

> This was the nature of my sickness. I was in torment, reproaching myself more bitterly than ever as I twisted and turned in my chain. I hoped that my chain might be broken once and for all, because it was only a small thing that held me now. All the same it held me....In my heart I kept saying "Let it be now, let it be now!" and merely by saying this I was on the point of making the resolution.

His agony increases until it becomes unbearable. And then a miracle happens. Off in the distance, he hears the clear, small voice of a child, singing with a divine innocence, and at that moment he experiences his conversion to Christianity:

> I probed the hidden depths of my soul and wrung its pitiful secrets from it, and when I mustered all before the eyes of my heart, a great storm broke within me, bringing with it a great deluge of tears....For I felt I was still the captive of my sins, and in my misery I kept crying "How long shall I go on saying 'tomorrow, tomorrow'? Why not now? Why not make an end of my ugly sins at this moment?...I was asking myself these questions, weeping all the while with the most bitter sorrow in my heart, when all at once I heard the sing-song voice of a child in a nearby house. Whether it was the voice of a boy or a girl I

cannot say, but again and again it repeated the refrain 'Take it and read, take it and read.'

Interpreting this as a divine command, Saint Augustine took up his book of Scriptures and read the first passage on which his eyes fell. As would happen to Petrarch atop Mount Ventoux, the words struck deeply into his soul. What he read were Christ's commands in Matthew 19:21, where he tells his listeners to go home and sell everything they own, give the money to the poor, and follow him because greater riches are in store in heaven. In one swift gesture in that garden, a setting that echoes the agony of Christ in the Garden of Gethsemane on the eve of the crucifixion, Saint Augustine abolishes in himself the mentality of the pagan universe. He articulates the experience so directly as the prime message of *Confessions* that he puts God in his heaven and humankind in the inanimate, comic universe where faith, not luck, is the basis for human happiness.

The conversion of a single individual may not seem like such an important matter in the grand scheme of either Christianity or the literary imagination. Yet Saint Augustine's conversion is a watershed moment in Western literature. *Confessions* represents a key shift in the imaginative landscape because it suddenly locates the setting for a narrative *inside* a character rather than *outside*. Where omniscient narrators describe the reactions of an Odysseus or an Aeneas, Saint Augustine allows us inside his mind and his thought processes both to tell us what he is thinking and to show us what he is feeling. His approach is overwhelmingly honest—almost to the point where the readers feel they are eavesdropping on a very private conversation—and that is part of what a confession should do as a literary form. If we feel uncomfortable, it is because the confessional voice and structure are meant to make us reflect critically upon our own lives, and our own flaws and weaknesses. For it is only by questioning our own lives that we might, in turn, become better people. To some, the confession might seem moralistic and didactic; yet the honesty and the candor of Saint Augustine's voice, and the harshness with which he treats himself, make us empathize with him and see his plight as our own.

Confessions presents us with a protagonist who, for all his flaws and his self-acknowledged weaknesses, is heroic. His heroism, of course, results from a mental struggle rather than a muscle-bound wrestle with the forces of nature. But there is something tremendously epic about this work, with its question of whether he will be able to complete his conversion, with the universal scope of the microcosm within his character, and with the persistent desire he feels to overcome whatever obstacles, either physical or intellectual, he encounters. When Saint Augustine succeeds in vanquishing his own demons, there is a powerful sense of a comic resolution and poetic justice.

Nowhere is this sense of poetic justice more evident than in the scene with his mother, Saint Monica, as they meet at the port city of Ostia just before the newly converted Saint Augustine embarks on his mission as a bishop. As they stand together on a balcony overlooking the port, with the sun setting before them, the two characters probe the meaning of a new imaginative universe, a new way of looking at the world that seems to open before them:

> ...suppose that the heavens and even his own soul were silent,
> no longer thinking of itself but passing beyond; suppose that his
> dreams and the visions of his imagination spoke no more and
> that every tongue and every sign and all that is transient grew
> silent—for all these things have the same message to tell, if only
> we can hear it, and their message is this: We did not make
> ourselves, but he who abides for ever made us.

Saint Augustine realizes the possibilities that might exist in this new way of looking at the world. It is a world without fate, without terror, a place where a person's inner landscape counts for as much as the outer landscape, a world where the value of individuals, whether fictional or actual, is based upon their ability to understand themselves and their place in the larger perspective. It is a world where a person's purpose is not merely to survive, but to grow and move closer to something that is divine and omnipresent in everyone. It is a world where hope is no longer locked in Pandora's box, but is in the heart and soul of every human. Saint Augustine realizes just what he has perceived:

And while we spoke of the eternal Wisdom, longing for it, and straining for it with all the strength of our hearts, for one fleeting instant we reached out and touched it.

And with that instant, the last evening of his mother's life on earth, Saint Augustine transformed the imaginative landscape and made possible not only the idea of the modern individual as we know him or her in society today, but the concept of the complete character. In this new world, humankind would be the battleground between good and evil. Every person would embody the search for happiness and poetic justice, the quest for morality, and the desire to examine the world and all it says through the scrutiny of critical thought, thus replacing the uncertainties and the dangers of an old and fearful imagination.

But the thread, rather than being weakened by this enormous shift in perspective, grows stronger from this point on. What Saint Augustine proved was that the process of self-discovery and the achievement of self-knowledge lay not through suffering or even intellect, but through the heart and a passionate understanding of what it feels. Others were moved by this, and their stories, narratives of personal journeys, become a metaphor and a motif for the quest to live life and to learn from it.

8

KNIGHT SCHOOL

The Quest of the Holy Grail
and *Sir Gawain and the Green Knight*

W H E N the major powers of Europe marched off to fight "the war that would be over by Christmas" in the early autumn of 1914, many did so under the patronage of the holy soldier Saint George. Attributed with the qualities of dedication, perseverance, and patriotism, he embodied the ideal role model for military-minded societies bent on defending their own Virgilian notions of territory and destiny. In *The Golden Legend*, Jacobus de Voragine tells us that Saint George was a "native of Cappadocia and a tribune in the Roman army" who one day arrived in the town of Silena in Libya—a place not far from Saint Augustine's abbey at Hippo. The town, we are told, was plagued by a "pestilential dragon" that lived in a nearby lake—perhaps a distant cousin of the biblical Leviathan who swallowed Jonah whole, a kind of latter-day Minotaur. In order to placate this dreaded beast, the townspeople were obligated to feed it regular sacrifices of food. But when the beast developed a taste for human flesh, the locals had to offer it the flower of their youth, down to the last remaining child, until it came time for the king to sacrifice his own daughter. In a replay of the myths of Perseus and Andromeda or Theseus and the labyrinth, Saint George arrived as the champion. De Voragine explains what happened next:

Bernardo Martorell. St. George Killing the Dragon. In this alternative rendering of the story related by Jacobus de Voragine, the hero saint, in the tradition of earlier mythical characters such as Theseus, slays his dreaded nemisis rather than taming it.

> Trembling, the young girl cried: "Flee, good lord, make haste and flee!" But George mounted his horse, armed himself with the sign of the cross, and bravely went to meet the dragon as it came towards him. Brandishing his lance and commending himself to God, he dealt the beast such a deadly wound that he threw it to the ground. He called to the princess: "Throw your

190

girdle round the dragon's neck! Do not be afraid, child!" She did as he told her, and the dragon followed her meekly as a puppy.

When Saint George and the young woman arrived back in the city with the monster on the leash, the entire populace was terrified. But Saint George calmed them by announcing, "The Lord has sent me to free you from the tyranny of the dragon. Only believe in Christ and be baptized, every one of you, and I will slay your dragon!" Just as in the story of Saint Augustine, the price of overcoming the last vestiges of the old pagan universe was faith. The townspeople, tired of monsters running their lives, were quite willing to profess their Christian beliefs and to trade the tragedy of appeasing nature for the comedy of controlling it.

The central idea behind the story of the champion knight—a figure who in the Christian universe succeeds where the Seven Champions of Thebes in Sophocles' *Antigone* failed—is that the hero serves as a stand-in/protector for the victim. Like Superman, the hero appears miraculously to fight the good fight when his services are required. And like the modern comic book protagonists, the hero always wins in the end, vanquishes the evil antagonists who threaten society, and lives to fight another day—all in the cause of justice, morality, order, and the comic universe.

Just as the tragic universe demands a price from characters for residing there, so too the comic universe exacts a fee. Comedy, in its very essence, is the pursuit of hope. In most narratives, the process of arriving at a destination or reaching a goal requires from the protagonist an enormous struggle—if the journey seems too easy, the reader may well turn away. What engages us is the plight of an Odysseus or an Aeneas, not just the possibility of a happy ending. Like the audience at a tragedy, we are watching how the characters dedicate themselves to their chosen ends. The pursuit of happiness, the desire to find resolution, and the longing to achieve poetic justice can be powerful motivators for protagonists. On their weary shoulders they carry not only their own desire to see things work out well in the end, but the aspirations of their audience or readers, who want to be reassured that the universe is safe and sound.

What seems to emerge from the literary role models established in the Classical stories of heroes—and in the Christian narratives of the faithful—is that comic resolution is worth the cost. Comedy, unlike tragedy, suggests that the choices an individual makes can alter the outcome of events—that the presence of desire, will, or adherence to some prescribed destiny can make even the impossible possible, if one is willing to pay the price. Simply put, the difference between tragedy and comedy is this: where tragedy finds its victims, comedy asks for volunteers.

This idea of volunteering oneself as the chosen sacrifice appeared at the beginning of the First World War, particularly in a famous sonnet by the English poet Rupert Brooke. In *The Soldier*, Brooke writes:

> *If I should die, think only this of me,*
> *That there's some corner of a foreign field*
> *That is forever England. There shall be*
> *In that rich earth a richer dust concealed,*
> *A dust whom England bore, shaped, made aware,*
> *Gave, once, her flowers to love, her ways to roam,*
> *A body of England's, breathing English air,*
> *Washed by the rivers, blest by suns of home.*
>
> *And think, this heart, all evil shed away,*
> *A pulse in the Eternal mind, no less*
> *Gives somewhere back the thoughts by England given,*
> *Her sights and sounds; dreams happy as her day;*
> *And laughter, learnt of friends; and gentleness,*
> *In hearts at peace under an English heaven.*

Ironically, fate and literature crossed paths in the life of Brooke, and in a cruel twist of fate he died the sort of literary, heroic death that his poem envisioned. In 1915, while part of the British Expeditionary Force in the Mediterranean, he developed a severe case of blood poisoning, died, and was buried as a hero beneath a laurel tree on the Greek island of Skyros. Also ironically, the poem he is best remembered for, *The Soldier*, replays the Virgilian edict of self-sacrifice, in which the protagonist is willing to give his life for his country. The powerful myth of the self-sacrificing hero, as it has been reenacted in more recent times, can be traced back to both the

Bible and *The Aeneid* through a series of stories written during the Middle Ages. This literary lineage, found in works by two unknown authors—*The Quest of the Holy Grail* and *Sir Gawain and the Green Knight*—form a type of literature known as the *romance*.

The modern-day concept of "romance" embodies everything from naked cupids on Valentine's Day cards and candlelit dinners with soft music to pot-boiler grocery store novels that feature lonely women and over-sexed men searching for love in the pink sunsets of Caribbean islands. What originally lay at the heart of romance, and an element that is still present today in the bastardized expression of the idea, is the notion of desire. Romances examine the issue of desire and how it interacts with human nature. The journeys that the knights undertake are quests: travels into both the world and the self. In *The Quest of the Holy Grail*, the knights embark not merely on a journey to find the chalice that may have been used at the Last Supper or the cup that caught the blood of the crucified Christ on Golgotha, but on a process of self-discovery whereby they learn whether they are stronger than their own weaknesses. In a sort of precursor to modern psychoanalysis, each of the knights is confronted by his own worst fears. If he manages to overcome that fear, he is allowed to progress to the next level of learning and to the next step on the road to moral perfection.

Of course, during this journey of self-discovery the goal is not always to learn what one thinks one desires, but what is most desirable from the highest possible level of moral and intellectual understanding. Some of the knights simply do not have the intellectual equipment to understand the challenge, let alone meet it and beat it. In *Sir Gawain and the Green Knight*, Sir Gawain fails the challenge that is put to him by the moral educational system of Providence. The story of the poem is a simple one. One Christmas, during Yuletide feasting at the court of King Arthur in Camelot, a rude knight dressed in green rides his stallion into the middle of the banquet hall and issues a challenge. The Green Knight declares that he will accept a blow from any knight at Arthur's court provided that his challenger will receive the Green Knight's blow exactly a year later:

No, it is not combat I crave, for come to that,
On this bench only beardless boys are sitting.
If I were hasped in armour on a high steed,
No man among you could match me, your might being meagre,
So I crave in this court a Christmas game....

If any in this household is so hardy in spirit,
Of such mettlesome mind and so madly rash
As to strike a strong blow in return for another,
I shall offer him this fine axe freely....

And I shall bide the first blow, as bare as I sit here....

> *Yet he shall have a year*
> *And a day's reprieve, I direct.*
> *Now hasten and let me hear*
> *Who answers, to what effect.*

Sir Gawain steps forward and accepts the challenge to uphold the honor of the court, declaring:

I am the weakest, the most wanting in wisdom, I know,
And my life, if lost, would be least missed, truly.

William Dyce. The Knights of the Round Table Departing on the Quest for the Holy Grail. Like the first day of school, everyone is dressed in their best apparel, but only three will make it all the way through the curriculum. Note the resemblance of the rearing horse to those in paintings of St. George slaying the dragon.

Sir Gawain volunteers because he realizes that he *is* weak, and because he understands that such a challenge is a learning process through which he can improve himself not only as a knight, but as a moral individual. He takes up the Green Knight's axe and cuts the horseman's head off in one blow. Much to everyone's surprise, the Green Knight picks up his head, thanks Sir Gawain very much for his efforts, and makes him promise to visit the Green Knight in a year's time to receive his blow. Gawain promises and the die is cast.

A year passes. Gawain spends the months living life to the fullest, expecting that he will become Camelot's next sacrificial victim. When he reaches a hospitable castle after a long, cold journey, the home of the Green Knight, he is accorded the kind of Homeric hospitality that we saw in *The Odyssey*. That night, while bedding in the special guest room, Gawain is seduced by the wife of the Green Knight, who offers him a special girdle that will make him immortal against the blows of her husband's axe. Valuing his own life and his own pleasure more than his honor, Sir Gawain accepts the gift and presents himself the next day for the knight's blow. Instead of severing Gawain's head, however, the Green Knight merely nicks him. Incredulous, Gawain asks why the knight has not killed him. The Green Knight responds that the Christmas game was really a test and that Sir Gawain has failed miserably:

> *For that braided belt you wear belongs to me.*
> *I am well aware that my own wife gave it you.*
> *Your conduct and your kissings are completely known to me,*
> *And the wooing by my wife—my work set it on....*

> *As the pearl to the white pea in precious worth,*
> *So in good faith is Gawain to other gay knights.*
> *But here your faith failed you, you flagged somewhat, sir.*
> *Yet it was not for a well-wrought thing, nor for wooing either,*
> *But for love of your life, which is less blameworthy....*

> *The first words the fair knight could frame were:*
> *"Curses on both cowardice and covetousness!*
> *Their vice and villainy are virtue's undoing."*

Gawain realizes his folly. Unlike Aeneas or Christ, he was unwilling to set his beliefs above his life. The deed is done, however, and he carries the stigma of his poor choices with him throughout his life. When Sir Gawain reappears as a character in *The Quest of the Holy Grail*, the mark of his cowardice, the scar from the Green Knight's blow, and the failure it signifies, remains with him and he is prevented from participating in the Grail ritual. His lack of awareness of the value of higher principles such as truth, honor, and sacrifice sets him off from the other knights, and he wanders in the labyrinth of the Waste Forest, a no-man's-land, where he is blind to the valors of the others. When Sir Gawain and his equally inept comrade Sir Hector meet up in the Waste Forest and question a hermit as to why they are unable to see any of the other knights who seek the Grail, the hermit reminds them of their past weaknesses:

These signs will never appear to sinners or men sunk deep in guilt, and never therefore to you, for you are the most heinous of sinners. Do not imagine moreover that the adventures now afoot consist in the murder of men or the slaying of knights; they are of a spiritual order, higher in every way and much more worth.

In the medieval world view, the acts of one's life were constantly kept in account. Indeed, according to folk beliefs, every individual carried a spiritual ledger in which the sins were balanced against the good deeds. At the day of judgment, the Almighty would open this account book and take the tally. In the world of Arthurian romance, past mistakes are what separate the worthy knights from the unworthy, and the way a knight can prove his worthiness is by placing faith, truth, and morality above all other concerns. In *The Quest of the Holy Grail*, for example, whenever a monk or a hermit appears out of nowhere to teach a knight the lesson of the situation, the correct answer is always the one that resides on the moral, ethical, or spiritual side of the issue. The moral purpose of the Arthurian legends is to demonstrate that strength of belief, above all other things, is what one should most desire, and the motto of the questing knight must always be "death before dishonor."

Honor, in the world of romance, is more than ethical intelligence:

it is a character's ability to read the situation he finds himself in and to interpret it correctly. What both the knights and the readers experience throughout this "knight school" is a process where one is constantly being tested and instructed in matters of morality. Throughout *The Quest of the Holy Grail*, most of the scenes are constructed according to a didactic process. The knights encounter a challenge, a situation that either stumps them or allows them to test their wits. The underlying question is always "What should I do?" And always, often right out of nowhere, an instructor appears— usually in the guise of a hermit, priest, or monk—to question the knight and replay the situation step by step. The examiner asks, "What did you just see or do?" The knight is forced into a position of critical self-examination where he must question not only his actions, but the motives for his behavior and his ability to interpret events.

The events are not meant to be read in the literal sense alone, but to be interpreted in the same way that we interpret the text of the Song of Solomon. As Saint Augustine learned from Saint Ambrose, a text is something that is meant to be penetrated, evaluated, questioned, and interpreted; in this way, a reader forms an understanding of it. Medieval authors believed that the more they crammed into a text in the way it might be interpreted, the more valuable the text became as an instrument of Christian didacticism. The most important works were those that sought to expand the reader's understanding, in the broadest possible terms. This standard for what is important in a text is still with us today in that we tend to measure whether a book is a literary masterpiece by the various ways it communicates timeless issues. Put quite simply, what distinguishes pulp fiction from great literature is how emphatically the work challenges us to interpret it.

Exegesis—the idea that a voice present in the narrative steps up to explain what is going on and to contextualize events for the reader— was not a medieval invention. In Sophocles' Theban plays, for example, the Chorus functions like a play-by-play commentator, keeping the audience members up to date with the narrative and telling them how to interpret events emotionally. More than just a mouthpiece for the audience's reactions, the Chorus is there to make sure that everyone is learning the same shocking realities about the nature of life. In *The Quest of the Holy Grail*, the monks, priests, and hermits serve almost the same function, but they take the role a step further. They offer the knight, and indirectly the reader, a glimpse inside the divine order of the universe. They footnote God's plan and act as commentators for Providence. Not only do they emphasize the distinction between right and wrong, but they also act as moral guides to assist the knights and the readers in the learning process.

The notion that literature is didactic and not merely emotive is something that arose from the study of theology. Authors and commentators such as Saint Augustine realized that both text and human action could be examined critically. The more one questioned what was written, the more texts provided meaning. This was particularly true for works that were written in a poetic manner, where the use of figures of speech such as similes, metaphors, and symbols begged the reader to interpret the text in multiple ways. By the time the authors of the Arthurian romances were writing their works, the process of reading a text on multiple levels had been well established by theologians, like Saint Ambrose, who were anxious to unlock some of the more complex meanings in the Bible. The romance authors borrowed from theology the four levels of interpretation. When an interpreter appears out of nowhere to question a knight about what he has experienced, it is to take him through these four levels of interpretation.

In the first level, the *literal* interpretation, the knight is simply asked to replay the situation in his mind and to sort out the narrative of the events. When Sir Gawain and Sir Hector meet up in the Waste Forest, wondering why they have not encountered any of their compatriots, a figure draped in red miraculously appears to them, and presents the two knights with an interpretation of a dream Sir Hector recently had:

Knights weak in faith and erring in belief, these three things you have just looked on are wanting in you: and this is the reason why you cannot attain to the adventures of the Holy Grail.

They listened awestruck to these words, and when they had sat in silence for a space, Sir Gawain spoke first and said to Hector:

"Did you understand that saying?"

"Indeed, sir, I did not, and yet I heard it clearly."

"In God's name," went on Sir Gawain, "we have seen such

things this night, both sleeping and waking that the best course open to us in my view, is to seek out some hermit or some man of God, who can tell us the meaning of our dreams and interpret what we have heard. And we will do whatever he advises; for else we shall but waste our time and energies, as we have done till now.

For those who have trouble understanding what is going on around them on a physical or literal level, school is out. Sir Gawain and Sir Hector are definitely not first-class students, and the miasma in which they wander is actually the fog of their own thinking.

The author of *The Quest of the Holy Grail* seems to be suggesting that the only thing separating the pagan, animate universe from the Christian, inanimate universe is the power of individuals to interpret events morally. The Waste Forest is full of surprises and magical circumstances that are intended to trick the knights and lead them into destructive deceptions. At times, in fact, the world of *The Quest of the Holy Grail* appears almost as dangerous as the sylvan woods of *Metamorphoses*. The defence against tragedy, however, is the ability to question, reason, and understand the world in a rational and analytical fashion.

When we examine a situation critically, we realize that events can reflect other meanings and other realities. The second level of interpretation is the *allegorical* reading. An *allegory* is an extended figure of speech in which the events in a narrative remind the knight or the reader of some other situation in some other text. The question here is not "What happened?" but "What does this look like?" An allegory has often been called an extended metaphor because it takes one broad picture and equates it with another broad picture. For example, the numerous paintings from the Middle Ages that depict Saint George slaying the dragon are actually allegories of faith triumphing over evil. The simple matter of a knight disposing of a neighborhood nuisance conjures up a number of possible associations: Christ descending to the underworld in the harrowing of hell; Jonah being swallowed by the whale and persevering through faith alone; Perseus or Theseus defeating a terrible monster that wrought havoc on society. In Book I of *Confessions*, Saint Augustine uses the theft of fruit from an orchard as an allegory of his sinfulness; we are supposed to remember the story of Adam eating the apple and bringing sinfulness into the world. In the case of *Sir Gawain and the Green Knight*, the entire story is an allegory that is meant to remind us of past failed heroes such as those Ovid depicts in Book VIII of *Metamorphoses*. Allegories in a text remind readers of what they already know or should know. They reward the well-read with associations, and point unprepared readers to other texts and further study that can help them acquire moral and interpretive skills.

In *The Quest of the Holy Grail*, the Grail itself is an allegory. It is the cup that may have been used by Christ at the Last Supper, but it is also a symbol for the power of faith to turn the world around. Following the miraculous appearance of the Grail floating through the banqueting hall of Camelot, the knights embark on their quest in part because their journey is an act of faith, and in part because the Grail demands the sacrifice of the very best individual the Arthurian world has to offer. By finding the Grail and then serving in a celebration of the Communion using the original Communion cup, the three best knights hope to restore the world to a state of Edenic equilibrium and to bring the fallen, winter-locked Waste Forest back to life again. What we are supposed to understand in this brush with an almost pagan vegetative-renewal myth is that the world needs a sacrifice to effect a second resurrection. When Galahad freely gives himself to bring the world back to life, we are meant to see through the allegory of the selfless knight to the story of Christ's passion and sacrifice.

Interpretation, however, is more than just a matter of unraveling the visual structures in language, such as symbols, metaphors, and even allegories. Interpretation, as Saint Augustine learned, is a matter of bridging the gap between what one knows and what one does. Knowledge is useless unless we make some attempt to apply it directly to life. The third level of interpretation, the *moral* reading, asks not only "What is happening" or "What does this remind you of?" but demands that the knight school student postulate laws that can govern real-life situations. When Sir Bors in *The Quest of the Holy Grail* is given the choice between rescuing his brother (who, like Byron's Mazeppa, is strapped naked to the back of a stampeding bronco) or rescuing a damsel in distress who is tied to a tree, he momentarily gives in to the instincts of the flesh and rescues the woman. Although she is not in the same amount of danger as his brother, Sir Bors realizes that rescuing the woman might entail some sort of reward, while rescuing his brother would only get him a pat on the back.

Sir Bors, the most intellectual of the knights and the one who eventually returns to Camelot to relate the legend of the Grail, can be forgiven for his brief lapse of moral interpretation. He is a victim of a trend that swept the Western imagination about the same time that the Arthurian romances were being written: *courtly love*. The tradition of courtly love contributes greatly to the contemporary notion of knights in shining armor rescuing damsels in distress—a notion that seems to have overcome the higher values of romance and reduced the mode to pulp fiction. In part an offshoot of Ovid's tales of heroes rescuing women from difficult situations in Book VII of *Metamorphoses*, and in part a result of the impact of the Song of Solomon upon Western attitudes to love, courtly love originated as a pragmatic system of manners at the twelfth-century court of Eleanor of Aquitaine, where it was used to keep sexual escapades from ruining life in the royal community. One of Eleanor's daughters, Princess Marguerite, instructed the royal chaplain, Andreas Capellanus, to construct a set of rules for how men should behave toward women in love and courtship. These rules became *The Art of Courtly Love*.

Capellanus constructs a dialogue between a man and a woman where the woman acts as the instructor. Suddenly, the whole question of love is addressed from a female perspective, and how women perceive love is far different from the way men consider the matter. Love, Capellanus says, is a form of suffering that comes from understanding how desire works:

Love is a certain inborn suffering derived from the sight of and excessive meditation upon the beauty of the opposite sex, which causes each one to wish above all things the embraces of the other and by common desire to carry out all of love's precepts in the other's embrace.

That love is suffering is easy to see, for before the love becomes equally balanced on both sides there is no torment greater, since the lover is always in fear that his love may not gain its desire and that he is wasting his efforts.

Capellanus presents the argument that women should be not simply outlets for lust, but objects of desire. The woman is a goal the man can win only if he proves his worth to her and wins her affections through a series of trials, labors, and endeavors. If *The Art of Courtly Love* did anything, it served to entrench in Western literature the idea that love involves progress toward a goal, replacing the Ovidian idea of love as simply a momentary emotion expressed through violence and wanton cruelty. Many authors who were approximately contemporary with the writer of *The Quest of the Holy Grail* built the notion of courtly love into their works. The heroes of such texts as *Le Roman de la Rose*, a popular long poem of the era, wake to find themselves filled with desire for an ideal of beauty that is seemingly impossible to attain.

This, then, is the tradition that Sir Bors is drawn into in his choice between his brother and the maiden. As a knight, he is sworn to uphold his honor, and part of that dedication is his obligation to assist those who cannot assist themselves. Of course, his choice is wrong. A hermit promptly appears and explains the meaning of his actions, from both a literal and an allegorical perspective. The correct answer is always the Platonic one: rescue the brother because friendship and brotherhood are much more lasting than the fickle whims of dalliance.

The moral reading of either fictional or actual reality requires a code of conduct—a set of rules that can be applied to all situations. This code became known as the chivalric code, a system of beliefs and laws for moral conduct that gives us our present-day concept of manners. Based partly on Christian virtues and partly on the principle of Virgilian honor, the chivalric code has come to govern everything from the conduct of the United States Marine Corps to the concept of defending one's honor in the ritual of dueling. It can be said that, at least indirectly, the authors of the Arthurian romances were responsible for the death in 1804 of Alexander Hamilton at the hand of Aaron Burr because both individuals felt that their honor had been violated by the other. The principle behind the chivalric code is that an individual must not only perceive the world through a set of moral laws, but defend those ideas to the death. Taken on a broad scale, this principle was one of the key drivers behind the start of the First World War. The shots fired by Gavrilo Princep on the quayside of Sarajevo did more than pierce the breasts of two Austrian royals: they also struck at the very foundations of an elaborate code of conduct that drew connections between the printed page and real life.

Although the theologians and authors of the Middle Ages realized that rationalism and critical thinking enabled people to distinguish between the animate and the inanimate universes, they realized as well that logic and analysis have their limitations. Even as Saint Augustine exhausted his critical capabilities when he overcame the Manichaean heresy, so the medieval theologians and authors came to the conclusion that there are things one simply cannot explain. To account for the fact that moral knowledge is sometimes attained through an experience that outstrips both language and reason, they came up with the fourth level of reading, the *anagogic*. The anagogic reading can best be explained by moments in Western thought when even great minds were overcome by the mystery and wonder of what they encountered. When Saint Augustine achieves clarity of thought after hearing the child's voice in the garden, or when Søren Kierkegaard in *Either/Or* can no longer reason his way to an understanding of God and "leaps" into the unknown by throwing his whole emotional and intellectual being into a comprehension that exceeds either analysis or logical comprehension, anagogic is in operation.

In *The Quest of the Holy Grail*, all the peregrinations and travails of the knights reach their apotheosis in the Grail ritual. The three lucky contestants who have survived innumerable tests and evaluations (Sir Bors, Sir Perceval, and the perfect Sir Galahad) are allowed to witness a ritual that is pure mystery. At Castle Corbenic, the destination they have been led to by the vision of the Grail, they witness a kind of Communion mass where the Grail is borne by Seven Virgins whose purity is unquestioned. Both the knights and the readers find the meaning of the situation difficult to grasp, perhaps for two reasons. By the time readers reach this climactic scene, the author expects them to have learned how to read allegorical situations and interpret them intellectually and morally. Yet the events of the Grail ritual pass before both readers and celebrants in a blur, as if the meaning of the rites being performed is intended to be lost in the sense of mystery. Like Saint Augustine, who is overcome at the moment of his resolution in the garden, Galahad is overwhelmed by the events that he is witnessing:

> Galahad drew near and looked into the Holy Vessel. He had but glanced within when a violent trembling seized his mortal flesh at the contemplation of the spiritual mysteries. Then, lifting up his hands to heaven, he said:
> "Lord, I worship Thee and give Thee thanks that Thou hast granted my desire, for now I see revealed what tongue could not relate nor heart conceive. Here is the source of valour undismayed, the spring-head of endeavour; here I see the wonder that passes every other!

Swept up in this moment of anagogic mystery, Sir Galahad feels his soul depart his body as Sir Bors and Sir Perceval stand in witness. What follows Sir Galahad's death is yet another unexplainable miracle:

> A great marvel followed immediately on Galahad's death: the two remaining companions saw quite plainly a hand come down from heaven, but not the body it belonged to. It proceeded straight to the Holy Vessel and took both it and the lance, and carried them up to heaven, to the end that no man since has ever dared to say he saw the Holy Grail.

The anagogic level suggests that literature can stretch the boundaries of the imagination, that a narrative can go into impossible regions where logic cannot explain the fantastic and where ideas are outstripped by the experiences they convey.

Although they attempted to mimic the structure of *The Aeneid*, the Arthurian romances, in particular *The Quest of the Holy Grail*, outdistance their model because they flirt with the fantastic. Where Virgil, and even Saint Augustine in his Roman way, called into question that which reason could not explain, the Arthurian romances suggest that nothing open to interpretation should be feared. The fantastic can be believable if we use our power to see through it. What these authors were attempting to do was to marry the pagan, animate universe of traditional epics such as *The Odyssey* with the inanimate Christian universe. And if the key to this marriage lay in the power of critical thought, then the challenge for medieval authors was to prove that the change in perception was part of the natural development of literature in the broader historical continuum.

To those who wrote and lived in the Middle Ages, the Dark Ages had not happened. Granted, they knew that, for a brief period, life had not gone well for European civilization. Christianity, however, had kept alive the very best of the past by preserving the important works and allowing the lesser writings to sink into oblivion. It was not until the Renaissance that critical minds such as Petrarch realized that the past had been much richer than anyone had recognized—and when this notion came into vogue, the explosion of learning and cultural activity associated with the intellectual "rebirth" of the fifteenth and sixteenth centuries gained its momentum.

In the meantime, most medieval authors viewed themselves as part of an unbroken continuum in which Rome had been subsumed into the greater glory of Christendom. In this continuum, medieval authors felt that they could pick up where Virgil had left off. Pious writers such as Boethius and Saint Augustine had indeed transformed the imaginative universe of Western literature, but only inasmuch as they had adapted the great works of the pagan past by readjusting the context in which those works were interpreted. The authors of *The Quest of the Holy Grail* and *Sir Gawain and the Green Knight* looked at the body of literature they had inherited from the past and found narratives that presented situations where a hero saves his people, both physically and morally, through the sum of all his abilities. And in the heroic structure they discovered a new means of communicating what they had to say—chiefly, that the world could be saved through the power of faith.

So powerful was the model of *The Aeneid* that it spawned a whole series of imitators, and these "Roman stories" (romances) came to include any work of literature that, like the epic, either embraced the world or recreated it through a series of carefully drawn episodes that were broad in scope. The idea of following a protagonist or a group of protagonists through a whole series of adventures, challenges, and conflicts inspired a form of literature that evolved toward the end of the Renaissance: the novel. What should be remembered is that the continental word for the novel is *roman*, a coincidence that reflects the Virgilian origins of this most popular of all literary genres.

Other medieval authors, conscious of a historical interruption in the cultural continuum following the collapse of the Roman Empire and the fall of Rome, were eager to find any evidence that might support their desire to link their own era to the glory of the past. One of the most important connections they found, although it is a highly questionable one because it lacks the essential ingredient of fact, was a work by a twelfth-century Welsh monk, Geoffrey of Monmouth, titled *The History of the Kings of Britain*. Lacking the documentary evidence that historians such as Livy or Plutarch had had at their disposal, Geoffrey of Monmouth fell back on the only source material at hand: stories and legends from the folk beliefs of the oral culture. As absurd as it may sound to today's factually minded historians, Geoffrey of Monmouth succeeded in collecting a body of stories that were powerful enough to influence not only the shape of European literature, but also an English playwright named William Shakespeare, who drew upon

Albrecht Dürer. Knight, Death and the Devil. This allegorical engraving is a Renaissance comment on the perils of temptation that would distract a questing knight. The world, as romance literature reminds us, is a place where one must maintain one's focus.

the stories in *The History of the Kings of Britain* for two plays: *King Lear* and *Cymbeline*. The point, of course, is that stories masquerading as history do not have to be true to be important. Indeed, quite often the stories that cannot be documented have the greatest effect on the literary imagination.

Geoffrey of Monmouth saw history as an unbroken thread, and perceived a connection between the events that had shaped the Britain of his own times and the fall of Troy. He tells a story of lineage that links the kings of England to the mythical character of Felix Brutus, a descendant of Aeneas' who occupied the island of Albion, latter-day England. A similar story was told by the Venerable Bede, the early English chronicler in his *History of the Church and the English People*, a coincidence that gave the legend considerable credence. In terms of the Roman continuum, England was well placed in a series of stories that became known as "The Matter of Troy." The poet who penned *Sir Gawain and the Green Knight* acknowledges the connection of his particular legend to the broader, Virgilian story in the opening stanza of his poem:

The siege and the assault being ceased at Troy,
The battlements broken down and burnt to brands and ashes,
The treacherous trickster whose treasons there flourished
Was famed for his falsehood, the foulest on earth.
Aeneas the noble and his knightly kin
The conquered kingdoms, and kept in their hand
Wellnigh all the wealth of the western lands.
Royal Romulus to Rome first turned,
Set up the city in splendid pomp,
Then named her with his own name, which now she still has:
Ticius founded Tuscany, townships raising,
Longbeard in Lombardy lifted up homes,
And far over the French flood Felix Brutus
On many spacious slopes set Britain with joy
  And grace;
 Where war and feud and wonder
 Have ruled the realm a space,
 And after, bliss and blunder
 By turns have run their grace.

The Gawain poet speaks glowingly of the pedigree of his people, and in these opening lines follows the pattern set by so many epic poets before him: the first thing that a reader must understand is the lineage of the protagonist. What was still missing was the other half of the new, post-pagan imaginative structure—the link with Christendom. That link was equally a matter for supposition. An obscure and unprovable legend claimed that England, the seat of the new Aeneas named Arthur, had been the first domain of Christendom. According to the legend, a tin trader named Joseph of Arimathea brought his young nephew, a carpenter's son named Jesus, with him on a business trip to England. The center for the tin trade at that time was an island located in a large, marshy area in present-day Somerset, an island called Avalon, the site of today's Glastonbury. There the young Jesus built his first church of clay and wattles and started preaching to the masses. When it came time for Joseph and his charge to return to the Holy Land, the young Jesus vowed he would come back and preach again from his church. Circumstances prevented him from returning. The idea, however, that England, and in particular the area around Glastonbury, formed the site of Christ's first church provided the English with a necessary sense of importance in the geographical scheme of Christendom. No longer would England be considered a backwater that had come upon the faith after the fact; instead, it could lay claim to being the birthplace of the beliefs that came to govern the world of the Middle Ages.

William Blake makes use of this same legend in *Jerusalem*, a famous poem that has often been excerpted from his larger work *Milton*. *Jerusalem* has become a mainstay of English nationalism, and William Perry's setting of the hymnlike lyric is a regular feature of such concerts as the Last Night at the Proms at Albert Hall—a musical celebration of all that is spiritually and morally British:

And did those feet in ancient time
Walk upon England's mountains green?
And was the holy lamb of God
On England's pleasant pastures seen?

And did the Countenance Divine
Shine forth upon our clouded hills?

And was Jerusalem builded here,
Among these dark Satanic Mills?

Bring me my Bow of burning gold:
Bring me my Arrows of desire:
Bring me my Spear: O clouds, unfold!
Bring me my Chariot of fire!

I will not cease from Mental Fight,
Nor shall my sword sleep in my hand,
Till we have built Jerusalem
In England's green & pleasant Land.

But the story does not end with that clay-and-wattle church some-where in Somerset. Following the crucifixion, Joseph of Arimathea and a band of his persecuted followers fled Israel and the tyranny of Roman oppression in order to practice their faith and spread the Gospel. In *The Quest of the Holy Grail*, the legend is explained:

Photograph of Rupert Brooke. This archetypal poet of the First World War created an almost self-fulfilling prophecy in his poem The Soldier, *and like a modern day Galahad was readily accepted by the public as an icon of self-sacrifice.*

> Two and forty years after the Passion of Jesus Christ, it happened that Joseph of Arimathea, the noble knight who took Our Lord's body down from the Holy Cross, left the city of Jerusalem accompanied by many of his people. It was Our Lord's command that set them on the road, and their wander-ings brought them at last to Sarras, a city held by King Evalach, who was then an infidel....Thereupon he set about expounding the doctrine of the New Law and the story of the Gospel, and unfolded to him the truth concerning Our Lord's Crucifixion, and His Resurrection also.

According to local legend in Glastonbury, Joseph is said to have returned to the site of his nephew's first church, and there, at the winter solstice, stuck his staff into the earth. The staff took root and bloomed, just as later versions of the same genus, the Glaston-bury thorn, continue to bloom each year at Christmas. Joseph is also believed to have brought with him to England the Grail: the cup or dish that serviced Christ either in the celebration of his life or in the moment of his death. According to *The Quest of the Holy*

Grail, Joseph passed the cup to his son, Josephus, who became the Fisher King of Castle Corbenic.

When the Fisher King is wounded and weak with old age, a vision of the Grail advertises for worthy candidates to replace him. The world of this weakened king is locked in a perpetual winter, and the lack of a willing victim is made all the more apparent by the pressing need for renewal and redemption. Sir Galahad's sacrifice of his earthly life, as we have seen, is an allegory for Christ's sacrifice to redeem humankind from the bondage of sin. But rather than rewrite the story of Christ's passion, the author of the Grail legend constructs an elaborate system where the vegetative decline of the world is really a metaphor for a pressing need for spiritual renovation.

T.S. Eliot, working with Jessie Weston's study of the Grail stories, *From Ritual to Romance,* recognized the need for a societal overhaul of spiritual and intellectual values following the waste of the First World War. In his long poem *The Waste Land,* Eliot shows the ethical and intellectual corruption of the world around him, the sexual sterility of the present set against the rich ritualistic depth of the past. For Eliot, the Waste Forest is modern-day London, and the only way out of it is to "give, sympathize and control." Without citing the Arthurian legends directly, Eliot constructs an allegory upon an

allegory with the purpose of taking the Western imagination back to its roots for the sake of spiritual renewal.

Eliot's message in *The Waste Land* is somewhat of a paradox. After all, when those troops marched into the trenches of the Western Front in the First World War, they believed that their cause, their sacrifice, was for a purpose. Certainly that is how society remembers this horrific moment in history in the various memorials and cenotaphs spread around the world. Rupert Brooke was only living up to the role model of Sir Galahad as he had learned it through such poems as Tennyson's *Morte d'Arthur* and through the images of knights that were so fashionable in Victorian art. So pervasive was the idea of the soldier as a modern-day Sir Galahad that British troops awaiting the signal to go over the top at the Battle of Ypres in 1915—the battle where poison gas was first used—believed they saw a vision of Saint George battling a dragon in the clouds above no-man's-land. Of course, the British propaganda machine exploited this apocryphal story in order to further the myth of sacrifice as a recruiting technique. And true to the structure and purpose of the Arthurian romances, the readership of those daily papers wanted to believe that events—whether apparitions in the clouds or mass slaughter in the mud of Flanders—could be read and could mean something. The dilemma appears to be this: that whenever the Western imagination strikes a note of moral imperative, it cannot relinquish the motifs of either Christ or Aeneas—heroes whose dedication and vision left them no other options than to serve a heaven that was quite willing to allow a sacrifice or two as part of the divine plan.

The writers of the Western imagination, however, soon discovered an alternative stance to either self-sacrifice or blind determination. The observer/hero, based more on Sir Bors than either Sir Galahad or Sir Perceval, suddenly became a standard motif when an exiled Florentine poet longed for both his native city and a vision of passionate redemption. And one day, as he took the long way home, he understood a vision of hell, purgatory, and heaven that would make romances pale by comparison. For love, faith, and hope, that Florentine wanderer, Dante Alighieri, set himself upon an imaginative quest not only to see the magnificence of God, but to understand the mysteries and complexities of the humane and the divine.

9

WHAT FRESH HELL
IS THIS?

Dante's *Inferno*

W H E N commenting on the difference between a poet in full command of his skills and one who is just learning his craft, T.S. Eliot remarked, "immature poets imitate; mature poets steal." Literary larceny, however, is more that just a matter of poets committing plagiarism. It is a question of the "mature" writer being aware of the context in which he or she is writing, of crafting a vision from the fabric of the tradition, of honoring those writers who have gone before by paying the highest possible tribute in literature—theft—and by translating that vision into the idiom of the present. No author works in a vacuum. When writers set pen to paper, regardless of their subject matter, they are extending a continuum, spinning out a new length of thread for the story, and repeating or rephrasing what has been said before. In that continuum, the works that have spoken most clearly and most emphatically about the human condition, works that have appealed to our sense of order, our longing, fear, and joy, become the measure of how those same subjects can be treated when they are refreshed by a contemporary retelling.

For those authors who perceive their works as an extension of the literary continuum, the text is more than merely a narrative; it is an implosion that draws to it the body of knowledge that the writers have inherited from their predecessors. When writers actively and consciously make reference in their texts to those works that have proceeded it, either by allusion, allegory, or quoted reference, they are practicing a policy of intertextuality, of writing their works not only through the power of their own knowledge and imagination but through the works of those who have gone before. Intertextual writing demands that the reader come armed with an extensive knowledge of what literature is, who the main authors are, how principal works have influenced the collective imagination that operates in literature, and what literature's key stories and themes have been. Just as Virgil read Homer and borrowed many of *The Odyssey*'s themes, structures, and even narrative events for *The Aeneid*, so writers throughout history have delighted in enriching and enhancing their own works by "stealing" from the texts they admire.

Literary intertextuality is an author's elegant, if sometimes pedantic, way of locating his or her own work in the rankings of what is important and what is not important, and of acknowledging the debt owed to earlier writers. From an author's point of view, intertextuality is a form of tribute. It is a way of pointing to those who have informed his or her vision. In its most subtle form—*allusion*—intertextuality is a polite way of admitting the influence and the importance of a forerunner. In a more aggressive stance, where writers quote directly from an earlier work, it is an admission that they cannot improve upon the way something was said in the past. But in its most overt form, when the former writer appears in the new work as a character, intertextuality is more than a tribute: it is the open acknowledgment that the great works of literature are actually a guide that can help one navigate the labyrinth of the imagination.

In Canto I of the *Inferno*, when Dante wakes to find himself lost "midway on my life's journey" and wandering helplessly in a valley that is part Waste Forest, part labyrinth, and part "valley of the shadow of death," he appears to be trapped. He is circled first by a Leopard, "nimble and light and fleet," which symbolizes the sins of the flesh; then by a Lion, "swift and savage," which represents the sins of the mind; and finally by a Wolf, "gaunt with the famished craving," which stands in for the sins of the soul. It seems as if all the sinfulness of the world has him cornered, and he is in a hopeless position. But luck intervenes and he stumbles through a crack in the earth "headlong down" where he is greeted by a familiar, although entirely unexpected, presence. The frightened faller asks the specter if he is a man or a ghost, and just when it appears Dante might flounder and lose himself in the immoral morass of the world, Virgil introduces himself:

It spoke: "No man, although I once was a man;
  My parents' native land was Lombardy
  And both by citizenship were Mantuan.

Sub Julio born, though late in time, was I,
  And lived at Rome in good Augustus' days,
  When false gods were worshipped ignorantly.

Poet was I, and tuned my verse to praise,
  Anchises' righteous son, who sailed from Troy
  When Ilium's pride fell ruined down ablaze.

But thou—oh, why run back where fears destroy
  Peace? Why not climb the blissful mountain yonder,
  The cause and first beginning of all joy?"

Virgil is referring to Mount Purgatory. Atop it sits the Garden of Eden which, according to legend, God removed far from the reach of humans after the fall of Adam and Eve. If Virgil is suggesting that Dante embark with him upon a quest for the biblical paradise, then the process of that quest, the learning experience, must therefore be to learn the nature of morality. Dante chooses Virgil both as his guide through hell and purgatory and as his moral teacher, because few other authors had taken such pains to explain in their writings the sacrifices necessary for the pursuit of happiness. To write an epic about a moral understanding of the way the world works, Dante realizes that he must turn to Virgil, who was confronted by exactly the same questions when he constructed the character of Aeneas. Dante appreciates the debt he owes to his literary predecessor—after all, Virgil solves in *The Aeneid* most of the imaginative problems that Dante is presented with in the *Inferno*—and pays him a tremendous tribute:

Thou art my master, and my author thou,
 From thee alone I learned the singing strain,
 The noble style, that does me honour now.

Literature is more than just a collection of engaging stories, Dante knows; the great works testify to the efforts of those who have attempted to make moral order from the chaos of the world around them. Just as Odysseus wanted his home, or Aeneas craved the peace and tranquillity of a homeland, or Saint Augustine struggled to find his spiritual home in God, so Dante recognizes that he can only attain inner peace if he is able to comprehend and witness the providential order that rules the universe. Literature is the desire to find a means of understanding the world—the desire to perceive that life is governed by order, if not by a grand author, wherein all the problems, struggles, fears, and torments will somehow work out to a beautiful resolution.

For Dante, the world was indeed a hard place to understand, and in many ways *The Divine Comedy*—made up of *Inferno, Purgatorio,* and *Paradiso*—is an attempt to retrieve those things that he loved and lost. From a very general perspective, *The Divine Comedy* is about humanity's search for what was lost at the time of the fall: the proximity to both God and divine grace. Like the Bible, it follows a comic structure. Dante, barred midway on his "life's journey" by the presence of sin, first undergoes a *nekusis* into the very depths of human experience through hell, where he is guided by his literary and moral master, Virgil. When he emerges from that depth, he finds purgatory, a great void that is neither life nor death, but a place of eternal waiting, indecision, and unpunishable misfortune. Yet from this nowhere-land, he rises further still into the arms of his divine sovereign, led by the light that he thought had gone out of his life, the object of his earthly and spiritual desires: Beatrice Portinari, a Florentine girl who had captured his heart when he was a young boy. Like the Bible, the narrative follows a decline and a gradual resurrection, and expresses the hope that, where the rule of Providence is wise and absolute, everything will work out with certainty and justice. But from a more personal perspective, *The Divine Comedy* is about how one comes to grips with loss. Through a profound use of intertextuality, Dante turns to both the entire scope of his literary learning and the sum experience of his life to answer the desires of his heart. And what his heart desires most is his native city, his lost love, and the peace of mind that comes from taking possession of one's own life.

The simple truth about Dante is that circumstances in his life prevented him from holding on to what he loved most. He grew up in Florence in a noble family that was associated with the democratic politics of the city. In Dante's time, Florence was split between three rival factions: the Ghibellines, whose aristocratic and non-Italian sympathies lay with the Holy Roman Emperor; the Black Guelfs, who were pro-Italian but supported an aristocratic and oligarchic system of government; and the White Guelfs, who believed in democratic, Italian government and who championed the pope. As a young nobleman, Dante was introduced to the cream of Italian society, and among those he met were intellectuals such as his fellow poet Guido Cavalcante, and the daughter of the Portinari family, the beautiful Beatrice. As Dante chronicles in *La Vita Nuova* (as we shall see in the next chapter), he fell in love with Beatrice while they were still children, only to see her wed to another in an arranged marriage. He was never capable of expressing his love for her in life, though he sought to glorify her in her death through his short poems and through the near-canonizing tribute that he pays her as his guide through paradise in the third part of *The Divine Comedy*.

Dante had a relatively secure life in Florence until 1302, when the Black Guelfs came to power. For reasons that are still not clear, Dante was exiled from Florence on pain of death for the remainder of his life. Forced to leave his beloved native city, he wandered Europe as a scholar and, after periods in Verona, Paris, and possibly Oxford, he settled in Ravenna. A line from Boethius' *The Consolation of Philosophy* seems to sum up the remorse that Dante must have felt at being separated from the place he loved most:

No wise man prefers being in exile, being poor and disgraced to being rich, respected, and powerful, and to remaining at home and flourishing in his own city.

This sense of remorse in exile comes through in the opening lines of Canto XXV of the *Paradiso*, where Dante laments his exile and the denigration of his talents by the ignorant clique that took control of his native city:

> *If it should chance that e'er the sacred song*
>   *To which both Heaven and Earth have set their hand,*
>   *Whence I am lean with labouring so long,*
>
> *Should touch the cruel hearts by which I'm banned*
>   *From my fair fold where as a lamb I lay,*
>   *Foe to the wolves which leagued against it stand,*
>
> *With altered voice, with altered fleece to-day,*
>   *I shall return, a poet, at my font*
>   *Of baptism to take the crown of bay.*

Gustave Doré. Poets in Limbo. This collection of notable figures from the Classical era entertain Dante during his visit to hell and embrace him as one of their own. The bald Socrates is seated to the right.

For Dante, the world is a labyrinth filled with three vicious animals—all representing sin. His goal is to seek wisdom through learning and through literature, and to find his way through that labyrinth, no matter how arduous. That, at least, is the point of the *Inferno*. As a story, it is filled with the pathos of one who is struggling to rise above both grief and the snares of a world that neither appreciates nor understands genius. And as all geniuses should, Dante believes in his abilities—a fact that comes through in the cheeky humor of the *Inferno* when he puts his enemies, especially the living ones, in the worst possible situations in hell. Dante seeks his way out of the *nekusis* that the world has imposed upon him, fully aware that his learning, his talents, and his ability to see far beyond any other poet of the time will ultimately allow him to triumph over his accusers.

So confident is Dante in his poetic abilities and his own personal sense of destiny that in Canto IV he places himself quite flatteringly among the pantheon of the greatest poets, whom he meets in hell. The great poets of the Classical era—those born outside the time of Christian grace, but who committed no sins of either the legal or poetic kind—are situated in an anteroom to hell and are engaged in a kind of writers' conference:

"Mark well the first of these," my master said,
  "Who in his right hand bears a naked sword
  And goes before the three as chief and head;

Homer is he, the poets' sovran lord:
  Next, Horace comes, the keen satirical;
  Ovid the third; and Lucan afterward.

Because I share with these that honourable
  Grand title the sole voice was heard to cry
  They do me honour, and therein do well.

Thus in their school assembled I, even I,
  Looked on the lords of loftiest song, whose style
  O'er all the rest goes soaring eagle-high.

And when they had talked together a short-while
  They all with signs of welcome turned my way,
  Which moved my master to a kindly smile;

And greater honour yet they did me—yea,
  Into their fellowship they deigned invite
  And make me sixth among such minds as they.

Confidence and self-congratulation aside, Dante is recognizing here that poetry is an on-going conversation between poets, where one learns from another. The twentieth-century British poet W.H. Auden noted, in one of his most famous observations, that "poetry is problem solving." Poets learn how to solve their own poetic problems, whether of form, content, or diction, by reading the works of their poetic forebears. When Dante cites the five major poets of the past—Homer, Horace, Lucan, Ovid, and Virgil—he is really saying to his reader, "These are the poets who have taught me how to solve my poetic problems through the example of their own work."

From Homer, Dante borrows the meaning of home. But if *The Odyssey* was about a man trying to find his way home, the *Inferno* is really a study of the realization that home has become unattainable. In Canto XXVI, as Dante and Virgil make their way through one of the inner circles of hell, a Malabowge where the counselors of Fraud are punished, they encounter the shade of Ulysses. Dante's response to the Bronze Age wanderer is to cast him, almost unsympathetically, in the Roman reading of his story. Odysseus is given his Roman name, and he is every bit the ne'er-do-well of both *The Aeneid* and *Metamorphoses*. Dante's Ulysses is worse than a knight-errant not only because of his dalliances with Circe, but because he has committed the worst sin of all in Dante's view: he has abandoned his friends. In what amounts to a poem within the poem of Canto XXVI, Dante's Ulysses recounts his final voyage and retells a story that is prophesied in the *nekusis* scene of *The Odyssey* and given a slightly longer telling in *Metamorphoses*. Ulysses tells how he sailed beyond Spain and Morocco with his elderly crew, and against the wishes of his comrades, he pushed west, eager to see the Isles of the Blessed, the Elysium of Classical mythology:

> *"Brothers," said I, "that have come valiantly*
> *Through hundred thousand jeopardies undergone*
> *To reach the West, you will not now deny*
>
> *To this last little vigil left to run*
> *Of feeling life, the new experience*
> *Of the uninhabited world behind the sun.*
>
> *Think of your breed; for brutish ignorance*
> *Your mettle was not made; you were made men,*
> *To follow after knowledge and excellence."*

At that moment, just when the landfall of the mountain is within their grasp, the fates or perhaps divine Providence intervenes, and Ulysses and all his comrades are drowned. The story ties in with the Homeric prophecies for Odysseus, that death will "come to him gently out of the waves" when he is in extreme old age.

What Ulysses cannot realize is that he and his men have arrived at the foot of the mountain where the earthly paradise of the Judeo-Christian mythology has been relocated. It is the same mountain that Dante spies in the distance as he enters the vestibule of hell in Canto III. The quest to find paradise or to become closer to God operates according to the same principles in the *Inferno* as it does in romance literature, and only the worthy may approach the moment when divine truth is within their grasp. Dante is attempting the same amalgam of Classical and Christian mythologies that the romances sought to achieve. For him, the ultimate goal of intertextuality is to recreate a larger mythical schema out of the material he has inherited from previous writers. In this sense, Dante is not merely rewriting past literature—at least not in the way that the authors of the medieval romances told moral Christian tales in the Roman manner—but instead creating a new super-mythology that speaks to both the pagan and the Christian pasts of the Western literary imagination. What is more important, however, is that Dante is busy creating his own personal mythology from the fabric of the past. He put Homer's protagonist in the middle of his epic about the Christian underworld for a simple reason: Ulysses was someone who, for all his faults, was like Dante. He wanted to go home.

Dante opens Canto XXVI with a strange reproach to his home city of Florence. His comments carry a heavy note of bitterness. After all, here was a city that should have embraced and celebrated his ideas and his talents, but instead chose to exile him and break his heart:

> *Florence, rejoice, because thy soaring fame*
> *Beats its broad wings across both land and sea,*
> *And all the deep of Hell rings thy name!*
>
> *Five of thy noble townsmen did I see*
> *Among the thieves; which makes me blush anew,*
> *And mightily little honour it does to thee.*

For Dante, Florence's fame was infamy; its name was ringing for all the wrong reasons. Though he holds out hope for Florence as he walks the paths of paradise in the *Paradiso*, he cannot overlook the feelings of shame and disgust that his great native city has engendered. Like a contemporary political exile who reads of his country's wrongs in the reports of Amnesty International, Dante can only wait and hope. He still believes that God will make things right for him in the end, and he follows his comic resolve with the faith that the works of his literary masters taught him.

Faith isn't the only lesson Dante learned at the feet of the earlier poets. These are the writers who solved the often perplexing logistical problems of presenting broad, extended narratives. Homer resolved the issue of how long a human voice could sing when, in *The Odyssey*, he chose to arrange his epic in a series of focused episodes—the concept that gives us the modern-day notion of the chapter. Virgil borrowed this notion for the "book" structure of *The Aeneid*, even though he intended his epic to be read rather than sung. In *The Divine Comedy*, however, Dante realizes that he is dealing with "heavenly song," that what he sees and experiences is coming to him not through Heliconian Muses, but through the inspiration of the Holy Spirit of the Christian tradition. As a result, he chooses to break *The Divine Comedy* into cantos, or "songs," instead of books, episodes, or chapters. By arranging his poem in this way, he is attempting to return the epic—especially after its reinvention and reinterpretation at the hands of the romance writers—to its origins as an extended lyric.

To heighten the poem's sense of lyricism, he chooses a unique verse form: terza rima. The terza rima stanza is composed of three lines with an *aba* rhyme scheme. But what makes the form so suited to Dante's epic purposes is that when the stanza form is repeated, *aba, bcb, cdc,* and so on, it gives the sonic impression of a movement forward. Homer had underpinned his lines with a steady and regular rhythm that was meant to mimic marching in *The Iliad* and the constant motion of the waves in *The Odyssey.* Dante, who also realized that an extended epic is often well served by an evident sonic movement supported by meter, verse form, and rhyme scheme, chooses the terza rima form because it gives, as the British critic Philip Hobsbaum has suggested, the impression of the voice constantly falling forward or moving upward.

This may seem a minor issue in the grand scope of *The Divine Comedy* until we consider that this is exactly what the poem's narrative is about: someone literally falling forward down through the depths of earth to the center of Hades, and then slowly making his way back up again through purgatory to paradise. In Dante's treatise on poetry and decorum, *La Vita Nuova,* he explains at some length that there should be a relationship between what a poem says and the way it says it. In expressing this belief in *The Divine Comedy*, Dante recognized the importance of marrying form to content to give the reader yet another layer of information about what a poem means. To modern readers, such a concept may not seem very important, but it became one of the perceptual keystones of the mentality that shaped the Renaissance.

Throughout the *Inferno*, the informed reader is constantly struck by a profound sense of familiarity—a result of Dante's tribute to and use of form and content from important works of the past. He borrows from previous narratives because they serve as imaginative benchmarks. The *Inferno* opens much like a medieval romance, for example, on a journey through a dark wood:

> *Midway this way of life we're bound upon,*
> *I woke to find myself in a dark wood,*
> *Where the right road was wholly lost and gone.*
>
> *Ay me! how hard to speak of it—that rude*
> *And rough and stubborn forest! there mere breath*
> *Of memory stirs the old fear in the blood;*
>
> *It is so bitter, it goes nigh to death;*
> *Yet there, I gained such good, that, to convey*
> *The tale, I'll write what else I found therewith.*

For Dante, life itself is a labyrinth, a dark wood, just as the Waste Forest of *The Quest of the Holy Grail* was both a quandary and a miasma. The pressures and the petty concerns of life appear to entangle him both emotionally and intellectually, and like Saint Augustine, he seeks that clarity, that "way through the maze," that will enable him to see the big picture and understand the purpose of his own existence. He calls the dark wood "that valley's wandering maze," as if death itself is the labyrinth. To navigate the maze, Dante uses the knowledge that he has gained from life and from literature. It is no coincidence that the most important authorial model available to him, Virgil, happens along when Dante the wanderer is most in need of a guide. Like a knight-errant, Dante feels the need for correction; yet what is astonishing is that he perceives literature, rather than theology or philosophy, as the container for moral ideas. It would almost seem that literature is the one defence against the Lion, the Wolf, and the Leopard.

Dante begs his poetic master to save him from the devouring beasts and worldly pressures that would destroy the imaginative mind and soul of the poet:

See there the beast that turned me back again—
Save me from her, great sage—I fear her so,
She shakes my blood through every pulse and vein.

For Dante, however, the sinfulness of the world works upon him like a neurosis—he simply cannot leave his problems behind and head straight for paradise, which sits on the mountain he can see in the distance. Just as Freud will suggest in the twentieth century, the recognition that one has problems begs the need to confront and overcome them. This need to understand both the good and the bad in the world is what is heroic about Dante's quest. His universe, whether it is the actual physical place or the literary imaginative creation, operates in a Boethian manner. There is a divine and good purpose to everything. And if the New Testament fails to offer a clear vision of how Providence deals with the inability of free-willed individuals to recognize the difference between good and evil, then the next best model for an afterworld built on the premise of moral justice comes from Virgil.

Virgil's Hades is a place where the psychoses of the upper world become the pains and torments of the afterlife. In what amounts to a statement that the punishment should fit the crime, Virgil's Shades endure a kind of divine retribution as a result of a system of moral justice. Dante constructs his hell in much the same manner, but he realizes that true justice is a matter of degree and that punishment in the next world must be tailored to the offender. Dante's hell is therefore much more stratified than Virgil's; the worse the sin, the lower the sinner seems to be cast into the quagmire of retribution.

When Dante begins his journey through hell with Virgil in Canto II, he is confronted by the famous message that is scrawled over the gates to the underworld:

Through me the road to the city of desolation,
Through me the road to sorrows diuturnal,
Through me the road among the lost creation.

Justice moved my great maker; God eternal
  Wrought me: the power and the unsearchably
  High wisdom, and the primal love supernal.

Nothing ere I was made was made to be
  Save things eterne, and I eterne abide;
  Lay down all hope, you that go in by me.

Dante's hell is a place of hopelessness, and although his journey will be a comic one—he is aimed at that high mountain in the distance, after all, and possibly even at heaven itself—he is about to witness a tragic world where, just as in the Sophoclean universe, there is no divine grace and no possibility of redemption. The inmates of the *Inferno's* nether regions are those who, with free will and in the presence of Christian grace, turned against God, denying the laws of both humanity and nature. Dante calls these souls "the miserable race," and notes that they "have lost the good of intellect." In other words, what lands a person in hell is stupidity:

And when I'd noted here and there a shade
  Whose face I knew, I saw and recognized
  The coward spirit of the man who made

The great refusal: and the proof sufficed;
  Here was that rabble, here without a doubt
  Whom God and whom His enemies despised.

Although the concept would not be expressed until the seventeenth century, when Blaise Pascal came up with his intriguing "betting man's" theory for the existence of God, Dante appears to have encapsulated the spirit of "Pascal's Wager."

Pascal was asked whether he could come up with a theory that would prove the existence of God. He worked on the problem, but realized, as had Saint Augustine and others before him, that the nature of God was too large and anagogic a construct for rational methodologies such as mathematics or philosophy. Instead, Pascal arrived at an idea that was based on the principle of a wager. He said that an individual should wager that God exists because the benefits of "winning the bet" (the kingdom of heaven and eternal bliss) far out-weighed the torments one would experience if one said God did not exist and then found out that he did. Reason dictates that in all things—but especially where the Almighty is concerned—it is better to be safe than sorry. Dante's lines in Canto III appear to express the same sentiment. Dante is surprised, however, by the scope of human folly—the number of people who went to the wicket, placed their bets, and lost: "It would never have entered my head," he notes. "There were so many men whom death had slain."

Hell, says Dante, was created for those whose free will overcame their natural instincts for good. The vestibule of hell, meanwhile, that area between the real world and the horrific business of punishment, contains the souls of those who are waiting to be assigned to lower regions, or the shades of beings who could not or would not distinguish between good and evil. In Canto III, the hapless non-believers suddenly find themselves mingled with the outcast neutral angels who did nothing when Satan rose against God in the mythological war in heaven:

> *They're mingled with that caitiff angel-crew*
> *Who against God rebelled not, nor to Him*
> *Were faithful, but to self alone were true;*

> *Heaven cast them forth—their presence there would dim*
> *The light; deep Hell rejects so base a herd,*
> *Lest sin should boast itself because of them.*

In Dante's world, faith is not a halfway measure. Hell and purgatory are filled with those who chose gray when given the options of black and white. As Virgil points out to his traveler, the vestibule of hell is a bit like an international airport, filled with those "from every country" who have suffered "beneath God's righteous ire."

At the conclusion of Canto III, Dante and Virgil arrive at the banks of the River Styx, that Rubicon that must be crossed. Once over it, there is no return. The boatman Charon, a figure that Dante has borrowed from Classical *nekusis* stories, refuses to take a living soul across the river. Virgil, however, silences the boatman with a powerful word—the first of many instances in the *Inferno* where Dante uses language as a theme. In *The Divine Comedy*, language is not merely the vehicle for telling the story, but the very source of meaning in the text. As the opening lines of the Gospel of John suggest, the word itself is sacred. Dante, like Saint Augustine, believes that the truthfulness of language is a key means to understanding and unlocking the mysteries of God; the misuse of language, therefore, is a crime against the Almighty. Canto XVIII, for example, deals with the Eighth Circle of Hell, the Malabowge where Flatterers and Frauds are permanently sequestered. In the Eighth Circle, Dante meets the Alessio Interminei, another White Guelf, whose blarney may have caused Dante some wrong:

> *I've seen thy face, dry-headed, up at home;*
> *Thou art Alessio Interminei, late*
> *Of Lucca—so, more eagerly than on some,*
>
> *I look on thee. He beat his pumpkin pate,*
> *And said, "The flatteries I spewed out apace*
> *With tireless tongue have sunk me to this state."*

In a world that still believed the medieval idea that faith and truth were a matter of what one professed, language was a very important element in the human character because what one said demonstrated what one was. Yet for all its sanctity, language, like reason or philosophy, cannot always express the full breadth and power of an idea or situation.

The insufficiency of language both intrigues and troubles Dante. Just as Virgil realizes that aspects of his narrative overwhelm him when he calls upon the Muses to assist him, so Dante realizes that even the vatic expression of a divine vision of the universe runs up against the limits of semantics and vocabulary. Early in Canto XXXIV, as he and Virgil pass through the most terrifying portion of hell, the area reserved for the betrayers of friends, which contains Judas, Brutus and Cassius, Dante is overcome by the horrifying spectacle. It is one of the few instances when words fail him:

How cold I grew, how faint with fearfulness,
Ask me not, Reader; I shall not waste breath
Telling what words are powerless to express;
This was not life, and yet it was not death...

Not only does Dante sometimes experience a profound semantic gap between what he can express and what he cannot, but he also understands that his entire poetic undertaking, its breadth, scope, and detail, is perhaps the greatest challenge ever presented to a poet. Cocky as ever, most of the time he feels he is up to it. Canto XXVII, which examines the circle where the sowers of Discord are confined, opens with a statement of his confidence in his own abilities:

Who, though with words unshackled from the rhymes,
Could tell full the tale of wounds and blood
Now shown to me, let him try a thousand times?

Truly all tongues would fail, for neither could
The mind avail, nor any speech be found
For things not to be named nor understood.

In other words, Dante is daring anyone to equal his efforts. He is open to challengers and certain of his poetic powers. The problem remains more than a semantic one, however; like Saint Augustine before him, Dante realizes that there are things that can not be expressed in language.

Even before it was finished, *The Divine Comedy* was considered something of a marvel. The Italian poet Boccaccio, who wrote one of the very earliest biographies of Dante (and who attempted at every turn to steal what he could from the Florentine poet for his own works such as *The Decameron*), tells the story of how some of Dante's friends discovered the manuscript for the poem while it was a work-in-progress. *The Divine Comedy* was only partially complete, and Dante, it appears, had abandoned the project for other duties during his exile:

This person read the cantos with admiration, though he did not know what they were; and, impelled by his exceeding delight in them, he carefully withdrew them from the place where they lay, and brought them to one of our citizens, by name Dino di Messer Lambertuccio, a famous poet of that time, and a man of high intelligence.... Upon reading them, Dino marveled no less than he who had brought them, both because of their beautiful, polished and ornate style, and because of the depth of meaning that he seemed to discover hidden under the beautiful covering of words.

What those first readers of *The Divine Comedy* discovered was that Dante's poem read like a work of theology. It appealed to their sense of interpretation on the four levels of reading—the literal, the allegorical/symbolic, the moral, and the anagogic—that were discussed in the last chapter. Yet *The Divine Comedy* seemed to beg readers to make up their own interpretations simply because, with the urgency of the narrative, Dante never seemed to pause to offer an exegesis of his ideas. As readers, we are on our own with the text; there are no sudden appearances by monks or hermits to give small sermons, no Chorus to offer a running commentary. Yet the meanings that Dante sought to present on all four levels are clear throughout his allegory, and he consistently gives the reader credit for being able to see through his poem to the larger ideas that he is attempting to communicate.

Of course, it is not hard for a reader to see just what hell is in the *Inferno*. The path upon which Virgil leads his pupil spirals downward through a whole series of levels until, in the depths of human depravity, they reach the center, where Satan gnaws upon the betrayers of friendship. Dante elaborates on Virgil's concept of hell by giving his netherworld an entire geography that seems a psychological extension of the torments and neuroses that afflict the imprisoned.

Put quite simply, and for want of a better metaphor, Dante's hell is shaped like a toilet. The vast area covers the Seven Deadly Sins (Pride, Envy, Avarice, Sloth, Wrath, Gluttony, and Lust) and makes allowance for some of the more particularized sins, such as Fraud, Simony (the selling of religious offices and indulgences), and Discord. The upper part of hell contains a series of circles where the landscape gradually slopes downward. In the first four circles, a region described in Cantos IV to VII, Dante presents those who suffer under the punishment of the Sins of the Leopard, the sins caused by desire, lustfulness, and uncontrolled appetites. In Canto IV, the First Circle of Hell, Dante enters a zone called Limbo, a place that contains the unbaptized, the neutral angels, and a collection of interesting personages from the ancient world who are known as the "righteous pagans." These individuals form a fascinating list of accomplished minds: Plato, Heraclitus, Euclid, and Ptolemy, as well as some major imaginative or literary characters such as Aeneas and Orpheus. The supposition is that these individuals were born outside the reach of Christian grace. Nonetheless, they did nothing wrong, and the power of their minds and the importance of their ideas put them in a position where they are free from torment to talk among themselves, just as they might have done atop the Necropolis in ancient Athens or in the Roman Forum. The *Inferno* led George Bernard Shaw to suggest that if he were given the choice between heaven and hell, he would choose hell because it contained far more interesting people, not merely a collection of Sunday School teachers and churchgoers.

In Canto V, when they reach the Second Circle of Hell, Virgil and Dante witness the ancient mythical figure of King Minos sorting out the throngs that have crossed the River Styx, and they see the Lustful being tossed on the wind. The Gluttonous are dealt with in the Third Circle (Canto VI); the Hoarders and Spendthrifts meet their torment in the Fourth Circle; and the Wrathful are punished in the Fifth Circle, in a scene not unlike mud wrestling:

And I, staring about with eyes intent,
Saw mud-stained figures in the mire beneath,
Naked, with looks of savage discontent,

At fisticuffs—not with fists alone, but with
Their heads and heels, and with their bodies too,
And tearing each other piecemeal with their teeth.

It is Dante's vision of torment that inspired the contemporary notions of how art depicts sinfulness, and it is his images that filled the imaginations of puritans with ideas of how the wicked might behave. Even rock videos have borrowed Dante's scenes to suggest what life on the edge is like—though such images more closely resemble a Saturday night in the French Quarter of New Orleans than a circle from Dante's medieval vision of punishment.

Beyond the Fifth Circle lies the city of Dis. This is the stronghold of the fallen angels, and in Milton's *Paradise Lost* it will be the seat of Satan's new kingdom in hell and the home of the Rebel Angels. In an expression of crusader-like paranoia about the onslaught of Islam against Christian Europe, Dante notes that the City of Dis is full of mosques:

And I: "Already I see its mosques arise
Clear from the valley yonder—a red shell
As though drawn out of glowing furnaces."

And he replied: "The flames unquenchable
That fire them from within thus make them burn
Ruddy, as thou seest, in this, the nether Hell."

As an imaginative construct, Dis is the opposite of the New Jerusalem. But its high ramparts, its angry population, and its unseemly social conditions suggest a vision that is more akin to the urban decay of the late twentieth century than to a place of torment. Dis is the opposite of Arcadia, as far away as one can imagine from the pastoral ideal of humans living in nature. The horrific appearance of this labyrinth-like city is merely a mask for a great plain that lies on the other side of the walls. It is on this plain that Dante places the suffering shades of Heretics, those who preached against the Gospel of the Truth and sought to alter it to their own ends.

It is here, in Canto X, on the Plain of the Heretics, that Dante meets the specter of the Ghibelline Farinata, who taunts the Florentine poet with a prophecy. While the underworlds of *The Odyssey* and *The Aeneid* were places where a protagonist could go to receive much-needed news of the world above, Dante's hell is still rife with the earth's troubles; Farinata prophesies Dante's exile from Florence and his wanderings, and offers him some small explanation for the journey he has embarked upon:

> *It seems you can foresee and prophesy*
> *Events that time will bring, if I hear right,*
> *But with things present, you deal differently.*
>
> *"We see," said he, "like men who are dim of sight,*
> *Things that are distant from us; just so far*
> *We still have gleams of the All-Guider's light...*
>
> *Sagely he bade me: "See thou mind and mark*
> *Those adverse warnings: now to what I say—"*
> *And here he raised his finger—"prithee, hark!*
>
> *When thou shalt stand bathed in the glorious ray*
> *Of her whose blest eyes see all things complete*
> *Thou'lt learn the meaning of thy life's whole way."*

The Plain of the Heretics not only marks the chance for Dante to receive the customary prophetic message that is part of every *nekusis*, but also represents a change in the shape of hell. From here, Virgil and Dante leave the region of the Sins of the Leopard and enter the darker region, that of the Sins of the Lion.

The Sins of the Lion—Suicide; violence against God, art, and nature; Fraud; and Usury—are sins of Pride, Aggression, and Obsession, where the victims are literally prey to their own worst instincts and ideas. The images of the Sins of the Lion often directly allude to *Metamorphoses* and Ovid's tales of terror in the face of hopelessness. In the Wood of the Suicides of the Seventh Circle (Canto XIII), for example, those who died by their own hands are not only hanging from the trees but have become the trees in horrific images of transformation:

> *We that are turned to trees were human once;*
> *Nay, thou shouldst tender a more pious hand*
> *Though we have been the souls of scorpions.*

233

Another figure explains the consequences of suffering from the torment of a change of state, and sums up what Ovid was trying to say in *Metamorphoses*:

> *When the wild soul leaps from the body, which*
> *Its own mad violence forces it to quit,*
> *Minos dispatches it down to the seventh ditch.*

Just as Ovid's stories were meant to show the folly of the gods and to warn humankind to revere its deities, so Dante's stories serve as stark reminders that the only reasonable course open to an individual's imagination and mind is that of balance, clarity, and Virgilian level-headedness.

The Eighth Circle of Hell is a far more complex arrangement. Virgil pauses in his trek to explain the arrangement of hell to Dante in Canto XI and warns his pupil that after they pass the region of the Sins of the Lion, both nature and the surrounding geography decline precipitously. The ever-declining circles suddenly give way to the sharp, long drop of the Eighth Circle or the Malabowges, a shaft that falls all the way to the frozen center of hell, the Ninth Circle. The Malabowges are a series of shelf-like structures where the tormented cling, beyond hope, to their sins—

the only things that are left to them. It is in this region of the Sins of the Wolf that Dante puts those he despises most: the panderers and the seducers, the simoniacs who by selling sacraments and church offices weaken the structure of Christendom, the sorcerers who corrupt beliefs, the barrators or people who sell public offices and corrupt the nation, the hypocrites and thieves and finally the sowers of Discord and the falsifiers. In Canto XXX, for instance, Dante tells the story of Gianni Schicchi, a clever Florentine lawyer who made a reputation for himself through his manipulation of the law and his trickery. In a farcical story that was later borrowed, though not directly from Dante, by Puccini for his opera *Gianni Schicchi*, the lawyer uses mimicry to deceive those who would contest a will in order to protect an estate that is comprised largely of ill-gotten gains.

Gustave Doré. The Suicides. In this Waste Forest of despair, the figures appear to have undergone a kind of Ovidian transformation that almost outweighs the horror of their actions and their unfortunate decisions.

But the worst of all crimes in the Dantean universe is the crime of betrayal. Dante may have been sounding a note against those who betrayed him, or perhaps he was simply taking up the great Platonic message that one should put friendship, honesty, and trust above all other virtues. In the Ninth Circle of hell, Dante places the greatest traitors of all time—Judas, who betrayed Christ, and Brutus and Cassius, who betrayed Julius Caesar. Dante offers an indictment of what he perceives to be the worst sin that humankind can commit by bringing the Classical and the Christian worlds together in a single image of despair and rage. The suggestion here is that the world operates on faith, and not just religious faith, but also the premise of trust between individuals. He sees that the whole basis for our culture, whether in literature or in society, is the need for individuals to cooperate with each other and learn from one another. When the sufferers in the *Inferno* offer up their own sad tales, they are presenting their stories as confessions, as statements of experience that might, one would hope, point the way toward a better realization of what humankind can be.

As Dante and Virgil emerge from this chilling and mind-boggling spectacle of human depravity, having witnessed the myriad weaknesses that riddle the human condition, readers might not be surprised if Dante contemplated the option of despairing and abandoning his journey. But as was prophesied to him, and as

he saw as he entered the gates of the land of the tormented, paradise, the vision of what is possible, lies off in the distance. Dante's decision to emerge and continue on his journey is an act of faith. He concludes the final Canto of the *Inferno* with his ascent back into the world of daylight and reason:

> *By that hid way my guide and I withal*
> *Back to the lit world from the darkened dens*
> *Toiled upward, caring for no rest at all,*
>
> *He first, I following; till my straining sense*
> *Glimpsed the bright burden of the heavenly cars*
> *Through a round hole; by this we climbed, and thence*
> *Came forth, to look once more upon the stars.*

The stars represent not just hope but God's constancy. They are a relieving and comforting image because they reassure Dante that there is still order in the universe and virtue in his journey. At the conclusion of Chaucer's *Canterbury Tales*, as the Parson completes his sermon on a vision of the New Jerusalem and the pilgrim band emerges from the labyrinth of Blean Wood just to the west of the English pilgrimage town, Chaucer pays a small tribute to Dante and notes that the stars are rising over the holy city. The point of a long and arduous journey, as both Dante and Chaucer tell us, is not merely to return home, but to realize a vision of something that one would not have thought possible at the outset. And if the path of a particular story might seem well travelled, it is because authors are continually seeking forms through which they can work their way toward a vision of reassurance in the order and beauty of the universe.

Jean Baptiste Carpeaux. Ugolino and His Sons. The unfortunate Ugolino, locked in the tower with his sons, weighs the fateful decision to consume his young. Dante uses the story not only to terrify his readers but to show the consequences of misguided beliefs.

Having witnessed the worst possible conditions of the human spirit, Dante is able to appreciate and understand what it means to strive for the highest state a human being can attain. It is almost as if the trip to hell clarifies for him the meaning of heaven. His determination to press on with his trek demonstrates courage, or perhaps simply the need to find and understand that comic resolution that faith would have one believe in. It would seem, as Dante suggests, that the need to love not only drives life but is its goal. In his beloved, Beatrice, Dante found both a symbol for and a personification of all that mankind might hope for in a complex universe. And if the journey itself is a metaphor for life, then the process of staying the course and living by the rules, if only to discover what one can learn or how it all works out, is worth more than the worst hell of it.

10

WHAT'S LOVE
GOT TO DO WITH IT?

Dante's *La Vita Nuova* and William Shakespeare's *Sonnets*

A T the start of the Middle Ages, the cathedral of Chartres in France was famous for having in its keep one of the most sacred relics in Christendom: the veil of the Virgin Mary. When a disastrous fire in 1194 destroyed all but the west front of the Romanesque church, a miracle happened that sent shock waves through European culture and resulted in a new way of looking at women. Sifting through the ashes, the townspeople found the veil intact. To them, it was a sign from heaven that God wanted the cathedral rebuilt and that the Virgin, the mother of Christ, was taking an active role in the affairs of the world. People believed that she wanted to speak to humankind and offer civilization the message of her sorrow, her patience, her beauty, and her love of humanity.

As news of the miracle spread throughout Europe, the Virgin Mary became the center of a developing aspect of Christianity: the cult of the Virgin. Within a decade of the fire, peasants flocked to Chartres from all over Europe, carrying large blocks of stone for the reconstruction of the place that would house her veil. Liturgies all over France were reworked to include hymns of praise to the Virgin. It is hard to comprehend today just how broad this fervor was, but it transformed the church. Suddenly, the stern figure of Christ the Judge, which had adorned the portals of so many sanctuaries, took second place to the figure of a young mother holding her tiny child, the future of the world in her arms.

As artisans crafted statues of the Madonna, according to how they pictured the attributes of the most beautiful woman who ever existed, so writers worked to glorify the mother of Christ. Literary versions of her life became best-sellers. The Virgin Mary was seen as a mother who suffered terribly when she witnessed the death of her beloved son on the Cross at Golgotha. In what became one of the most famous hymns of the thirteenth century, "Stabat mater dolorosa," a lyric that was eventually put to a stirring setting by the composer Rossini, the suffering of the Virgin Mary is chronicled by an anonymous Franciscan monk:

There stood the Mother deeply sorrowing
At the Cross-side, tears outpouring
As they hanged her Son, her Christ;
How her heart was gravely groaning,
Wracked with pain and full of moaning
As the swords inside her sliced.

The poem speaks of the terrible suffering that the Virgin must have experienced as she watched her oldest son die a terrible death. The writer wonders just what she was feeling, and offers to interject himself into her situation in order to share and ease her pangs.

The identification of the Virgin with humanity, both as an intercessor saint and as a mortal who was chosen to bear a divine child, lay at the core of the early Virgin hymns. Soon the idea of shared suffering became a matter of praising this exceptional mortal, as in the Middle English poem *I Singe of a Maiden*:

I singe of a Maiden
That is makeless;
King of all kinges
To hir Sone she ches.

He cam all so stille
Ther his Moder was,
As dew in Aperille
That falleth on the grass.

He cam all so stille
To his Modres bour,
As dew in Aperille
That falleth on the flour.

He came all so stille
Ther his Moder lay,
As dew in Aperille
That falleth on the spray.

Moder and maiden
Was nevere non but she,
Well may swich a lady
Goddes Moder be.

In the hands of medieval poets, particularly the English ones, the Virgin Mary was not only a *cause célèbre* but a reason for humankind to endure the challenges and problems of a fallen world. She was so special that she made even death and the hardships of the earth seem worthwhile. In one of the most famous medieval English lyrics, *Adam lay yboundin*, which we first visited in chapter 1, Adam is thanked indirectly for his sinful fall from paradise because his misdemeanor enabled the world to know the beauty and grace of the Virgin Mary: "Ne hadde the appil taken ben, the appil taken ben," the poet wrote, "Ne hadde never our Lady a ben hevene quen."

Twisted logic aside, the impact of the Virgin Mary upon the collective psyche of Europe was enormous. She was a breath of fresh air to the Christian mythos that was struggling to fill the vacuum caused by the loss of earlier pagan mother-figure cults. She brought to Christianity a wonderful sense of motherly comfort and understanding that had been absent in its early stern, paternalistic structure.

Soon, just about every church in Europe had a minstrel/wordsmith on hand to write hymns for special occasions when it was deemed necessary to invoke the benevolence of the Virgin. Taking some broad hints from the songs of praise that the lover sings to her beloved in the Song of Solomon, these minstrels usually described the Virgin Mary from her head down to her waist, with specific attention paid to her facial features, and from her toes up to the tops of her legs. This practice of describing the beloved codified the process of singing the praises of a woman. The point was to glorify her beauty by identifying her most stunning attributes—an approach that is still present in contemporary songs when a male singer talks about a woman's eyes or lips or hair.

The cult of the Virgin resulted in a whole new way of looking at women; if hymns were effective in celebrating and pleasing the Mother of God, it followed that the same method could be used to catch the attention of a mortal maiden. Within a century of the rebuilding of Chartres, and especially throughout the south of France in the Provençal region, the inheritors of those early minstrels were performing for secular purposes, their talents most often employed by young courtiers who wanted to make good marriages or improve their extra-curricular relationships, in the same manner that Ovid had offered advice to his readers on matters of love in the *Ars Amatoria*.

Love at the courts, as Andreas Capellanus suggested in *The Art of Courtly Love,* had to be codified, highly stylized, and extremely secretive to avoid discovery and scandal. After all, reputations were at stake. However, the writers also realized that the process of wooing and winning a young woman's hand was not so much a matter of singing her praises and celebrating her virtues as it was of convincing her of the importance of a relationship. This posed certain difficulties since, as a rhetorical structure, the lyric simply did not measure up to the challenge of presenting both a problem and a solution; the lyric was meant for celebration rather than persuasion.

Toward the latter part of the thirteenth century, the Italians arrived at a poetic solution to the problem. They constructed a fourteen-line poetic form that was brief enough to make an emotional impact through the power of reason, persuasive enough to examine an issue with logic and intelligence, and lyrical enough to suggest the hint of song through a statement that was intended to be spoken rather than sung. The form itself, at least as it was devised by its early Italian practitioners, had a rhyme scheme that approximated song: *abbaabba cdecde*. The English language, however, has problems sustaining a rhyme for more than three words—four pushes the limits of what the language can do. So instead of following this pattern, the English poets who toured Italy as part of their education returned to their court with the best of Italian poetics firmly in their command and created a rhyme scheme that would function within the range of their own language: *ababcdcdefefgg*, with the final pair forming a couplet to drive home the poem's conclusion by creating an echo effect.

The new poetic form was the *sonnet*. Its brevity allowed it to be written on a small scrap of paper and slipped, surreptitiously and beyond the sight of prying eyes, into the hand of the beloved at a court function. Like the *samizdadt* editions of the twentieth century, which sought to keep free literary expression alive during horrible totalitarian regimes, the sonnet was a secretive, personal, and private way of saying things that others ought to hear but could not, for reasons of social and political decorum. Rather than being a song in the stillness of a summer night, the sonnet was a whisper of meditation, a passing thought in the continuous stream of argument and consideration that underlies the rational world. The word *sonnet* was derived from the Italian notion for sound, *sonnetta*, an origin that underpins the very spoken nature of the form. The point behind the sonnet was that the reader could hear the persona reasoning out loud, though in a private and reflective matter. Rather than song, the intent was argument. The first eight lines, or *octave*, were designed to present a problem, to study the ramifications of a situation from as many angles and ideas as possible. The remaining six lines of the sonnet, or *sestet*, were meant to convey the solution.

One of the most famous sonnets, William Shakespeare's *Sonnet 18*, follows the octave/sestet model:

Shall I compare thee to a summer's day?
Thou art more lovely and more temperate:
Rough winds do shake the darling buds of May,
And summer's lease hath all too short a date:
Sometimes too hot the eye of heaven shines,
And often is his gold complexion dimmed;
And every fair from fair sometime declines,
By chance or nature's changing course untrimmed;
But thy eternal summer shall not fade
Nor lose possession of that fair thou ow'st,
Nor shall Death brag thou wander'st in his shade
When in eternal lines to time thou grow'st;
  So long as men can breathe or eyes can see,
  So long lives this, and this gives life to thee.

In the first line, the persona is confronted with a problem: how can he compare someone to a summer's day, especially if, as he suggests in the second line, the person who is the object of the comparison is so much more lovely? Love poetry, it must be remembered, is praise based on the flattery of comparison. On the surface, the comparison in *Sonnet 18* seems flattering and apt. But as the sonneteer puts the question to the test, he realizes that even a summer's day can be problematic: on such a day the weather can be too hot or it can be overcast, cloudy, and gray. The other problem with a summer's day is that it is temporal. It soon fades away, taking with it all its beauty and turning abundance into decay. Nature's course, the poet realizes, is the pursuit of entropy, not the lasting monument to beauty that surface appearances would have us believe.

But despite all the problems of the octave, the persona believes, with a certain cockiness that is suggested by the voice, that he has the solution. The sestet opens with the announcement, in line 9, "But thy eternal summer shall not fade." The persona proves that by putting the good qualities of the person he admires into the immutable form of a poem, he will protect those elements worth praising from the ravages of time. He concludes, "So long lives this, and this gives life to thee," because the person to whom the poem is addressed will "grow'st" in "eternal lines to time." What occurs in *Sonnet 18* is more than just the presentation of a problem and its solution: what Shakespeare is arguing through the stasis of the lines and the words, through the Edenic present of the text itself, and through the constant recognition that the beauty of every summer is repeated each year, is that poetry is a place where there is no time. If he can record his beloved's attributes in the context of verse, then those attributes, the very core of the individual's personality, will become immortal.

The recognition that poetry has the power to immortalize its subject, if only because the printed words of a poem tend to outlast those things that they describe, is one of the fascinating ideas that lies at the heart of literature. No matter what happens in the world outside the cover of a book or beyond the margins of a printed page, the page or the book itself does not change. Poetry, the literary genre most suited to praise, has always been recognized as a

Unknown. Allegorical Portrait of Dante. Dante holds open the pages of Canto XXV of the Paradiso, *in which he laments that his great talents as a poet and scholar have been all but ignored by his native city. In the distance, Paradise sits atop Mount Purgatory, surrounded by a ring of fire. Perhaps no man is a prophet in his own times.*

way of making important events, such as the founding of home-
lands or the eruption of cataclysmic wars, endure in the cultural
continuum. And if works such as the Song of Solomon in the Bible
taught both readers and writers that the means of celebrating love
lay in the poetic medium of praise, then poetry is the literary genre
associated most often with the relationship between the lover and
the person or thing he or she loves. The idea that poetry is the
primary vehicle for expressing love has been ingrained on our
cultural psyches. It is the reason greeting cards are frequently written in poetry, why even toddlers exchange Valentines bearing cute
little rhymes that suggest feelings they cannot possibly have, and
why ditties such as "Roses are red, Violets are blue" play such an
important role in the way we express our affection for one another.

Dante was an early advocate of the belief that love was something that found its best literary expression through the art of
poetry. In *La Vita Nuova* he sought to show his readers the

connection between what one feels and how one expresses that feeling in literature. The work itself is essentially a creative-writing handbook, a guide in which he intersperses his poems with biographical reflections on his own experience. It is a unique and rare glimpse behind the scenes of a literary work, where an author explains why he has made certain choices and what events or ideas triggered certain works. Dante wants his readers to enter his poems, and he is willing to allow his private nature a public airing in order to instruct his readers on how they might write poems themselves.

The poems in *La Vita Nuova* take three forms: sonnets, which Dante uses to explore the philosophical and intellectual ramifications of his feelings; songs, or *canzones*, which are reflections that commemorate, in elevated language and tone, key moments of perception for him; and ballads, which are celebratory songs about his lady. In between the poems, however, Dante has written prose that almost follows the scholastic model of Saint Augustine's *Confessions*. In these prose interludes, essentially introductions to each poem, Dante provides a biographical commentary in which he examines his feelings about love, as well as passages of exegesis that offer technical explanations for what he is doing. By attempting to define the relationship between literature and life, Dante creates a work that is a cross between Aristotle's *Poetics* and Saint Augustine's autobiographical introduction to the book of Genesis. Although Dante intended the poems to be the key features of the work, it is in fact the biographical writing for which *La Vita Nuova* is best remembered, simply because that portion of the book offers a rare glimpse inside the life of a poet who did so much to evolve and broaden the scope of literature.

As a creative-writing handbook—one of Dante's key reasons for crafting *La Vita Nuova*—the book attempts to show the pragmatic underpinnings of the sonnet form. Sonnets, he believed, were rational responses to those aspects of one's emotional life that could not otherwise be fathomed. In the tradition of early Italian sonneteers, Dante recorded his reflections on love, its problems, and its challenges in a series of poems that he circulated among his closest friends. The poems were his observations on a difficult situation: he loved a woman he could never have. Writing poetry was his way of understanding the relationship between his emotions and the social constraints that society imposed upon him.

The poems were also Dante's attempt to put his memory in order. Like Saint Augustine, who believed that memory was the repository of the divine and a means to understanding the glory of God, Dante saw memory as a book, a place where the past never changed and to which one could return to relive life with those who had been lost. Dante believed that, through poetry, he could regain the world that continually retreated before him and infuse his personal past with a "new life." In this new life, those individuals who were most precious to him would be his guides. If the world around him seemed a loveless place, the world of the memory—that avenue to God and the divine kingdom—would be governed by love.

Dante opens *La Vita Nuova* in much the same thematic fashion that Saint Augustine opens the *Confessions*:

> In the book of my memory, after the first pages, which are almost blank, there is a section headed Incipit vita nova (here begins the period of my boyhood).

Using Saint Augustine's *Confessions* as his model for an autobiographical statement, Dante came to realize that his response to life was not so much an admission of his sinfulness as it was an opportunity to praise God for the glory of his creation and for the moments in Dante's life when he was able to experience divine love. Where Saint Augustine's defining childhood moment is the theft of the apple from the orchard, a moment that casts him in the role of the sinner, Dante's defining pre-pubescent moment comes when he first lays eyes on Beatrice Portinari, the daughter of a Florentine merchant. Dante fell in love with Beatrice instantly. However, in the words of the twentieth-century novelist Graham Greene in a story of childhood infatuation, "The Innocent," such premature experiences have a "terrible inevitability of separation because there *can* be no satisfaction."

Dante first saw Beatrice crossing a square in Florence. He was nine years old at the time, and she slightly younger:

Nine times the heaven of the light had revolved in its own movement since my birth and had almost returned to the same point when the woman whom my mind beholds in glory first appeared before my eyes. She was called Beatrice by many who did not know what it meant to call her this. She had lived in this world for the length of time in which the heaven of the fixed stars had circled one twelfth of a degree toward the East. Thus she had not long passed the beginning of her ninth year when she appeared to me and I was almost at the end of mine when I beheld her.

For Dante, Beatrice is the embodiment of all good. Their lives, intertwined because of the way he perceives her, are not measured in earthly years but by celestial movements, as if to suggest that heaven itself has ordained their existences, moving the planets to create the sort of sign that is suggested in Genesis of the Bible. Dante would have us believe that in every possible way, this is a relationship that has been preordained as a miraculous event that glorifies Beatrice as the saint-redeemer who has come to lead him to the "new life" beyond this realm.

Gustave Doré. Beatrice. As with Shakespeare, there are no reliable likenesses of Beatrice. Suffice to say that she provides that structure of beauty into which any artist or poet might pour the features of his own beloved.

Dante's beatification of Beatrice is based on a number of ideas. He reads her name, Beatrice, both as a divine pun and as a signal of godly numerology. The first syllable, "Bea," means good or holy. The second syllable, "trice," means thrice, so she is "thrice good," an embodiment of the holy Trinity in name. The first three letters, when multiplied by the number three (thrice times b-e-a), equal the number nine (or the holy number of three multiplied by three). Dante meets her in his ninth year. All of this, he feels, is part of her beauty and the attraction she holds for him. She is not merely a human but a heavenly exemplar of goodness, beauty, and grace.

Had Dante actually succeeded in wooing her, it is doubtful that Beatrice would have achieved the divine status that he bestows upon her. The very fact that she was unattainable, that Dante could not express his feelings directly to her, is part of what makes her holy. In Beatrice, Dante creates a character who is more than the rose at the center of the *hortus conclusus* in the romances and more than Don Quixote's object of courtly love. She is also more than a Heliconian Muse who inspires his poetry, though she does serve that purpose as the object of his highest desires and as the subject matter for his sonnets and songs. But in addition, she is a moral guide, in the same way that Virgil is Dante's moral guide in the *Inferno*. When it comes time in *The Divine Comedy* for the Roman poet to take leave of his follower, it is Beatrice who greets the celestial traveler and acts as his tour guide through the crystal spheres of the kingdom of heaven.

Events in the conscious world kept Dante from fully realizing and expressing his love for Beatrice, but the unconscious world was the servant of his desires. Like many of the dreamer protagonists of romances such as *Le Roman de la Rose* or medieval allegorical poems such as Chaucer's *House of Fame* or Langland's *Piers Plowman*, Dante is able to encounter Beatrice more directly through the medium of dreams. In Section III of *La Vita Nuova*, Dante describes a dream that reflects the reality of his first glimpse of Beatrice. When he sees her for the first time, she is clothed in a crimson dress. When he first dreams of her, she is draped in a crimson robe:

> As I thought of her I fell asleep and a marvellous vision appeared to me. In my room I seemed to see a cloud the colour of fire, and in the cloud a lordly figure, frightening to behold, yet in himself, it seemed to me, he was filled with a marvellous joy. He said many things, of which I understood only a few; among them were the words Ego dominus tuus [I am your Master]. In his arms I seemed to see a naked figure sleeping, wrapped lightly in a crimson cloth. Gazing intently I saw it was she who had bestowed her greeting on me earlier that day. In one hand the standing figure held a fiery object, and he seemed to say, Vide core tuum [Behold your heart].

Rather than inspiring erotic notions in Dante, the appearance of Beatrice in his dreams, or even in public, fills him with feelings of divine love. She is more a medium for the expression of high values and moral goals than a sexual object. In Section XI, Dante explains that whenever she appeared before him in public, he was filled with a "flame of charity which moved me to forgive all who had ever injured me." For him, Beatrice is a saintly presence, a moral guide who sets the tone for the remainder of his imaginative life:

> When she was on the point of bestowing her greeting, a spirit of love, destroying all the other spirits of the senses, drove away the frail spirits of vision and said: "Go and pay homage to your lady"; and Love himself remained in their place.

Beatrice's love, as Dante perceives it, is *agape* or godly love, rather than *eros* or physical love. As a moral being who expresses that love through his sonnets or songs, Dante realizes that his beloved is a guide for him. Although the real Beatrice Portinari probably had no notion that such an amount of meaning had been read into her being, she is, for Dante, the embodiment of the moral universe. In order to express his love for her, Dante sets himself, like Sir Galahad, upon a quest for spiritual purity, the goal of which is achieving the divine love of God that can be bestowed upon him only through his desire for Beatrice.

Beatrice even provides the inspiration for *The Divine Comedy*, at least according to what Dante has to say in Sections XLI and XLII of *La Vita Nuova*. In Section XLI, he presents a sonnet that he is moved to write upon learning of her death:

> *Beyond the widest of the circling spheres*
> *A sigh which leaves my heart aspires to move.*
> *A new celestial influence which Love*
> *Bestows on it by virtue of his tears*
> *Impels it ever upwards. As it nears*
> *Its goal of longing in the realms above*
> *The pilgrim spirit sees a vision of*
> *A soul in glory whom the host reveres.*
> *Gazing at her, it speaks of what it sees*
> *In subtle words I do not comprehend*
> *Within my heart forlorn which bids it tell.*
> *That noble one is named, I apprehend,*
> *For frequently it mentions Beatrice;*
> *This much, beloved ladies, I know well.*

The vision of Beatrice ascending into heaven, wrapped in divine glory, is too much for him. He's overcome, not only by grief but by the overwhelming moment of anagogic perception that his dream expresses to him, and he vows not to speak of her in poetry until he has the means to do it in a grand fashion befitting the highest principles of the art. If she is to be near God and he is to speak of her, he resolves to do it only in a form that is divine:

> After this sonnet there appeared to me a marvellous vision in
> which I saw things which made me decide to write no more of
> this blessed one until I could do so more worthily. And to this
> end I apply myself as much as I can, as she indeed knows. Thus,
> if it shall please Him by whom all things live that my life
> continue for a few years, I hope to compose concerning her
> what has never been written in rhyme of any woman. And then

may it please Him who is the Lord of courtesy that my soul may go to see the glory of my lady, that is of the blessed Beatrice, who now in glory beholds the face of Him qui est per omnia secula benedictus (who is blessed forever).

It is at this moment in *La Vita Nuova* that Dante resolves to write *The Divine Comedy*. Rather than grieve over the death of Beatrice, he chooses to replace the elegiac with the comedic—in other words, he decides that, in his mind and in his memory and ultimately in his poetry, Beatrice must continue to live and speak to him as if she were alive.

The paradox at work in *La Vita Nuova* is that Dante could not bring himself to declare his love for Beatrice during her lifetime. She made an arranged marriage at a young age and eventually died in childbirth. What is even more piteous, perhaps as piteous as the sight of a young boy at a junior high school dance who cannot ask the girl of his dreams to dance with him, is that life afforded Dante a series of opportunities to speak directly to Beatrice and he simply blew them. He is asked by one of his friends in Section XVII of *La Vita Nuova*: "What is the point of your love for your lady since you are unable to endure her presence?" Indeed, Dante was almost apoplectic whenever Beatrice appeared. She seems to have sensed that the young Alighieri may have been attracted to her, but his paralytic fear of confronting her in anything but the peaceable distance of the memory or the page continually got the better of him. In a scene that Shakespeare replays in Act I of *Romeo and Juliet* (where Mercutio and Romeo slip uninvited into a party so that Romeo can glimpse Rosaline, his beloved of the moment), Dante and a group of friends appeared uninvited at a party where Beatrice was in attendance. He narrates his response to the situation:

I felt the beginning of an extraordinary throbbing on the left side of my breast which immediately spread to all parts of my body. Then, pretending nothing was wrong, I leaned for support against a fresco painted in a frieze round the walls of the house. Afraid that other people might notice how I was trembling, I raised my eyes and as they rested on the women gathered there I saw among them the most gracious Beatrice.

> Then my spirits were so routed by the power which Love
> acquired on finding himself so close to this most gracious being
> that none survived except the spirits of vision; and even they
> were driven from their organs because Love himself desired to
> occupy their noble place in order to behold her who inspired
> such wonder.

In a moment of absolute adolescent panic, with his heart pounding
and his palms sweating, Dante freezes. He is mocked by a group of
women at the party, including Beatrice, for his gawking, his trembling, and the seizure of his wits. Dante remarks that the whole
episode was the result of having "set foot in that part of life beyond
which one cannot go with any hope of returning." When he
confronts the living Beatrice, he is struck dumb because, even at
that young age, Dante understood the nature and the power of
love.

In Section XXV of *La Vita Nuova*, Dante defines what he
perceives to be the nature of love. It is partly a traditional reading
of the subject and partly a subjective response to the frustrating
circumstances of his own life. For him, love is an "accident in
substance," not merely a thing or a moment but the result of living
one's life and hoping for the best in all things. Like other medieval
writers, Dante viewed love as a personification. In Dante's case,
Love is a man who directs his heart toward Beatrice. But Dante
also sees love as an emotional expression that is communicated in
the language of his age—whether it is a feeling or an abstraction,
it is something that speaks through where he is and what he is. By
locating Love as a question of language, Dante raises an important
issue. He explains:

> ...in ancient times the theme of love was not taken as a subject
> for verses in the vernacular but there were authors who wrote on
> love, namely, certain poets who composed in Latin [perhaps
> Ovid is who he has in mind here]; this means that among us
> (and no doubt it happened and still happens in other countries,
> as in Greece) those who wrote of love were not vernacular but
> learned poets. It is not many years ago since the first vernacular
> poets appeared. I say poets because composing rhymes in the

vernacular is not so different from writing verses in Latin, due proportion being borne in mind.

What Dante is addressing here is the emergence of national languages as a medium for poetry. From his vantage point in the late Middle Ages, Dante was writing in a world where the governing language of learning and literature was still Latin. However, Latin was, day by day, becoming more and more a remote, specialized language of either the church liturgy or scholarship. It certainly was not a personal language, a tongue in which one could converse either with one's private thoughts or with the object of one's affections. The Italian language, a tongue that had been considered too commonplace and vulgar for the high art of poetry only 150 years before Dante's birth, was now being used to express everything. Dante, like his contemporaries, seized upon the opportunity to use a language that remained relatively unexplored to create not only new poems, but an entirely new literature. The new life that Dante alludes to in his title is more than just the life of love; it is the expression of a new literature that would speak not just to clerics and scholars but to the people of his nation. And if he found confidence by either expressing his personal reflections on love or finding the kingdom of God through the guidance of an Italian-speaking woman in an Italian-language poem, then perhaps the entire nation could recognize endless possibilities in the expression of its own national understanding of things.

At the heart of Dante's belief in his native tongue (the "vulgar tongue" that he perceived as an untried instrument of incredible beauty and power in his treatise *De Eloquentia Vulgaria* or "On the Eloquence of the Vulgar Tongue") lies the realization that national destiny was tied to language. If Italy or even his native city of Florence were to be reborn, he had to speak to his own people directly in their own tongue. Dante was a morning star of the concept of national literature, as well as a herald of nationalism and linguistic determination that would shape not only the Reformation but the course of nineteenth- and twentieth-century history. By writing love poems in their own languages, and by declaring to the world that national tongues defined not only the individual but the borders of a continent, Dante and his contemporaries redrew the map of Europe.

By the time the Renaissance reached its full height in the courts of northern European nations, the sonnet had blossomed into one of the key practices of contemporary poetry. As nations began developing and enlarging their literary canons in their own "vulgar" tongues, the sonnet was recognized as a refined expression that balanced both emotion and consideration, the hallmark of young Aeneas-type courtiers who, for want of a better quest, made love into a courtly game. The form also became appreciated for its intellectual content. After all, the octave and the sestet, the idea of a cause-and-effect relationship at work in the emotions, appealed to a society that was inching its way toward the scientific revolution, where, eventually, the entire system of nature would be explained in the consequential rhetoric of physical laws.

Because Italy, the center of Europe's wool-dying industry, was the hub of fashion as early as Dante's time, the more fashionable aspects of Italian culture also spread throughout the rest of the continent. Dante's successors, such as the energetic Petrarch, were known for their poetry as well as for their scholarship and their dissemination of great ideas through the revival of lost books. Like Dante, Petrarch undertook the the task of chronicling the adoration of his beloved, a woman named Laura, and in a series of remarkable sonnets and *canzone*, raised her to a level just short of the beatification that Dante had bestowed on Beatrice.

The mark of a genuine gentleman in the Renaissance was not merely the length of his sleeves or the cut of his cloth but his ability to express himself eloquently both on and off the page. One of the mandatory means of expression was the ability to write intelligent and well-crafted poetry. While the rest of Europe was struggling to evolve poetic forms that would convey all the grace, elegance, and eloquence of refined, mannered society, the Italians had perfected the notion of metrical verse.

What the Italians recognized was that in spoken language, there were certain syllables that were pronounced more heavily than others. When the words were arranged in the right order, these weighted and unweighted syllables gave a poetic line a rhythm and a regular beat. Suddenly, prosody—meter, rhyme, and verse form—became fashionable. So appealing to the ear was this revival of traditional poetics—a notion that went all the way back to Homeric poetry but that had been lost to the alliterative traditions of northern Europe—that the smart poets at courts such as that of Richard II of England began to write in that manner.

One of the poets in that court in the late fourteenth century, a young diplomat named Geoffrey Chaucer, spent some extra time in Italy while on a mission in 1372 and learned just what the Italians had rediscovered. It would not be beyond conjecture to say that English poetry changed forever on an October day in 1372 when both Chaucer and Petrarch were in Padua. Could they have met? The matter is open to speculation. In any case, when Chaucer returned to England the following year, he wrote what is considered the first English *novel*, albeit in metrical verse, *Troilus and Cresseida*. What Chaucer realized when he read Italian poetry was that the English language could not cope with the bevy of rhymes and the long, melodious lines that Petrarch had crafted. English syntax dictated that the natural rhythm of speech was the iambic foot or measure, where each individual unit of pronunciation amounted to a lightly stressed syllable followed by a heavily stressed syllable.

Chaucer also discovered that English syntax dictated that a phrase could last only so long before it required a break, in the form of a comma or a period. This need to break or breathe determined how long a poetic line could continue without leaving the reader gasping for breath at the end of it. Rather than create an eight-foot line as the Italians had done, Chaucer shortened it to five units, a pace that seemed to fit nicely with the sound of his native tongue. In that instant, the iambic pentameter (or "five-foot") line was born, and almost everyone from Shakespeare to Seamus Heaney has used it ever since. It is the natural rhythm for English poetry.

In the 1500s, following a seventy-year disruption caused by the War of the Roses, the English refocused their attentions on courtly culture, and visits to Italy or tours for the education of intelligent young nobles became the order of the day. Courtiers such as Thomas Wyatt and Henry Howard, Earl of Surrey, rediscovered the sonnet and raised the form to a new level of excellence. In 1557, Wyatt's and Surrey's sonnets were gathered by Richard Tottel in a volume titled *Tottel's Miscellany*, a book that served as a landmark in the English canon for the sonnet form. *Tottel's Miscellany* raised the sonnet above the level of private utterance and made it into a public poetic form. Just as readers had overheard Saint Augustine's confessions to his God, so the readers of Tottel's small volume were allowed to listen in on the emotional musings of men who were both poets and key political figures of the time—Surrey for the fact that he was executed on a questionable charge of treason and Wyatt for his role in the life and love affairs of Anne Boleyn.

The tradition of the sonneteer court poet reached its apotheosis through the works of Sir Philip Sidney, a young soldier who seemed to sum up what a courtier should be at the court of Elizabeth I. Sidney produced an eloquent extended series of sonnets, *Astrophel and Stella*, which examined the nature of a love affair and included the famous line, "'Fool,' said my Muse to me, 'look in thy heart and write'." But *Astrophel and Stella* suffers from the same problem as Shakespeare's *Hamlet*: it is a work of literature that debates an issue that can never really be resolved. Sidney asks, should one commit to a life of love or should one remain distant and virtuous? In the end, the character of Astrophel simply abandons his musings because there is no clear-cut solution. *Astrophel*

Unknown. Sir Philip Sidney. The typical courtier with an air of the elegant continental gentleman about him.

and Stella was one of the earliest examples of the *sonnet sequence*, a series of continuous musings that investigates the issue of love. The very nature of the sonnet suggests consideration and meditation on a specific idea. However, as most authors of sonnet sequences discover, although the form appears to sustain a narrative, it carries more philosophy than plot in the individual poems.

The problems inherent in the sonnet sequence are the issues that make William Shakespeare's *Sonnets* so intriguing and so mysterious. As a work of English literature, it remains to this day a mixture of the Gordian knot and the Sphinx's riddle, in that it appears to present a story that teases the reader with questions about who the figures in the poems are, what they are doing, and what the resolution of their dilemma was. As individual poems, the sonnets are linguistically dense, tightly crafted, and often allusive to one another—a fact suggesting that some portions of the 154 sonnets comprising the collection may have been fragments of smaller sequences that Shakespeare wrote and abandoned.

Unknown. William Shakespeare. In truth, we really don't know what Shakespeare looked like. He has been pictured as everything from a red-haired scholar to a dark-haired country squire. In this portrait he is depicted as a dark, brooding bohemian. As is often the case with scholarship, the colder the trails, the hotter the interest.

The publishing history of *The Sonnets* presents even more questions. The poems were likely collected and published without Shakespeare's consent, and they are probably not a reflection of his intent or even a complete collection. According to some early sources, Shakespeare's sonnets were circulated among his friends. By the time he presumably wrote them—between 1593 and 1596, and surely no later than 1609, when they were collected and published by Thomas Thorpe—the sonnet form had already fallen into decline. Life at the court of an aging queen had lost some of its splendor, and Shakespeare was not a courtier but a public poet who made a living speaking in his own language to the masses. The secretive quality of the sonnets somehow made them seem less important in comparison to his other accomplishments.

The poems that Thorpe presents appear to tell a story, though this may not have been the poet's intention. *Sonnets 1 to 126* describe the persona's relationship with a young man. These poems contain advice on matters of love, life, and the lasting importance of friendship—that old Platonic notion—in the face of the mutability and entropy that time inflicts on human beings. In *Sonnets 1 to 17*, the persona addresses the issue of procreation. He tells his young friend that it is important to marry, to have children, and to lead a settled life. *Sonnets 18* to *126* are a series of celebrations of the young man's life, beauty, and future. A competing poet who had vied for the young man's affections in *Sonnets 28* to *38* again rears his head in *Sonnets 79* to *86* and displaces the persona as the focus of youth's literary attentions. With *Sonnet 127*, however, a strange, dark lady, who mingles passion with loathing, enters the picture. She appears to have been the mistress of the persona of the poems, and she is bad news. The young man is warned against her, though he has become ensnared in her clutches. Just when it appears that *The Sonnets* are about to present a resolution to the tangled web of this four-way relationship, the sequence breaks off into two concluding sonnets about Cupid that bear little resemblance, linguistically or thematically, to the other poems in the collection.

There are innumerable theories as to who the supposed characters of *The Sonnets* are. The problem of the dramatis personae is further complicated by the fact that the collection bears a cryptic dedication:

TO THE ONLY BEGETTER OF
THESE ENSUING SONNETS
MR. W.H. ALL HAPPINESS
AND THAT ETERNITY
PROMISED
BY
OUR EVER-LIVING POET
WISHETH
THE WELL-WISHING
ADVENTURE IN
SETTING
FORTH

T. T.

Who was W.H.? Was he Henry Wriothesley, the Earl of Southampton, as some critics suggest? Was he William Herbert, the Earl of Pembroke, as others would maintain? Or was he a friend of Thorpe's, who, as an admirer of Shakespeare's poems, financed the edition but had nothing to do with the poet other than publishing his work? As cryptic as this notice may be, with its use of initials and its allusion to a life journey for the financier of the edition, the truth of the matter is that the characters themselves, if they are indeed characters, have very little to do with the content or the arrangement of the poems. And it is the arrangement of the poems that presents the real, concrete mystery of *The Sonnets*.

A sonnet sequence often takes the shape of an on-going conversation, usually with oneself, as the poet considers and reconsiders his ideas and his situation. But *The Sonnets* seem to represent a portion of a two-way conversation, a debate between two poets competing for the favor of the young man who is addressed in the collection's first phase. Poetic dialogues are not uncommon. In this century, the novelist Muriel Spark evolved one with the poet Howard Sergeant, who was her lover after the Second World War. Spark and Sergeant answered one another's unconscious dreams with poems, and when seen in a sequence, the poems fit together thematically and imagistically. The poems, however, were never published as a dialogue but appeared instead in separate volumes, rearranged by different editors, so that they display little of their original connection. What were interlocking images become merely cryptic statements when the poems are taken out of their original context.

This may be the case with *The Sonnets.*

Sonnet 24 opens with a discussion of how the persona desires to see the world with a painterly eye:

> *Mine eye hath played the painter and hath stelled*
> *Thy beauty's form in table of my heart;*
> *My body is the frame wherein 'tis held,*
> *And perspective it is best painter's art.*
> *For through the painter you must see his skill*
> *To find where your true image pictured lies,*
> *Which in my bosom's shop is hanging still,*
> *That hath his windows glazed with thine eyes.*

The *conceit*, or extended image, is that the persona is a painter who perceives and depicts the young man's virtues. He asks the young man for trust. What follows, from *Sonnet 25* to *Sonnet 28*, is a series of "Slumber" poems that talk of the evening falling, the stars appearing, and the persona resting carefully, safe in the knowledge that he is first in the young man's favor. The well-known and aforementioned *Sonnet 29*, however, is a morning-after statement. In the cold light of day, the persona realizes that he has been—or could be—excluded from his position of prominence with the young man. An emotional exile, the persona considers his situation and concludes that he would give up all the riches in the world and the power of a king if only he could hold on to the friendship of his young friend:

> *When in disgrace with Fortune and men's eyes,*
> *I all alone beweep my outcast state,*
> *And trouble deaf heaven with my bootless cries,*
> *And look upon myself and curse my fate,*
> *Wishing me like to one more rich in hope,*
> *Featured like him, like him with friends possessed,*
> *Desiring this man's art, and that man's scope,*

With what I most enjoy contented least;
Yet in these thoughts myself almost despising,
Haply I think on thee,—and then my state,
Like to the lark at break of day arising
From sullen earth, sings hymns at heaven's gate;
  For thy sweet love remember'd such wealth brings
  That then I scorn to change my state with kings.

The arrangement of the poems then leads the reader through a series of "judgment" sonnets, in which the persona is tried by Fortune (a very Boethian notion), by Memory (*Sonnet 30*'s "When to the sessions of sweet silent thought / I summon up remembrance of things past"), by Love (in *Sonnet 31*), and by Death (in *Sonnet 32*). The legalistic language and imagery of *Sonnet 30*, in particular, with its constant allusions to justice and accounting ("sessions," "summon," "cancelled woe," "expense," "grievances," "sad account," and "I new pay as if not paid before"), suggest that at this point in the story, the persona is undergoing a severe trial.

Suddenly, however, there is the troubling presence of *Sonnet 33*. *Sonnet 33* simply does not fit the sequence. Its opening line, "Full many a glorious morning have I seen," is completely out of sync with the issues that have been discussed in the previous sonnets. The persona is confronted with an image of perspective, of standing atop a mountain and watching the glories of nature with a painterly eye. The question is, where did this new train of thought come from? Is it a return to the conceit of *Sonnet 24*, or is it a response to a completely new issue that may have been raised by a competing poet to whom the sonnets were replies? The drastic shift between *Sonnet 32* and *Sonnet 33*, and the anomaly of the "Cupid" sonnets, suggests several things: the poems in *The Sonnets* are out of order; they are an incomplete selection from several sequences Shakespeare may have written; or the collection is only one half of a much broader picture in which another competing poet, of whom Shakespeare speaks, dictates the course of a "singing match" by shifting topics or raising images to which Shakespeare felt impelled to reply.

All mysteries aside, the sonnets continue to speak eloquently to readers on the theme of how life itself is engaged in an ongoing struggle with time and entropy. Throughout the sequence, the persona perceives time as not only the enemy of youth but the antagonist of life. As the discourses evolve, a philosophy takes shape that declares the purpose of poetry is not merely to celebrate love or to praise the attributes of a beautiful person but to present a means of challenging the course of nature by creating an alternative world where there is no time.

The great battle with time opens in *Sonnet 6*, where the persona warns the young man:

> *Then let not winter's ragged hand deface*
> *In thee thy summer ere thou be distilled:*
> *Make sweet some vial; treasure thou some place*
> *With beauty's treasure ere it be self-killed.*

He concludes the sonnet with the warning that the young man must not himself be "death's conquest and make worms thine heir." There are ways to battle time: procreation, memory, and friendship. In a statement not unlike the famous Latin maxim *Amor vincit omnia*, the persona challenges time in the final lines of *Sonnet 19*: "Yet do thy worst, old Time: despite thy wrong, / My love shall in my verse ever live young."

For Shakespeare, the sonnet was both a vehicle for praise and a defence against time, the force that he believes to be most hateful to the world. He realizes, as he states in *Sonnet 18*, that poetry is a vehicle for timelessness; a single line can capture the essence of a life once lived and preserve it forever in the Edenic present of the literary text. If life on earth is destined to slip away, then it is only through poetry that one can glimpse what eternity and immortality really are.

Just as Dante sought to pursue his heaven through praise for Beatrice, or as the faithful of Europe conveyed the heavy stones to Chartres Cathedral as an act of devotion to the queen of heaven, so Shakespeare realized that there could be an alternative to "nature's changing course." What lies at the root of all these stories is the human need to define what heaven really is, to nurture its design, and to execute the crafting of it while the clock continues to run.

11

WHOSE LIFE IS THIS?

Giorgio Vasari's *Lives of the Artists*

W H E N novelist James Joyce was approached by an admirer who wanted to "kiss the hand that wrote *Ulysses*," he recoiled from the person in shock and dismay. "No," he replied. "It has done other things as well!" The problem is that, as a twentieth-century writer, Joyce lived in an age when the cult of celebrity formed the basis for public approval. If a person is famous, so the cult of celebrity suggests, then that person must be important. The figure at the center of this acclaim is made legendary, often out of all proportion to reality, by the power of good publicity and sound public relations. Stories are spread about celebrities that make them seem unique and beyond the ordinary. They are portrayed as having special gifts—good looks, personal magnetism, charisma—and lifestyles that the rest of us only dream of having. To add to the sense of wonder that surrounds a celebrity, the same system conjures up an air of elusive mystery, be it through the allure of sexiness or the iron gates of a mansion that shut out the rest of the world from the lifestyle of the rich and famous.

In order to promote and market its motion pictures, Hollywood seized upon the apparatus of the cult of personality. The plethora of movie magazines during the twenties, thirties, and forties under-lined the fact that public personalities evolved through elaborate corporate personality-making machines that marketed certain individuals with a fervor that outdistanced even the most arduous of religious frenzies. Modern-day hagiographies evolved around vague notions of glamour. Clara Bow, the "It Girl," and others like her, lay at the heart of these new secular hagiographies.

The key to understanding hagiographies, whether of the religious or the secular kind, is realizing that the allure of the mysterious, the idea of what is special and worthy of attention, speaks volumes about what a society considers most important. The reality is that the cult of celebrity is the voice of a society's dreams. When a society suddenly adopts a figure as the center of attention, it may be because that figure embodies exactly what individuals in that society wish they could become. When celebrities rise to power, they take their fans with them, at least imaginatively, and when they fall, either through stupidity or tragedy, the result is equivalent to the kind of catharsis that Sophocles built into the notion of tragedy. When the crowds gathered for a candle-lit vigil outside the Dakota building in New York the evening after John Lennon was shot, for example, they were gathering to express the kind of grief that is witnessed only in the context of a tragic catharsis.

The star-making machinery of Hollywood, of course, is far from being a twentieth-century phenomenon. In fact, the penchant for portraying real personalities in literary biographies is an old one that has its roots in the studied reading of Roman history that Plutarch provided in his *Makers of Rome*. Plutarch chose to profile the lives of older, legendary figures such as Coriolanus (and his profile then became one of the chief sources for Shakespeare's tragedy *Coriolanus*) and more contemporary figures such as Brutus, Mark Antony, and Julius Caesar. These individuals were all significant because they had shaped the destiny of Rome, by either praiseworthy or nefarious means. The structure of each "life" was simple. Plutarch began by presenting a picture of the person's past, his upbringing, the events that shaped the personality behind the actions. He then went on to show how these individuals had influenced much larger events. But these were not simple curricula vitae; each life was intended to comment on the individual, to show what was important and memorable about that particular personality. Even Plutarch's choice of who to include and who to exclude was a significant comment on the nature of what his own society deemed important—and such judgment a role in shaping a nation. Plutarch's perspective is very Virgilian and very Roman, but it set the standard for the way in which the literary genre of *lives* functions. Throughout literary history, lives act as a barometer for what society considers important, for what a society deems heroic, and for what individuals dream of becoming. Lives serve as as a useful reflection of the values of the world they describe.

The *Legenda Aurea* by Jacobus de Voragine, for instance, tells us that his society considered the acts of the saints, the matter of faith, to be the most important issue. *Foxe's Book of Martyrs*, published in the wake of the turmoil of the English Reformation, during the reign of Mary I, offers testimony to the necessity of standing up for one's beliefs. In John Aubrey's *Brief Lives*, the author chronicles the major figures of the English Renaissance in a strange mixture of politics and culture. His choice of subjects—everyone from Thomas More to Shakespeare—gives a clear picture of what the age of Elizabeth was all about, both spiritually and intellectually. Samuel Johnson implied that poets were the most accomplished and most fascinating individuals that eighteenth-century England had to offer when he penned his *Lives of the Poets*. And when Anna Jameson, the Canadian pioneer traveller and literary socialite, wrote what became a best-seller in Victorian England, it was a book about the lives of the English monarchs, a small testament to the fact that the Victorians valued tradition and class-conscious power above other attributes.

Out of this tradition comes the modern notion of celebrity. When Americans dreamed of the icons of the "everyman," the Gary Coopers and Clark Gables who appeared larger than life on the movie screens of the mid-century, Hollywood easily found the avenue by which social iconography functions and evolved the myth of celebrity from the profession of screen-acting. This tradition comes down to us today in the pages of personality magazines, those glossy gossip rags that favor pictorial representation over written text. This would suggest that we live in a world that has become increasingly more visual and far less print- and idea-oriented—a bathetic cry from the print-based iconography of the intelligentsia that was evident in such early twentieth-century works as Lytton Strachey's *Eminent Victorians* or even John F. Kennedy's *Profiles in Courage*.

Needless to say, when Giorgio Vasari produced his three-volume *Lives of the Artists* in the sixteenth century, the subject matter spoke eloquently to the fact that his society valued a new way of seeing the world that was rapidly transforming the fabric and structure of the European imagination. Vasari also believed that the guides to freedom for his native land, Italy, were a certain group of gifted individuals who could perceive a perfection in both art and nature that the rest of the fallen world was too spiritually impoverished to comprehend. On these individuals, the artists of his time, Vasari conferred the highest recognition possible through the art of a chronicle that was, to some extent, an eye-witness account of an important moment in history.

In his life of Michelangelo, Vasari turned, quite consciously, to the model of *acta sanctori* provided for him by the literature of hagiography. When he writes about Michelangelo's birth, the language and images take on a profound aura of the miraculous. The heavens themselves appear to have conspired to bring Michelangelo to the people of Italy:

> So in the year 1474 in the Casenino, under a fateful and lucky star, the virtuous and noble wife of Lodovico di Leonardo Buonarroti gave birth to a baby son.... The boy was born on Sunday, 6 March, about the eighth hour of the night; and without further thought his father called him Michelangelo, being inspired by heaven and convinced that he saw in him something supernatural and beyond human experience. This was evident in the child's horoscope which showed Mercury and Venus in the house of Jupiter, peaceably disposed; in other words, his mind and hands were destined to fashion sublime and magnificent works of art.

In a society that was looking for miracles, of either the spiritual or the secular kind, the arrival of artists such as Michelangelo made an enormous impact. The artist embodied what Vasari's society wanted: Italians who were challenging the status quo of artistic perception, and by doing so, were making a powerful statement not only about their own individuality but about the distinct nature of their nationality. The artist was a redeemer, artistically and politically, in that he had given expression to something vital about an entire society that had long been repressed by outsiders. By articulating what his society deemed most important, Vasari chronicled a moment in Western history when the nature of perception changed.

Vasari was born in the Tuscan town of Arezzo in 1511, just shortly after the apex of the Italian Renaissance. Professionally, he dedicated his life to art, first as a pupil of such masters as Michelangelo and Andrea del Sarto, and then independently. Although he was an accomplished painter in his own right, it was his interest in writing about the lives and works of other artists that won him fame. The publication of *Vitte de' piu eccellenti pittori, scultori ed architetti* (published in 1550 and enlarged in 1568) garnered Vasari enormous international acclaim as both a scholar of the visual arts and a critic who opened the works of the Italian masters to the imaginations of European readers. So powerful and engaging were his lives of the artists that Italian art became the new standard for taste and culture, along with the measure for material success, wealth, power, and prestige among the competitive courts of northern European monarchs.

If the creative achievements of the individual artists were not enough to capture the reader's imagination, Vasari's near-beatification and fascinating, larger-than-life portrayals surely were. The artist was to Renaissance Italy what the saint had been to England of the Middle Ages or the movie star or sports hero has been to North America in the twentieth century. The impact of these painters on Italian society—and on Italian nationalism—was not lost on Vasari, and he portrayed them as celebrities who talked back to popes, dictated terms to kings, and rose above the realm of mere mortals through the power of their creative gifts and their energetic, individual personalities. These were not mere mortals but supermen who lived above the mundane level of daily life. In his life of "Raphael of Urbino," Vasari writes:

> In short, Raphael lived more like a prince than a painter. The art of painting was supremely fortunate in securing the allegiance of a craftsman who, through his virtues and his genius, exalted it to the very skies. It is fortunate also in having disciples today who follow in the footsteps of Raphael. For he showed them how to live and how to combine virtue and art....

Vasari often tends toward hyperbole in his descriptions of the artists because he is so caught up in the energy and excitement of the milieu of which he was a part. He realized that these artists were not only producing fine pictures, buildings, or sculptures; they were changing the way human beings looked at the world and they were doing it in an Italian manner. What they were evolving was a new national style that set artistic standards for both the visual and

Michelangelo. The Dream of Human Life. This is Michelangelo's heroic idea of the relationship between humankind and divine inspiration. Here, humankind may possess the world, which rests upon a Pandora's box of tragic and comic personas. Hopeful and idealistic, the underlying message is that humankind can improve things.

the written arts. And it was the nature of Italy that made it all happen. In his first preface to *Lives of the Artists*, Vasari shows how the place itself spawned the overthrow of weaker, alien artistic practices that had invaded and corrupted the spirit of his people:

> The men of that time had no experience of anything better than those imperfect productions, which were regarded as great works of art, villainous though they were. And yet, helped by some subtle influence in the very air of Italy, the new generations started to purge their minds of the grossness of the past so successfully that in 1250 heaven took pity on the talented men being born in Tuscany and led them back to the pristine forms.

The year 1250 was a benchmark date that Vasari set for the beginning of what he considered to be the birth of modern painting in Italy. It is conveniently located between the births of the two founding fathers of Italian art, Cimabue and Giotto, at the outset of an era that marked the beginning of the new style. Vasari argues that the old style, a blend of the German Gothic and the remnants of the old Roman expression, was the result of bad design and foreign influences on the otherwise sound and intelligent Italian way of seeing things. Vasari sees the coming of Giotto, in particular, as a moment when the clouds of misperception cleared. That one individual, to Vasari's mind, had the power to alter not only the way art had taught him to see things but the way others would perceive the world through art:

> For after many years during which the methods and outlines of good painting had been buried under the ruins caused by war it was Giotto alone who, by God's favour, rescued and restored the art, even though he was born among those incompetent artists. It was, indeed, a great miracle that in so gross and incompetent an age Giotto could be inspired to such good purpose that by his work he completely restored the art of design.

Vasari believed that what separated the Middle Ages from the Renaissance was the realization that the world could be transformed by a single individual who saw something in a new way and articulated that vision through a work of art. On a grand scale, the Renaissance was about a new way of seeing, and this new way of seeing impacted both the visual arts and literature.

The belief was that Italians had invented not only a new system of perception but also a means of expressing that perception, wherein their ideas could be conveyed to the world with almost the same qualities of clarity, detail, and level-headedness that God had brought to the creation of all things in nature. These artists, according to Vasari, were reflections of God because they seized what nature had given them and improved upon it, thus making a good thing even better. In his preface to *Lives of the Artists*, Vasari draws the parallel between the artist and the Creator:

> I am sure that anyone who considers the question carefully will come to the same conclusions as I have reached above: namely, that the origin of the arts we are discussing was nature itself, and that the first image or model was the beautiful fabric of the world, and that the master who taught us was that divine light infused in us by special grace, which had made us not only superior to the animal creation, but even, if one may say so, like God Himself.

In Boethian terms, the artist recognized that God had made the world in the spirit of goodness, but the world had, alas, fallen with Adam and was a lesser version of what it once had been. It was the duty of the artist to take over from there and improve things through a secondary act of creation, which would bring mankind closer to an understanding of the perfection that had once been part of nature.

On the opening page of *Lives of the Artists*, Vasari explains the relationship between the artist and God:

> Now the material world in which God worked to fashion the first man was a lump of clay. And this was not without reason; for the Divine Architect of time and of nature, being wholly perfect, wanted to show how to create by a process of removing from and adding to material that was imperfect in the same way that good sculptors and painters do when, by adding and taking

away, they bring their rough models and sketches to the final perfection for which they are striving. He gave his model vivid colouring; and later on the same colours, derived from quarries in the earth, were to be used to create all the things that are depicted in paintings.

Of course, God had the power of divinity behind his act of creation, while humankind was at a slight disadvantage because people were, after all, mortal. The way to improve upon the limitations of human capabilities was to improve the way one looked at the world. The miracle of Italian art, Vasari believed, was the divinely inspired gift of a new perception. By turning perception into a science rather than just allowing it to be happenstance, and by realizing that what the hand crafted was a product of what the eye saw, the artists of the Italian Renaissance transformed the very process of seeing.

The trained eye, Vasari believed, was a matter of achieving a moral way of looking at the world, a vision not unlike that which we saw in chapter 8. The artist, like the questing knight, had to possess *virtù*, a balance of goodness and intelligence that would allow the artist to make a kind of moral and intellectual order from his perceptions. *Virtu*, to the Renaissance way of looking at the world, was more than merely "virtue," the pale, twentieth-century anglophone version of the concept that entails goodness. To the Italians of the Quattrocento, it was a type of intelligence that today would commonly be called "smarts." *Virtu* meant that an artist embodied a balanced combination of perception, intelligence, and pragmatic skills that would assist him in translating high ideals into concrete realities.

These skills came into play in a number of different aspects of the artistic process. The first of these aspects was *disegno*. Roughly translated, the word means "design," but in the Renaissance, the concept was more than merely drawing an idea out on paper to see how it might look. Vasari very carefully points out, in the opening passage of his life of Giotto, that that artist's primary contribution to art had been to throw out the awkward and misconceived "design" of the Gothic perception and replace it with a fresh structure that honored both intelligence and nature. *Disegno* was the concept behind the artistic idea, the imaginative structure that embraced more than a mere reflection of nature to the point where, like Dante's texts, an idea could contain various levels of meaning and perception. What the beholder was meant to see in the *disegno* of a work was the brilliance of the idea, the originality of the artist's approach to the subject matter, and the directness and clarity of the planning of a work of art.

The second important element in the scheme of *virtù* was the question of *natura*. When the Renaissance artists looked at the world, they did so, as Shakespeare's Hamlet suggests when he discusses the art of dramaturgy, as if they were holding "as t'were a mirror up to nature." The closer the work of art could come to reflecting that spark of divine creation, the exactness, detail, and vitality that God demonstrated in all natural things, the closer the artist would be to honoring God in the artistic process. Art, the Renaissance painters believed, had to reflect nature. This was not merely an argument for representationalism or even the twentieth-century notion of magic realism, but a perception that art should be an extension of nature, with the elements that comprised the beauty and wonder of the world reworked into a stunning new creation that outlived the constraints of temporality. When Vasari describes that most famous of all Italian Renaissance canvases, the *Mona Lisa*, he takes pains to point out that Leonardo was catching something in nature that no one else could portray:

> If one wanted to see how faithfully art could imitate nature, one could readily perceive it from this head; for here Leonardo subtly reproduced every living detail. The eyes had their natural lustre and moistness, and around them were the lashes and all those rosy and pearly tints that demand the greatest delicacy of execution. The eyebrows were completely natural, growing thickly in one place and lightly in another and following the pores of the skin. The nose was finely painted, with rosy and delicate nostrils as in life. The mouth joined to the flesh-tints of the face by the red of the lips, appeared to be living flesh rather than paint. On looking closely at the pit of her throat one could swear that the pulses were beating. Altogether this picture was painted in a manner to make the most confident artist—no matter who—despair and lose heart.

Leonardo was attempting to do more than merely render a life-like portrait of the Mona Lisa. What the artist was trying to do, just as Shakespeare was attempting in *Sonnet 18*, was to find a way through art to create something that existed beyond the normal bounds of temporality. It is no wonder, therefore, that when Vasari speaks of the artists of his era he does so with a fervent recognition that what they accomplished on canvas or in stone was nothing short of a miracle. These were men who were testing and pushing the accepted boundaries of nature.

Vasari in fact suggests that Michelangelo's creations, especially his sculpture of David, ranked with the miraculous acts of the saints. When a previous artist abandoned a block of marble because he thought it was flawed and beyond use, Michelangelo worked around the flaw in the stone to create a work of art that took on a life of its own:

As I said, the marble had been flawed and distorted by Simone, and in some places Michelangelo could not work it as he wanted; so he allowed some of the original chisel marks made by Simone to remain on the edges of the marble, and these can still be seen today. And all things considered, Michelangelo worked a miracle in restoring life to something that had been left for dead.

If a work of art such as Michelangelo's *David* appeared so realistic that it seemed to breathe, it was a miracle directly attributable to the supernatural skill of the artist. Yet the work of art was also an extension of the personality of the artist. When a Florentine nobleman criticized Michelangelo for making the statue's nose too large for the size of the figure's face, the sculptor responded with a bit of showmanship and pretended to chip away at the statue, letting marble dust fall from his hand without removing a single grain from the work. "Ah, that's much better," said the nobleman. "Now you've brought it to life."

Leonardo da Vinci. Mona Lisa. In order to capture her enigmatic smile, Leonardo hired dancers and musicians to keep the otherwise sulky debutante amused. Napoleon was so enraptured by her smile that he kept the painting in his bedroom.

A work of art, these artists believed, had to convey not only a sense that it reflected nature or was an improvement on nature but also a profound sense of balance and proportion. The art of the late Roman Empire had abandoned the sense of natural proportion that was evident in nature. Vasari loathed the works of what he called the "barbarian" artists, the invaders from northern Europe who had perverted the natural Roman inclination toward balance in all things. In his first preface to *Lives of the Artists*, Vasari noted that "foreign" art was generally poor, and in many ways symptomatic of what was wrong with his beleaguered country:

Such was the condition of the arts of design before, during and after the period when the Lombards ruled Italy as despots. Precious little was done, but the practice of the arts did at least continue, and so did their decline. The work produced could not have been more awkward or more lacking in the qualities of design.

What lies beneath Vasari's observation is the fact that, in his mind at least, design was equated with nationality. The Italian way of doing things had become perverted, and if Italy were to end its misfortunes by throwing off the yoke of foreign domination, it had to do so by reviving the essence of what it meant to be Italian. As Vasari saw it, that essence was a question of a vision that could perceive the world through a balanced and rational eye. The qualities of greatness that Virgil expressed in moral terms were, to Vasari, matters of perception. That perception had been distorted by the Gothic vision. In a Gothic frieze, for example, a general might be depicted with a large head to show his importance; his foot soldiers would have small heads to show that they were of lesser stature. To Vasari, this disproportion was an abomination because the artist was not reflecting nature; he was using a sycophant's criteria based more on abstract notions of power than on what the eye saw. Vasari realized that, starting with Giotto, Italian artists were discovering the verity that lay at the heart of late Hellenistic art.

This pointed him to the third attribute in the schema of *virtù*, which was *decoro*. This word comes down to us in the contemporary idiom as either "decorum," the proper way of doing things, or "decor," a design term applied liberally by interior-decorating magazines that urge home owners to color coordinate their cushions with their sofas. But to Vasari, *decoro* suggested that the eye of the artist, that supreme instrument upon which the Renaissance was founded, was capable of perceiving harmony when the various parts of a work of art were presented together.

What was needed, Vasari and his contemporaries recognized, was a return to the ancient ideas of balance and proportion. When they examined the remnants of the Roman past, they realized that the Romans had had a much different and much keener sense of what was good and what was bad in art:

Before that, during the years after Rome was sacked and devastated and swept away by fire, men had pillars, and carved columns; but until the period we are discussing they had no idea how to use or profit from this fine work. However, the artists who came later, being perfectly able to distinguish between what was good and what was bad, abandoned the old way of doing things and started once again to imitate the works of antiquity as skillfully and carefully as they could.

To Vasari, the ancient works of art, those produced in Greece and Rome in Classical times, were of supreme importance. The Gothic era was the problem because there had been no consensus as to how works of art should be shaped. In Classical art, all aspects of the work functioned together to please the eye of the beholder, making a statement that art itself was a reflection of, if not a metaphor for, a higher system of organization. If *decoro* was exercised, nothing in a work of art would seem out of place and the entire entity would reflect the intelligence and beauty of the principles behind the design, as well as the divine order of nature.

In the process of applying the ideas of *disegno*, *natura*, and *decoro*, the artist was obligated to exercise both moral and intellectual judgment, or *iudizio*. *Iudizio* was more than merely a matter of good taste or doing the right thing in the right place in a work of art. *Iudizio* reflected the notion that the artist had considered all of his options, as was his privilege in a universe that governed by free will, and had chosen righteous vision as the moderating principle behind his work. In his life of Filippo Brunelleschi, Vasari notes that the artist's personality and his artistic vision were essentially one and the same, and his sense of personal good judgment was reflected in what he did:

> Moreover, Filippo was endowed with outstanding personal qualities, including such a kind nature that there was never anyone more gentle or lovable. He was dispassionate in judgement, and he never allowed his own advantage or the interest of his friends to blind him to merit and worth in others. He knew himself, he let others benefit from his success, and he was always ready to help someone in need. He was a forthright enemy of all vice and a friend of the virtuous. He never wasted his time, but was always working to help others, either directly or indirectly; and he would go round on foot visiting his friends and was always ready to serve them.

Artistic judgment, as Vasari attempts to show us, was more than a reflection of artistic intelligence. It was the expression of a type of morality that lay behind the work itself, the belief that art was made not just in the service of the world but in the cause of heaven. It announced to the beholder that the artist was choosing a path of presentation that would lead the viewer closer to an understanding of the wonder of God and the splendor of his creation. As the eleventh-century French Abbot Suger of St. Denis had realized, art was one of the ways in which God spoke to humanity, showing humankind a reality that was far greater than anything the earthly world could offer. The artists that Vasari hailed in his book were instruments of God, archangels of perception who articulated a higher vision to the world through their individual command of artifice.

Although the artists were expressing a higher reality, each had his own way of communicating what he saw. In *Lives of the Artists*, Vasari goes to great lengths to explain how each artist was unique. There is Giotto, the pioneer. Brunelleschi is depicted as a spunky little underdog whose vitality and energy enable him to overcome enormous obstacles. And then there are the later giants, those who appear when the ascendancy of Italian art reaches its apotheosis: Raphael, the angelic young Adonis; Leonardo, the restless intellect; and Michelangelo, the star of the team, who embodies both physical strength and mental finesse. What makes each of these individuals stand out within the pantheon of Italian art, as Vasari points out, is the way in which their personalities were reflected in what they did and how they saw and interpreted the world. This, Vasari recognized, was *maniera*, the idea that each artist has his own style of expression that, like a fingerprint, belongs to no one else. *Maniera* is the mark of individual identity in a work of art, be it the style of a painting or the way in which an author writes. Individuality of perception and skillful execution of a subject lie at the heart of *maniera*, or style. In his preface to Part III of *Lives of the Artists*, Vasari offered an explanation of what he meant by style:

And then the artist achieves the highest perfection of style by copying the most beautiful things in nature and combining the most perfect members, hands, head, torso, and legs, to produce the finest possible figure as a model for use in all his works; this is how he achieves what we know as fine style.

Maniera is the embodiment of the artist's own *disegno, decoro, natura*, and *iudizio*. It is as recognizable to the eye of the beholder as a familiar face is in a crowd.

When style becomes the issue of content, however, we tend to look at a work of art and claim that it is highly mannered, overdone to the point where the form of expression means more than the ideas that are being expressed. Style, however, is one of the first things a reader or a beholder notices about a work of art. When we talk of "style," particularly in relation to a literary text, we are referring to the author's manner of conveying what it is that he or she has to say. Ernest Hemingway, for example, has a completely different style of writing from his American contemporary William Faulkner. The question is, what makes it different? On the level of how the authors express themselves grammatically, the differences in style between Hemingway and Faulkner are enormous. Hemingway's grammatical pattern always returns to his "base" or regular *syntax* (sentence structure), a subject, verb, predicate pattern. Hemingway's prose always appears "terse" because this pattern is the most direct manner of grammatical arrangement in English. The directness of such a structure implies a sense of reportage and factuality that Hemingway emphasized by steering clear of adverbs whenever he could. Faulkner's syntax, on the other hand, usually consists of a sentence that begins with a subordinate clause, followed by an appositive statement or qualifying interruption, followed by a principal clause that contains the subject and the verb, followed by another subordinate clause with yet another appositive statement. This structure of expression, which Faulkner hoped would reflect the workings of the inner narrative of memory, is often labelled "melodious" or "lyrical" because the concepts, even within a single sentence, tend to flow in a continuous stream. Whether on the printed page or on a canvas, style, or *maniera*, is a matter of how the artist approaches the structure of expression.

If the style of a work of art is difficult to interpret, if it seems to keep the beholder or reader at arm's length because it is jarring, remote, or inaccessible, it is, as Vasari suggests, because the artist has not exercised *grazia*, or gracefulness. *Grazia* suggests fluidity, ease, and appropriateness beyond *decoro*. In a work such as Michelangelo's *David* or Leonardo's *Mona Lisa*, *grazia* approximates the animating power of the divine inspiration that created mankind in Genesis 2—that is, it is as if the artist has breathed life into it. It also suggests that the artist has made an attempt to welcome the beholder or the reader by pleasing the eye or the ear with a clarity of expression and an elegance of execution that make the work inviting. But *grazia* goes beyond mere gracefulness of expression. If the way in which the artist has presented his work— the *maniera*, the *disegno*, the *natura*, and the *decoro*—is invisible, if it fails to be the central issue of the work, then the artist has managed to roll all of the Vasarian attributes into one perfect and unified statement, and has achieved the kind of perfection that God brought to his creations.

The artist, Vasari believed, was in possession of all these attributes as a kind of knowledge or understanding of what art must do if it is going to impact the consciousness of a nation or an entire race. The Roman poet Horace in his *Ars Poetica* had claimed that poets were the unacknowledged legislators of the race—a statement that Samuel Johnson wove into his novel, *Rasselas* (as will be discussed in chapter 15), and that Percy Bysshe Shelley claimed as a maxim for all poets in his *Defence of Poetry*. What Horace, Johnson, and Shelley were announcing was that artists have the power to affect their societies through possession of a complete knowledge of art. Artistic expression, they believed, was not enough. The artist had to be someone who understood the whole picture: what he was saying in his particular work of art, how he was doing it, why he was creating his work, and what his creation would ultimately mean in the much broader context of culture. In *Lives of the Artists*, Vasari claimed that the milieu of the times, born from the soil and air of his beloved Italy, was creating a new breed of artists who were known as *cognoscenti*, or those who approached their arts from the most complete sense of knowledge that they could acquire. These artists were professionals who valued what they did and who were working not just from inborn skill but from the knowledge that they were part of a continuum in which one artist passed along his discoveries and ideas to the next, who would then improve upon his inheritance. The goal of this process of learning, improving, and refining was perfection, and Vasari believed that this had been achieved by Michelangelo.

The pursuit of perfection is not an unworthy goal, by any means.

What the Italian Renaissance artists encountered, however, were the problems that ensue from overreaching one's capabilities. Vasari describes Leonardo's attempt to cast a large, bronze equestrian statue only to have the whole process turn into a grand disaster. He sums up the story by quoting Petrarch: "The desire outran the performance." Yet it is from this notion of the pursuit of perfection that Robert Browning (that great observer of Renaissance personalities) drew what has become one of our favorite modern-day maxims: "[A] man's reach should exceed his grasp, / Or what's a heaven for?" Nowhere is this more aptly communicated than in Leonardo's famous Vitruvian Man, the drawing that depicted the fact that a man's reach was usually equivalent to his height. What such perceptions concluded was that human beings were the measure of all things, a notion that lies at the heart of the Renaissance. If the Renaissance achieved anything, it was the realization that the world, at least in terms of perception, was a domain that humans could shape. If the raw materials of nature could be transformed through the power of perception, then, perhaps, so too could the seemingly coincidental course of human events. It was all a matter of how one examined things.

True to the spirit of the Renaissance as an age of "seeing," Niccolò Machiavelli in his dedicatory epistle to *The Prince* explains that politics, especially the tricky question of how Italy can overcome her captors and be restored to greatness, is all a matter of how one perceives things. In a passage that could just as easily have come from Vasari's discussion of perception, Machiavelli strikes a conceit about the view from the mountain top versus the view from the valley:

Nor I hope will it be considered presumptuous for a man of low and humble status to dare discuss and lay down the law about how princes should rule; because, just as men who are sketching the landscape put themselves down in the plain to study the nature of the mountains and the highlands, and to study the low-lying land they put themselves on mountains, so, to comprehend fully the nature of the people, one must be a prince, and to comprehend fully the nature of princes one must be an ordinary citizen.

What Machiavelli learned from the tenor of his times, and especially from what the artists of his time had expressed, was that if one adjusted the framework or structure of one's perception, then the way the world appeared within that system also changed. The great gift of the Renaissance appears to have been the idea that the world is a matter of what one sees and what one makes of it.

What this meant to both contemporary and later writers was that ideas and not institutions shaped the world. Gradually, the process that the Renaissance had begun, a process of allowing individuals to alter their own frameworks of perception in order to express an individual spirit, was translated into Martin Luther's Reformation statement that "Each man meets God on his own terms," and William Blake's decree at the heart of the Romantic era, "I must create a system, or be enslaved by another man's." What Vasari was ultimately articulating was the possibility that systems of thought, systems of perception and interpretation, lay within the scope of the individual personality, and that it was the individual who could and would determine the shape of the world. Although this idea would not be given a complete airing until the late seventeenth century, when it was articulated by John Locke, Vasari nonetheless realized that enlightened individualism lay at the core of his era's mentality.

By defining exactly what it was that his society considered important through the process of writing about artists' lives, Vasari was also subtly suggesting, if not teaching, that each of us could be our own best critics and readers. In *Lives of the Artists*, he presents not merely descriptions of the works or the events behind the works, but the process by which each man became an artist. The reader of *Lives of the Artists* was being asked to form a morality of perception, a system of discernment that would teach one how to approach a work of art and understand the complexities and the beauties of what it had to say.

Even more important, Vasari's ideas about how a painting or sculpture were to be "read" laid a framework for the concept of taste that, by the eighteenth century, operated in the fields of both visual art and literature. Though it is usually consigned to the realm of art history in the contemporary literary canon, *Lives of the Artists* is a work of literature, and an expression of some of the key notions behind the practice of contemporary literary criticism. After all, when we approach a text, we are expected to interpret and understand what we encounter. We are asked to respond to it and decide whether it is good or bad. We judge it in terms of its design, its style, its sense of verity or believability, the ease of the author's expression, and the issue of whether the book meets our expectations in terms of form, genre, and inventiveness. We are constantly being asked to cast an artist's eye on what we encounter, and to fill our minds with as much knowledge as we can so that the next work of art will seem all the more pleasing to us.

Perhaps it comes down to that handful of dust that appeared to fall from David's freshly sculpted nose. The principle of freedom says that everyone is entitled to an opinion, and the more that opinion is informed, the better equipped the individual is to critique the world and maintain that freedom. In other words, everyone's a critic.

12

WHO'S RUNNING
THIS PLACE?

Machiavelli's *The Prince* and More's *Utopia*

I N 1507, when a German cartographer was drawing the first outlines of the New World on a chart that would point navigators through the great unknown to a place that was just taking shape in the minds of Western Europeans, he labeled the recent discovery "America," after the Florentine merchant explorer Amerigo Vespucci. Vespucci, taking a cue from the Renaissance enthusiasm for seeing new things, had already undertaken two voyages to the New World, in 1499 and 1502, on the advice of an acquaintance of his, a Genoan named Columbus, who had sold an expanded vision of the world to the Spanish. Unbeknownst to the German cartographer, who had heard only of Vespucci's adventures, Columbus had been the first to reach the New World in 1492. It was Vespucci, though, who took the honor of having a continent named after him.

The point of this small historical anomaly is that a large portion of the newness of this world resided not in certainties and tangible realities but in a process of discovery that opened a *terra incognita* of dreams and possibilities to the imagination. Into the vacuum, that no-place, that open-ended question, rushed all manner of speculations as to what might exist "out there," beyond the traditional and accepted systems of belief. Perhaps the great beyond to the west of Europe would offer strange worlds that contained the solutions to everyone's problems. Perhaps, just perhaps, things were better somewhere else.

Shakespeare seized upon this notion for his farewell comedy to the theater, *The Tempest* (which we will discuss in the next chapter). *The Tempest*, inspired by early accounts of navigators who reached the island of Bermuda, is a play about speculation, about what might exist in a new world if that world were totally separate from the old one. After the storm that opens the play, when the various groups of characters wash ashore on Prospero's island, a wise old courtier, Gonzalo, speculates openly about what the perfect society in the perfect land might be like:

> *I' th' commonwealth I would by contraries*
> *Execute all things; for no kind of traffic*
> *Would I admit; no name of magistrate;*
> *Letters should not be known; riches, poverty,*
> *And use of service, none; contract, succession,*
> *Bourn, bound of land, tilth, vineyard, none;*
> *No use of metal, corn, or wine, or oil;*
> *No occupation; all men idle, all;*
> *And women too, but innocent and pure;*
> *No sovereignty.*

When another character in the group, Antonio, points out that this perfect society would border on anarchy ("The latter end of his commonwealth forgets the beginning"), reasoning that no perfect society can come from the fabric of a fallen world, Gonzalo replies that his vision of a new world stems from a much more positive view of nature:

> *All things in common nature should produce*
> *Without sweat or endeavour. Treason, felony,*
> *Sword, pike, knife, gun, or need of any engine*
> *Would I not have; but nature should bring forth,*
> *Of its own kind, all foison, all abundance,*
> *To feed my innocent people.*

He concludes by arguing, "I would with all perfection govern, sir, / T'excel the golden age." The vision of the new world that Gonzalo outlines is an amalgam of the Classical notion of Arcadia outlined by Ovid in the *Metamorphoses*, where man lived in harmony with nature during a Golden Age, and the medieval fantasy of the Land of Cockaigne, a place not unlike a contemporary holiday resort, where all things were provided by a beneficent and fruitful nature.

What underpins Gonzalo's picture is the belief that his people are "innocent." In Shakespeare's view, the innocent possess a kind of vision that sees through worldly matters with a clarity and a sanity that is often mistaken for foolishness. When the others in Gonzalo's party mock his ideal society, he thinks nothing of it. His mind is set on opening the world around him to the possibility of something better. When Alonso accuses him of talking of "nothing," Gonzalo responds that the very essence of the ideal is its power to evoke an imaginative vision from nothing.

What Shakespeare is alluding to in Act II, Scene i of *The Tempest* is the concept of utopia that had been outlined by Sir Thomas More in his satirical philosophical dialogue, *Utopia*. More is aware that in *Utopia*, he portrays a place that does not exist; yet the verity and detail with which his protagonist, Raphael Nonsenso, describes that new world make it seem exceedingly real. In his introductory poem to *Utopia*, More explains that the word "utopia" literally means "no place," from the Greek words "u" for "no" and "topos" for place:

> *Noplacia was once my name,*
> *That is, a place where no one goes.*
> *Plato's Republic now I claim*
> *To match and beat at its own game;*
> *For that was just a myth in prose,*
> *But what he wrote of, I became,*
> *Of men, wealth, laws a solid frame,*
> *A place where every wise man goes:*
> *Goplacia is now my name.*

At its root, More's *Utopia* was an in-joke among a group of learned gentlemen, the Humanists, who had carried the message of the Renaissance to Northern Europe, where the arts of literary scholarship were just awakening. More couched his work in the form of a *satire*, a work intended to critique the institutions of a society through the power of humor, and to bring about the reform of those institutions through the force of critical examination. Satire, to our contemporary world, has taken a rather bathetic turn. It is now a means of lampooning politicians or entertaining an audience with weak-minded skits that skirt contemporary issues. But to the Humanists, satire was a serious business. Satire allowed writers such as More or the translator Desiderius Erasmus (who penned a response to *Utopia* titled *Praise of Folly*) the opportunity to say what law and the political correctness of the times would not permit them to express directly.

More's England was a place that faced some serious problems, and More knew just how serious they were. Though he had started out as a simple page in the household of an archbishop, More went on to earn an Oxford education, a job in the foreign service, and a seat in Parliament—all before becoming a protégé of Henry VIII's Cardinal Wolsey, who helped More secure the positions of Speaker of the House of Commons and eventually Lord Chancellor of England. The problems that More faced in England were enormous. Thousands of tenant farmers had been displaced from their traditional lands when powerful landlords evicted them under a series of measures known as the Enclosures. The cities, as a result of this displacement, swelled, crime rates soared, and poverty became a national problem. In a situation that would be repeated in countless North American cities in the late twentieth century, London, in the nascent stages of the Industrial Revolution, was faced with throngs of homeless people in the streets and lacked the wherewithal to remedy the situation. The sudden redistribution of wealth into the hands of a ruling elite, the burgeoning international economy, and the first inklings of a new class of educated bourgeoisie all contributed to a realization that the world was changing.

What changed the most, however, was the fact that when people lived together, they no longer formed just a town or a village but a new concept—society—and that such an aggregate operated by discernible laws and probabilities. The ultimate irony of the age was that the notion of science—the ability to observe humans and nature, to define the laws by which they operated, and to predict what might happen next—gave rise to the possibility that people could tinker with human existence and with nature and shape destiny, society, and the world to their own ends.

In Book I of *Utopia*, the character of More (who is interviewing the rugged and well-traveled mariner Raphael Nonsenso about his journey to Utopia) comments on the theory that society can be shaped by ideas. He resurrects the ghost of Plato's *Republic*, that ancient text that argued society should be run by those who knew what they were doing, that kings should be philosophers and philosophers should be kings:

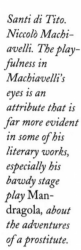

Santi di Tito. Niccolò Machiavelli. The playfulness in Machiavelli's eyes is an attribute that is far more evident in some of his literary works, especially his bawdy stage play Mandragola, *about the adventures of a prostitute.*

> You know what your friend Plato says—that a happy state of society will never be achieved, until philosophers are kings or kings take to studying philosophy. Well, just think how infinitely remote that happy state must remain, if philosophers won't even condescend to give kings a word of advice!

Raphael agrees with More and adds, "If only people in power would listen to them." This may have been a very subtle acknowledgement on More's part that his *Utopia* was, to some degree, a response to a small book that had been written in Italy two years before he began his work in 1516. That book was an attempt by a philosopher to offer advice to a king, or at least a prince, on how to run a state according to the principles of science and logic. The little Italian book, which immediately became a best-seller, scandalized Europe by countering many of the key assumptions by which Christendom operated; it was a slim volume that would shape ideas of nationalism, leadership, and power, and would challenge the notion that Aeneas-like virtue was the key to good government. The book that so troubled More was *The Prince* by an unemployed Florentine statesman named Niccolò Machiavelli.

Having risen in the ranks of the Florentine government as an administrator, Machiavelli received his moment in history when, in 1492, the people of Florence rose up against their princely "dictators," the Medici family, and exiled them from the city. In that moment, the old desires of Dante and the White Guelfs were suddenly fulfilled, and a democratic system of government was installed at the head of a republic.

In 1498, Machiavelli was made Second Chancellor and oversaw the foreign and diplomatic services for the republic—no small task

since Florence was the center of the wool-dying industry in Europe and thus in a position of considerable economic power.

In his foreign-service role, Machiavelli had the opportunity to travel all over Europe, to meet with some of the leading political figures of the age, and to observe first-hand how the various systems of power worked to the advantage or disadvantage of their nations. He travelled extensively with Cesare Borgia as that fated figure came close to uniting Italy and casting out the various powers that vied for position on the Italian peninsula. In 1507, Machiavelli was accorded the task of organizing a state militia, which he later commanded at the siege of Pisa (an experience that would find its way into the pages of *The Prince,* where he argued for a national "people's" army over highly paid mercenaries).

Machiavelli's fortunes, however, took a serious turn for the worse when, in 1509, after his people's army was defeated by a Holy League, the Medici were reinstalled in Florence. Machiavelli was imprisoned, tortured (he was hung up for three months with his arms tied behind his back and walked with a stoop for the remainder of his life), and then excluded by decree from further participation in public life. Facing poverty, he retired to the isolation of his country house and attempted to earn a living as a writer. It was his writings that he thought would reinstate him in Florentine public life, and to win the favor of the Medicis, he decided on a gamble. In 1513, he sat down and put his experience as a statesman on paper. The result was *The Prince*.

Machiavelli addresses the book to "Magnificent Lorenzo de Medici," but the book was originally intended to be dedicated to another member of the Medici family, and the existing dedication is confusing. In reality, this individual is not Lorenzo the Magnificent, the employer of artists and princely prince who had ruled Florence prior to the republic. The person to whom *The Prince* was actually dedicated was a younger member of the Medici family who bore the same name; he was the only one who would grant the outcast Machiavelli an audience. Just at the moment Machiavelli was about to present the book to Lorenzo, however, another favor-seeker entered the room and gave him a pair of hunting hounds. Lorenzo is said to have laid the book down without thanking Machiavelli and gone off to play with the dogs. Disgusted, Machiavelli went home to his house in the country. Lorenzo apparently never read the book. If he had, it might have changed the course of his life and Florentine history. He might have become a true Machiavellian prince. Instead, he was assassinated several years later.

Machiavelli is perhaps one of the most misunderstood authors in the Western canon. His poor reputation can be attributed directly to a series of misreadings and misinterpretations that have been piled upon *The Prince*. The abuse heaped upon his little book by those who considered such a clear-minded view of politics to be scandalous and sacrilegious soon evolved into outright scorn for the author. The term "machiavell" entered the English language to indicate one who used cruelty in an unbridled fashion for political ends—a measure that Machiavelli had in fact sought to temper with his advice. The term soon evolved to mean anyone who was a "devil" in terms of breaching the laws of nature and God. When Shakespeare wrote his play *Richard III*, for example, he portrayed that particular prince as a dark, monstrous machiavell, antagonistic to God, who killed not only little boys but his own brother to get ahead. (In fact, period documents suggest that Richard III was a good and popular king who was overthrown by a questionable alliance of greedy political factions. Shakespeare's character is based on a propagandist chronicle of Tudor history that was written to dispense with the Plantagenet family once and for all. The Tudor apologist was none other than Thomas More—Henry VIII was so pleased with the job More had done on Richard that he gave him Richard's old home, Crosby Hall, and allowed More to move the building from its former location along the Strand in London to a riverside lot in Chelsea, immediately next door to Henry's palace.)

The one thing that Machiavelli could not be accused of was dishonesty. *The Prince* was a frank examination of the nature of power, how it was won, how it was held, and how one might apply laws or almost scientific principles to the matter of government. As a volume of "advice," *The Prince* was to be a guide to the management of power for leaders. Its literary form as a "how-to" book was little more than an extrapolation of Machiavelli's experience in government based upon the rhetorical structure of process analysis.

The other literary foundation for *The Prince* was the Italian use of the *ricordi*. *Ricordi* had evolved in Florence during the thirteenth and fourteenth centuries when men of power, in order to secure their family's fortunes for future generations, had collected and recorded their observations about how they thought life worked. These maxims became a valued source for worldly knowledge in the southern Renaissance. Banking giants such as Luca Pitti or Gregorio Datti, who were among the first to evolve the principles of debit and credit accounting (as well as the audit, where someone read the account books out loud while the bankers listened—hence the notion of the "audit," or hearing of the accounts), passed on their wisdom to their family members and others. One must remember that wisdom in the Renaissance ranked with conspicuous consumption and political savvy as a means of maintaining the appearance of power. (Francesco Guicciardini, a contemporary of Machiavelli and a patrician Florentine statesman who worked for the papacy, left a very clinically minded account of how he perceived the realities of the world in his *Ricordi*, a book alongside which *The Prince* pales by comparison as a textbook for cold-hearted political behavior.) What lay at the heart of the literary form of the *ricordi* was Vasari's belief that knowledge and understanding (*virtù*) could be passed both from one person to another through the power of the written word and from one generation to another, until the ultimate goal of freedom could be achieved.

The problem with Machiavelli's *The Prince*, and perhaps the point that earned him the most scorn from some readers in European Christendom, was his argument that the ends justified the means. In political terms, this meant that a prince must do whatever was necessary to safeguard the destiny of his state. In Book XV of *The Prince*, a chapter titled "The things for which men, and especially princes, are praised or blamed," Machiavelli attempts to cut through the blurring effects of epideictic (the rhetoric of praise and blame) to a much more frank vision of how a society should operate:

> The fact is that a man who wants to act virtuously in every way necessarily comes to grief among so many who are not virtuous. Therefore if a prince wants to maintain his rule he must learn how not to be virtuous, and to make use of this or not according to need.

A prince should not be virtuous? This concept flew in the face of all the ideals that had been articulated in romance and in its literary predecessor, *The Aeneid*. Yet what lay at the heart of Machiavelli's contention was the very core of the character of Aeneas: that single-minded sense of destiny, that commitment to the goal of a secure homeland, and the desire for a leader to wear blinkers against the distractions of the temporal world. Just as Aeneas sailed away from Carthage and turned his face away from the suicide of Dido, so too would Machiavelli's prince govern with a directness of vision that would ultimately protect the state. Cruelty was not to be avoided:

> I believe that here it is a question of cruelty used well or badly. We can say that cruelty is used well (if it is permissible to talk in this way of what is evil) when it is employed once for all, and one's safety depends on it, and then it is not persisted in but as far as possible turned to the good of one's subjects.

Machiavelli concluded that for a prince, at least, it was better to be feared than to be loved, because fear was a better motivator for loyalty than generosity. When the coffers of a prince ran dry, Machiavelli argued, his flatterers would turn elsewhere for their material needs, and the security of the state would be undermined. This was a cold-hearted vision of how a prince should behave, but Machiavelli also advised a modicum of humanity:

> Nonetheless, a prince should be slow to take action, and should watch that he does not come to be afraid of his own shadow; his behaviour should be tempered by humanity and prudence so that over-confidence does not make him rash or excessive distrust make him unbearable.

There was a balance to be achieved, Machiavelli believed; the prince should be feared but not hated, and cruelty, a reality in all the courts of Europe (though it was not admitted), was a necessary means to that end.

In order for the prince to maintain power, Machiavelli asserted, he must avoid liberality, the generosity that in some remote way echoed the notion of Christian charity, whereby supporters and flatterers were rewarded for minor services. This, Machiavelli declared, was dangerous, for such insincere supporters would soon turn their allegiances elsewhere. And those who usually had their hands out for such tokens were the nobles. Machiavelli makes it quite clear that these individuals are expendable and unnecessary:

> And the man who becomes prince with the help of the nobles finds it more difficult to maintain his position than one who does so with the help of the people.

The key, Machiavelli argued, was that the people desired not to be oppressed, while the nobles, for their own ends, desired to oppress the people. He suggests that the prince rule by the power of the people, because they would take orders, whereas nobles were in a position to challenge authority:

> A man who becomes prince by favour of the people finds himself standing alone, and he has near him either no one or

very few not prepared to take orders. In addition, it is impossible to satisfy the nobles honestly, without doing violence to the interests of others; but this can be done as far as the people are concerned. The people are more honest in their intentions than the nobles are, because the latter want to oppress the people whereas the people only want not to be oppressed.... Again, a prince must always live with the same people, but he can well do without the nobles, since he can make and unmake them every day, increasing and lowering their standing at will.

What must be remembered about Machiavelli is that he was, first and foremost, a democrat in his beliefs and his profession, and that *The Prince*, a work about political expediency, was actually triggered by Machiavelli's need to find employment. Following the book's publication, he wrote several other key works, including *The Discourses*, in which he examined the various types of government that had evolved in the Western world, along with the value of democracy and the proud heritage of the Roman ideal of a people's state. Until Alexis de Tocqueville penned *Democracy in America* in the early nineteenth century, *The Discourses* was considered one of the chief texts on the evolution and practice of democracy.

Hans Holbein. The Ambassadors. Put your eye to the upper right hand corner of the illustration and look directly across the surface of the page. A memento mori *replaces the worldly, almost arrogant twosome. The effect is known as* anamorphosis, *and is yet another Renaissance expression of the idea that what one sees is all a matter of how one looks at it.*

For all its bleak sense of *realpolitik*, however, *The Prince* is a textbook not for tyranny, but for the evolution of democracy, although it has seldom been viewed as such. In order to perceive this notion at work in *The Prince*, one must look beneath the surface of both the structure and the argument of the work. In reality, it is a cleverly written guide book that, if followed to the letter, would have resulted in the return of the Florentine government to the people. Books I to XI of *The Prince* are a series of classification discussions in which Machiavelli examines the various types of states and analyzes their structures. He examines hereditary principalities, or older states, where succession was achieved through generations of tight rule; composite principalities, or states composed of newly conquered territories; new principalities, where the political process has produced a nascent state; constitutional principalities, such as the Florentine republic that he served; and ecclesiastical principalities, chiefly the Vatican. Books XII to XIV deal with the issue of the militia, with Machiavelli concluding that mercenaries could not be trusted and that national security would be achieved only if a nation were defended by a people's army in which the soldiers sought to protect their own best interests.

He then launches into an examination of how a prince might hold a state once he acquires it—the process of management. The nobles, as has already been discussed, are not to be trusted; if possible they should be weakened and disliked by the people. In time, the nobility would fade away, and the power structure would consist only of the prince and his people. After all, it was the people who installed the prince, and the prince's gestures, even those that made him feared rather than loved, were intended to maintain the loyalty of the masses. This raises the issue of what happens when the prince dies. To whom does succession pass? Machiavelli leaves this question unanswered. It is a glaring flaw in the otherwise superb reasoning that he built into *The Prince*, and if the absence of a suitable answer begs the question "What comes after the prince?" then perhaps the only logical answer is "the people."

Still, the ultimate problem facing a prince, as Book XXV

outlines, is not the process of statecraft or even the questions of how to shape an army or who to favor in a politcal structure, but the old Classical notion of *fortuna*. In his own lifetime, Machiavelli had witnessed the rise and fall of Cesare Borgia, the fall of Savonarola, and the collapse of the Florentine republic. He knew, as the monarchs of Europe discovered in the summer of 1914, that the events of a single day can alter the political structure of a nation or a continent. In other words, *fortuna* could make or break a leader:

> I am not unaware that many have held and hold the opinion
> that events are controlled by fortune and by God in such a way
> that the prudence of men cannot modify them, indeed, that
> men have no influence whatsoever. Because of this, they would
> conclude that there is no point in sweating over things, but that
> one should submit to the rulings of chance.

Boethius had argued in *The Consolation of Philosophy* that fate and fortune were entirely in God's hands; all events were part of a divine plan wherein the universe was working toward an eventual reconciliation between God and humans at the end of time. In this system, all fate was good because it came from God. Realizing the goodness at work in the universe was merely a matter of persuading oneself toward a positive interpretation of events. Machiavelli almost buys into Boethius' argument. He realizes that fortune is something controlled by the Almighty, yet he stops short of the idea of Christian submission. Instead, he flies in the face of the theology of his times and suggests events are something that human beings can mitigate and manipulate to a large degree, if not control completely:

> Nonetheless, because free choice cannot be ruled out, I believe
> that it is probably true that fortune is the arbiter of half the things
> we do, leaving the other half or so to be controlled by ourselves.

The key to success, Machiavelli believed, was more than just having a sense of the importance of seizing the moment, although the ability to recognize what moment to seize was an art in itself:

This is inevitable unless those who have suddenly become princes are of such prowess that overnight they can learn how to preserve what fortune has suddenly tossed into their laps, and unless they can then lay foundations such as other princes should have been building on.

What Machiavelli was declaring was that humans, not God, could dictate the course of events by possessing a political version of Vasari's *virtù*, or the intelligence to read the world, interpret the signs, prepare for events, turn the events to one's own ends, and maximize one's potential and security. This went far beyond the Boethian notion of acceptance. This was the declaration of the power of the individual that had been expressed as a subtext in *The Aeneid*, examined as a theme in Saint Augustine's *Confessions*, and was at work as a curriculum priority in the knight schools of medieval romances. The individual in possession of enlightened free will could challenge even God's order in the universe. All that individuals needed to do was to aim high, keep their goals squarely in front of them in a Virgilian fashion, and maintain constant vigilance by reading and interpreting the political landscape. And if the Virgilian quest for a secure homeland was ever going to come to pass, political *virtù* was the means by which it would occur.

This notion of free will immediately upset the Christian scholars of Europe. Machiavelli, after all, was arguing against the notion of Christian resignation. Fate, he suggested, was not something one should merely accept. One should question, observe, and if possible reshape the circumstances of the world to one's own ends. The idea of altering one's destiny, of improving on what God and nature had provided, was startling, and did much to draw a line of demarcation between the Italian Humanists in the Petrarchan tradition and the northern Humanists such as More and Erasmus.

But if the northern Christian Humanists were upset with Machiavelli's thinking on matters of destiny and fate, they were totally livid at his suggestion that the next savior would have to be an armed prophet. In Machiavelli's final exhortation to the prince—a cry for a savior figure to redeem Italy from its bondage and to reawaken the glory of the Italian spirit—Machiavelli echoed

the old sentiments of loyalty, duty and perseverance that Virgil had expressed:

In order therefore that Italy, after so long a time, may behold its saviour, this opportunity must not be let slip. And I cannot express with what love he would be welcomed in all those provinces which have suffered from these foreign inundations, with what thirst for vengeance, with what resolute loyalty, with what devotion and tears. What doors would be closed to him? What people would deny him obedience? What envy would stand in his way? What Italian would refuse him allegiance? This barbarous tyranny stinks in everyone's nostrils. Let your illustrious House understake this task, therefore, with the courage and hope which belong to just enterprises, so that under your standard, our country may be ennobled, and under your auspices what Petrarch said may come to pass:

> *Virtu' against fury shall advance the fight,*
> *And it i' th' combate soon shall put to flight:*

For th' old Romane valour is not dead,
Nor in th' Italians brests extinguished.

The savior, Machiavelli argued, would be an individual who possessed all the criteria of *virtù* and who resembled Aeneas more than Christ. The armed prophets, those great leaders of history who had redeemed their peoples, including Moses, Cyrus, Theseus, and Romulus, had exercised cunning and intelligence but were also not afraid to defend themselves by military might when called upon to do so. In his own time, Machiavelli had witnessed the disaster brought upon Florence when it followed the political precepts of an unarmed prophet, Fra Girolamo Savonarola, whose short-lived success was more a matter of faith than of stable statesmanship.

Hans Holbein. Portrait of Erasmus. In this profound study of the humanist character, Erasmus quietly pens yet another work. Erasmus' views of how a prince should behave were a direct response to Machiavelli's.

The problem with Machiavelli's arguments about armed prophets being successful and unarmed prophets being disastrous was that Christendom perceived the greatest prophet of all time to be an unarmed leader—Christ. Machiavelli's position, although he did not state it directly, was that Christ had been a failure. His people remained in bondage, and he died a victim of his people's conquerors. Only the persuasiveness of his message won him any success, and that success belonged to his conquerors, the Romans, who converted to Christianity under Constantine only when it became a military expedient:

> That is why all armed prophets have conquered and unarmed prophets have come to grief. Besides what I have said already, the populace is by nature fickle; it is easy to persuade them of something, but difficult to confirm them in that persuasion.

When *The Prince* was read, especially by those close to the seats of power in Europe (such as More at the court of Henry VIII), the immediate reaction was that Machiavelli was the devil incarnate. In truth, Machiavelli simply swept the gauze of decency from the true workings of Renaissance politics and simply expressed a vision of the realities he had witnessed first-hand while on diplomatic missions throughout the continent. Nonetheless, despite his candor and frankness about how one could manipulate political realities, Machiavelli was branded as the most evil man alive.

The problem with *The Prince* was that it gave exposure to the great lie, the theory (expressed first by Plato in *The Republic*) that society operated by a very different system of beliefs than was apparent to the general populace. When the first copies of *The Prince* circulated among the network of scholars and men of power throughout Northern Europe, there was an immediate need to respond to it in some way. More chose to structure his response in the form of a joke among his group of intellectual friends. What must be remembered about the nature of jokes, as Freud pointed out in the twentieth century, is that they are often masks for more complex statements, deflections of deeper truths, and more challenging and unnerving ideas.

The joke underlying *Utopia* was that it was a story of no-place, a land that could not possibly exist. To the literalist, Utopia would seem a beautiful, ideal land, removed from the sufferings and hardships that made daily life in Renaissance England a challenge, as well as a place that presented enticing possibilities as a model for social reform. But what was quite evident from the wit with which More conveyed his story was that the place was too good to be true. Gold was in abundance, so much so that criminals were made to wear gold chains as punishment. Like Gonzalo's ideal commonwealth in *The Tempest*, all things were provided: health care, schooling, defence, and social-support systems. Labor was required, but only in so much as it would support the collective good. In short, what More removed from his equation was the very thing Machiavelli had built into his: human nature. It was similar to the vision that Marx and Engels would later construct in their *Communist Manifesto*; More's *Utopia* depicted an ideal society that could not accommodate the natural human drives toward self-interest and greed.

More, the interviewer character in *Utopia*, questions Raphael about the plausibility of such a system. He foresees that a society that cannot make allowances for human nature will collapse under its own illusions of perfectability. In his comments, More sounds a note of warning for communal societies that would not be fully understood until the Iron Curtain collapsed in 1991:

I don't believe you'd ever have a reasonable standard of living under a communist system. There'd always tend to be shortages, because nobody would work hard enough. In the absence of a profit motive, everyone would become lazy, and rely on everyone else to do the work for him. Then, when things really got short, the inevitable result would be a series of murders and riots, since nobody would have any legal method of protecting the products of his own labour—especially as there wouldn't be any respect for authority, or I don't see how there could be, in a classless society.

Raphael responds with a line that Khrushchev might have used during the Kitchen Debate with Richard Nixon:

You're bound to take the view, for you simply can't imagine what it would be like—not accurately, at any rate. But if you'd been with me in Utopia, and seen it all for yourself, as I did—I lived there for more than five years, you know, and the only reason I ever left was that I wanted to tell people about the New World—you'd be the first to admit that you'd never seen a country so well organized.

The problem with Utopia, as More is well aware, is that it is illogical; yet the very things that make it illogical, the absence of human nature and the fact that it seems to operate more by theory than by natural dynamics, is part of the joke. What More does in *Utopia* is show us the ideal society in order to launch a satirical barb at his own world. The book was as much an attempt to point out what he considered to be wrong with England of the sixteenth century as it was a response to *The Prince*.

Structurally, *Utopia* is quite like *The Prince*. Where Machiavelli's text opens with a dedicatory epistle, *Utopia* begins with a fictitious exchange of letters among a circle of friends—friends who, from the start, know better and are in on the joke. More also employs a new genre that was just beginning to take hold in English literature: exploration writing. The first accounts of voyages, such as those by Columbus or Vespucci, were mandatory scientific reading among the European intelligentsia in More's day. The problem with early exploration writing, however, was that such accounts triggered fanciful ideas rather than the strong urges for economic expansion that evolved later in the century. The early exploration texts were read much as today one reads the more outlandish works of contemporary science fiction; the circumstances that the mariners described often exceeded the boundaries of the European imagination. More consciously flirts with the boundaries of the fantastic in *Utopia*. In his introduction to the dialogue with Raphael, More the character explains:

> We did not ask him if he had seen any monsters, for monsters have ceased to be news. There is never any shortage of horrible creatures who prey upon human beings, snatch away their food, or devour whole populations; but examples of wise social planning are not so easy to find.

What More was drawing upon was a working knowledge of a 1322 bestseller by John Mandeville, *The Travels of Sir John Mandeville*. In that account, the merchant-traveler Mandeville ventures beyond the Holy Land, that imaginative heart of the medieval world, into the bizarre, uncharted realms of *terra incognita*. Part journey account but mostly fantastic fiction, *The Travels of Sir John Mandeville* featured reports from far-flung places of strange human-like creatures who had no heads or who were part animal.

In describing such places in accordance with his "flat earth" theory of geography, Mandeville played upon the medieval fear of the unknown, a fear that ranked with the fear of death. This same fear almost prevented Columbus from sailing west in search of China in the belief that the world was round. What Mandeville's book established, and what More consciously drew on for *Utopia*, was the somewhat Homeric concept that the world is a strange place, and that the farther one went from the known, the more fantastic it became. By following this example, More locates his satirical commentary in a world that is still, imaginatively, medieval. In that mentality, the outreaches of the world were realms where the laws of nature as European man knew them no longer operated, and where the imagination was wildly unbridled. In the late eighteenth and early nineteenth centuries, this notion of what exists at the fringes of the known world, and therefore at the threshold of the imaginative realm, would supply the foundation for Gothic literature. In More's *Utopia*, guessing at what might be out there also provided the cornerstone for a sub-genre that we commonly term today "speculative fiction." Speculative fiction is one of the reasons why science fiction, an offshoot of the Gothic, so often crosses paths with social satire; in speculative fiction, the author goes beyond the process of societal comparisons (the root of satire) and tests the limits of what is either possible or conceivable. This blurring of the distinction between speculative fiction and societal satire enabled later authors such as Aldous Huxley in *Brave New World*, George Orwell in *Nineteen Eighty-four*, and Margaret Atwood in *The Handmaid's Tale* to present visions of societies where the fantastic had become nightmarish.

When utopias become nightmares they are dystopias. Essentially what the sub-genre of horror draws upon is the potential for the ideal to become the hellish. For every type of utopia, there is a dystopia that represents, at least metaphorically, the ideal turned upside down. The vision of heaven that John Milton presents in *Paradise Lost* finds its dystopian equivalent in Pandemonium, that kingdom of hell over which Satan presides as a rebel ruler (see chapter 14). When Arcadia comes apart at the seams, it becomes a place of death, suffering, and entropy. The Land of Cockaigne, the place of plenty where there is no need for laws or order, is given its dystopian airing in William Golding's novel *The Lord of the Flies*, where a group of castaway school boys revert to a terrible form of barbarism. The Perfect Moral Commonwealth of Plato's *Republic* or Book IV of *Gulliver's Travels* is turned upside-down by Orwell in *Nineteen Eighty-four*, where the protagonist, Winston Smith, struggles to maintain his individuality in a society that would crush every evidence of human nature. The Rational Republic, where everything should operate according to logic or the laws of science, becomes a nightmare state of science out of control in Aldous Huxley's *Brave New World* or Samuel Butler's *Erewhon* (an anagram of "nowhere"—a small joke on More's joke). And the kingdom of heaven itself, that divine city of the New Jerusalem, the ultimate utopia, finds its dystopic mirror image in the idea of eternal perdition.

Utopias and dystopias locate the world of the story not merely in physical space but in that part of the mind where philosophy and the imagination merge, where speculation, based on sound foundations of knowledge, is allowed free rein. The underlying question behind these works is "What if?" More's *Utopia* exists at the boundaries of believability. The narrative, as More realizes, must be told by someone who has knowledge both of the real world and of the imaginary place. As a character, Raphael is described in terms a Humanist would understand:

> He's really more like Ulysses, or even Plato. You see, our friend Raphael—for that's his name, Raphael Nonsenso—is quite a scholar. He knows a fair amount of Latin and a tremendous amount of Greek. He's concentrated on Greek, because he's mainly interested in philosophy.... He wanted to see the world, so he left his brothers to manage his property in Portugal— that's where he comes from—and joined up with Amerigo Vespucci. You know those *Four Voyages* of his that everyone's reading about? Well, Raphael was his constant companion during the last three, except that he didn't come back with him from the final voyage.

The suggestion here is that this new world is the product of informed interpretation, an interpretation that is formulated from a sound knowledge of Europe as well as the newly discovered land of the Utopians. When Raphael offers his observations about Utopian society, they are meant to be comparisons to English society. Book I of *Utopia*, for example, offers a view of how the economics of Utopian society operate, yet this view is really an "anti-description" of the English system. While the principles of enlightened self-interest and greed are rampant in the society of More's time, *Utopia* presents a classless, property-less community where human nature and materialism take a back seat to "the common good." This is really the notion of Christian charity taken to its outside limits as a rule for the operation of an entire society:

> In Utopia, where there's no private property, people take their
> duty to the public seriously. And both attitudes are perfectly
> reasonable. In other "republics" practically everyone knows that,
> if he doesn't look out for himself, he'll starve to death, however
> prosperous his country may be. He's therefore compelled to give
> his own interests priority over those of the public; that is, of
> other people. But in Utopia where everything's under public
> ownership, no one has any fear of going short, as long as the
> public storehouses are full. Everyone gets a fair share, so there
> are never any poor men or beggars. Nobody owns anything, but
> everyone is rich—for what greater wealth can there be than
> cheerfulness, peace of mind, and freedom from anxiety?

The underlying concept, and one that is often forgotten in many readings of *Utopia*, is that More was talking about a world that could not possibly exist outside the realm of the hypothetical, that an imaginary world as a hypothesis is meant to address glaring needs and concerns in his contemporary society. The imagination is a safe place for the satirist, because it allows the broadest range of extreme ideas while providing the security of a world that is well within the writer's control.

Ultimately, what More is satirizing in his discussion of Utopian economics is the hypocrisy of charity within his own time. Christian charity told individuals to suppress their natural instincts toward

Painting after Hans Holbein the younger. Sir Thomas More. Beneath the calm confidence in More's eyes, one can detect a savvy and a sharpness of perception that is haunting. This was, after all, the man who steered the helm of English politics until his falling-out with Henry VIII.

possessiveness. At the same time, the church rewarded those who were best equipped to deliver generous gifts because they had been self-interested enough to accumulate vast wealth. More's faith and dedication to the church, for which he was eventually beheaded, placed him in a position where he was obligated to honor the practices of his religion while also acknowledging its inequities. Coincidentally, at the time *Utopia* was published, a German monk named Martin Luther was openly arguing for a reform of the relationship between church and society. Luther, a scholar and adherent to Saint Augustine's idea of the enlightened individual critiquing not only himself but the world around him, approached the same problems as More, yet he did so through direct and open argument, not through satire. This openness, a kind of late medieval *glasnost*, was what triggered the Reformation. Anyone raising the same issues a hundred years earlier would have been burned as a heretic, but Luther was allowed to have his say because the temper of the times dictated that ideas and beliefs should be openly argued and tested.

The Reformation lurks in the background of *Utopia*. The same issues that drove Luther to nail the ninety-five theses to the church door in Wittenberg were being discussed by the Humanist scholars. Should church practices be reformed? Should ordinary people have access to the text of the Bible in their own languages? What role should icons play in the perception of God? How tolerant should the church be of other faiths or of variations within Christian beliefs? Should individuals be able to approach God directly on their own terms rather than through the medium of a priest?

In Book II of *Utopia*, Raphael explains the religious practices of the Utopians in terms that would be *au courant* to those within More's circle:

> On the same principle, their churches contain no visual representations of God, so that everyone's left free to imagine Him in whatever shape he chooses, according to which religion he thinks best. Nor is God addressed by any special names there. He is simply called Mythras, a general term used by everybody to designate the Supreme Being, whoever He may be. Similarly, no prayers are said in which each member of the congregation cannot join without prejudice to his own particular creed.

What More is suggesting, through the inversion argument of satire, is that the Utopians have found the remedy for the religious problems of their world and are practicing a kind of Protestantism where, according to Luther's tenet, "Each man meets God on his own terms." Though More is commenting on a world on the cusp of the Reformation, he is, in his thinking, clinging to a world and a mentality that were shaped by fifteen hundred years of Christianity. More's playfulness and sense of wit in expressing his views on Christianity, either directly or through satire, locate him in a great debate that raged throughout the northern and southern Renaissance, the debate between the Ancients and the Moderns.

As Vasari illustrated in *Lives of the Artists*, the Ancients of the Classical, pagan era had achieved magnificent artistic and intellectual accomplishments through the way they perceived the world. Their vision, Vasari claimed, was unfettered by any notions of accepting the world for what it was; rather, they believed that the world was what one could make of it, a lump of clay waiting to be shaped by the power of individual will and brilliance. The Modern era, the era that began with the rise of Christianity, changed the imaginative and perceptual mechanisms by which the European mind comprehended and experienced life. The ideas of Boethius, for example, may have spared the collective imagination the perils and sufferings implicit in tragedy; yet the notion of divine grace as the force that shaped the world also suggested that one should simply accept what one encountered as the will of God. More, as a thinker, is caught between the Ancient and the Modern perceptions. On the one hand, he sees that there are problems in the world and he attempts to correct them through the art of satire. On the other hand, he is willing to put his life on the line for his belief in the status quo of faith.

More's Utopians, meanwhile, are quite like the Ancients in their beliefs and in their knowledge:

> Until we arrived, they didn't know the name of any famous
> European philosopher. And yet they'd discovered much the
> same principles, in music, logic, arithmetic, and geometry, as
> those early authorities of ours. But though in most things

they're on a par with the Ancients, they're no match for the Moderns when it comes to logic.

Later, in Book II, More again picked up this theme, discussing the Utopians in light of the debate of the Ancients versus the Moderns:

> You see, I can't help thinking that they must be of Greek extraction, since their language, though otherwise like Persian, contains some traces of Greek in place-names and official titles. I presented them with several Greek texts—for when I started out on the fourth voyage I didn't intend to come back for a very long time, if at all, so instead of packing a lot of things to sell, I took on board a pretty large trunk full of books. I gave them most of Plato, even more of Aristotle, and Theophrastus's work on botany....

As this passage suggests, More believed that the net sum of human knowledge, ideas from both the pagan and the Christian worlds, could revive in humankind all of the greatness that had been lost from the past. Yet More was far less cautious in his praise of the Ancients than Machiavelli. For More, the Ancients were a group who presented knowledge that could be useful to the Christian ideal; for Machiavelli, the Ancients were smarter and more effective in their political ideas because they did not allow their thinking to be mitigated by ideas such as divine grace, forgiveness, or hope.

The debate of the Ancients versus the Moderns lies at the core of the Renaissance. It was a debate that would rage even into the eighteenth century, when Jonathan Swift would write his satirical essay "The Battle of the Books." Although by Swift's time the Scientific Revolution had gained tremendous force, and this debate had become merely a matter of intellectual speculation, the issue as to who was wiser remains at the core of both *The Prince* and *Utopia*. Still, for both Machiavelli and More, the solution was simple: society was something that could be controlled through the power of ideas. More perceived a perfect moral commonwealth where, by consensus, people could agree upon a specific set of ideals and live by them, just as they might live by faith in the Christian world.

Machiavelli, however, placed little weight upon consensus or even collective cooperation. For him, leadership was the key. The enlightenment of a leader, the ability to create organization at the top of society rather than throughout the masses, was the key to liberty and security.

What More and Machiavelli prove is a concept not unlike that discovered by the painters of the southern Renaissance: namely, that the shape of the world can be determined by intellectual and imaginative activity, and that the *disegno* of ideas in the imaginative world can have a direct impact on how both individuals and societies conduct themselves. In other words, the dreams of literature can become the realities of life. Both *The Prince* and *Utopia* are part of a broad category of writing known as the literature of ideas. In the literature of ideas, the text, whether imaginative or discursive, becomes a vehicle for argument so that the literary form serves as a mask for persuading the reader to a particular point of view. Samuel Johnson's *Rasselas*, Voltaire's *Candide*, and Mary Shelley's *Frankenstein* are all part of this broad spectrum, as are the novels of D.H. Lawrence (such as *Women in Love*) and those of Graham Greene (such as *The End of the Affair*). Contemporary readers tend to take a writer's expression of philosophical concepts as par for the course. But what lies at the root of the literature of ideas is the fact that the written word is more than merely a form of entertainment; it is also a vehicle for didactic intentions that can effect changes not just in the mind of the reader but in the world. The principle that what is written can impact the shape of the world is something we have learned from the Renaissance ideal that books are a means to sharing and debating information.

In an information-intensive world such as the one we currently live in, it is almost a moral obligation of the individual to consume as many different ideas as possible to possess a well-rounded knowledge of what is happening. The educated individual is no longer a guarantor of freedom for a society, but is a necessity in free societies that need to keep pace with information overload. The decisions that shape our world are based on our ability to comprehend as many different ideas as possible. To accommodate that concept, we've become accustomed to viewing all forms of literature, not just philosophy, as forums for debate and vehicles for ideas.

What this means is that writers are arbiters, if not legislators, of their place and time, and writing is a means of addressing and improving the world. Both *The Prince* and *Utopia* demonstrate that the writer must have an individual and a public moral conscious-ness, because what the writer says will make not only for better readers but for a better world in which those readers can live. But true to the spirit of the Renaissance, where the issue of how one perceives things lay at the core of just about everything, More and Machiavelli's entire worlds could be shaped from ideas—good or bad. It became one of the duties of the writer to show readers not only the range of alternatives but the process by which they could distinguish between them through the exercise of critical thought.

13

MAKING SOMETHING
FROM NOTHING

William Shakespeare's *King Lear* and *The Tempest*

———————————————————

P ERHAPS the most ubiquitous forms of architectural ornamentation in theaters are the masks of tragedy and comedy. They appear in the frieze work over the stage as traditional emblems of drama, and they are there for a purpose: to remind audience members that what they will witness on the stage will cover a range of emotional possibilities. The masks are also there because what the audience sees is an illusion, the process of making something from nothing. Originally, these masks, or personas, were donned by actors on the stages of the Classical Greek theater to denote characterization; they were mouthpieces through which the actors spoke to portray specific dramatized individuals. But the masks also represented the essence of theater, the ability to create illusions, to convince the audience that the imaginative reality of the play was as real as anything in the world beyond the stage.

Saint Augustine's admonitions against the nature of theater, where the audience offers real emotions in response to illusions, lies at the core of drama. In Book III of *Confessions*, as we saw in chapter 6, Saint Augustine argues for a recognition of the difference between dreams and consciousness and between illusions and reality. He perceives the illusions of the stage in the same vein as the illusions that take place in our unconscious dreams, and he pleads for the ability to recognize the boundaries between the two worlds:

> They were dream substances, mock realities, far less true than
> the real things which we see with the sight of our eyes in the
> sky or on the earth. These things are seen by bird and beast as
> well as by ourselves, and they are far more certain than any

image we conceive of them. And in turn we can picture them to ourselves with greater certainty than the vaster, infinite things which we surmise from them. Such things have no existence at all, but they were the visionary foods on which I was then fed but not sustained.

It is essential that a reader or a theater-goer be able to tell the difference between reality and illusion, he maintains, because the structure of knowledge, the way things are presented or expressed, is as important as the content. In other words, when we go to the theater and ask to be presented with an illusion, we should be aware that what we are witnessing is only "play," or the demonstration of an alternative, imaginative reality that is completely artificial and has been constructed solely for the purpose of entertainment.

In *The Tempest*, Shakespeare demonstrates that the role of the dramatist is to mediate and control the action so that events can be brought to a conclusion, either as a resolution (in the case of a comedy) or as dashed hopes (in a tragedy). *The Tempest* is a play about resolution, about how one mediating force that governs the action can make events work out to a just and rewarding conclusion. In the play, about a dispossessed king and his attempts to win back his throne, the protagonist, Prospero, manipulates events through the use of illusion. He blinds his enemies to the truth of their situation, separating fathers from sons and kings from courtiers, until each character is ready to acknowledge what the truth really is.

However, in *The Tempest*, illusion is more than merely a means to justice: it is a way to celebrate the verities of love, devotion, and understanding that form the basis for human existence. When Ferdinand, the only son of the king of Naples (Prospero's old adversary), falls in love with Prospero's daughter, Miranda, he is faced with a series of labors. Like a courtly lover, he proves his worth to the young maiden by freely submitting to her father's will. Eventually, Ferdinand triumphs, and Prospero celebrates the betrothal of his only daughter to his enemy's only son in a joyous moment of comic reconciliation.

The celebration takes the form of a *masque*, a small "spectacle" or song and dance that provides an interlude in the dramatic action

of the play. For the masque, Prospero conjures the spirits of three Classical goddesses, Ceres, Iris, and Juno, who bless the union of the two young lovers with bountifulness, youthful beauty, and domestic security. At the masque's conclusion in Act IV, Scene i, Prospero offers an exegesis of what he, Ferdinand, and Miranda have just witnessed:

> *Our revels now are ended. These our actors,*
> *As I foretold you, were all spirits and*
> *Are melting into air, into thin air;*
> *The cloud-capped tow'rs, the gorgeous palaces,*
> *The solemn temples, the great globe itself,*
> *Yea, all which it inherit, shall dissolve,*
> *And like this insubstantial pageant faded,*
> *Leave not a rack behind. We are such stuff*
> *As dreams are made on, and our little life*
> *Is rounded with a sleep.*

In essence, what Shakespeare is saying is that drama is a form of conjuring, an extended illusion, if not an extended metaphor, where the imagination is asked to animate the inanimate and to create the appearance of life where none existed. In reality, the play is only an illusion, and, like a utopia, a "no-place," an imaginative construct that reaches beyond itself and grabs hold of either the emotions or the intellect, which are part of the real world.

The dramatist in this context is a magician, a conjurer who uses all his knowledge and "charms" to cast a spell upon the audience. This spell carries the viewers' collective imagination beyond the confines of the theater through the power of the drama. When Prospero mentions "the great globe itself, / Yea, all that it inherit," Shakespeare is punning on the name of his own theater, the Globe, which was located on the south bank of the Thames in London. The implication, although slightly allusory, is quite simple: the stage is a place that can become any place, and it is a platform where the dramatist can recreate the entire world through the power of words and actions. To do this, the dramatist begs upon one of the central ingredients of drama—the *suspension of disbelief*, whereby the audience is asked to set aside Augustinian critical faculties (discerning the difference between reality and illusion) and, for the length of the drama, buy into the idea that the stage is Prospero's magical desert island and the sound of timpani in the props house is really the crash of thunder in a violent sea storm.

In a rare moment when Prospero (who is in many ways a mouthpiece for the dramatist) steps outside the illusion and addresses the audience directly and frankly about the nature of illusion, Shakespeare takes his leave of the playwright's art. In this farewell speech to the theater he explains just how the dramatist's use of illusion works:

Now my charms are all o'erthrown,
And what strength I have's mine own,
Which is most faint. Now 'tis true
I must be here confined by you,
Or sent to Naples. Let me not,
Since I have my dukedom got
And pardoned the deceiver, dwell
In this bare island by your spell;
But release me from my bands
With the help of your good hands.
Gentle breath of yours my sails

Must fill, or else my project fails,
Which was to please. Now I want
Spirits to enforce, art to enchant;
And my ending is despair
Unless I be relieved by prayer,
Which pierces so that it assaults
Mercy itself and frees all faults.
As you from crimes would pardoned be,
Let your indulgence set me free.

Shakespeare is saying that the dramatist draws upon the same area of the human imagination that is home to religion. Like a prayer, a play is an evocation of the audience's ability to believe in an illusion to the point where it seems a reality. Yet beneath this believable illusion, there is nothing tangible other than the script, the actors, the props, and the costumes.

Both *The Tempest* and *King Lear* stem from the notion that the "insubstantial pageant," the spectacle of drama, is all a matter of nothing. When Gonzalo offers his vision of a utopian society in Act II, Scene i of *The Tempest*, Alonso, the king of Naples, responds in a fairly literalist fashion: "Prithee no more. Thou dost talk nothing to me." Shakespeare, well aware that More's *Utopia* is a story of no-place, in which a better world is merely imagined, has Gonzalo reply that he realizes such political speculation is idle chatter, but that "they always used to laugh at nothing." The machiavell, Antonio, who overthrew Prospero and usurped the dukedom of Milan, responds nastily, "'Twas you we laughed at," mocking Gonzalo and the noble intentions of his imagination. Gonzalo, however, turns the tables on Antonio, and paints him as a literalist who cannot tell the difference between political strategy and passive speculation: "Who in this kind of merry fooling am nothing to you: so you / may continue, and laugh at nothing still."

What Gonzalo is saying is that "nothing" is not to be scoffed at. The political world of the English Renaissance, as Shakespeare realized, was a time and a place where nothing meant a great deal. Nothing, in the political spectrum, was not a vacuum or an absence of power but a strange, obtuse way of acknowledging the presence of something that could not be discussed directly for fear of political repercussions. The idea of nothing, especially in *King Lear,* was a conceit for expressing what one could not say as well as for suggesting the specter of tragedy. The "nothing" of Gonzalo's speech represents the concept of the ultimate no-place, a political vacuum where there is neither leadership nor political control.

The greatest fear in the Renaissance mind was not tyranny—in fact, Machiavelli's *The Prince* argues that tyranny is an option on the road to democracy—but anarchy. The vacuum of power that occurs when an individual is displaced, homeless, and insecure was perceived as the worst situation of all. Perhaps this fear was simply an echo of the medieval mentality, where everyone had a place and where displacement, as suggested in Anglo-Saxon poems such as *The Wanderer* or *The Seafarer,* was the worst fate God could hand to an individual. It is no accident that Shakespeare locates one of his bleakest tragedies, *King Lear,* not only in a world where power and control absent themselves in favor of nothing, but in a negative universe, that land on the debit side of zero, where nothing fills the vacuum caused by the sudden absence of sovereignty. As a result, all of nature goes awry.

Shakespeare's *King Lear* tells the story of an elderly king who decides to divide his kingdom among his three daughters, Goneril, Regan, and Cordelia. All the daughters need do to acquire their third is to express in words their love for their father. Cordelia, however, realizes that words can be hollow: "my love's / More ponderous than my tongue," she says.

Lear, of course, falls into the trap that Machiavelli warns against: a prince should never listen to flatterers. When asked by her father what she has to say for herself to win his affection and a part of the kingdom, Cordelia gives an honest answer: "Nothing, my lord." Lear responds with a statement that becomes the major theme of the play: "Nothing will come of nothing." In the world of *King Lear,* the universe operates in terms of negative integers. Lear banishes Cordelia, and having dispersed his political power among his two remaining daughters, casts himself and his courtiers on their mercy. Goneril and Regan prove to be very un-Homeric hosts. They strip Lear of his remaining retainers, turn him out into the cold, cruel world, and fight with each other in a power struggle. In other words, the whole stability of the world comes undone and the worst nightmare of the Renaissance is realized.

The story on which Shakespeare based *King Lear* was not a tragedy but a comedy of errors in which an elderly king, Leir, divided his kingdom in portions among his three daughters. The source is the famous Welsh text by Geoffrey of Monmouth, *The History of the Kings of Britain*, which indirectly locates the story of the politically injudicious Leir as a "Matter of Troy" and includes a sub-plot that embraces the Grail legend. In Monmouth's version, Leir celebrates his diamond jubilee by dividing his kingdom among his three daughters. He describes the story of his Leir in the following manner:

> Leir ruled the country for sixty years. It was he who built the city on the River Soar which is called Kaerleir after him in the British tongue, its Saxon name being Leicester. He had no male issue, but three daughters were born to him. Their names were Goneril, Regan and Cordelia. Their father was very fond indeed of them and above all he loved Cordelia, his youngest daughter. When he felt himself becoming a really old man, he made up his mind to divide his kingdom between these three daughters and to marry them to husbands whom he considered to be suited to them and capable of ruling the kingdom along with them. In an attempt to discover which of the three was most worthy of inheriting the larger part of his realm, he went to them each in turn to ask which of them loved him the most.

When Cordelia refuses to flatter him, Leir marries her to the king of France (rather than banishing her), and watches as Goneril and Regan create anarchy by fighting each other for the lion's share of the nation. Cordelia, on hearing that her father is in a desperate situation, returns to Britain with the Frankish army, destroys her two sisters, restores the fortunes of her father, and rules the kingdom with him happily ever after.

The terrifying message for Shakespeare in Monmouth's version of the legend, however, is that the French get control of England. In a world where emerging nationalism could in itself sustain a drama (as in *Henry V*), Lear's break-up of the kingdom represented an unspeakably awful strategy. But in the source story, the Franks are the lesser of the two evils: order of any kind is preferable to civil war. Monmouth's story of misadventure is a comedy where everything works out to a just resolution in the end.

The question, then, is why did Shakespeare make *King Lear* into a tragedy? The answer may be that Shakespeare wanted to examine the essence of tragedy, probing beyond the six Aristotelian attributes (plot, character, language, thought, spectacle, and song) to a much darker, Sophoclean notion of what the world is like when everything goes wrong. The concept of "nothing" in the world of *King Lear* is more than just the empty feeling that results from a tragic catharsis—it is the opposite of everything. If, in a Christian universe, all events are part of a grand comedy, then in an ancient, pagan world, a Sophoclean world, tragedy is the negation of life, nature, and human will, a nothingness that depicts how awful things can be on the negative or "anti" side of the universe. To achieve this, Shakespeare constructs both a plot where everything works according to the opposite of what should be, and an entire universe and language of negativity, as well as a mentality of negation, where we look into "a glass darkly" to witness an inversion of everything that is sane, natural, and intelligent.

In the opening scene of *King Lear*, one of the first things that Kent says to Gloucester is "I cannot conceive you," a linguistic foreshadowing of the negativity at the heart of the play. Shakespeare's constant use of "neither/nor" constructions, the negating of words by using the prefix "un," and Lear's constant inability to see reason are only part of the negative equation. In this system, evil appears to triumph over good and illegitimacy over legitimacy. The subplot involving Gloucester's sons—the legitimate Edgar and the bastard Edmund, an eschatological pairing of opposites in the form of brothers—suggests that the world of the play is a perverse one, where the excesses of court life have permeated society and upset the natural laws by which the community should operate. In Act I, Scene ii, as Gloucester queries his evil son Edmund about the false and damning evidence that will indict the good son Edgar, Edmund replies, "The quality of nothing hath not such need to hide itself. Let's see. Come, if it be nothing, I shall not need spectacles."

What lies at the root of this negativity is a weakness of perception on the part of the tragedy's victims, Lear and Gloucester in particular. In these characters, that great Renaissance virtue—intelligent and informed sight—is transformed into either perceptual or physical blindness. The Fool warns Lear about the perils of giving away all his riches when he sings:

Fathers that wear rags
  Do make their children blind,
But fathers that bear bags
  Shall see their children kind.

Lear doesn't get the message, so the Fool resorts to the clarity of a prose statement to explain the folly of his king's ways:

We'll set thee to school to an ant, to teach thee there's no labouring i' th' winter. All that follow their noses are led by their eyes but blind men, and there's not a nose among twenty but can smell him that's stinking.

When Gloucester becomes the victim of misfortune at the hands of Edmund, he is blinded and set adrift in the world. In a page that is taken from Sophocles' Theban plays, physical blindness, if not cognitive blindness, results from trusting the wrong idea or placing too much importance in one's confidence. Blindness in *King Lear* comes not from failing to see but from seeing something that is not there—a kind of nothing. Lear perceives gratitude in his two eldest daughters where there is none. Gloucester perceives a plot by Edgar that does not exist. Of the outcast and downfallen in the play, only the Fool is able to see things clearly. Indeed, even the sun, that "eye of heaven" from Shakespeare's *Sonnet 18*, has been blinded by eclipses, as Gloucester remarks to Edmund in Act I, Scene ii:

These late eclipses in the sun and moon portend no good to us. Though the wisdom of nature can reason it thus, yet nature finds itself scourged by the sequent effects. Love cools, friendship falls off, brothers divide. In cities mutinies; in countries, discord; in palaces, treason; and the bond cracked 'twixt son and father... We have seen the best of our time.

All the world, it would seem, is afflicted by a kind of tragic flaw; the light is eclipsed by darkness and a pervading blindness prevails. Edmund refers to it as a time akin to the fall of man from the Garden of Eden, an upset of nature that has thrown everything off balance "like the catastrophe of the old comedy." Indeed, Lear's intellectual blindness is a metaphor for a presiding darkness in nature that obscures the true meaning of things so that nothing is what it seems and the entire world is cast into shadow.

Lear himself, as the king of this world, is a metaphor for what has gone wrong with nature and a microcosm of the world itself. A microcosm is a human being viewed as epitome of the universe, a personification of nature where the essential ingredients of the world are reflected on a small, observable scale within a single individual. Shakespeare makes Lear fulfill this role by having him reflect imbalances that manifest themselves in a series of "disorders." As an individual, a king, and a microcosm, Lear contains in his character all of the four *elements*—earth, air, fire, and water—that were considered to be the essential ingredients of the world according to the ancient Greek philosopher Heraclitus. These elements were normally balanced within nature, but when one attempted to usurp or take precedence over the others, the result was a natural disaster. These elements within a human being were known as *humors*. If they were balanced within a personality, then the individual was said to be in good humor; if they were out of kilter, then the result was a malady or a particular type of negative personality. Ben Jonson, a contemporary of Shakespeare, wrote a play about the nature of human temperament, *Every Man in His Humour*, where he depicts the individual personality as being a matter not only of Virgilian level-headedness but of a balance of internal chemistry that is reflected in behavior types. Lear, the microcosm of the universe, experiences four distinct periods in which each of his elements goes out of balance. The result is disorder both within Lear's personality and in nature.

Air, being hot and moist, was associated with the blood. When an individual's temperament suddenly became hot, short-tempered, or extremely passionate, that individual was said to be *sanguine*. The ruddy-cheeked Wife of Bath, who set out on her pilgrimage to Canterbury to find her sixth husband in Chaucer's prologue to *The Canterbury Tales,* is said to be sanguine—passionate and hot-blooded. In *King Lear,* Lear's short temper at the home of Regan, a moodiness that Regan uses to dismiss her father from her home, is his sanguine period.

Fire was associated with hot and dry conditions, and those who possessed passionless, dry, arid personalities were said to be *choleric.* The choleric aspect of the humors was associated with the yellow bile of the digestive systems; when an individual was violently dyspeptic (sick to his stomach), it was said that his body was attempting to rid itself of an excess of choleric humor. When Goneril and Regan realize that their father is out of humor, or imbalanced in his thinking, shortly after he gives away his kingdom in Act I, Scene i, Goneril describes his advancing years as "the unruly waywardness that infirm and choleric years bring with them." Old age is perceived as a "drying out of the human spirit," a withering in which the body acts much like a dry leaf that has fallen from a tree.

Water, the element of cold and moist conditions, was given the name *phlegmatic* when applied to personalities. It was associated with green matter in the body, with pus and infections; when the body produced too much nasal waste, it was said that the personality was attempting to expel an excess of phlegm. Certainly the storm scene in Act III, Scene ii, is Lear's phlegmatic period. Outcast, stripped of his power, his dignity, and his sanity, he experiences a period of madness as nature unleashes a violent tempest. He huddles with the Fool, Kent, and the dispossessed Edgar, orphans of the storm, in a small shelter on the heath. As nature rages against them, Lear rages against the world, and his inner madness is reflected in the outer madness, the imbalance, of the physical world that is completely out of its humors:

> *Blow, winds, and crack your cheeks. Rage, blow.*
> *You cataracts and hurricanoes, spout*
> *Till you have drenched out steeples, drowned the cocks.*
> *You sulph'rous and thought-executing fires,*

Vaunt-couriers of oak-cleaving thunderbolts,
Singe my white head. And thou, all-shaking thunder,
Strike flat the thick rotundity o' th' world,
Crack Nature's moulds, all germains spill at once,
That makes ingrateful man.

In his pitch and fever, Lear asks that the entire world be destroyed, and that his madness unleash a second flood that would wash all humankind away.

The final element, earth, was represented in the human makeup as black bile, the cold and dry end of all life and all things that are consumed to sustain life. Associated with excrement, this element was given the name *melancholy* and associated with despair, depression, and numb withdrawal from the world. When Lear appears dead to the world shortly before he recovers his senses, he experiences his melancholy phase. In Renaissance art, particularly in English portraiture from Shakespeare's period, melancholy was often associated with love-lorn young men, who struck a pose with a hand either to their cheek or under their chin, suggesting that they were musing on a broken heart or on the complexities of a universe that had left them defeated. Albrecht Dürer's famous engraving "Melancholia" portrays an angel with one eye cocked toward heaven. She is surrounded by all the instruments of science and learning, but in a fit of exasperation or ennui does not know what to do with them. Goethe extrapolated the theme of the melancholic personality in his novel about despair, ennui, and suicide, *The Sorrows of Young Werther*. What both the pose and the state of mind of melancholia suggest is a boredom that stretches beyond the "woe is me" of a character and into the dark depths of unquenchable longing, a state of mind that becomes the malaise of the world in Chekhov's *Uncle Vanya*.

Albrecht Dürer. Melancholia. All the instruments of science and invention lie idle while the angel wrestles with the darker side of its nature with a look of "Now what?" in its eye. Advancement, the etching suggests, is available only if we are prepared to take action to make it happen.

Tragedy, in Shakespeare's view, was more than mere blindness, being out of balance with the elements, or even a matter of being tested by the elements, although Edgar acknowledges that tragic victims come under the intense scrutiny and pressures of a nature that is out of order. In Act III, Scene iv, at the height of the storm and in one of the most desperate moments in the play, Edgar laments:

...through fire and through flame, through ford and whirlpool, o'er bog and quagmire; that hath laid knives under his pillow and halters in his pew, set ratsbane by his porridge, made him proud of heart, to ride on a bay trotting horse over four-inched bridges, to course his own shadow for a traitor. Bless thy five wits, Tom's acold. O, do, de, do, de, do, de. Bless thee from whirlwinds, star-blasting, and taking.

In these very Anglo-Saxon-sounding words, a cry for help from the depths of privation and despair, Edgar is suggesting that to bear the weight of tragedy is to come under that ancient, horrible specter of fortune, the same force that drove Oedipus to blind himself in Sophocles' play.

In terms of the theme of fortune, *King Lear* is Shakespeare's attempt to rewrite Sophocles. The world of the play, that dark, blind, imbalanced cosmos, is a realm that lacks any notion of Boethian grace. It is almost as if there is no God, no comedy, and no redemption in *King Lear*. The universe that Shakespeare portrays is the very heartland of tragedy, a place that is pagan almost beyond belief, where human beings are victims of some absurd, indefinable, higher power. The blinded Gloucester, a victim of both plot and fortune, remarks in Act IV, Scene i: "As flies to wanton boys are we to th' gods; / They kill us for their sport."

This is a universe where the pagan again rears its head, in spite of Saint Augustine and in spite of Boethius. Shakespeare seems to be freely admitting that tragedy is not possible in a Christian universe where God would ordain a just resolution to all action and where suffering, no matter how great or how unexplained, is always for a purpose. In the world of *King Lear*, the gods rule in place of God. Like the Thebes of Sophocles' Theban plays, it is a land governed by fortune.

In Act II, Scene iv, the Fool refers to "Fortune, that arrant whore." The Fool is wise enough to have read his Boethius. He realizes that Fortune is fickle, and that a Job-like fall from a pinnacle position is inevitable. The Fool is also wise enough to know that Fortune, like the stock market, runs in cycles, and it can be perceived as a great wheel:

> Let go thy hold when a great wheel runs down a hill, let it break thy neck with following. But the great one that goes upward, let him draw thee after.

All one has to do, the Fool believes, with considerable patience and wisdom, is to wait until things improve. Even patience, however, has its limits. The view from the bottom of the heap, as Edgar laments in Act IV, Scene i, is bleak and dismal. Yet even in the darkest moments of a pagan, tragic universe, there is still the element of hope—that one small blessing from the gods that did not escape Pandora's box:

To be worst,
The lowest and most dejected thing of fortune,
Stands still in esperance, lives not in fear,
The lamentable change is from the best;
The worst returns to laughter...

World, world, O world!
But that thy strange mutations make us hate thee,
Life would not yield to age.

If the only consolation in the world of tragedy is faint hope, then perhaps the Machiavellian dictum, cognizance above all, is the functioning maxim in the Lear universe.

This begs the question: what makes a character fall? If one is searching for the source of misfortune in tragedy, there are several possibilities. Gloucester's statement that we are "flies to wanton boys" would suggest that the first reaction to tragedy is to blame it on the gods. But as Cassius points out in Shakespeare's *Julius Caesar*, "the fault dear Brutus is not in the stars but in ourselves." Tragedy, as common sense would suggest, is the product of a weakness or an oversight in the tragic protagonist, a character flaw that is known as the *tragic flaw*. Lear's flaw is his blindness. His desire to retire exposes that flaw; retirement means that he must relinquish power. His blindness to the ramifications of his actions is astounding; he brings down not only himself, but his entire world. In the end, what remains after the final battle is a world reduced to next to nothing.

Edgar offers a *dénouement*, or aftermath statement, that seems excessively understated in the face of the overwhelming tragic spectacle that the audience has just witnessed:

The weight of this sad time we must obey,
Speak what we feel, not what we ought to say,
The oldest hath borne most; we that are young
Shall never see so much, nor live so long.

In a remnant land that Albany (Goneril's hen-pecked husband) calls "a gored state," the downfall of the world was brought about both by folly and madness on the part of Lear—all of it seemingly unnecessary—and by poor kingship. Albany offers the crown of the kingdom jointly to Edgar and Kent (as if it were his to offer), but Kent declines it because of his age and his impending death ("I have a journey, sir, shortly to go"). The entire universe, it would appear, has suffered what Shakespeare in his historical tragedy *Richard II* calls "the second fall of curs'd man." It would appear, from Shakespeare's reading of the situation, that the world was brought down by hubris that expressed itself as a physical and spiritual blindness.

The only one who sees through this folly is the last person one would turn to for clear thinking: the Fool. In Act I, Scene iv, Goneril refers to the jester as "All licensed Fool," someone who says whatever he wants because he has no need for dishonesty. He achieves, long before anyone else in the play, what Edgar longs for in his closing speech: to "speak what we feel." It is the Fool's sense of personal honesty, his integrity in the face of absurdity, that makes him the only character in this dark world who really knows who he is. Everyone else suffers an identity crisis during the massive shuffling of positions and ranks that takes place during the course of *King Lear*, but the Fool remains firm in his low social standing. When Lear fails to grasp the directness of the Fool's wisdom and his intelligent commentary on the stupidity of their predicament, the Fool chastises him with a little declaration of that Classical Greek virtue—know thyself:

Thou wast a pretty fellow when thou hadst no need to care for her frowning. Now thou art an O without a figure. I am better than thou art now: I am a fool, thou art nothing.

The Fool's sense of identity seems almost out of context, but this is an inverted world, where fools are wise and kings are foolish. Shakespeare has drawn upon an older notion of foolery than the one we tend to acknowledge in our contemporary use of the word. In present-day idiom, to be a fool means to act with stupidity, to lack the insight and information necessary to make correct decisions. In the world of *King Lear*, however, Shakespeare's Fool is a wise, if not holy, innocent, a figure uncorrupted by the airs and pomposities of a political world. Like Cordelia, whose part can be played by the same actress as the Fool because the two characters never appear in the same scene, the Fool sees the world with a clarity that is unappreciated by others. When he offers advice to Lear in Act I, Scene iv, his philosophy is one of simplicity and practicality rather than elaborate reasoning:

> *Have more than thou showest,*
> *Speak less than thou knowest,*
> *Lend less than thou owest,*
> *Ride more than thou goest,*
> *Learn more than thou trouest,*
> *Set less than thou throwest;*
> *Leave thy drink and thy whore,*
> *And keep in-a-door,*
> *And thou shalt have more*
> *Than two tens to a score.*

When Lear replies that "This is nothing fool," it is because all he hears is a strained, run-out rhyme scheme and not the content. In other words, Lear and his tragic courtiers are constantly caught in the formality of structure and fail to consider content. When asked by the Fool if Lear can make use of nothing, the king responds with his hubristic maxim that "Nothing can be made out of nothing." Kent realizes that the Fool's observations may contain some element of wisdom when he points out to Lear, "This is not altogether fool, my lord." But it is too late: Lear has already made his fatal error. He need not have split his kingdom to remain secure; yet out of the nothing of that unnecessary action, he reduced his whole existence to nothing, thus fulfilling the prophecy of his own words. And if Lear is anything, he is a bad student. The Fool keeps offering him the schooling he needs to recognize just how the real world operates, but Lear, playing another kind of fool, fails to listen. "Prithee, nuncle," says the Fool, "keep a schoolmaster that can teach thy fool to lie. I would fain learn to lie."

Through his blindness to the realities of the world, Lear fails to

obey the principles of kingship that Machiavelli stressed: cognizance, *virtù* and tight security. But the root of tragedy in *King Lear* is a negation of order. The audience's heart breaks when Lear appears in the final scene of the play, carrying the body of his beloved Cordelia. To this shock and horrific loss, Lear exclaims: "And my poor Fool is hanged." To scrap any form of order is to leave the world open to anarchy, and to make victims of everyone caught within the ill fortune of the circumstances.

The Tempest, on the other hand, is a play about how a king makes something out of nothing by conjuring spirits, directing characters to ends that are his own and not theirs, and by establishing order where none previously existed. The play tells of a dispossessed king who is marooned, along with his infant daughter and a library of conjuring books, on a magical island. His evil brother, who has masterminded the situation, usurps his throne. Many years later, with the young girl grown almost to adulthood, the marooned king, Prospero, seizes the chance to manipulate events to his satisfaction, manufacturing a terrible storm just off the coast of his island. During that storm, a ship carrying his brother, Antonio; his adversary, Alonso; his adversary's son, Ferdinand; and their court and servants is dashed by the waves until it spills its passengers into the sea. The castaways wash ashore on Prospero's island, and events unfold until the dethroned king has won back his kingdom and worked out a political resolution to his problems.

As a play, *The Tempest* is Shakespeare's most sociological. He portrays the various levels of society to show how each class operates by its own set of principles. Natural man is represented by Caliban, a strange creation of nature rather than nurture, who has been portrayed in stage productions of *The Tempest* as everything from a native North American to a half-fish-like being. The manual or existential level of society, those who are defined by what they do, is represented by the mechanicals: Stephano, a drunken butler, and Trinculo, a jester who lacks some of the finer social graces that were portrayed by Lear's Fool. Political man is represented by the collection of statesmen and princes that includes Alonso, the king of Naples; his brother, Sebastian; Antonio, the usurper of the crown of Milan and Prospero's brother; and a gaggle of hangers-on such as Adrian and Francesco. In addition, Shakespeare has opted to present two higher orders of being: the intellect (represented by Prospero and Gonzalo) and the spirit (portrayed by Ariel, Prospero's servant of the supernatural).

Despite all these classifications, Shakespeare shows that there are essentially two types of individuals: those who control others and those who are controlled. When the slave, Caliban, joins forces with Stephano and Trinculo for a drunken revel (unlike the comic revel, which is celebrated with the virtues of music and dance in a masque), the three attempt to rise in revolution against their masters and create their own state. In a vision of what mob rule might be like, Shakespeare puts into Caliban's mouth a profession of violence:

Why, as I told thee, 'tis a custom with him
I' th' afternoon to sleep; there thou mayst brain him,
Having first seized his books, or with a log
Batter his skull, or paunch him with a stake,
Or cut his wesand with thy knife. Remember
First to possess his books; for without them
He's but a sot, as I am, nor hath not
One spirit to command. They all do hate him
As rootedly as I. Burn but his books.

James Barry. King Lear and Cordelia. Lear's heart breaks as he enters with Cordelia's body. Lear exclaims, "And my poor Fool is hanged." Oddly enough, Cordelia and the Fool never appear in the same scene and it is possible to have the same actress play both characters—a fact that many productions ignore.

Caliban may be a brute, but he is smart enough to realize that the power behind Prospero lies in his ability to control circumstances through a series of magic texts that allow him to conceive of a world as he would have it. In this world where power comes not from force of arms or courtly appearances but from the imagination, the great strength that Prospero wields comes through his ability to harness the spirit world, represented by Ariel. Ariel performs Prospero's will; in fact, the sprite is an extension of his will. With each command, Prospero vows that Ariel will soon be set free, and when his final bidding is done, that freedom is finally granted. Ariel is allowed to go back to the elements, and fades away as Prospero announces that all his "charms are now o'erthrown."

What Shakespeare is saying, in both *King Lear* and *The Tempest,* is that the new world we all wish for begins in a twofold manner. On the one hand, it must be shaped from the cognizance and understanding of the limitations of this world. It must be given the same checks on human nature that one would exercise in the management of power. And good managers are, after all, argus-eyed. They maintain the kind of vigilance that Machiavelli saw as the basis for *virtù*. But Shakespeare also seems to be saying that comic possibilities result from the marriage between our cognitive abilities and our imaginations. Our desire to see the world work out according to our own passions for poetic justice can create amusing circumstances. That land of happiness, that destination of human dreams, is a matter of choice and free will, a question of how one is going to perceive the world, a matter of masks. It comes down to the individual to decide how to achieve happiness.

Prospero, the ruler of a magic island, is a metaphor for the notion of authorship, of how an imagination can shape and direct events to make a desired resolution possible. Happiness, Shakespeare likes to believe throughout his plays, is not a matter of living by a set of illusions but of reaching a hard-earned understanding of the world. Contrary to Saint Augustine's warnings about the theater, the stage is a realm where illusion makes understanding possible by putting the audience in touch with its own terrors, its own joys, and its own ability to rely on human instincts to see something better in the world. Experience, as Edgar suggests in the final lines of *King Lear,* is the greatest educator. It teaches that clarity and honesty, saying what one feels rather than what one thinks one should say, are the most stable foundations for a better world. In the end, as Prospero suggests in his final speech, the only real goal of the dramatist is to give the audience what it wants, so that "the purpose of playing, both at first and now," as Hamlet advises the Player King in *Hamlet,* is more than "to hold as 'twere a mirror up to nature." The purpose of playing, if the dramatist's "project" is not to fail, is to "please." And few things please an audience as much as seeing, in a vision that rises out of the emotional wreckage of tragic catharsis, a comic preview of a place and time that just might be possible if given enough play in the imagination.

Sir Joseph Noel Paton. Caliban. Paton's Caliban looks more devilish than many theatrical renderings of the character. Caliban has been depicted on stage in a vast variety of manners— from a frog-like creature to a Russian serf and a North American Indian. He is a metaphor for the downtrodden, who cannot express their desire for liberty in an articulate manner.

14

A BETTER PLACE
THAN THIS

John Milton's *Paradise Lost*
and Jonathan Swift's *Gulliver's Travels*

---

*Richard Westall.
Milton Compos-
ing* Paradise
Lost. *In this
stylized early
nineteenth-
century depic-
tion, Milton's
daughters are
dutifully taking
dictation in a
spacious, Gothic
hall setting. The
reality was far
different. The
rooms of the
house at Chal-
font St. Giles
were dimly lit
and it is a
wonder that the
girls did not go
blind along with
their father.*

SHORTLY after the publication of *Gulliver's Travels* in the autumn of 1726, Jonathan Swift wrote to his friend, the poet Alexander Pope, slightly bemused at the initial reaction his book of four satirical travel stories had received. An Irish bishop, a learned man of sound reputation, examined Swift's new work of fiction and, according to Swift, said the book was "full of improbable lies, and for his part he hardly believed a word of it."

This must have amused Swift, which is why he drew the comment to Pope's attention. *Gulliver's Travels* is the story of a wandering seaman who travels first to a land where he is surrounded by a race of little people, then to a nation of giants, next to a flying island where the people are consumed by science, and finally to a land where human beings run about like wild beasts and the sanest creatures afoot are rational, platonically minded horses.

To Swift, the bishop's reaction must have been nothing short of pure triumph, for *Gulliver's Travels* was a work of witty and humorous satire in which he attempted to deflate the ills of his world by exposing the flaws of reason that govern human thought. The fact that the bishop missed the point, that his reaction blended into the mass of stupidity the work sought to expose, was only part of the joke Swift was sharing with Pope, because in reality, there is no record of an Irish bishop making such a comment. In fact, the bishop may simply have been part of an attempt by one writer to gloat over a new work to another. The deadpan nature of the satirist, Swift realized, was the key to success in writing a satire, and when the real or imaginary bishop took the bait, hook, line, and sinker, Swift could pride himself on that little moment of superiority every satirist dreams of achieving.

John Milton did not fare as well with the publication of *Paradise Lost*. In 1652, Milton, who served in the parliamentary government of Oliver Cromwell following the overthrow and execution of Charles I in 1649, went totally blind from overwork. To make matters worse, he lost his second wife and his only son within a matter of months in 1658, then was briefly imprisoned when the

monarchy was restored in 1660. A political outcast, just as Machiavelli had been when the Florentine republic fell to the Medici,
Milton was more or less unfashionable in the world of the Restoration. When the plague hit London in 1665, he decided to cut his
losses and move his third wife and two remaining daughters to a
house in south Buckinghamshire, in the village of Chalfont St.
Giles. In that house, a small, melancholy place with tiny windows
(what need did he have of light?), he waited out the plague by
dictating an epic poem to his daughters. When no one was available to take his dictation, Milton would memorize up to forty lines
at a time and hold them in his head. The scope of information that
the blind Milton carried around with him in his memory is unparalleled. Into his masterwork he poured the lifetime of reading and
learning that had ruined his sight.

Originally, Milton had intended to write an epic about
Arthurian romances, and he chose as his medium the iambic lines
of English speech set in the elevated form of Virgilian blank verse.
But Milton soon had second thoughts about creating another
poem that would recount the matter of Troy, a theme that had
been recounted so often in previous eras. According to Edward
Phillips' 1694 account, *The Life of Milton*, the first passage Milton
composed in that lightless house in Buckinghamshire was an invocation in which he called both for inspiration and for the light to
enable his vision to see greater things:

> *O thou that with surpassing glory crown'd!*
> *Look'st from thy sole dominion, like the god*
> *Of this new world; at whose sight all the stars*
> *Hide their diminish'd head; to thee I call,*
> *But with no friendly voice; and add thy name,*
> *O Sun! to tell thee how I hate thy beams*
> *That bring to my remembrance, from what state*
> *I fell, how glorious once above thy sphere;*
> *Till pride and worse ambition threw me down,*
> *Warring in Heaven, against Heaven's glorious King.*

Milton had intended this to be the opening of his new work, a poem
not merely about the moral questing of knights and the schooling of

intellects but about the entire nature of the universe—part cosmological mythology, part heroic epic, a blend of the Bible and Virgil. Milton took as his theme the grand notion of humankind's fall from the Edenic state, as the Bible outlines in Genesis 2–4. As Phillips explains, Milton had considered writing a much different poem, one that would evoke pity and cathartic suffering from Anglo-Saxon readers, who would see the world as a bleak, miserable, and despairing place, cut off from the beauty and bounty of divine grace:

> But the height of his noble fancy and inventions began now to be seriously and mainly employed in a subject worthy of such a Muse, *viz.* a heroic poem, entitled *Paradise Lost*, the noblest in the general esteem of learned and judicious persons of any yet written by any either ancient or modern. This subject was first designed a tragedy...

However, instead of opening his tragedy with the first passage he wrote, Milton saved the lines for Book IV, and decided that what he would create would be the first half of a divine comedy, a history of time that would show the reader, in much the same Boethian way that the medieval poem *Adam lay yboundin* had argued, that fate was the result of a good and all-seeing Providence, and a God who had a master plan for His cherished creation. Perhaps to mitigate his own suffering and to find, through the writing of an epic, the answers to the questions of his own unfortunate life, Milton transformed his tragedy into a comedy.

According to legend, as the epic stretched to almost eighteen thousand lines, his daughters' patience wore thin. When he had completed the manuscript for the enormous work, he had difficulty finding a printer for it. First, there was the matter of his political unpopularity. Second, there was about as much call in the publishing world of 1666 for a highly academic epic about the battle of good and evil and the future of humankind as there is today. The third problem he faced came as a result of the Great Fire of London, which started in a baker's shop in Pudding Lane on September 2, 1666, and raged out of control for four days, devastating over four hundred acres of urban real estate and destroying over thirteen thousand houses. Much of the destruction centered on the area around St. Paul's Cathedral, where the majority of English printers and publishers were located. In the end, Milton found a publisher named Samuel Symons in Aldergate in London, but to persuade him to issue the work in ten books, Milton agreed to one of the all-time worst contracts in publishing history. He received £5 for delivery of the manuscript and was promised another £5 when the first edition sold out. Milton revised the work for a 1674 edition, adding Books XI and XII, for which he was paid another £5. He should have received a successive payment of £5 when the second edition sold, but he did not live long enough to see the money: he died of gout shortly after the second edition was published. In all, Milton's revenue from *Paradise Lost* was the absurdly small sum of £15.

To make matters worse, upon the publication of the initial, ten-book version of *Paradise Lost* in 1667, his friend Thomas Ellwood, the first person to read the new epic, suggested that he write a sequel and complete his intended comic structure. To live up to his intention to portray the complete divine plan of the Almighty, Milton wrote another, somewhat shorter epic, *Paradise Regained*. When he completed *Paradise Regained*, he showed the manuscript to Ellwood and said, "This is owing to you; for you put it into my head by the question you put to me at Chalfont, which before I had not thought of." If Milton's struggles prove anything, it is that the life of an author is seldom an easy one.

The first edition of *Paradise Lost* in 1667 opened with a Latin verse provided by Milton's former secretary, the English poet Andrew Marvell. The Latin poem is something of an advertisement for Milton's poem, a kind of early movie trailer, where the plot, the design, and the other virtues of the work are openly lauded. Marvell speaks of the poem's "vast design" and how he grew to like the project's "success." The opening lines of Marvell's commendatory verse make direct reference to the size of the accomplishment and to the challenge of Milton's blindness:

> *When I beheld the Poet blind, yet bold,*
> *In slender Book his vast design unfold,*
> Messiah *Crown'd,* God's *Reconcil'd Decree,*
> *Rebelling Angels, the Forbidden Tree,*

Heav'n, Hell, Earth, Chaos, All; the Argument
Held me a while misdoubting his Intent,
That he would ruin (for I saw him strong)
The sacred Truths to Fable and old Song
(So Sampson *grop'd the Temple's Posts in spite)*
The World o'erwhelming to revenge his sight.

To Marvell, the poet's blindness is both a testament to his imaginative strength and proof that *Paradise Lost* is a vatic poem, a work inspired by divine insight.

Milton had examined the issue of his blindness in a sonnet written as early as 1655 but published only a year before *Paradise Lost*, the famous *When I Consider How My Light Is Spent* (also known as *On His Blindness*). As in many of his poems, but particularly in *Paradise Lost*, Milton asks his maker why he has imposed certain challenges. What he desires to understand, more than anything else, is the nature of God's plan. In *When I Consider How My Light Is Spent*, Milton attempts to make sense of that plan through the most discursive of poetic forms, the sonnet:

When I consider how my light is spent
Ere half my days, in this dark world and wide,
And that one talent which is death to hide,
Lodged with me useless, though my soul more bent
To serve therewith my Maker, and present
My true account, lest he returning chide;
"Doth God exact day-labour, light denied?"
I fondly ask; but Patience, to prevent
That murmur, soon replies, "God doth not need
Either man's work or his own gifts; who best
Bear his mild yoke, they serve him best. His state
Is kingly. Thousands at his bidding speed
And post o'er land and ocean without rest:
They also serve who only stand and wait."

The question that may have perplexed Milton was, "Wait for what?" The answer may be divine inspiration. Like Tiresias in Sophocles' Theban plays or even Demodocus of *The Odyssey*, the blind man is a seer who is able to look inward through the gift of imaginative sight and see a world that is far more complex and splendid than anything the sighted can perceive.

Certainly, Milton understands the weight of literary tradition he must bear when, in Book III of *Paradise Lost*, he reflects not only on his own loss of eyesight but on the issue of poetic sight:

> *With other notes than to th'* Orphean *Lyre*
> *I sung of* Chaos *and* Eternal Night,
> *Taught by the heav'nly Muse to venture down*
> *The dark descent, and up to reascend,*
> *Though hard and rare: thee I revisit safe,*
> *And feel thy sovran vital Lamp; but thou*
> *Revisit'st not these eyes, that roll in vain*
> *To find thy piercing ray, and find no dawn.*

Milton realizes that his blindness has a purpose: he is part of a long line of seers who coped with enormous quantities of poetic material and shaped their vision around the strength of a grand inner sight. Such inner sight is mandatory, Milton understands, if a poet is to approach the epic tradition and meet its incredibly high demands:

> *So were I equall'd with them in renown,*
> *Blind* Thamyris *and blind* Maeonides,
> *And* Tiresias *and* Phineus *Prophets old.*
> *Then feed on thoughts, that voluntary move*
> *Harmonious numbers; as the wakeful Bird*
> *Sings darkling, and in shadiest Covert hid*
> *Tunes her nocturnal Note.*

The seer, remember, is a receptacle or a medium for divine inspiration, a conduit through which higher truths pass on their way to human ears. Milton realizes that the light that has been denied to his eyes now shines inward, and that "the mind through all her powers" irradiates the world for him so that he "may see and tell" both an earthly narrative and "Of things invisible to mortal sight." All Milton need do as a poet to receive the gift of divine sight and see heaven in his mind's eye—that place he calls "the Fountain of Light"—is to ask for assistance when he needs it.

In the opening lines of Book I, Milton calls upon the "Heav'nly Muse," not the pagan spirits of the Classical helicon but the Holy Spirit itself, to assist him as he attempts to "justify the ways of God to men" by illumining "What in me is dark." *Paradise Lost*, then, is more than a history of time. It is a story that attempts to portray the struggle between good and evil, the battle between the metaphorical forces of light and darkness, and the way in which faith and patience reveal the splendor of God's creation. Milton attempts to bridge the inherited conventions of Classical pagan poetry and the mythography of the Bible. This goes a step beyond Dante, who struggled to amalgamate the pagan and the Christian conventions of the epic while reaching for a new literary cosmology. *Paradise Lost* would be a modern epic, one conceived, shaped, and articulated from a new, post-Renaissance view of the imaginative world. If Vasari articulated the laws by which the seeing eye perceived the world, Milton would articulate the vision by which the inner eye perceived the imaginative landscape in a fresh and reordered sense.

The Reformation—and its premise that each person meets God on his or her own terms—became the foundation for Milton's argument. For Milton, there would be no guides through the cosmos, no intercessors or intermediaries. *Paradise Lost* was to be the statement of a clear, single voice articulating a clear, single poetic vision. In *Paradise Lost*, the individual, whether the narrator or Adam, would speak directly to his Creator with an openness and directness that are evident in the Bible and in Saint Augustine's *Confessions*. In the end, what Milton created was a modern, intimate epic, as much a story of a personal struggle to find meaning and purpose in the hardships of life as Saint Augustine's *Confessions* was an individual's attempt to comprehend his own personality.

Nowhere in *Paradise Lost* is this notion of the intimate epic more evident than in Book IX. At that point, Adam is given the choice of either staying on in Paradise without Eve, who has been condemned for her crime of yielding to the temptations of the serpent, or leaving Eden and making his way in the cold, cruel world. In one of the most touching passages of the poem, Milton hints at the grief he must have felt on having buried two wives in his life, and the difficulties of maintaining a third marriage that bore the pressures of his infirmity. In a speech that sounds almost like the abdication message of Edward VIII, Adam explains his choice to Eve, who is shaken by the fact that the first man would rather give up eternal life in paradise than live without the woman he loves:

> *How can I live without thee, how forgo*
> *Thy sweet Converse and Love so dearly join'd,*
> *To live again in these wild Woods forlorn?*
> *Should God create another* Eve, *and I*
> *Another rib afford, yet loss of thee*
> *Would never from my heart; no, no, I feel*
> *The Link of Nature draw me: Flesh of Flesh,*
> *Bone of my Bone thou art, and from thy State*
> *Mine never shall be parted, bliss or woe.*

Eve, for Milton, becomes the icon of womanhood. Not only is she described in Book IV as walking "hand in hand" with Adam, she is also given the conventional treatment accorded to the beloved in the Song of Solomon or the Virgin Mary in a troubadour's poem: she is described from head to foot according to the conventions of love poetry:

> *Shee as a veil down to the slender waist*
> *Her unadorned golden tresses wore*
> *Dishevell'd, but in wanton ringlets wav'd*
> *As the Vine curls her tendrils, which impli'd*
> *Subjection, but requir'd with gentle sway,*
> *And by her yielded, by him best receiv'd,*
> *Yielded with coy submission, modest pride,*
> *And sweet reluctant amorous delay.*
> *Nor those mysterious part were then conceal'd,*
> *Then was not guilty shame: dishonest shame*
> *Of Nature's works, honor dishonorable,*
> *Sin-bred, how have ye troubl'd all mankind*
> *With shows instead, mere shows of seeming pure,*

And banisht from man's life his happiest life,
Simplicity and spotless innocence.

It would seem that Milton is in love with Eve, with her beauty, her innocence, and her erotic presence and "coyness." He intends her to be a model for all women, in the same way that the Virgin Mary (who could not appear in this poem, as she would have represented a pro-Catholic theological slant) in the Provençal hymns of the eleventh century represented all womanhood. Eve is the fascination that all men cannot live without, and she provides the basis for the intimacy and love that Milton perceives as the binding element in human behavior.

What makes Milton's characters engaging in what would be an otherwise stagy narrative is their humanity. The pathos of Adam's statement, the profound power of human love, and even the power of human weakness make the epic dynamic. The final lines of the poem, as Adam and Eve leave the garden together and enter the unknown world, where toil and eventually death will seize them, capture the frailty and devotion that Milton perceived as the elements holding humankind together:

The world was all before them, where to choose
Thir place of rest, and Providence thir guide:
They hand in hand with wand'ring steps and slow,
Through Eden *took their solitary way.*

Even the central characters, in particular Satan, fascinate and captivate the reader with their depth of human passion.

Herein lies one of the central problems of *Paradise Lost* that has troubled readers from the outset: evil, for all its peculiarities and idiosyncrasies, is almost more fascinating than good. When the rebel angels fall from heaven in Book I, they are cast into hell. Milton describes their place of imprisonment as a dark, gloomy dungeon, a place not unlike the Tower of London cell that he occupied briefly during the Restoration:

The dismal Situation waste and wild,
A Dungeon horrible, on all sides round
As one great Furnace flam'd, yet from those flames
No light, but rather darkness visible
Serv'd only to discover sights of woe,
Regions of sorrow, doleful shades, where peace
And rest can never dwell, hope never comes
That comes to all; but torture without end
Still urges, and a fiery Deluge, fed
With ever-burning Sulphur unconsum'ed:
Such place Eternal Justice had prepar'd
For those rebellious, here thir Prison ordained
As far removed from God and light of Heav'n
As from the Centre thrice to th' utmost Pole.

Like Dante's hell, Milton's infernal region is a place without hope, and his reference to the hopelessness of the rebel angels' situation is a small nod to Dante's eschatologically organized place of punishment. But Milton's hell is not delineated, probably because his purpose is not to show the sins of man but the way in which evil takes shape and constantly reorganizes itself like a government following a revolution. To this end, Milton makes his hell into a

parliament, not unlike the parliament of which he was a part during the Civil War. In Book II, as the fallen angels debate what they should do next and each of the major figures of hell speak in their turn, the speeches are composed of empty, rhetorical gestures. In its scope and its deliberations, hell is a place of much talk but little action. It is also a place cut off from the divine light of the imagination that Milton calls upon for inspiration. It is a literalist's lock-up. Milton makes it quite clear that if heaven is a place driven by intelligence, creativity, and the power of the imagination, then hell, or Pandemonium, as it is called in *Paradise Lost*, is a place of vengeful willfulness:

> *What though the field be lost?*
> *All is not lost; the unconquerable Will,*
> *A study of revenge, immortal hate,*
> *And courage never to submit or yield:*
> *And what is else not to be overcome?*
> *That Glory never shall his wrath or might*
> *Extort from me. To bow and sue for grace*
> *With suppliant knee, and deify his power*
> *Who from the terror of this Arm so late*
> *Doubted his Empire, that were low indeed,*
> *That were an ignominy and shame beneath*
> *This downfall...*

Satan, the leader of the rebel angels, announces his intention to wage a constant war upon God and his creations for having cast him out of heaven during a cosmic civil war. His banner cry is, "Better to reign in Hell, than serve in Heav'n," and in a kind of perverted piece of Boethian-style logic, he declares:

> *The mind is its own place, and in itself*
> *Can make a Heav'n of Hell, a Hell of Heav'n.*
> *What matter where, if I be still the same,*
> *And what I should be, all but less than hee*
> *Whom Thunder hath made greater? Here at least*
> *We shall be free...*

Unknown. The war in heaven. From an eighteenth century edition of Paradise Lost. *The troops are gathered in a heroic arrangement, arrayed for battle and posed for aesthetic purposes. The figure in the center is meant to be Aeneas-like in his stature.*

Satan's declaration to his fallen troops is an attempt to rouse them from the stupor they experience after the fall. It is couched in a new, defiant form of rhetoric, the rhetoric of revolution and overthrow, which must have taken readers by surprise when they opened *Paradise Lost* for the first time in 1667; yet it is the same rhetoric that Milton heard in the Puritan-minded parliaments that challenged the authority and sanctity of Charles I. Couched as it is in the language of defiance, this rhetoric of revolution embraced a new concept: liberty and freedom could be achieved by the overthrow of existing power structures, and the ends, as Machiavelli suggested, justified the means. From Satan's point of view, his ends are liberty and freedom, the right of self-determination, and the abolition of existing political orders.

If this sounds familiar to modern readers, it is because two key minds of the modern world—Thomas Jefferson and Karl Marx—turned to Books I and II of Milton's *Paradise Lost* when they laid the imaginative foundations for their own new worlds. Usurpation and revolution had been traditionally taboo subjects in the order-oriented Western imagination up to the time of Milton. To overthrow a king, as Shakespeare suggests in his history plays *Richard II* and *Henry IV*, was to challenge an order established by heaven and to act, as Boethius would see it, in an evil manner contrary to the laws of nature. It is no accident, then, that when the early leaders of the American Revolution were evolving their ideas in the State House of Virginia, they turned for their visual symbols to *Paradise Lost*. The banner that was originally carried into battle by the uprising colonials was a flag bearing a serpent and the motto "Don't Tread On Me," a symbolism that reflected Milton's motifs more than any biblical connection. When Jefferson challenged the right of kings in the Declaration of Independence, he went to great lengths to explain that rights issued only from "the Law of Nature and of Nature's God." Men were "endowed by their Creator with certain unalienable rights," and these included "life, liberty, and the pursuit of happiness." Marx, on the other hand, cared less for religious justification than he did for the bourgeoisie, and he suggested that the proletariat's "ends can only be achieved through the forcible overthrow of all existing social conditions." In other words, Marx considered nature and God to be sidebars to human affairs, and thus made an easy target of himself for the Bible-thumping opponents of "Godless Communism."

Ideology and revolution aside, what Milton accidentally created in *Paradise Lost* was a new type of literary character: the dark hero. In fact, the major question that confronts the reader of *Paradise Lost* is the question of who exactly is the protagonist. One would assume that, because God has a divine plan that unfolds through the narrative, he is the protagonist. Like Prospero in *The Tempest*, he is the stage-manager of all the action, the author of the events, and the inspiration that articulates the action through the medium of the poet. Quite evidently, Milton intended God to be his protagonist, and for him, the issue would not have been a question.

But there are other candidates. Milton explains in Book VII, during an interlude in which the Archangel Michael offers Adam a lesson in explanatory mythology, that God imagined the world but it was Christ who was the artist. This may have been Milton's indirect attempt to poeticize the fact that the book of Genesis features two creation stories: in the first, an artist makes the cosmos and the world; in the second, a judging and governing God presides over human beings in the Garden of Eden. The plan for *Paradise Lost* and its sequel, *Paradise Regained*, suggests that Christ's sacrifice is the reason man will return to God and evil will eventually be vanquished. In Book IV, Christ offers himself up in much the same way that Galahad presents himself as a worthy victim in *The Quest of the Holy Grail*:

> *Behold mee then, mee for him, life for life*
> *I offer, on mee, let thine anger fall;*
> *Account mee man; I for his sake will leave*
> *Thy bosom, and this glory next to thee*
> *Freely put off, and for him lastly die*
> *Well pleas'd, on me to let Death wreck all his rage;*
> *Under his gloomy power I shall not long*
> *Lie vanquished; thou hast giv'n me to possess*
> *Life in myself for ever, by thee I live,*
> *Though now to Death I yield, and am his due*
> *All that of me can die, yet that debt paid,*
> *Thou wilt not leave me in the loathesome grave...*

But I will rise Victorious and subdue
My vanquisher, spoil'd of his vaunted spoil...

Then with the multitude of my redeem'd
Shall enter Heav'n long absent, and return,
Father, to see thy face...

If, for his love of humankind and his bravery, Christ is considered the protagonist of *Paradise Lost*, it is a well-earned accolade, based not only on the character's strength but on the foreshadowing that his promise carries with it. Milton had hoped the reader would identify with the admirable characters of the poem such as God and Christ, and failing that, at least identify with Adam and his dedicated love for Eve.

But *Paradise Lost* presented the character of Satan as a figure full of intense passion. He is seductive to contemporary readers for the fire and vitality with which he expresses his rage and his determination. That is why (as will be discussed in chapter 16) Satan passed through the hands of Gothic writers such as Mary Shelley and was recreated as a new breed of character, the *anti-hero*. Anti-heroes in literature are fascinating because they play against our moral expectations by being both bad and clever at the same time. Like Goethe's Faust or Egmont, or even like the rogue Odysseus, such characters struggle against forces of goodness that they cannot hope to overthrow, yet they do so with such fervor and single-mindedness that readers are attracted to them. Anti-heroes draw upon the same impulse that makes one yield to the spectacle of tragedy.

Milton builds this strange attraction into his description of Satan, perhaps as a reminder to the reader that the weakness in the human character that Saint Augustine warned against in his arguments about the nature of illusion, reality, and the theater is the same flaw that would tempt a moral reader into sin:

Thir dread commander: he above the rest
In shape and gesture proudly eminent
Stood like a Tow'r; his form had yet not lost
All her Original brightness, nor appear'd
Less than Arch-Angel ruin'd, and th' excess

Of Glory obscur'd: As when the Sun new ris'n
Looks through the Horizontal misty Air
Shorn of his Beams, or from behind the Moon
In dim Eclipse disastrous twilight sheds
On half the Nations, and with fear of change
Perplexes Monarchs.

Milton goes on to note that Satan still possesses "dauntless courage" and "considerate Pride." And strangely, it is Satan who undergoes the mandatory *nekusis*, or trip to the netherworld, that is typically the domain of the hero. When Satan decides to journey to earth in Book II, to open a second front on God, the trip is an "anti-*nekusis*" or a voyage to the world of life, rather than to the realm of death. Milton is trying to show that everything Satan does is of a metaphorically inverted or contrary nature. Yet despite its contrariness, Satan's journey is described in heroic terms, almost like an odyssey. As God watches the progress of the fallen angel's voyage through the cosmos, the leader of the rebel angels is described as a solitary, wandering figure, much like Cain:

So on this windy Sea of Land, the Fiend
Walk'd up and down alone bent on his prey,
Alone, for other Creature in this place
Living or lifeless to be found was none...

Mary Shelley later makes use of this passage for *Frankenstein* when the Daemon—the Fiend, as he is called by Victor Frankenstein—wanders the earth as an outcast. In this passage, which describes Satan's stop in the empty regions that will eventually become Chaos, Milton paints a picture of a dark figure in a desolate landscape. Writers of the later Romantic era, those who had lived through the political and moral complexities and ambiguities of the French and American revolutions, used the dark hero in the solitary landscape as a means of evoking both a chill of fear and a note of alienation. Yet no matter how far later authors evolved their dark heroes, characters such as Heathcliff in *Wuthering Heights* or even the Daemon in *Frankenstein* owe a small portion of their makeup to Milton's Satan. He is drawn in such a way as to challenge the reader into questioning and examining the difference between good and evil. And just as the medieval romances tried to show the reader how to make a moral decision based on faith, intelligence, and adherence to the vision of a larger goal, so *Paradise Lost* uses Satan to test the reader's faith, intelligence, and ability to discern between the literal purpose of a character and the moral message he conveys.

The high-epic quality of *Paradise Lost* is achieved by Milton through his use of elevated language, through the poetic form of *blank verse*, and through the structure of the narrative. The poem is extremely episodic in its treatment of events, though each book tends to end with a note of suspense that makes the reader want to move further through the narrative. Like *The Odyssey*, the story begins *in medias res* with the fall of the rebel angels onto the fiery lake. This is followed in Book II by the parliament of Pandemonium, where the proceedings of hell resemble the broadcasts from a modern government. These two books are set in the linear time of the narrative, though the paradox is that Milton is writing about a world before the fall of humankind and therefore before time existed. Instead of making this into a narrative problem, Milton realizes that it frees him to have the events of his story take place on a series of simultaneous planes, a framework that is exactly the nature of the epic form.

Book III shifts the scene to heaven, where a discussion between God and Christ is under way, and where Christ promises to sacrifice himself for humankind. What Book III underlines is Milton's notion of predestination, the Protestant view that God has a plan for the universe and that faith is the key to embracing, understanding, and accepting what he has in store.

In Book IV, the scene shifts again. Satan arrives in the newly formed paradise and, through his envying eyes, the reader is taken on a tour of Adam and Eve's blissful state. Milton's paradise is a lush, Arcadian vision that owes more to Classical literary notions of the Golden Age and to Virgil's *Eclogues* than it does to the Eden of Genesis. It is described as a "Silvan Scene," "verdurous," and "loaden with fairest Fruit." Borrowing his phraseology from the Bible, Milton tells us that paradise is:

A Heaven on Earth: for blissful Paradise
Of God the Garden was, by him in the East
Of Eden *planted....*

The garden does not represent all of Eden. Milton believes that Eden was the name for the first state of the world, and that a corner of it was set aside as a *hortus conclusus*, a miniature Land of Cockaigne where nature provided everything for the first humans and where they and the animals coexisted in a peaceable kingdom. With passages of lush description, Milton paints a vision not unlike those that were being created by the Restoration landscape architect Inigo Jones, who favored slightly wild parkland stretching into broad prospects, instead of the small, ornamental gardens that for centuries had been the artistic interpretation of paradise:

Flow'rs worthy of Paradise which not nice Art
In Beds and curious Knots, but Nature's boon
Pour'd forth profuse on Hill and Dale and Plain...

Groves whose rich Trees wept odorous Gums and Balm,
Others whose fruits burnisht with Golden Rind
Hung amiable, Hesperian *Fables true,*
If true, here only, and of delicious taste:
Betwixt them Lawns, or level Downs, and Flocks
Grazing the tender herb, were interpos'd,
Or palmy hillock, or the flowr'y lap
Of some irriguous Valley spread her store,
Flow'rs of all hue, and without Thorn the Rose:

Milton almost goes overboard in his description of paradise because he wants to heighten the sense of loss that the reader will feel when Eve and Adam are cast out.

The feeling of grief over the loss of paradise is further heightened by Milton's use of suspense. Books V to VIII form a large digression in the narrative that begins after the Archangel Raphael issues Adam an all-points warning that Satan has escaped from hell and may show up in the garden. Raphael stays and talks to Adam and Eve, reciting a virtual encyclopaedia of explanatory mythology concerning the natural history of the world. Book VI digresses yet again to tell of the story of the war in heaven, its causes, its major events, and its results, and to provide the background information to Book I. Book VII offers the story of the creation by Christ, who acts on God's advice and direction. Book VIII offers even more additional material, explaining the structure of the heavens and the situation of earth in relation to the rest of the cosmos. Milton seizes this opportunity to talk about why God always seems so remote to humankind and to present a half-baked version of the Copernican universe:

Giulio Romano. St. Michael and the Devil. As in the battle between St. George and the dragon, the battle between St. Michael and the Devil is an eschatological allegory where good is pitted against evil. St. Michael appears heroic though tangled in the serpent's tale, a left over from the Devil's appearance in Paradise Lost *and* Genesis.

God to remove his ways from human sense,
Plac'd Heav'n from Earth so far, that earthly sight,
If it presume, might err in things too high,
And no advantage gain. What if the Sun
Be the centre of the World, and other Stars
By his attractive virtue and their own
Incited, dance about him various rounds?

Having provided more background to the story in the form of explanatory mythology, and having heightened the sense of suspense by delaying the forward movement of the narrative, Milton moves on with the events of his story. When it picks up again in Book IX, the events of the fall are described. Satan, disguised as a serpent, tempts Eve and she eats of the fruit of the tree of knowledge. The fall of humans through the acquisition of

knowledge would suggest that innocence is a lack of awareness, a state of intellectual numbness in which one simply accepts, without question, one's circumstances. Milton realizes this is a simplistic view. His pre-fall Adam and Eve are intelligent beings who question, acquire knowledge, and learn where they are and how they came into being. Knowledge, in Milton's view, is the consciousness of limits. In paradise, there were no limits, no time, no lifespan, and no death. Perhaps this is why Eve feels the taboo against the fruit of knowledge is meaningless:

> *O Sacred Wise, and Wisdom-giving Plant,*
> *Mother of Science, Now I feel thy Power*
> *Within me clear, not only to discern*
> *Things in thir Causes, but to trace the ways*
> *Of highest Agents deem'd however wise...*
>
> *Those rigid threats of Death; ye shall not Die:*
> *How should ye? by the Fruit? it gives you Life*
> *To Knowledge: By the Threat'ner? look on mee,*
> *Mee who have touched and tasted, yet both live,*
> *And life more perfet have attain'd than Fate*
> *Meant mee, by venturing higher than my Lot.*

What knowledge entails, as Milton's ironic statement would have us believe, is the capacity to overreach ourselves in such a way that we become self-destructive. Mary Shelley considers these words when she writes *Frankenstein*; for her, science is the fruit of the tree of knowledge, the capacity of humankind to overreach its bounds or its "lot" in life and attempt to be God without bearing the moral responsibility of the divine. Indeed, in a comment that shows both humankind's naivety and its inability to measure up to the Almighty, Adam tells Eve that he believes God will not destroy them for their transgression:

> *Nor can I think that God, Creator wise,*
> *Though threat'ning, will in earnest so destroy*
> *Us his prime Creatures dignifi'd so high,*
> *Set us over all his Works, which in our Fall*

For us created, needs with us must fail,
Dependent made; so God shall uncreate,
Be frustrate, do, undo, and labor lose,
Not well conceiv'd of God, who though his Power
Creation could repeat, yet would be loath
Us to abolish, lest the Adversary
Triumph and say; Fickle their State whom God
Most Favors, who can please him long?...

The perplexed Adam is sadly mistaken, and the scene shifts in Book X back to Pandemonium, where Satan celebrates his triumph as sin and death enter the world.

Had Milton left *Paradise Lost* at Book X, it would have been an anomaly: a tragic epic. Epics, by their very nature, reward readers for having endured their length by presenting or promising the justice of a satisfactory resolution. For the second edition, Milton added Books XI and XII, and *Paradise Lost* became a comic poem. In Book XI, just as the dispossession of Adam and Eve from paradise is taking place and the Archangel Michael is leading them from the garden, he pauses and takes the first man on a short journey to the top of a mountain, where he shows him a vision of the future. In the history lesson that Book XI becomes, Adam is shown the hardship of the world, but with the promise of something better at the end of time—the New Jerusalem. Yet the message is quite clear, and the note of tragedy that has been struck continues to echo. Once paradise is lost, it is lost forever. Though new horizons present themselves, and though Christ's sacrifice will ultimately redeem humankind, the human race can never truly go home again. Blissful grace gives way to restless wandering, just as eternal life and innocence give way to death and sin. No matter how hard they may search for that lost garden, the best that humanity can do is to discover or imagine surrogate paradises, utopias, and strange new worlds. The New Jerusalem is *not* Eden, and although it may symbolize a promised return to God, it also implies a return that comes via the price of worldly experience and human suffering. What is lost with paradise is innocence.

The voyage of humanity toward a better destiny than that allotted to them after the fall has been one of the chief dreams of the imagination. Boethius thought we could convince ourselves of a better direction merely by believing in the underlying goodness of the world. Saint Augustine championed the avenue of moral self-criticism as a means of retrieving what remained of humanity's contact with divine grace in a fallen world. Medieval romance presented the idea that a better world would be built upon the moral education of a Christian soul, and More considered evolved systems of public morality to be the key to social improvement. Machiavelli embraced the science of politics as a means to his end and stated that reality was something the fortunate individual could learn to control and shape to improve a nation.

With this tradition behind him, Jonathan Swift set out to explore the imaginative possibilities of an Everyman figure who sets forth on voyages for profit or discovery, only to learn that paradise and a happy society might be beyond the grasp of human nature. *Gulliver's Travels* examines what it means to be out of one's context, to feel different, and to attempt to see the world through a set of fresh perspectives that are just as limiting and human-centric as those of Swift's own society. The ability to step outside ourselves, "to see ourselves as others see us," as Robert Burns the Scottish poet would put it, is a gift from God that allows glimpses of the ways in which the world might be different, if not better.

At its heart *Gulliver's Travels* is a satire, an attempt by Swift to reform his society by exaggerating its weaknesses and flaws. His attacks are leveled against religion, politics, the legal system, human vices, bodily habits, fashion, industry, and science. Nothing escapes his piercing wit. Despite the voraciousness and vicious-ness of his satire, however, Swift never launches into *invective*, a form of satire that defames its subject without pointing to correc-tive measures. Nor does he engage in *splenetic*, which is satire that attacks a person by getting personal. His line of argument, however, particularly in Book IV, does border on a *jeremiad*, a form of satire in which the satirist is sad or remorseful over the state of his society. Jeremiad, like all satire, is a developed and highly styl-ized form of *irony*, in which the work seems to be saying one thing while really meaning another. Irony is a complex way of speaking that demands that the reader read not merely interpretively but inferentially—in other words, read through and beyond a text to grasp its meaning. What we are meant to do when we read *Gulliver's Travels* is to see the Lilliputians of Book I as contemporary Englishmen, the Laputians of the flying island of science and logic of Book III as the continental Deists, and the Houyhnhnms, the Platonic horse-beings of Book IV, as paragons of what human nature should be. Satire views the world slightly askance, through a fun-house mirror, where there is just enough distortion to allow the viewer to see the reality behind the reflection. A satirist is one who looks at life and institutions from a distance, and who is willing to depict reality not just as he sees it but as it would be seen if it could be altered for the better.

Swift believed that satire was "one of the illnesses he suffered throughout his life." Born in Dublin of Anglo-Irish background, he was a member of the educated ruling class of Ireland, the Ascendancy, and he served as dean of St. Patrick's Cathedral in Dublin until his death in 1745. As a churchman, however, he was constantly confronted by the ills of English rule in Ireland. During a serious famine in 1729, when Irish children were dying in droves, he penned a satirical essay, "A Modest Proposal," in which he suggested that they would make tasty meat dishes for English tables. He discussed how to prepare the children and how they should be served. To an English public expecting the gospel truth from a cleric of such high position, Swift's observations were an outrage. Surely the English were not cannibals. But Swift had made his point: the Irish were suffering under English laws.

Even though it was the Age of Enlightenment, these were not times in which an author could speak freely. Swift had difficulties with the publication of *Gulliver's Travels*, as had Milton with *Paradise Lost*. The first edition of the book outraged Swift when he found that his friends who had seen it through the press had allowed the printer to make serious cuts to the text for fear its language would inflame certain individuals and cause irrevocable political problems for its author. What made the cuts even harder to bear was that many of them were made by one of Swift's closest friends and a fellow satirist, Alexander Pope, a figure who was not prone to withholding his sentiments on most topics. It was not until 1735 and the second edition that Swift was able to restore much of his original text and give *Gulliver's Travels* the satiric bite he had intended.

The question for Swift was how to challenge the moral assumptions of his time. In a stroke of brilliance, he perceived that it was language that was flawed—an observation that Saint Augustine attempted to express in the *Confessions*. It is no accident of narrative that the first thing Gulliver does when he arrives in each new world is to learn its language. Language gives him access to what people are thinking, while also allowing him to delve into the most essential structures that govern the society. In Laputa, for example, the language is so difficult to pronounce that it baffles even the proficient linguist Gulliver. In Houyhnhnmland the Houyhnhnms whinny like horses:

> In speaking they pronounce through the nose and throat and their language approaches nearest to the High Dutch or German, of any I know in Europe; but is much more graceful and significant. The Emperor Charles V made almost the same observation, when he said that if he were to speak to his horse, it should be in High Dutch.

The story is that the Emperor Charles V said that he would "speak to his God in Spanish, his mistress in Italian, and his horse in German." What Swift appears to be saying is that the Houyhnhnms speak a language that is not far from the contemporary dictum of some of the first naturalist philosophers of the Enlightenment, chiefly Gottfried Leibniz, who argued in his philosophy of Optimism that in all things, there was a necessity for the truth, and this was "the best of all possible worlds." Swift's subtle allusion to Optimism (a matter that was lampooned by Voltaire in *Candide* and that will be discussed in chapter 15) as an ingredient in Houyhnhnmland suggests that the world of Book IV may be what "the best of all possible worlds" would look like. Indeed, Houyhnhnmland, which closely resembles Plato's republic of philosopher kings, is a reason-based society that values truth, friendship, and clear thinking. The question for Swift, then, was how could such a rational republic be achieved? Was science the route for humankind or would science ultimately prove destructive? What possibilities lay in the old, ancient virtues that had been expressed by the Greek philosophers? In some ways, *Gulliver's Travels* amounts to a debate between the Ancients and the Moderns, a debate that Swift himself lampooned in his treatise "The Battle of the Books."

In the end, Swift seeks to settle the issue through a critique of the various forms of reason that operated in the social systems of his times. In *Gulliver's Travels*, there are several types of reason at work. In Book I, when Gulliver makes his first voyage and lands on the island of Lilliput, reason is a means by which the little people of that place defend their positions, no matter how absurd that position may be. They use reason, particularly extreme positions of theology and political theory, to explain all manner of absurdities. They believe that if they are buried on their heads, they will be standing at the day of judgment. The island's great political-religious debate is about at which end a person should open his hard-boiled egg, and the controversy between the Big-Endians and the Little-Endians is meant to reflect Swift's disgust at the debate between the high and the low church.

In Book III, Swift examines Laputa, an entire society that lives by scientific reason. This presents an opportunity for him to consider how humans use science. The Laputians have, for example, found a way to make their island fly. But they use this knowledge to rain terror from the sky on their enemies—a small allusion to the *auto-da-fé* of the eighteenth century—until, in retaliation, their adversaries raise church spires. The Laputians are terrified that the bottom of their island will be pierced, and they leave their enemies alone.

For Laputians, everything is a matter of mathematics and science. Gulliver recounts a banquet and how mathematical theorems rather than culinary skills dominated the event:

In the first course there was a shoulder of mutton, cut into an equilateral triangle, a piece of cold beef into a rhomboides, and a pudding into a cycloid. The second course was two ducks trussed up into the form of fiddles; sausages and puddings resembling flutes and hautboy, and a breast of veal in the shape of a harp. The servants cut our bread into cones, cylinders, and parallelograms, and several other mathematical figures.

The Laputians are so bound up in scientific thought and astronomy, in fact, that they do not even watch where they are going. To avoid injuring themselves or bumping into walls or objects, they employ a group of people known as Skruldrubs, who knock them on the head with a round mallet. Gulliver notes that the Laputians are so obsessed with mathematics and science that they have lost all semblance of imagination—a virtue that Swift perceives as being the highest order of reason.

Swift links reason directly to language in Book IV of *Gulliver's Travels*. The Houyhnhnms believe that reason is the basis for goodness and friendship, and language is the means by which the rule of compassionate reason is established. Gulliver observes the sanctity in which the Houyhnhnms hold reason:

...so their grand maxim is to cultivate *reason*, and to be wholly governed by it. Neither is *reason* among them a point problematical as with us, where men can argue with plausibility on both sides of the question; but strikes you with immediate conviction, as it must needs do where it is not mingled, obscured, or discoloured by passion and interest.

Reason, the Houyhnhnms believe, is more than a mere system of logic or argumentation; it is also a generosity of spirit and ideas that forms the basis of friendship:

Friendship and *benevolence* are the two principal virtues among the Houyhnhnms, and these are not confined to particular objects, but universal to the whole race....They preserve *decency* and *civility* in the highest degrees, but are altogether ignorant of *ceremony*....They will have it that *nature* teaches them to love the whole species, and it is *reason* only that maketh a distinction of persons, where there is a superior degree of virtue.

Morality is something that comes through the practice of honesty and the use of a language that is honest in its semantics and grammar:

> For he argued thus: that the use of speech was to make us understand one another, and to receive information of facts; now if anyone *said the thing which was not*, these ends were defeated; because I cannot properly be said to understand him; and I am so far from receiving information, that he leaves me worse than in ignorance, for I am led to believe a thing *black* when it is *white*, and *short* when it is *long*. And these were all the notions he had concerning that faculty of *lying*, so perfectly well understood, and so universally practiced among human creatures.

The Houyhnhnms are troubled when they learn from Gulliver that in his world, there are individuals who are paid to lie: lawyers:

> I said there was a society of men among us, bred up from their youth in the art of proving by words multiplied for the purpose, that *white* is *black*, and *black* is *white*, according as they are paid. To this society all the rest of the people are slaves.

Swift is arguing the point that Saint Augustine was also trying to make: language can become a vehicle for morality only when it is used morally. The problem, as Gulliver acknowledges through his misanthropy at the conclusion of the work, is that morality is something one must learn from the world, from the Odyssean experience of "seeing the cities of many men and learning their ways."

Swift uses the voyage story only as a framing device, a context into which he sets his attempts to explore the ills of his own society. He realizes that his duty as a satirist is to present ways that those ills may be addressed. In chapter 7 of Book IV, Gulliver articulates Swift's purpose:

> But I must freely confess that the many virtues of those excellent quadrupeds [the Houyhnhnms] opened my eyes and enlarged my understanding, that I began to view the actions and passions of man in a very different light, and to think the honour of my own kind not worth managing...

Ultimately, Gulliver's voyage account is an attempt to reform his species. There is something in the satirist, a belief that things will get better in the end, that is hopelessly idealistic. It is a view of life that holds that literature serves a higher comedic purpose, that it shows readers the possibilities the future holds if only the moral instincts of the imagination are heeded.

The idea that the world can be improved, either through the patience of faith or the faith of the imagination, lies at the heart of both *Paradise Lost* and *Gulliver's Travels*. Swift, in the spirit of adventure and enlightenment, believed that one must go out into the world and explore it, challenge it, and discover just what it has to offer. If there is a moment of disappointment presented by the character of Lemuel Gulliver, it comes when he arrives home and does nothing to improve humankind. He simply goes and lives in his stable with his horses, unable to keep human company or stand the smell of human bodies. However, Swift accomplishes what Gulliver does not by writing his book, though as a work of literary legislation, it has not changed the world. The irony of *Gulliver's Travels* is that it has often been consigned to the realm of children's literature, but perhaps that is where it is most effective. The better world that humankind longs for, both Swift and Milton would argue, is something that begins in a state of innocence. The question Johnson and Voltaire ask, as we will see in the next chapter, is whether or not innocence is a good thing. Whatever the case, the memory of a peaceable and uncomplicated time and place is always there as a reminder, a possible destination for the next journey.

15

JUST HAPPY TO BE HERE

Samuel Johnson's *Rasselas*
and Voltaire's *Candide*

A T the height of the Seven Years War in North America, as the Age of Reason seemed anything but, the most popular board game in the British colonies was an early prototype of modern-day Snakes and Ladders. In the Game of Life, as it was known, a player rolled the dice and moved his marker along the board. He would land on an array of occupational and emotional possibilities that would provide opportunities for other players in the game to offer jests, jabs, and mocking remarks. In the space of a few turns, a player could move from being "The Angelic Boy" to the "The Debaucher" or "The Indigent." The game was meant to be a commentary on how the choice of direction in life could determine not only one's status in society but one's happiness.

Epistemological philosophers of the Age of Reason—the philosophers who sought to understand how they knew what they knew—arrived at the idea that happiness was an occupational matter, a perception that was more elaborate than our contemporary sense of job satisfaction and a little less complex than the Greek sophist concept of "know thyself." René Descartes declared that "to be was to do," a forerunner of Sartre's existentialist idea of "man is defined by what he does." To the eighteenth-century mind, the process of doing something both defined a person and dictated public identity and self-comprehension. One of the marvelous concepts that the eighteenth century gave to the Western imagination was the notion of possibility, that an individual, such as Daniel Defoe's Moll Flanders, could start off in the worst circumstances and, through a series of strange coincidences and developments, end up very well off. It was an age when the possibilities of science, society, and the imagination were suddenly open to an ever-increasing audience. The novelists of this period loved the idea of poetic justice, that life presented one with the opportunity for comic resolution.

Although rank and inherited position still held sway, the old idea that one's birth determined social standing and status was gradually being eroded by the rise of the middle class; what one did with one's life counted more and more toward the issue of success. The road to success, if not the road to heaven, seemed to be paved either with rubble or with gold, depending on whether one was happy or not. And after all, what was happiness? It was a fresh concept that asked individuals to question their existence, critique it, measure it both spiritually and materially, and evaluate the positives and negatives in the search for satisfaction, self-assurance, and security.

Gottfried Wilhelm Leibniz, who is credited, along with Isaac Newton, with the invention of calculus, evolved a philosophy in which he perceived the hand of God at work in all things, as a creator and as a divine mathematician. Leibniz's philosophy, a view that was not far from the extreme mathematical positions that Swift satirized in Book III of *Gulliver's Travels*, suggested that because the universe was governed by a complex system of laws that appeared to work logically and mathematically, nature was therefore a reflection of the perfection of God. The universe was perceived as a collection of individual parts, or "monads," as Leibniz called them. Each monad was the irreducible form of a thing, and all the monads were connected in one large, complex, machine-like structure that worked logically. As God was good, something he demonstrated in the mathematical correctness of nature, then everything was as good as it could be, and our world must therefore be "the best of all possible worlds."

What evolved in the eighteenth-century mind was essentially paradoxical. On the one hand, philosophers sought order, balance, and elaborate systems in nature. They believed that their systems would ultimately reflect the goodness of God, the order of the universe, and the ideal state of humankind, if only people were willing to exercise reason and logic. On the other hand, the problems

of society continued. England and France launched an enormously costly war for the dominant position on the colonial front. The Seven Years War was perceived by many as sheer folly, or, as Voltaire expressed it in *Candide*, a matter of extreme absurdity:

"'Tis another sort of madness," said Martin. "You know these two nations are at war for a few acres of snow in Canada, and that they are spending more on this fine war than all of Canada is worth. It is beyond my poor capacity to tell you whether there are more madmen in one country than in the other...."

What seems to have resulted from this paradox between philosophy and reality in the minds of eighteenth-century writers were two very different stances. There were those who maintained a position taken by the Scottish philosopher David Hume (who wanted to be a writer and never really succeeded), who argued that beliefs were based on the imagination and not on reason; morality was not something that could be argued, because convictions were based on feelings rather than on logic. In the end, said Hume, nothing can be known for certain. Human existence was the question and not the answer. Writers such as Samuel Johnson adopted

Hume's position, and that is why a work such as *Rasselas* examines how one pursues questions rather than how one arrives at answers.

Johnson wanted to believe there were certain principles in the universe that one could trust: faith, friendship, justice, and love. His novel tells the story of a young prince, Rasselas, who becomes bored with life while living in a perfect world, an enclosed *hortus conclusus* nation that resembles Houyhnhnmland or Arcadia. With his mentor, Imlac, his sister, Pekuah, and her handmaiden, Nekayah, Rasselas leaves his home in Happy Valley and enters the world with one question: *what is the way of life?* He undertakes the pursuit of happiness, only to find that no one is happy because each situation has its limitations and drawbacks. The imagination is not to be trusted because it expresses an uncertainty principle. Johnson believed that somehow, reason must triumph over the imagination and the universe must be an ordered place where individuals find happiness:

Benjamin West. The Death of General Wolfe. Alas, the only one in the picture who was actually at the Battle of Quebec in the Seven Years War was Wolfe. The rest of the individuals were subscribers who paid to be painted into West's canvas.

> There is no man whose imagination does not sometimes predominate over his reason, who can regulate his attention wholly by his will, and whose ideas will come and go at his command. No man will be found in whose mind airy notions do not sometimes tyrannise, and force him to hope or fear beyond the limits of sober probability. All power of fancy over reason is a degree of insanity; but while such power can control and repress, it is not visible to others, not considered as any deprevation of the mental faculties: it not pronounced madness but when it comes ungovernable, and apparently influences speech or action.

Human beings can be happy, claims Johnson, if humanity is willing to live life according to reason, inquiry, and humane logic. But as Rasselas and his party discover, happiness is hard to find.

On the other side of this philosophy–reality paradox were writers such as Voltaire, who perceived a vast discrepancy between the capacities of reason and the realities that the exercise of reason was intended to correct. Through the use of satire in his novel, *Candide*, Voltaire sought to deflate Leibniz's concept of the perfect, mathematical universe. The characters in *Candide* are scattered by the forces of evil and violence. Unspeakable acts of barbarism are

committed against the protagonist, Candide, his love interest, Cunegonde, and his mentor, Dr. Pangloss. Throughout it all, in a fit of
belief that borders on insanity, Pangloss maintains his Optimistic
position that this is "the best of all possible worlds." In his attack on
the philosophy of Optimism, Voltaire outlined his position:

"O Pangloss!" cried Candide. "This is an abomination you had
not guessed; this is too much, in the end I shall have to
renounce Optimism."
   "What is Optimism?" said Cacambo.
   "Alas!" said Candide, "it is the mania of maintaining that
everything is well when we are wretched."

For Voltaire, philosophical inquiry was absurd in a world where
survival was a fundamental issue for most people. He held that the
best individuals could do was to look after themselves, their own
world, and mind their own business. To demonstrate his point, he
bought a house at Ferney, just on the edge of the Swiss border, and
proceeded to plant over four hundred trees in the belief that his
actions would give shade and tranquility to later generations. There
was also an element of political savvy in his choice of real estate.
His garden house at the end of the property was in Switzerland.
Whenever the French authorities came after him for something he
had written, he could sit in peace at the end of his garden and wave
to his pursuers from the safety of a neutral country.
   The twentieth-century English poet W.H. Auden memorialized
Voltaire's border-riding in *Voltaire at Ferney*:

Almost happy now, he looked at his estate.
An exile making watches glanced up as he passed,
And went on working; where a hospital was rising fast
A joiner touched his cap; an agent came to tell
Some of the trees he'd planted were progressing well.
The white alps glittered. It was summer. He was very great.

Far off in Paris, where his enemies
Whispered that he was wicked, in an upright chair
A blind old woman longed for death and letters. He would write

"Nothing is better than life." But was it? Yes, the fight
Against the false and the unfair
Was worth it. So was gardening. Civilize.

In his subtle way, Auden is making the point that as a writer, Voltaire took the art of satire to an entirely new level. For Voltaire, satire was not merely an agent to suggest reform of some of humankind's more absurd institutional creations and follies, as Swift might have suggested; it was also a powerful weapon for social change that could target and destroy the very structures on which modern Europe had evolved. Voltaire signed most of his letters with the vehement declaration, "Ecrasez l'infame" or, "Wipe out the evil thing," a message leveled at those in society who propagated injustices in the name of tradition. The vehemence with which Voltaire expressed himself in this salutation became well known, causing one French nobleman to remark, "Who is this Monsieur l'Infame?"

There was something enormously attractive about Voltaire's response to the world around him, and he garnered the attention of the rich and famous. Catherine the Great sent him gifts. Frederick the Great was a regular correspondent, and Samuel Johnson's wandering biographer, James Boswell, came to visit. A wax figure that Madame Tussaud modeled from life and that was displayed at the London waxworks until the 1970s caught the sense of defiance through intellect that marked all of Voltaire's writings, in particular *Candide*, a satirical novel that he wrote in three days in 1751 but did not publish for another eight years.

One of the great coincidences of literary history occurred in 1759 when Johnson and Voltaire, in two separate countries that were locked in a life-and-death struggle for control of North America, and without either having prior knowledge of what the other was doing, published two startlingly similar books. The books were successful beyond their authors' expectations, becoming instant best-sellers and hotly debated material for discussions on the need for social and spiritual renewal. In the case of each novel, the settings were exotic, part of a new vogue called *orientalism* that sought to dislocate the reader by placing the action in the realm of the unfamiliar. Both volumes examined the world through philosophical narratives, and both involved the journeys of young ingenue protagonists who go in search of happiness and encounter the world in all its hardship and struggle. Although Johnson and Voltaire reach very different conclusions and their perspectives are from two opposing spheres—Johnson the Christian Modern and Voltaire the satirical Ancient—the two works have become synonymous with their age. Both reflect the *esprit du temps*, the ethos of an epoch that perceived the possibility of happiness as being just beyond the human grasp.

The similarity between the two works was not lost on Johnson's biographer James Boswell, who recorded the coincidence in the April 1759 entry in his *Life of Johnson*:

Sir Joshua Reynolds. Samuel Johnson. Reynold's portrait captures Johnson in a moment of speculation, perhaps as he is formulating a witticism. Johnson has his finger squarely on the page, and the cock of the head and tilt of the eyes suggests that, like Rasselas and his company of wanderers, he has his sights set on a vision of something beyond this world.

None of his [Johnson's] writings has been so extensively diffused over Europe; for it has been translated into most, if not all, of the modern languages. This Tale, with all the charms of oriental imagery, and all the force and beauty of which the English language is capable, leads us through the most important scenes in human life, and shews us that this stage of our being is full of "vanity and vexation of spirit."...Voltaire's *Candide*, written to refute the system of Optimism, which it has accomplished with brilliant success, is wonderfully similar in its plan and conduct to Johnson's *Rasselas*; insomuch, that I have heard Johnson say, that if they had not been published so closely one after the other that there was not time for imitation, it would have been vain to deny that the scheme of that which came latest was taken from the other.

As Boswell notes, the two works were written for entirely different reasons. Voltaire tried to refute the absurdity of Leibniz's attempts to explain the complexities of the world through mathematical theories, just as Swift had done with Gulliver's narrative of the voyage to Laputa. But Voltaire's inclinations go much deeper; he argues that God is not as much at work in the world as the Optimists believe, and that the distance between heaven and earth that Milton pointed out suggested God was absent from his offices of grace and goodness when events such as the devastating Lisbon earthquake of November 1755 took place. However, where Milton had confronted the disasters and upheavals of his time with the

368

question, "Where was Man?" Voltaire responded to the Lisbon earthquake with the question, "Where was God?"

Johnson wrote *Rasselas* for entirely different, almost small-scale reasons. As a young man, he had left his widowed mother in Lichfield to seek his fortunes, first in Birmingham and later in London, abandoning her and the poverty they shared in that provincial town. He eventually returned to Lichfield, where he started a small but less than prosperous grammar school, but he

soon set out for London again with one of his students, a would-be actor named David Garrick, who would later revolutionize the English stage. When his mother died in 1758, Johnson was overcome with guilt for what he had done. He went to the market square in his home town and stood there for three days as penance for his ungrateful act of selfishness. To pay for his mother's funeral, he penned *Rasselas* during the evenings of a three-week period. The story is about an individual's quest for happiness, and an answer to the restlessness and worldliness that had drawn his younger self to London.

As Boswell points out, both *Candide* and *Rasselas* share a fascination with the eighteenth-century vogue for *orientalism*. Like the late twentieth-century fascination with South American or postcolonial literature, the idea of oriental stories was to locate the action in the realm of the exotic and the unfamiliar. Just as More and Swift had used the possibilities of new worlds as a means of delineating social characteristics and philosophies, the practitioners of orientalism attempted to dislocate the reader's sensibilities and expectations within the context of discoveries. In the case of *Rasselas*, the story begins in Abissinia, a locale that embraced all the sense of otherness that Johnson needed. His first book, published anonymously in 1736, was a translation of a French novel set in Abissinia. The literary idea of Abissinia, or Ethiopia, carried connotations of the medieval Prester John legend and the hint that the characters hailed from an exotic cul de sac of Christendom.

Most of the main action in *Rasselas* is set in Egypt and Asia Minor, as the prince's party roams in search of "the way of life"; as a result, the story offers a subtle echo of a crusade, a quest, or an exodus. The twentieth-century author James Hilton borrowed much of Johnson's setting for his novel *Lost Horizons*; the difference between it and *Rasselas* is that in Johnson's work, the characters are trying to leave their happy and protected world, while in Hilton's book, the characters are attempting to get back to an ideal, womb-like state.

Rasselas opens in a place called Happy Valley, the Edenic seat of the Abissinian kings:

> The place, which the wisdom or policy of antiquity had destined for the residence of the Abissinian princes, was a spacious valley in the kingdom of Amhara, surrounded on every side by mountains, of which the summits overhang the middle part. The only passage, by which it could be entered, was a cavern that passed under a rock, of which it has long been disputed whether it was the work of nature or of human industry. The outlet for the cavern was concealed by a thick wood, and the mouth which opened into the valley was closed with gates of iron, forged by the artificers of ancient days, so massy that no man could, without the help of engines, open or shut them.

Happy Valley is a strange mixture of familiarities within the context of the exotic. It is partly the Garden of Eden, a place removed from the general situation of humankind and shut off with barriers. It is also, metaphorically, the cave from Plato's parable about the search for enlightenment and understanding. Whatever Happy Valley may be, it presents in *Rasselas* a metaphor for a place where everything is satisfied except for curiosity, a Land of Cockaigne in need of the variety and change that are part of existence in the rest of the world:

> The valley, wide and fruitful, supplied its inhabitants with the necessaries of life, and all delights and superfluities were added at the annual visit which the emperour paid his children, when the iron gate was opened to the sound of musick; and during eight days every one that resided in the valley was required to propose whatever might contribute to make seclusion pleasant, to fill up the vacancies of attention, and lessen the tediousness of time. Every desire was immediately granted.

The problem with Happy Valley and its utopian environment is the same problem that confronts so many utopias: tedium or ennui. As Anton Chekhov suggested in his nineteenth-century play *Uncle Vanya*, or as George Bernard Shaw parodied in his twentieth-century work *Heartbreak House*, ennui is the malaise of paradise. Herein lies the paradox of Eden that Johnson struggles with: if paradise is a place without change, a refuge from the cycles of time and natural entropy, is it really a perfect place?

Human nature, as Johnson argues in *Rasselas*, is based on change, and the continual process of learning something new, of discovering what is different, and of adapting one's understanding of the world on a daily basis form the fabric of life. Perhaps the most important message of *Rasselas* is uttered by the prince's sister, Nekayah, in chapter XLVII, as the party wearies of its continuous traveling and searching:

> Such, said Nekayah, is the state of life, that none are happy but by anticipation of change: the change itself is nothing; when we have made it, the next wish is to change again. The world is not

yet exhausted; let me see something to morrow which I never saw before.

This statement—that change is good and that life is a matter of continual learning—seems to reside at the heart of Johnson's own philosophy. It was Johnson, after all, who made the famous pronouncement about the plethora of energy and activity in his chosen city: "When a man is tired of London, he is tired of life."

What the oriental, exotic, secure setting of Happy Valley seems to represent, at least metaphorically, is the idea of numb perfection, a place that can accommodate human dreams but not human desires. For Johnson, desire and dreams are two different things. Dreams are part of that untrustworthy realm that, as Hume suggested, lies beyond the grasp and mediation of reason. The imagination is useful up to a point because it inspires curiosity, but beyond that, it is ungovernable. The quest undertaken by Rasselas and his entourage is triggered by "fancy," by imagining what might lie beyond Happy Valley:

> I fancy that I should be happy if I had something to pursue. But, possessing all that I can want, I find one day and one hour exactly like another, except that the latter is still more tedious than the former. Let your experience inform me how the day may now seem as short as in my childhood, while nature was yet fresh, and every moment showed me what I never had observed before. I have already enjoyed too much; give me something to desire....I shall long to see the miseries of the world since the sight of them is necessary to happiness.

Desire is a natural human inclination, the idea that there is always something to pursue that will lead one to better places, deeper understandings, and more certain beliefs. Yet desire and dreams, as Johnson would have us believe, are at odds with one another, and thus happiness is something that one can always pursue but never really attain. Life, in this context, is a quest, a search, a learning process. "Surely," comments Rasselas in chapter XVI, "happiness is somewhere to be found." Rasselas searches for a happiness that "must be something solid and permanent, without fear and uncertainty." But no matter how hard the characters search, happiness is mitigated by the realities of life in a harsh world. Individual choice is a factor in one's favor in the pursuit of happiness, but it is limited to the lucky few. Most, Johnson argues, live by necessity:

> Very few, said the poet, live by choice. Every man is placed in his present condition by causes which acted without his foresight, and with which he did not always willingly co-operate; and therefore you will rarely meet one who does not think the lot of his neighbour better than his own.

If *Rasselas* has one shortcoming as a work, it is that the goal at the end of the quest seems to lie beyond Johnson's capacity to explain to his reader. Happiness, Johnson realizes, is almost a matter for dialectic; the presence of unhappiness offers a measure against which an individual can determine his own happiness. At its heart, this idea is part of the eighteenth-century notion that happiness is something one strives to attain through the power of imagination and desire. When it came time for Thomas Jefferson to articulate the purpose of his new, *Aeneid*-styled nation, he chose not only the principles of enlightened individualism proposed by Locke but also the notion of the questing heart that lies at the core of *Rasselas*, so that his "self-evident truths" of life and liberty included "the pursuit of happiness."

Happiness, Johnson believed, was an adherence to the laws of nature. Humans had to recognize their place in the universe, to contextualize and adjust themselves to the world in order to strike a reasonable and logical balance between desire and imagination. Three years after the publication of both *Candide* and *Rasselas*, Jean-Jacques Rousseau would publish his *Social Contract*. In that 1762 volume, Rousseau declared that "Man was born free, and everywhere he is in chains," a pronouncement that lay at the heart of the French Revolution. What Rousseau was calling for, more than merely an overthrow of the *ancien régime* in France, was a recognition of the balance between man and nature that would lead to the happiness of the individual. Johnson also recognized the profound importance of natural laws:

Nothing is more idle than to inquire after happiness, which nature has kindly placed within our reach. The way to be happy is to live according to nature, in obedience to that universal and unalterable law with which every heart is originally impressed; which is not written on it by precept, but engraven by destiny, not instilled by education, but infused at our nativity...deviation from nature is deviation from happiness.

Johnson severely distrusts the idea that the imagination points to the happy "way of life" by showing individuals their context within God's creations, but he nonetheless acknowledges that those who are happy are those who have struck a balance between the world of reality and the world of dreams. Such an individual, in Johnson's view, is a poet.

Rasselas' tutor and mentor is the poet Imlac. Imlac, like Odysseus, has seen the cities of many men and learned their ways. He is worldly but knowledgeable. His view of poetry is that it is an avenue to learning, a practice that venerates and seeks to understand nature—a role for the poet that, in our contemporary society, we might consign to the scientist:

The business of the poet, said Imlac, is to examine, not the individual, but the species; to remark general properties and large appearances: he does not number the streaks of the tulip, or describe the different shades in the verdure of the forest. He is to exhibit in his portraits of nature such prominent and striking features, as recall the original to every mind; and must neglect the minuter discriminations, which one may have remarked, and another have neglected, for those characteristicks which are alike obvious to vigilance and carelessness.

But for Johnson, the poet is more than a mere natural scientist of rhyme. He is a student of the world, in much the same way that Rasselas is a student of the world; he is someone who attempts to learn the ways of humankind and to articulate a vision of common truths that can help others to navigate the labyrinthine perils of life. In a statement that Rainer Maria Rilke echoes in *Letters to a Young Poet*, Imlac declares that:

To a poet nothing can be useless. Whatever is beautiful, and whatever is dreadful, must be familiar to his imagination; he must be conversant with all that is awfully vast or elegantly little...for every idea is useful for the enforcement or decoration of moral or religious truth; and he, who knows most, will have most power of diversifying his scenes, and of gratifying his reader with remote allusions and unexpected instruction.

The poet was to be the eyes and ears of a society that pursued not only happiness or even scientific knowledge but moral justice, spiritual clarity, and ethical interaction. It was the poet who would be the guide in the pursuit of happiness—an idea not lost on those United States presidents who have prominently featured poets at their inaugurations. The role of the poet, for Johnson, was a high calling:

He must divest himself of the prejudices of his age or country; he must consider right and wrong in their abstracted and invariable state; he must disregard present laws and opinions, and rise to general and transcendental truths, which will always be the same: he must therefore content himself with the slow progress of his name; contemn the applause of his own time, and commit his claims to the justice of posterity. He must write as the interpreter of nature, and the legislator of mankind, and consider himself as presiding over the thoughts and manners of future generations; as a being superior to time and place.

Johnson borrows the notion of the poet as a "legislator of mankind" from the *Ars Poetica* of the Classical Latin poet Horace. Horace argued that the impact of literature, and especially of poetry, was to transform the way in which readers saw themselves and the world. In altering opinions, pursuing truths, and offering a sound basis for the growth of individual judgment and moral interpretation, the poet was essentially "legislating" the imagination, providing new outposts of ideas for future readers and writers to build upon. Percy Bysshe Shelley, in his *Defence of Poetry*, takes the notion a step further—he states that poets are "the unacknowledged legislators of the world," a pronouncement that realized the diminishing role of poetry in a world where science, nationality, and mass politics were playing an increasing role.

Like Horace and Shelley, Johnson sees the poet's role as a key one, because the poet would enable the questing individual, the pursuer of happiness, to acquire a clearer vision of the foundations of personal peace of mind. That peace of mind, Johnson concludes at the finale of *Rasselas*, was not something that could be found in this world. The wearied Nekayah concludes that happiness is something that must be sought in one's faith and beliefs, not in the occupations of earthly existence: "To me, said the princess, the choice of life is become less important; I hope hereafter to think only on the choice of eternity."

In the end, the entire party of Abissinian wanderers returns to Happy Valley to contemplate their futures and what they have seen, no happier and presumably no wiser than they were when they departed. The pursuit of happiness led nowhere except to the realization that the individual must recognize in himself what he holds dear, what he believes in, and where he wants to go with it if he is to navigate the twists and turns of the world.

Boswell, in his *Life of Johnson*, perceived that the purpose of *Rasselas* was, to use Milton's words from *Paradise Lost*, to "justify the ways of God to men" and to show that the paths of inquiry, not just glory, lead to the recognition of heaven:

> Though the proposition illustrated by both these works [*Candide* and *Rasselas*] was the same, namely, that in our present state there is more evil than good, the intention of the writers was very different. Voltaire, I am afraid, meant only by wanton profaneness to obtain a sportive victory over religion, and to discredit the belief of a superintending Providence: Johnson meant, by shewing the unsatisfactory nature of things temporal, to direct the hopes of man to things eternal. *Rasselas*, as was observed to me by a very accomplished lady, may be considered as a more enlarged and more deeply philosophical discourse in prose, upon the interesting truth, which in his *Vanity of Human Wishes* he had so successfully enforced in verse.

Boswell, however, appears to have missed part of the point Voltaire was trying to make in *Candide*. Voltaire sought, through his "candid" and frank protagonist, who can see neither the dangers nor the evils of the world, to show just how much the human spirit can take before it is broken.

In a vision that stemmed from Boethius' concerns about how evil can exist in the world, Voltaire portrayed a world where only the human spirit enables an individual to survive and focus attention on a discovery of what is true and lasting. The love of Candide's life, Cunegonde, seems to sum up the misery of the human condition:

> I have grown old in misery and in shame, with only half a back-side, always remembering that I was the daughter of a Pope; a hundred times I wanted to kill myself but I still loved life. This ridiculous weakness is perhaps the most disastrous of our inclinations; for is there anything sillier than to desire to bear continually a burden one always wishes to throw on the ground; to look upon oneself with horror and yet to cling to oneself; in short, to caress the serpent which devours us until he has eaten our heart?

The world of *Candide* is a cosmos of desperation. Extremes of violence and hardship are imposed upon the characters, almost as if Voltaire takes a great glee in seeing his literary creations tortured, mutilated, and broken; yet though they endure an incredible array of suffering, they do not break. Where *Rasselas* is a gentle story in which characters move through a world that is teetering on the brink of tedium, *Candide* is a novel in which the characters survive, only to learn how hard the world can be. Where Rasselas and his band of wanderers embark on a student tour of life, Candide and his compatriots experience life as an ongoing nightmare. Through it all, however, they endure. The point of life, summed up by a Turk whom the characters encounter in the final chapter, seems simple enough:

> "I have only twenty acres," replied the Turk. "I cultivate them with my children; and work keeps at bay three great evils: boredom, vice and need."

The maxim of "To be is to do" is at play in the post-Cartesian universe of *Candide*. The characters are not in search of a way of life, but rather in need of a safe place, a fixed purpose, and the intellectual well-being that comes from not having to worry about the forces of evil in the world. The novel posits several contrasting points of view about how the individual should confront life. On one hand, there is Dr. Pangloss, the dreamy-eyed Optimist who is willing to endure any amount of suffering gladly because it is all for the best. There is Martin, the servant to Candide, who represents the old view of Christian patience, of waiting for better things to come whenever they should be made available to humankind. Then there is Candide, who, in the manner of a David Hume, has no opinions whatsoever other than the idea that human beings, whether good or evil, should define their own circumstances and live happily within their own limitations.

In one of the novel's most famous remarks, Candide announces the moral that life has taught him through all its suffering and hardships: "I also know," said Candide, "that we must cultivate our gardens." The remark, one that sent Louis XVI and Marie Antoinette into the back forty of Versailles to play peasants in a tiny cottage, suggests that humanity has strayed from the lost innocence of its primal, Edenic state. In that fallen condition, terrible things occur not simply in the name of evil but as a result of confusion, impaired thinking, dogmatism, and systematic philosophy:

> "You are right," said Dr. Pangloss, "for, when man was placed in the Garden of Eden, he was placed there *ut operaretur eum*, to dress it and to keep it; which proves that man was not born for idleness."
>
> "Let us work without theorizing," said Martin; "'tis the only way to make life endurable."

As Martin seems to be pointing out, reason alone cannot return man to his Edenic state. Life, in Voltaire's opinion, is something one must experience and sort out for oneself. No theory, no system will organize human beings better than if they simply look after their own business and cultivate their own gardens. In this sense, happiness is all a question of degree.

When Candide and Martin arrive in Eldorado, they enter a world that is patterned quite closely and consciously on Thomas More's Utopia. It is also a creation that was informed by the legends of the Seven Cities of Gold and the disastrous New World quest of the De Soto expedition. Eldorado allows Voltaire to create a parable on the nature of greed. The landscape is paved with gold and jewels. There is no private property and no severe laws, and everyone lives in a state of bliss. Candide is impressed by this group of people, and openly acknowledges to Martin that the Eldoradians are the happiest people he has met on earth. Still, he chooses to flee Eldorado when he has the opportunity, because the wealth that he can carry away with him would enable him to become richer than any European monarch. In the end, however, greed leads to folly, and Candide and Martin lose all their riches, moving on to the next set of adventures and misadventures.

Voltaire's ideas found their appropriate literary expression in the *picaresque novel*. The picaresque novel, a Spanish invention, follows the exploits of a character through a vast series of improbable situations and adventures. The picaresque protagonist is often naive, yet it is this sense of naivety that enables him to survive his adventures and misadventures. The *novel* itself, an extended narrative in either prose or poetry, originally carried the connotation of being a "new" type of story. (Indeed, the term comes from the French word *nouvelle*.) Originally, as we saw earlier, any extended narrative in prose or poetry was referred to as a "roman," or a story in the Roman fashion. In the late Renaissance in France, several authors attempted to infuse the roman with a new vitality and energy. No longer would the form be a device purely for moral education—although many novelists in the eighteenth century, including Samuel Richardson, author of *Pamela*, and Daniel Defoe, in *Moll Flanders*, sought to use the form this way. Instead, the reborn roman was to be employed for entertainment, a novelty that would attract and hold readers' attention by transporting their imaginations rather than playing purely to their need for self-improvement.

In this sense, *Rasselas* is very much a roman and *Candide* is a novel. Both fall within the category of the "novel of ideas," works of extended narrative that serve as vehicles for important ideas. But while Johnson instructs in a didactic voice, Voltaire challenges.

Both works address the question of what it is to be happy, how one might go about finding happiness, and what that happiness might be like if one were wise enough or fortunate enough to discover it.

In the end, however, the books are works of fiction. Though fiction is not supposed to be held accountable for the way in which stories impact on reality, both works had a significant influence on two major revolutions of the eighteenth century, when truths, ideas, and philosophies suddenly became the means by which new worlds could take shape. Both books point to that elusive concept of what might be out there if only humanity would challenge its collective imagination. Both writers dream that a better world might be possible. Perhaps that world is Happy Valley, the womb-like state of innocent bliss that was abandoned at the beginning of time or at the beginning of the individual's life. Or perhaps happiness is something that can be learned from an understanding of the misery of the world.

Joseph Wright of Derby. An Experiment on a Bird in the Air Pump. The iconography of the Age of Reason—the sage, the apparatus, and the intent learners— is surrounded by elements of a far more emotional vision of the world—the broody clouds out the window, the terrified little girls, and the smitten lovers. More than capturing an act of science, Wright appears to have rendered a historical moment of transition in thought and ethos.

In any case, as Britain and France struggled with the notion of pursuing happiness, they were also engaged in a war of almost global proportions, fought mostly in a new world across the ocean. Although Voltaire saw North America as "a few acres of snow," he also perceived it through the philosophy of Optimism as a better world than the "best of all possible worlds." In the movie version of *The Wizard of Oz*, the protagonist Dorothy, one of the most North American of all literary characters, remarks, after returning to consciousness from her imaginative and concussive journey to another, better world, "If I ever go looking for my heart's desire, I will never look farther than my own backyard," a summation of the quest for happiness that paraphrases Candide's notion that "we must cultivate our gardens."

The philosophical certainty that both Johnson and Voltaire challenged in their works did not produce the happiness that thinkers such as Leibniz envisioned. Instead, it produced more questions until even the physical laws of nature—the heart of science—came under scrutiny and criticism. It soon became apparent to writers such as Mary Shelley that the only reliability in the universe was curiosity and the only answer another question.

16

IT WAS A DARK
AND STORMY NIGHT

Mary Shelley's *Frankenstein*

I N 1768, the English artist Joseph Wright of Derby painted
what has become an emblem of the scientific revolution. His
canvas, *An Experiment on a Bird in the Air Pump*, which now
hangs in the National Gallery in London, depicts an evening soirée
of science where a gray-haired philosopher attempts to show the
effect of a bell jar and an air pump upon a white dove. At the center
of the painting, the dove flutters helplessly inside the jar, more a
victim of circumstance and human power than of any enlightened
ideas. Two little girls to the right of the picture's focus weep as
another man presumably tries to explain that the creature is going

to die for the acquisition of knowledge. To the left of the painting, two young people, possibly lovers, gaze into each other's eyes, unperturbed by the moment of revelation that is about to take place in front of them. A pensive-looking younger man to the right of the canvas appears to muse on whether the pursuit of scientific knowledge is really worth the price of the bird's life; he is deep in contemplation, his hands raised to his chin in a gesture that is partly meditative and partly melancholy. And at the extreme right of the picture, a boy is pulling a window curtain across a scene of stark, moonlit desolation. The clouds partially cover the moon, the sky is moody. It was a dark and stormy night....

Wright's painting is as much a critique of the scientific enlightenment of the eighteenth century as it is a testimony to the period. The center of the painting, the man of science, seems to be surrounded by individuals who are caught up in other concerns: the besotted lovers, the perplexed and meditative young man, the sentimental and terrified little girls. The painter appears to be saying that the emotionalism of the era has supercharged the atmosphere of the room, and the storm of challenge and revolution that is mounting has almost as much force as the dark and foreboding clouds seen through the window. As Wright was painting his canvas, the ideas of the scientific revolution were being challenged. The Newtonian perception that the universe was an ordered and magnificent engine of divine design, expressed in more philosophical terms by Leibniz, was gradually being challenged by poets, who saw the ordered universe as a place where everything but the human spirit was explained. And it was the inexplicable human spirit, the ferocity of emotions, the play of sentiment and the unexplored regions of the passions that began to fascinate the poets of the late eighteenth century.

By 1796, as the American experiment in democracy was gaining strength and turning the new world into a nation, and as the French Revolution upset the almost deistic order of the *ancien régime*, plunging France into the Terror, the English poet William Blake offered his own critique of the Age of Reason. As Blake saw it, it had been a dismal failure because its thinkers had sought to systematize humankind and the human spirit in ways that were not meant to be. Jean-Jacques Rousseau had suggested the need for universal individual liberty, but Blake saw that even Rousseau's philosophy was far too systematic to accommodate the free spirit in each human being. This is why Blake rejected philosophy and its logic in favor of a new entity that he recognized as the divine spark in humankind: the imagination. In a short poem, Blake suggested that the Enlightenment's flaw had been its inability to empower the imagination:

Mock on, Mock on, Voltaire, Rousseau;
Mock on, Mock on, 'tis all in vain.
You throw the sand against the wind,
And the wind blows it back again.

God, for Blake, was not a system that could easily be explained away. In fact, Blake made the pronouncement that in many ways encapsulates the nature of the late eighteenth-century reaction against systematic thought: "I must create a system, or be enslaved by another man's." Blake was thoroughly Protestant in his thinking, especially in his belief that each person must meet God on his or her own terms, and that people should forge a personal perception of God from their own inclinations toward morality and goodness. Like Saint Augustine, he perceived the immensity of God, the struggle of the human mind to comprehend the scope and complexity of nature, and the power of the imagination to grasp, if only for a fleeting, anagogic instant, the wonder and glory of the Almighty. In reason, any system of logic is limited to the strength of its premises—a line of argument can go only as far as its point of origin will allow it. Medieval philosophers and theologians had recognized the limitations of reason, and settled upon the notion of anagogic. But even anagogic could not go the distance in explaining the true nature of the universe, and the poignant reasoning behind satire, that jesting, barbing, and baiting raid on folly, could not address the key issues that still troubled the human spirit. When something inexplicable, something immense or preponderant, took shape in the mind, it was frightening. Evil, terror, vastness, and infinite goodness were perceived as somehow beyond the capabilities of human reason to explain logically and philosophically. As Blake saw it, the eighteenth century was "sand against the wind," and the spirit of the Almighty, personified by that wind, would blow "it back again."

In this line of thought Blake was merely extending an argument in literature that had been present since the late Classical era. In the first century, the Greek thinker Longinus claimed that there were moments in literary texts when something grand, magnificent, terrifying, or awe-inspiring took place and sent a shiver through the reader, an ecstasy or *ekstasis*, a feeling not quite as emptying as a catharsis but which sprang from the same source in the emotions. To this moment Longinus applied the term *sublime*, from the Latin word *sublimis*, meaning "lifted up," "eminent," or "aspiring." The sublime has been associated with an array of artistic styles. It has been applied to anything that is "elevated" and excessively dignified such as *Paradise Lost*, and to anything that produces terror and nervous excitement such as horror films. Simply put, the sublime in literature is what a reader experiences when he or she utters an interjection of exclamation, surprise, or alarm; the "wow" of a text.

True to eighteenth-century fashion, philosophers made an attempt to understand the sublime by examining the epistemology of the astonished reaction. In 1757, Edmund Burke published *A Philosophical Enquiry Into the Origin of Our Ideas of the Sublime and the Beautiful*, a work that attempted to address and understand those moments when a reader or a beholder is overcome by powerful emotions. What on the surface may appear to be a rather dry reaction to the "wow" of literature and art today forms the basis for our appreciation of experiential thrills from the horror films of Boris Karloff to high-tech amusement-park rides. What concerned Burke was the idea that human beings react on impulse to things that trigger extreme excitement:

> The passion caused by the great and sublime in *nature*, when
> those causes operate most powerfully, is Astonishment; and
> astonishment is that state of the soul, in which all its motions
> are suspended, with some degree of horror. In this case the
> mind is so entirely filled with its object, that it cannot entertain
> any other, nor by consequence reason on that object which
> employs it. Hence arises the great power of the sublime, that far
> from being produced by them, it anticipates our reasonings, and

hurries us on by an irresistible force. Astonishment, as I have said, is the effect of the sublime in its highest degree; the inferior effects are admiration, reverence and respect.

The key to Burke's definition of the sublime is nature. Nature, God's work of art and humankind's work-in-progress, was, for Burke and his fellow-travelers, the source for all that could be perceived as sublime. As the eighteenth century wore on, poets in particular came to place less and less value in science, reason, and logical systems, and more and more value in the organic structures of nature and human nature. Botanists might have been able to classify the various genera of plants and study the life cycles of vegetation, but they were at a loss to explain just what made the flower come to life, or as Dylan Thomas would say in the twentieth century, "The force that through the green fuse drives the flower." Nature was one big moment of astonishment. The size, the scope, the power, and the vitality of the world baffled the mind. And those who wanted to observe the world in its splendor and vastness had only to seek out a place to practice the fine art of solitude. The theory was that being alone with nature would produce the same sense of awe, wonder, and even terror that one might feel being locked in a broom closet with an elephant: an experience of being overpowered, crushed, and transmogrified all in one instant. As Burke suggests, looking on nature not only turns the mind to God, it literally freezes the thoughts of the thinker in a state of awe, lifting the beholder out of reality and into an aura of contemplation and deep reflection that is far beyond any reasonable or logical interpretation.

In 1798, William Wordsworth and Samuel Taylor Coleridge published *Lyrical Ballads*, a slender volume of poetry that revolutionized not only English verse but the imaginative structures of literature. In that collection, Wordsworth attempted to articulate in poetry just what Burke had described in philosophy. In the poem *Lines Composed a Few Miles above Tintern Abbey*, he melded the theory of the sublime with his personal experiences during a walking tour from his native Lake District to Wales:

For I have learned
To look on nature, not as in the hour
Of thoughtless youth; but hearing oftentimes
The still, sad music of humanity,
Nor harsh nor grating, though of ample power
To chasten and subdue. And I have felt
A presence that disturbs me with the joy
Of elevated thoughts; a sense sublime
Of something far more deeply interfused,
Whose dwelling is the light of setting suns,
And the round ocean and the living air,
And the blue sky, and in the mind of man:
A motion and a spirit, that impels
All thinking things, all objects of all thought,
And rolls through all things. Therefore am I still
A lover of the meadows and the woods,
And mountains; and of all that we behold
From this green earth; of all the mighty world
Of eye, and ear—both what they half create,
And what perceive; well pleased to recognize
In nature and the language of the sense
The anchor of my purest thoughts, the nurse,
The guide, the guardian of my heart, and soul
Of all my moral being.

Benjamin Robert Haydon. William Wordsworth. The elder, mature Wordsworth well past the era of Romantic fervor. Here, he is caught in a moment of philosophical speculation, perhaps musing on lines that would become part of the expanded Prelude.

For Wordsworth, the observation of nature produced a kind of natural high through which an individual could "see into the life of things." This was a means by which a person could get in touch with himself and the world around him, as well as with the Almighty.

Nature was perceived as everything beyond the artificial, the clinical, and the contrived. Nature was the original state of humankind, the last glimpse of Eden, and the closest thing to divine grace that humanity had at its disposal. Entering nature was, for Wordsworth, a trip not only into the sublime but into the realm of anagogic. In a few lines that echo the Song of Solomon in their imagery and beauty, he attempts to explain just what he felt when he found the time to be alone with the landscape:

386

I came among these hills; when like a roe
I bounded o'er the mountains, by the sides
Of deep rivers, and the lonely streams,
Wherever nature led—more like a man
Flying from something that he dreads than one
Who sought the thing he loved. For nature then
(The coarser pleasures of my boyish days,
And their glad animal movements all gone by)
To me was all in all.—I cannot paint
What then I was.

Literary legend has it that as *Lyrical Ballads* was being prepared for the press, Wordsworth walked into his printer's shop and said, "Set this," dictating the entire work from memory. Although the poem is structured in highly formal blank verse, the same elevated structure of expression that Milton chose for *Paradise Lost*, the facts of its composition suggest that what Wordsworth was attempting to do was to link the art of written poetry to the tradition of *oral* verse.

Because poetry is so often associated with the printed page, we tend to forget that the roots of the art lie in the sung or spoken word. Poetry, even today, is meant to be heard; the words "rhythm" and "rhyme" both have their origins in the Greek word for "measured motion."

In the 1802 preface to *Lyrical Ballads*, Wordsworth explained that the poet is "a man speaking to men" and that his poems were "the real language of men in a state of vivid sensation," a comment that directly links his poetry to the ideas of Burke. Wordsworth believed that "Poetry is the breath and finer spirit of all knowledge," and that the poet is

Caspar David Friedrich. The Wanderer above the Mists. The Burkean landscape is a mighty setting for this dark-clad figure with his back turned, diffidently, to the viewer. Like the traditional Cain figure or Coleridge's Ancient Mariner, he is the archetypal outcast shunted to the periphery of a harsh and powerful nature.

> the rock of defence of human nature; an upholder and preserver, carrying everywhere with him relationship and love. In spite of difference of soil and climate, of language and manners, of laws and customs, in spite of things silently gone out of mind and things violently destroyed, the poet binds together by passion and knowledge the vast empire of human society, as it is spread over the whole earth, and over all time...Poetry is the first and last of all knowledge...

In Wordsworth's view, the poet articulates human nature because "the poet thinks and feels in the spirit of the passions of men." Poetry expresses the core of the imagination, that little shard-memory of Eden, because it was "the real language of nature," the "image of man and nature" built up through the accumulation of pleasurable experiences. Wordsworth's connection of pleasure and poetry (art) may not seem like such an important issue until one realizes that Freud's twentieth-century schema for the human mind was based completely on this notion. As we shall see in chapter 17, Freud declared that art and civilization were extensions of our need to protect and curb our own desires and pleasures. Both Freud and Wordsworth would agree that one of the most important forms of pleasure comes from our ability to recognize beauty in art and nature.

Added together, the elements at work in the minds of late eighteenth- and early nineteenth-century writers—the idealization of nature, the fascination with the sublime, the desire to challenge

static systems of order and logic—forged a new vision in literature known as *Romanticism*. Partially a reaction against the staid, systematic reasoning of the Enlightenment, in which everything had a place and the universe was supposed to work by predictable laws and plans, Romanticism offered its practitioners the kind of imaginative liberty that reflected the notions underlying the American and French revolutions. Romanticism took as its prime metaphor not God the clockmaker, as the Deists had done, but the uppity human of Classical mythology, Prometheus, who stole fire from the gods only to be chained to a mountainside as eternal punishment. Prometheus was a revolutionary, part Satan from *Paradise Lost*, part Caliban from *The Tempest*, and part Napoleon—characters who consciously challenged authority and attempted to create their own systems.

In its lighter manifestations, Romanticism expressed the hopefulness of natural renewal described by the innocence of the lamb in Blake's *Songs of Innocence*:

> *Little Lamb, who made thee?*
> *Dost thou know who made thee?*
> *Gave thee life and bid thee feed,*
> *By the stream and o'er the mead;*
> *Gave thee clothing of delight,*
> *Softest clothing, wooly, bright;*
> *Gave thee such a tender voice,*
> *Making all the vales rejoice?*
> *Little Lamb who made thee?*
> *Dost thou know who made thee?*

It also gave voice to the sudden and surprising beauty of Wordsworth's golden daffodils:

> *I wandered lonely as a cloud*
> *That floats on high o'er vales and hills,*
> *When all at once I saw a crowd,*
> *A host, of golden daffodils;*
> *Beside the lake, beneath the trees,*
> *Fluttering and dancing in the breeze.*

In its darker, more sinister expressions, the Romantic perspective could become synonymous with unbridled passions, such as in Blake's *The Tyger*:

Tyger! Tyger! burning bright
In the forests of the night,
What immortal hand or eye
Could frame thy fearful symmetry?
...
When the stars threw down their spears,
And water'd heaven with their tears,
Did he smile his work to see?
Did he who made the Lamb make thee?

Either way, the supposition beneath the Romantic vision of the world was that God did indeed make the universe, but that the imperfect, the evil, and the terrifying were as much an expression of the divine will as the good, the beautiful, and the innocent. And if goodness and order seemed slightly boring, there were, at least, thrills to be found in disorder and the sublime.

The ability to find pleasure in the sublime, Wordsworth argued, was merely a matter of "learning to look on nature" and to appreciate the splendor of the landscape. The poet's purpose was not merely to articulate the wonder and astonishment that comes from interacting with nature but to show others how to find that same experience when they looked at the world:

> ...there is no necessity to trick out or to elevate nature: and, the more industriously he applies this principle, the deeper will be his faith that no words, which his fancy or imagination can suggest, will be compared with those which are emanations of reality and truth....it is impossible for the poet to produce upon all occasions language as exquisitely fitted for the passion as that which the real passion itself suggests....

Although Wordsworth seems to be admitting to moments of speechlessness when he looks on nature, he is locating poetry directly in the context of the Burkean notion of the sublime.

What Wordsworth does not discuss in his preface is the fact that Burke sees nature as a kind of two-edged sword; it can be both divinely beautiful and terrifyingly evil. And while Wordsworth was conjuring a vision of nature that was dreamy, there were other writers who looked on nature, its laws, and its structures as potentially nightmarish. The same imagination that could glorify the natural beauty of the Wye Valley a few miles above a ruined monastic building could also express frightening visions of the unnatural, the horrific, and the abominable. Such was the scope of the imagination.

Richard Roth-well. Mary Shelley. It is hard to believe that this serene face belonged to an individual who challenged the notion of man's relation-ship to God.

In response to the skepticism of Hume, Johnson, and other eighteenth-century thinkers, a number of poets in the late eighteenth century began to explore the notion of disorder, and to question what lay not just at the core of the mind's eye but in the peripheral vision of conscious dreaming. What they saw there was more than outside the explicable order of things; it was terrifying.

On a summer night in 1816, as she tried to sleep in a Swiss castle, Mary Shelley, the wife of Percy Bysshe Shelley, experienced a vision of just what that part of the mind's eye had to offer:

> When I placed my head on my pillow, I did not sleep, nor could I be said to think. My imagination, unbidden, possessed and guided me, gifting the successive images that arose in my mind with a vividness far beyond the usual bounds of reverie. I saw—with shut eyes, but acute mental vision—I saw the pale student of unhallowed arts kneeling beside the thing he had put together. I saw the hideous phantasm of a man stretched out, and then, on the working of some powerful engine, show signs of life, and stir with an uneasy, half-vital motion.

In that instant and with that vision, the novel *Frankenstein* began to take shape. Mary Shelley's realization that something terrifying and emotionally stimulating lay at the edge of the imagination in that half-waking, half-dreaming state of reverie locates *Frankenstein* in that twilight world of human consciousness where anything is possible. Shelley, however, was not entirely original. By examining what is good and what is evil in the world, by challenging the boundaries between science and the imagination, she

was echoing a tradition in literature that could be traced back to Boethius and even to Ovid and the animate universe of Classical literature.

In *The Consolation of Philosophy*, Boethius argued that the order of nature and morality, the laws by which the world worked, were splendid and divine codes that had been set forth by God as part of his plan. An individual who obeyed those laws was good. But there were those, Boethius noted almost in passing, who challenged the natural order of things, who operated morally, ethically, and imaginatively outside the boundaries of what God permitted. These individuals he deemed "evil."

The presence of evil, especially within a fictional world such as one finds in a novel, can be the result of two things. In the Christian view, it is delayed or forestalled poetic justice. God will act eventually, but he simply hasn't gotten around to it yet. This view holds that the ultimate resolution of evil, the comeuppance for an antagonist, is the Day of Judgment at the end of time. In the animate, Classical universe, however, evil is much harder to define, because everyone is a victim in some way and therefore no one is undeserving of sympathy or pity. What Mary Shelley did in

Frankenstein was to construct a psychological and eschatological bridge between the pagan, animate universe and the Christian, inanimate one. As a narrative, *Frankenstein* challenges early nineteenth-century notions of morality because it places its two protagonists, the scientist Victor Frankenstein and his creation, the Daemon, in a murky world where each represents a form of sympathetic self-interest. In other words, the morality is confusing because no character is totally evil and no character totally good.

The familiar plot of *Frankenstein* is now almost a cliché. A young student of science decides to investigate the roots of the life source and find that divine spark that animates the dust of a human being. Taking some inspiration from the eighteenth-century interest in the practice of "galvanism," or attempts at animating dead material by applying electrical currents, Mary Shelley perceived the possibility that humans could intercede where only God had tread, playing recreator or even creator to a new species of beings in an act that would be both horrific and sublime:

> Frightful it must be; for supremely frightful would be the effect of any human endeavour to mock the stupendous mechanism of the Creator of the world. His success would terrify the artists; he would rush away from his odious handiwork, horror-stricken. He would hope that, left to itself, the slight spark of life which had received such imperfect animation would subside into dead matter, and he might sleep in the belief that the silence of the grave would quench forever the transient existence of the hideous corpse which he looked upon as the cradle of life. He sleeps; but he is awakened; he opens his eyes; behold, the horrid thing stands at his bedside, opening his curtains and looking on him with yellow, watery, but speculative eyes.

Of course, once Frankenstein has created his being out of dead human remains, he cannot remove the spark of life. Instead, he fails to take responsibility for his creation, abandoning the Daemon to the world. What the Daemon learns from human existence is that the universe is an ordered place where a Divine Creator rules over those creatures he loves. The only problem is that the Daemon alone, as an unnatural creation who is outside the order of nature, has no place in this ordered universe. His solitude is not Wordsworthian contemplation but the lonely, outcast exile of a Cain. Faced with a creator who will not acknowledge or take responsibility for his creation by loving him, the Daemon sets out on a path of havoc and, like Satan in *Paradise Lost*, attempts to wreak vengeance on his master and his master's world. The question is, who is evil? Is it Frankenstein, for attempting to play God by perverting science and breaking the laws of nature? Or is it the Daemon, for going on a killing spree in order to torment his creator?

At the heart of this two-way conundrum, Shelley establishes an opposition between real, reasonable, factual science and imaginative, speculative science. She appears to be suggesting that science is a matter not merely of proof and logic but of aspiration and imagination, a place where the implausible is just as worthy of investigation as the possible. In other words, in *Frankenstein*, the true battles occur both between the creator and his creation and between reason and the imagination. In the realm of reason, everything has to be pinned down factually and logically, but in the realm of the imagination, there are no such rules, and anything is possible. This is the core of the horror Mary Shelley wanted to convey. Underlying this horror is an idea that was argued by Theophrastus Bombastus Paracelsus, a sixteenth-century metaphysician and alchemist who believed in an elixir of life that could reanimate dead matter. Science, at least in Mary Shelley's view, especially the speculative kind practiced by Paracelsus, is as much part of the imagination as it is part of the logical side of the human mind.

What seems to percolate within the mythology of *Frankenstein* is the fascination with the pursuit of the implausible. The novel opens with a *framing narrative*, a sub-story in which Mary Shelley sets the themes and tone for the work and introduces the protagonist and the antagonist. The story concerns a young, energetic Englishman named Walton, who has embarked on a journey of polar exploration on a ship that, like Sir John Franklin's H.M.S. *Erebus* and H.M.S. *Terror* of the ill-fated 1848 expedition in search of the Northwest Passage, has become trapped in the ice. Walton, in a letter to his sister back in England, explains that the pursuit of the Northwest Passage represents the frontier of physical science, the chance for humans to assume greater dominion over the world. It is part realization of a dream and part study:

> This expedition has been the favorite dream of my early years. I have read with ardour the accounts of the various voyages which have been made in the prospect of arriving at the North Pacific Ocean through the seas which surround the pole. You remember that a history of all the voyages made for purposes of discovery composed the whole of our good Uncle Thomas' library. My education was neglected, yet I was passionately fond of reading. These volumes were my study day and night, and my familiarity with them increased that regret which I had felt, as a child, on learning that my father's dying injunction had forbidden my uncle to allow me to embark on a seafaring life.

The barren wastes of the Arctic provide the novel with the most sublime and terrifying landscape an imagination could conjure. In contrast, there is Walton in the cocoon of his ship, embarking on a potentially deadly journey with an air of innocence and naivety.

Mary Shelley may have based part of the rewritten version of her novel on accounts of the Ross Expedition, which returned in 1818 to England after having its ships crushed in the massive ice floes of the Arctic Ocean. Ross, unlike Franklin, adapted to the Arctic. He abandoned notions of civilization for the practicalities of survival. Where Franklin took little notice of the Inuit and perished along with all of his crew—many the victims of cannibalism—Ross and his party of survivors learned how to adapt, donning parkas and mukluks, and building kayaks. They were eventually rescued with little loss of life. The Ross Expedition supported Rousseau's contention that the "noble savage," the Calibans of the world, did have something to teach the Western mind, if only the Western mind would listen and adapt. Franklin, like Shelley's Walton, went into the Arctic with a kind of disconnected innocence; he and his crew took along stage props, a library of several thousand books, and a printing press. Both Walton and Frankenstein, for their part, approach science as if it were a legend to be dreamed rather than an experiment to be cautiously tested.

In *Frankenstein*, the pull of the imagination on the reasonable and the rational seems to support the argument that science and myth are closely linked, as they are in the explanatory mythology of Genesis (where the imagination covers for the deficiencies of methodology in accounting for how the world came into being). The imagination functions in much the same way as a scientific investigation; the key difference is that each realm of the mind has a different way of testing its premises. Both imaginative narrative and science, however, are, rhetorically and epistemologically speaking, "process analyses," step-by-step progressions where each idea or event allows the mind to move on to the next idea or event.

This cause-and-effect relationship is quite evident in the story that seems to lie at the heart of *Frankenstein*, the sixteenth-century Jewish legend of the Golem of Prague. When the Jewish community in that Czech city were threatened by gangs of anti-Semites, their rabbi, Jodah Low Ben Bezalel, constructed a clay man and, by walking around it three times and reciting the mystical names for God from the Talmud, brought the thing to life. It was hoped that this new creation would act as a champion for the community, a defender who would be impervious to the enemies' blows and who would obey its maker as devout humans obeyed theirs. The word "golem" in the Talmudic tradition was also the name applied to the body of Adam, the first man, before God had breathed into the creation, inspiring the dust with life. The Golem was successful at first, but like a plague out of Pandora's box, it took on a life of its own and soon turned on the community it was intended to serve. The animation of the clay was undone only when the magic spell was reversed by walking around the Golem three times in the opposite direction and reciting the names of God in the opposite order.

Shelley was aware that what she was detailing in her novel was a kind of modern Golem story, in which man placed himself in the position of the Almighty as a master of life and death. The subtitle for *Frankenstein*, "The Modern Prometheus," suggests that the outer boundaries of science presented a means of copying the skills of God. The novel has been interpreted by contemporary scholars as a parable against everything from vaccinations to the atom bomb. The ethical crux of the novel's argument, however, is quite simple: humankind must bear responsibility for its actions just as God must be accountable for his divine plan.

Frankenstein is a creator who wishes to have nothing to do with his creation. When the Daemon confronts Frankenstein, he is rebuffed:

"Devil," I exclaimed, "do you dare approach me? And do you fear the fierce vengeance of my arm wreaked on your miserable head? Begone, vile insect! Or rather, stay, that I may trample you to dust! And oh! That I could, with the extinction of your miserable existence, restore those victims whom you have so diabolically murdered!"

"I expected this reception," said the daemon. "All men hate the wretched; how, then, must I be hated, who am miserable beyond all living things! Yet you, my creator, detest and spurn me, thy creature, to whom thou art bound by ties only dissoluble by the annihilation of one of us. You purpose to kill me. How dare you sport thus with life? Do your duty towards me, and I will do mine towards you and the rest of mankind."

In the enmity that evolves between Frankenstein and the Daemon, Mary Shelley finds a metaphor for the relationship between people and their creator that is, in many ways, based on a plot line that her father, the novelist William Godwin, developed in his novel *Caleb Williams*. In *Caleb Williams*, the honest servant/protagonist after whom the work is titled is wrongly accused of dishonesty by his sinister, dark-clad master, Mr. Falkland. He pursues the frightened and fleeing Williams to the bitter end, though the servant is eventually able to prove his innocence and resolve matters with a modicum of justice.

In Shelley's case, the dynamic of the pursuer and the pursued becomes a much larger issue. Indeed, it is the same issue that fascinated Milton in *Paradise Lost*: what are the ways of God to man? When Victor Frankenstein first conceives of his creation, he is tempted not merely by the fruit of knowledge but by the thought of the power that such an act of creation would offer him:

A new species would bless me as its creator and source; many happy and excellent natures would owe their being to me. No father could claim the gratitude of his child so completely as I should deserve theirs. Pursuing these reflections, I thought that if I could bestow animation upon lifeless matter, I might in process of time (although I now found it impossible) renew life where death had apparently devoted the body to corruption.

What lies at the heart of Frankenstein's ambitions is a reversal of the laws of nature that have been established by God. His intentions are essentially evil in the Boethian sense, because he is seeking to overturn the order by which the world operates. The idea of the unnatural, the forces in the universe that seek to pervert or invert the accepted order of things, was given its most important airing in Milton's *Paradise Lost*, and Mary Shelley draws heavily on the great English epic as a source for her novel.

In her preface to the 1818 edition of *Frankenstein*, Shelley suggests that the purpose of her novel is to "preserve the truth of the elementary principles of human nature," chiefly the tragedy of *The Iliad*, the magic and imaginative dreaming of Shakespeare's *A Midsummer Night's Dream* and *The Tempest*, and, most especially, the cosmological concerns of Milton's *Paradise Lost*. It is no coincidence that Milton's epic forms the backbone of the Daemon's education. While hiding out for several months in the loft of a peasant's cottage, the Daemon makes use of a small library—these are educated peasants and not some run-of-the-mill, ignorant, rural proletariat. Teaching himself to read, he indulges in some of the classics, including Plutarch's *Lives* and Goethe's story of a melancholy, suicidal youth, *The Sorrows of Young Werther*. But it is *Paradise Lost* that has the most profound impact. In his narrative to Walton, the Daemon explains that Milton taught him the relationship between a creator and his creation. In other words, he takes *Paradise Lost* both literally and personally:

"But *Paradise Lost* excited different and far deeper emotions. I read it, as I had read the other volumes which had fallen into my hands, as a true history. It moved everyone feeling of wonder and awe that the picture of an omnipotent God warring with his creatures was capable of exciting. I often referred the several situations, as their similarity struck me, to my own. Like Adam, I was apparently united by no link to any other being in existence; but his state was far different from mine in every other respect. He had come forth from the hands of God a perfect creature, happy and prosperous, guarded by the especial care of his Creator; he was allowed to converse with and acquire knowledge from beings of a superior nature, but I was wretched, helpless and alone. Many times I considered Satan as a fitter emblem of my condition, for often, like him, when I viewed the bliss of my protectors, the bitter gall of envy rose within me."

Frankenstein expands on a central issue of Milton's poem in that Books I and II of *Paradise Lost* depict a world that is neither natural nor supernal, a metaphorical inversion of order and divine design. Like *Paradise Lost*, *Frankenstein*'s use of antithetical settings and ideas contributes to the work's ability to turn our assumptions of natural laws and order on their heads. As a character, the Daemon is the quintessential dark hero who seeks not only a passionate readjustment of the hand he has been dealt in life, but revenge on the one who created him. In the Daemon, emotions prevail over reason and redress over acceptance. Like Satan in *Paradise Lost*, he is fascinating, sympathy-evoking, and high-strung.

As a work of fiction, *Frankenstein* is considered to be one of the chief expressions of a literary vision that emerged during the late eighteenth century in reaction to the rule of reason and in partial response to the need to recognize the organic and natural in human behavior. If the Age of Reason was a period that revived the balanced orderliness of the Classical, Virgilian perception, especially for its intellectual and visual metaphors, then the Romantic era turned for its ideas and images to the Middle Ages. Suddenly, organic metaphors, metaphors drawn from nature and its cycles, were more appealing and interesting than reflections of mathematical theories.

What the return to nature pointed out to writers of the Romantic era, both imaginatively and psychologically, was that characters, experiences, themes, and settings could reflect growth, order, and hope, as well as entropy, disorder, and despair. It was as if the Romantics were attempting to undo the Age of Reason by creating a vision antithetical to the notions of the previous hundred years. This vision became known as the *Gothic*. It took its visual metaphors from the ruined and overgrown abbeys and castles of the Middle Ages, and its imaginative cues from Books I and II of *Paradise Lost*. The Gothic represented a world in which perfection was somehow inverted. Gaston LeRoux, for example, in his *Phantom of the Opera*, places in the basement of the Paris opera house a network of rivers that are convenient, dark, and mysterious passageways for the disfigured architect, Eric. That underworld is, by allusion, Milton's Pandemonium, but it is also an inversion of the Garden of Eden in which four rivers flow from the Fountain of Life, an anti-paradise that represents crushed hopes, despair, and vengeful intentions. The Gothic—a tradition that embraces everything from the notions of dissolute lineage in Edgar Allan Poe's "The Fall of the House of Usher" to the murderousness of the lovelorn in William Faulkner's "A Rose for Emily"—is a broad term that has been applied to many works of the imagination that seem to lie outside the Virgilian expectations of order, balance, and reason. With its invention, literature became something that could express the full range of human experience, the evil as well as the good. Beyond what Boethius had suggested, evil could exist not merely as a moral foil for didactic purposes but as a complete and fascinating entity that was just as real and complex as the good.

In writing *Frankenstein*, Shelley was attempting to understand both good and evil within the same context, to test the limits both of knowledge and of the imagination. What she perceived was a world that was as dark and mysterious as the drawing room in Wright's painting. She believed science could take humans to places and experiences that could be dreamed of only in the imagination. The only question that remained was a matter of how far one could or should go, and it would take a twentieth-century psychiatrist, Sigmund Freud, to discover such limits. Like Theseus, Freud would offer a solution to the labyrinth of the imagination and a means of confronting the horrific Minotaur within it.

17

THE COUNTDOWN

Sigmund Freud's *Civilization and Its Discontents*
and Virginia Woolf's *A Room of One's Own*

T HERE was a hush to the darkness shortly before the sun came up on the morning of July 19, 1945. In the desert outside Los Alamos, New Mexico, a thunderstorm had rolled through the dry, flat plain, and the rumblings of the heavens almost trembled and echoed off the mountains. A voice began a final countdown on loudspeakers in preparation for a scientific test. Just as the numbers were descending into single digits, a local radio station broadcasting on the same frequency was suddenly picked up by the sound system, and the countdown was drowned out by the strains of Tchaikovsky's *Nutcracker Suite*. When the countdown reached zero, humankind unleashed the first atomic explosion.

Writing in 1928 in his study *Civilization and Its Discontents*, Sigmund Freud confronted the question of whether humans would allow the strange union of science and political power to lead the species to the brink of extinction. Freud was justifiably concerned; he had witnessed the cataclysm of the First World War, treating survivors for neurasthenia, or shell-shock, a state in which individual imaginations replayed their traumas over and over again to the exclusion of either reason or sanity. He had seen the decline of nineteenth-century Romanticism, the failure of the worship of nature to protect people from their baser instincts. Yet beyond all this, he saw the future of the species as a question that could be answered either for survival or against it:

The fateful question for the human species seems to me to be whether and to what extent their cultural development will succeed in mastering the disturbance of their communal life by the human instinct of aggression and self-destruction. It may be that in this respect the present time deserves a special interest. Men have gained control over the forces of nature to such an extent that with their help they would have no difficulty in exterminating one another to the last man.

Despite his pessimistic concern for the future of humanity, Freud believed that the "Heavenly Powers" of "eternal Eros," or divine love would somehow reassert themselves in the nick of time, and human beings would find their way back to the sanity that authors had tried to harness in their great books.

The American novelist William Faulkner took a much more positive view, a view he claimed had been shaped both by human nature and through a lifetime of reading literature in an effort to understand the human spirit. On December 10, 1950, at the outset of the Cold War, when America and the Soviet Union were struggling for nuclear supremacy and the Frankenstein-like secrets of the atomic bomb were quickly spreading to every nation, Faulkner addressed the Swedish Academy as he was presented with the Nobel Prize for Literature:

I believe that man will not merely endure: he will prevail. He is immortal, not because he alone among creatures has an inexhaustible voice, but because he has a soul, a spirit capable of compassion and sacrifice and endurance. The poet's, the writer's, duty is to write about these things. It is his privilege to help man endure by lifting his heart, by reminding him of the courage and honor and hope and pride and compassion and pity and sacrifice which have been the glory of the past. The poet's voice need not merely be the record of man, it can be one of the props, the pillars to help him endure and prevail.

What Faulkner believed was that our literature—a constant affirmation that we exist in body, mind, intellect, and soul—was our best defense against the inherent barbarism of our baser instincts. That barbarism would extinguish not only the record of mankind but the continuous process of discovering just what that record could tell us. In other words, our best defense against ourselves is the civilizing power of the voice of the poet or the writer. For Freud as well, culture, literature, and the civilization that the arts helped to create represented an important buffer that served to hold our "inclination to aggression" in check:

> In consequence of this primary mutual hostility of human beings, civilized society is perpetually threatened with disintegration. The interest of work in common would not hold it together; instinctual passions are stronger than reasonable interests. Civilization has to use its utmost efforts in order to set limits to man's aggressive instincts and to hold the manifestations of them in check by psychical reaction formations.

Humans, for Freud, were brutish creatures driven by passions and desires, beings who used violence to satisfy those desires and who could be properly refined and made peaceable only through a set of protective layers that had evolved in the human consciousness.

What Freud argued was that human knowledge might ultimately redeem people from their baser instincts because all thought was an extended metaphor. Epistemologically, the way human beings think was considered to be a series of connections where one sensation was added to another to create a single thought, a pattern identical to the way a vehicle establishes a new meaning when it is attached to a tenor to create a metaphor. The newborn child, Freud stated, grows hungry not long after its birth. Its mother feeds it by putting a breast in the child's mouth, and the child instinctually knows to suck on the breast, filling its infant stomach with milk and creating a new sensation of satisfaction. The child soon realizes that the breast in the mouth is the cure for the pangs of hunger in the stomach, and by relating one sensation with another, it forms a vital relationship with its mother. Essentially, we think in metaphors, Freud argued, almost to the point where all knowledge is metaphor, the basis for poetry and literary expression.

Our progression from breast-feeding to *Remembrance of Things Past* is something Freud perceived as being truly remarkable. In Freud's view, the mind was something like a Chinese box, entities within entities, with each element making its own peculiar

Christian Schad. Portrait of Doctor Haustein. The alien-like shadow in the background is that of the doctor's mistress. The message, however, is more than a mere skeleton in the doctor's closet; it suggests that each of us carries with us a dark interior presence of something far more primeval than our super-egos would have us believe.

contribution to the complete structure of the human psychological machinery. The innermost components comprised our baser instincts: our need for survival, self-preservation, and the animal instincts for self-sufficiency. The outer layers contained the more refined aspects of the human personality, so that the outermost level of the mind, something Freud called the *superego*, gave us the ability to interact communally through the complexities of law, religion, ethics, and the arts. As complex as the mind may have appeared, with each of its various layers representing a different driving aspect of the human personality, Freud maintained that at its core lay something extremely primeval, instinctual, and animal. This core he called the *id*, the place where the human personality stores the will to survive and procreative sexual urges. In Freud's theory, the id was what made the human mind work. He was so emphatic about the importance of sexuality that generations of readers have labeled him a kind of dirty old man of psychology.

In truth, Freud believed that literature, and even our ability to perceive beauty—even the beauty of truth as Keats perceived it—was a result of our desire to control and focus our procreative urges for the sake of our own survival. If we were merely seething masses of sweaty sexual desire, which he called the *libido*, we would do nothing else but procreate. Ultimately, that would be self-destructive, because we would behave like helpless animals and not evolve into a position where we could protect ourselves by taking control of the world around us. Instead of just being raw hormones raging in search of the next sexual fix, Freud argued, the libido was an educated entity, informed not merely by desire but by an under-standing of how we endeavor to survive. We grow and increase our chances for survival by gradually enlarging our understanding of ourselves. This increased understanding is based on our ability to make metaphors from our experience—the same process that lies at the root of literature. Metaphors are the product of our ability to compare two separate images or ideas (the vehicle and the tenor) in our minds, to see how those things relate to one another, and to draw a conclusion (the metaphor) that teaches us a new idea. Freud seems to have evolved his understanding of epistemology (the philosophy of how we know what we know) not from science but from reading literature.

Freud believed that, when we are born, our minds are essentially repositories for sensations and information, waiting to be filled. The first stage in our development is what Freud termed the oral stage, a psychological response to sensual stimuli brought on by the introduction of food (breast-feeding) in our first hours of existence. The child equates the breast in the mouth with the easing of pain and the coming of satisfaction. The metaphor that evolves from this is the idea of fulfillment.

Since, as Freud noted, we are always learning from both the intellectual world and the sensations we experience, the next major stage of development occurs in later infancy, when we become aware of our internal functions, especially our bowel movements. This he called the anal stage, and it represents an attempt to impose control over our bodies. This is an aspect of our psychology that prompted Thomas More to note that the Utopians take great pleasure in the sensations of a bowel movement; that same aspect, in its more demented expressions, can be seen in the senile and misanthropic Jonathan Swift modeling small animals from his feces, and Gulliver's admiration for horse-like creatures who dropped their excrement freely and aspired to a much different concept of self-control.

The third stage, the phallic stage as Freud called it, develops when we become aware of our gender equipment. The connection between awareness of our sexual identities and our literary inclinations may not be obvious until one considers that the sonnet, that rhetorical poetic form where a persona examines and debates profoundly human concerns, resulted from the nearly erotic manner in which the poets of the troubadour tradition praised the Virgin Mary. Love poetry, in particular, appears to be an expression of desire and a celebration of sexual awareness. In *La Vita Nuova*, for example, Dante is inspired to write poetry not simply because he wishes to practice the art but because he has a prepubescent erotic dream of the naked Beatrice draped in crimson and being carried away by a mysterious figure, who may be either love or death.

These three stages of development, however, do not make up a human personality or provide an individual with enough psychological equipment to construct the grand metaphors that are literature, religion, and civilization. Yet all the experiences we encounter before the age of three are fundamental in shaping the individuals we become. At the root of Freud's theory of how the mind is built is the late eighteenth-century concept of innocence that was articulated by William Blake in *Songs of Innocence* and *Songs of Experience*. To Blake, childhood was a formative period and also a time when the individual mind was uncorrupted by the cares, pressures, and immoralities of the world. To Freud, however, the notion of innocence, of a period in human development when we see the world through a kind of Lear's Fool–like clarity, is not really an issue—innocence, Freud would argue, is a poeticization of personality. As the mind develops and builds its various layers, the individual acquires an *ego*, the net sum of his or her experiences. As Freud notes in *Civilization and Its Discontents*, "There is nothing of which we are more certain than the feeling of our self, our own ego." The ego is the individual's personality and identity; it is as much a result of the continuous narrative that we tell ourselves about ourselves as it is a result of nature. "This ego appears to us as something autonomous and unitary," Freud explained, "marked off distinctly from everything else."

But individual personalities would not, he argued, guarantee the survival of the species. Human beings need to interact, and they do this through consensus, belief, and common ideals. To account for the presence of literature, law, and religion in society—attributes he named *civilization*—Freud suggested that a final level existed in the mind of each individual, a level that permitted group interaction. This level he called the *superego*. The superego, Freud believed, was the mechanism in the mind that allowed us to formulate and accept the ideas of a group, and to acknowledge a consensus on matters that, at first glance, do not necessarily have anything to do with our need to survive. It was in the superego that humankind evolved the notion of art and beauty. Beauty, Freud felt, was an offshoot of our need to find happiness:

We may go from here to consider the interesting case in which happiness in life is predominantly sought in the enjoyment of beauty, wherever beauty presents itself to our senses and our judgment—the beauty of human forms and gestures, of natural objects and landscapes and of artistic and even scientific creations. This aesthetic attitude to the goal of life offers little protection against the threat of suffering, but it can compensate for a great deal. The enjoyment of beauty has a peculiar, mildly intoxicating quality of feeling. Beauty has no obvious use; nor is there any clear cultural necessity for it. Yet civilization could not do without it.

Freud's idea of beauty comes in the wake of Wordsworth's *Lines Composed a Few Miles above Tintern Abbey* and of that very nineteenth-century observation of John Keats in *Ode on a Grecian Urn*: "'Beauty is truth, truth beauty,'—that is all/ Ye know on earth, and all ye need to know." Beauty, in effect, is a form of truth because the perception of beauty, as Freud sees it, is one of the things that makes us happy. Beauty, or the appreciation of it through art and culture, was viewed as a surrogate for our instinctual drives, our unmitigated desires, which became crass and out of line in complex modern societies. James Joyce in *A Portrait of the Artist as a Young Man* puts this message in the mouth of his protagonist, Stephen Dedalus, when Stephen tries to explain to the flirtatious Eileen why he wants to be an artist instead of blindly settling for the domesticity of marriage and propagation. Eileen does not seem to understand. Stephen makes his message even more remote and complex by phrasing his objections to routine life in the form of a highly stylized poem, a villanelle:

Are you not weary of ardent ways,
Lure of the fallen seraphim?
Tell no more of enchanted days.

Your eyes have set man's heart ablaze
And you have had your will of him.
Are you not weary of ardent ways?

Above the flame the smoke of praise
Goes up from ocean rim to rim.
Tell no more of enchanted days.

Our broken cries and mournful lays
Rise in one eucharistic hymn.
Are you not weary of ardent ways?

While sacrificing hands upraise
The chalice flowing to the brim.
Tell no more of enchanted days.

And still you hold our longing gaze
With languorous look and lavish limb!
Are you not weary of ardent ways?
Tell no more of enchanted days.

Had Freud been leaning over Stephen Dedalus' shoulder, he would have explained that Eileen's "ardent ways," which express themselves as flirtation and the murkiness of romantic longing, are working against the intent of the superego, that drive for artistic achievement and god-like perfection that stands outside the baser concerns of the sex-driven ego. The superego's function is to provide a social buffer to the mere need to procreate, to offer something timeless as an antidote to the temporality of life and the teeming biological frenzy that life would become if one could not take time out to read a good book or visit an art gallery. This is why cultural development is often at odds with one's personal drives. The artist, therefore, just as Joyce states in *A Portrait of the Artist as a Young Man* or in *Ulysses*, has to stand outside the order of a biologically driven society and provide the necessary distraction of civilization. Freud notes:

> So, also, the two urges, the one towards personal happiness and the other towards union with other human beings must struggle with each other in every individual; and so, also, the two processes of individual and cultural development must stand in hostile opposition to each other and mutually dispute the ground.

Stephen Dedalus' declaration of a kind of artist's creed seems entirely plausible, almost as if Joyce in 1906 is anticipating what Freud will write in *Civilization and Its Discontents* in 1928:

> I will tell you what I will do and what I will not do. I will not serve that in which I no longer believe, whether it call itself my home, my fatherland, or my church: and I will try to express myself in some mode of life or art as freely as I can and as wholly as I can, using for my defence the only arms I allow myself to use—silence, exile, and cunning.

William Holman Hunt. The Awakening Conscience. Fun and games in the parlor. In this Victorian rendering, the superego engages in mortal combat with the libido. Which one will win?

Happiness, in these terms, was not merely the process of taking satisfaction from art or pretty Welsh landscapes, but of working toward the establishment of a personal system of understanding (as Blake declared when he said "I must create a system, or be enslaved by another man's") that allows an individual to extend the all-too-easily codified and structured boundaries of what society accepts as a norm for civilization, its collective superego. In other words, the artist who sees things freshly works toward keeping his culture lively and his fellow human beings happy.

Freud defined happiness as a necessary illusion—he was, after all, a product of nineteenth-century ennui, that spiritual malaise and uncertainty that made one question the purpose of existence. However, happiness, whether delusional or not, was absolutely necessary if humanity was to accomplish anything more than mere survival. In fact, evolution depended on our ability not only to pursue happiness but to find some measure of it along the way. The pursuit of happiness, as eighteenth-century thinkers such as

As he that taketh away a garment in cold weather, so is he that singeth songs to an heavy heart.

Voltaire, Johnson, and Jefferson taught us, was a necessity because the idea of happiness represented the possibility that we could be secure from the ills of the world. Freud also tied the pursuit of happiness to the need to believe there was an overriding order and sanity to the universe. Freud realized, as Saint Augustine had in *Confessions*, that humankind possessed a form of hopeful necessity in wanting to believe God kept the cosmos in a balanced order. Religion, its laws, its ethics, and its moral standards, was really an expression of that old Virgilian desire for balance, security, and sanity in life. But where religion served to codify morals and beliefs, literature acted as the means by which the ideas of the imaginative aspect of the human personality were passed from one generation to the next, and arranged in such a way as to create a "tradition," a continuum of stories, ideas, forms, structures, expressions, and motifs. The ongoing story that appears to be told through literature, the story of human life and human dreams, was, according to Freud, a reflection of the personal story that each of us tells ourselves in the process of defining who we are:

> The superego of an epoch of civilization has an origin similar to that of an individual. It is based on the impression left behind by personalities of great leaders—men of overwhelming force of mind or men in whom one of the human impulsions has found its strongest and purest, and therefore often its most one-sided expression.

Just as Saint Augustine perceived the life of the individual as a microcosm of the life of the world, so too did Freud understand that our individual personal narratives were microcosms of larger narratives we keep retelling in literature. What the accumulation of these stories produces is a group consciousness that forms our culture. The purpose of culture, said Freud, was to offer people a suitably neutral ground, a place in the mind or the imagination driven by something above and beyond the baser animal instincts of the id or the ego. The paradox, however, is that even though the artistic impulse seems at odds with the procreative impulse, as in the case of Joyce's protagonist, it is actually in the service of humanity's survival. Freud attempted to explain what he meant by this apparent contradiction:

> At one point in this enquiry I was led to the idea that civiliza-
> tion was a special process in the service of Eros, whose purpose
> is to combine single human individuals, and after that families,
> then races, peoples and nations, into one great unity, the unity
> of mankind. Why this has to happen, we do not know; the work
> of Eros is precisely this.

Literature, in other words, is more than merely an entertainment—
it is an expression of happiness that represents the power of love
itself. The Prioress, Madame Eglantine in Chaucer's *The Canterbury Tales*, is described as wearing a brooch at her throat that seems
to suggest that she is a natural "romantic" at heart and an addict for
courtly love romances. The brooch, Chaucer tells us, bears the
Latin inscription *Amor vincit omnia*. And just as the twentieth-
century English poet Philip Larkin concluded his poem *An Arun-
del Tomb* with the statement, "What will survive of us is love," so
Freud appears to be offering a similar tribute to the human capacity both to procreate and to maintain and honor those things that
are beautiful, timeless, and redeeming. Love, to paraphrase Saint
Paul in 1 Corinthians 13, is not destructive.

The problem with literature, though, is that it does portray some
of the most troubling aspects of life. Freud realized that the presence of tragedy in literature, of human beings' ability either to
destroy themselves or to destroy others, was not merely a warning
that was meant to refine and define morality and codified behavior.
Classical tragedy, or "ill-luck" as Freud called it, was depicted in
literature in order to "enhance the superego" or make it more
keenly aware of its duty to provide a buffer between humankind
and its baser animal instincts:

> The field of ethics, which is so full of problems, presents us with
> another fact: namely that ill-luck—that is, external frustration—
> so greatly enhances the power of the conscience in the super-ego.
> As long as things go well with a man, his conscience is lenient
> and lets the ego do all sorts of things; but when misfortune

befalls him, he searches his soul, acknowledges his sinfulness, heightens the demands of his conscience, imposes abstinences on himself and punishes himself with penances...Fate is regarded as a substitute for the parental agency. If a man is unfortunate it means that he is no longer loved by his highest power; and threatened by such loss of love, he once more bows to the parental representative in his super-ego—a representative whom, in his days of good fortune, he was ready to neglect.

If Freud's observations about the nature of tragedy and fortune sound familiar, it is because they almost directly echo the words of Boethius in *The Consolation of Philosophy*. The power of fate to reverse the fortunes of an individual's life, the need to blame some higher power for the downfall, to look to the stars rather than ourselves, is what comprises the core of spectacle in tragedy. What Freud does not explain, however, is how the individual seeks a remedy to tragedy through the power of reason. Boethius does not blame his metaphorical parental power. Instead, he reasons that it is his perception of events that needs adjustment, and in the end, he conquers, or at least mitigates, tragedy by his ability to pursue the thought of happiness, no matter what. The tragedy that we see in Sophocles' Theban plays or Shakespeare's *King Lear*, or the near-tragedy that we encounter in the Christian religion through Christ's sacrifice, are reminders of how close we can allow ourselves to come to destruction. The message seems to be that we must take control of the world and of our lives by taking control of our imaginations and reasoning our way toward the happiness and order we instinctively desire but are unable either to express or achieve. Freud, like Faulkner, believes that this will eventually happen, and that human beings will not merely endure, they will prevail.

Literature, in this schema, is a means of externalizing our fears, our challenges, and our imaginative development. As the contemporary British writer D.M. Thomas points out in *The White Hotel*, his novel about a Theseus-like quest through the labyrinth of the mind that Freud undertakes to cure one of his patients, the mind is a maze. The psychoanalyst attempts to penetrate that maze and to slay the Minotaur of mental illness that lies at the puzzle's heart. In one of the early sections of *The White Hotel*, Freud writes to C.G. Jung about the treatment of shell-shock victims from the First World War, individuals who were suffering from neurasthenia, an obsessive repetition of extreme fear and excessive violent absurdity wherein the patient's inner ego cannot explain to the id why it is that the superego has allowed events like bombardments and poisonous gas attacks to threaten the individual's survival.

W.H.R. Rivers, one of Freud's contemporaries, a British medical officer who had been one of the pioneers in the new science of anthropology and who had done extensive research into tribal customs in Borneo, believed that the way to cure a patient of neurasthenia was to allow him to confront his experiences and psychological traumas through the externalizing power of art. During the First World War, Rivers was placed in charge of a number of young British officers who had been severely shell-shocked and were being treated at hospitals in the Borders region of England. At the hospital of Craiglockart, Rivers had considerable success in persuading some of his more literate patients to externalize their sufferings and the horrors they had witnessed by

Augustus Leopold Egg. Past and Present No. 1. Even in the ennui of a nineteenth-century drawing room, tragedy can strike. The sharp division between innocence, on the left, and experience on the right, delineates the difference between childhood and the world of adult realities. The mirror in the center of the painting is troubling because it reflects the world of the viewer.

writing poetry. Among those who responded to Rivers' treatment were Siegfried Sassoon, Frank Prewett, and Wilfred Owen, and the poetry they produced provided them with the ability to study their suffering in the way that Saint Augustine learned to appreciate the beauty of drama by separating his experience of the play from his emotional interpretation of it. Owen was able to arrive at a profound understanding of his war experience, an understanding that culminated in his declarations that "all the poet can do today is to warn," and "the Poetry is in the pity." What these declarations meant was that literature was not merely a vehicle with which to assert moral conventions, as Virgil might have argued, but a barometer for society that informed the world just how far it could go with either self-destructive insanity or the illusions that came from not paying attention to the imagination.

George Bernard Shaw, in his play *Heartbreak House*, a rewriting of Anton Chekhov's play *Uncle Vanya*, suggested that the causes of the First World War lay in the social and imaginative malaise that crept into European society during the nineteenth century. For Shaw, the ruling classes in Europe were composed of two groups: those he placed in Horseback Hall, the upper classes who spent their lives fox-hunting and ignoring the intellectual life they had inherited from previous generations, and those he placed in Heartbreak House, the educated bourgeoisie, who buried their minds in romantic notions of art that had little to do with the realities of the world around them. Disgusted by the carnage that a hundred years of ennui and silliness had wrought on European society, Shaw exclaimed:

The nice people could read; some of them could write; and they were the only repositories of culture who had social opportunities of contact with our politicians, administrators, and newspaper proprietors, or any chance of sharing or influencing their politics. But they shrank from contact. They hated politics. They did not realize Utopia for the common people: they wished to realize their favorite fictions and poems in their own lives; and when they could, they lived without scruple on incomes which they did nothing to earn.

As Shaw saw it, the nineteenth century had missed a glorious opportunity to set humankind on the path that the imaginative thinkers of the past had intended. Industry, rather than creating a better society, had opted instead for the destructive powers of a war machine. When Captain Shotover, one of the leading characters of *Heartbreak House*, confronts his lack of money, he is urged by his daughter, Mrs. Hushabye, to put his talents toward inventions that will generate income:

CAPTAIN SHOTOVER: Only £500 for that lifeboat! I got twelve thousand for the invention before that.

MRS. HUSHABYE: Yes, dear; but that was for the ship with the magnetic keel that sucked up submarines. Living at the rate we do, you cannot afford life-saving inventions. Can't you think of something that will murder half Europe at one bang?

Beneath Shaw's biting, satirical flippancy, the message seems to be that the capitalist system of economics had driven Europe not only to the brink of destruction but to the point where the end of civilization seemed inevitable.

The same year that Freud wrote *Civilization and Its Discontents*, the English novelist Virginia Woolf was asked to deliver a speech to women students at Cambridge. In her speech, she decided to examine literary history from the perspective of anti-history, the process of investigating what might have happened to the world had events worked out differently. In one memorable passage, she supposed what the male-dominated world of literature might be like had Shakespeare had a smarter sister who also wrote:

Let me imagine, since the facts are so hard to come by, what would have happened had Shakespeare had a wonderfully gifted sister, called Judith, let us say. Shakespeare himself went, very probably—his mother was an heiress—to the grammar school, where he may have learnt Latin—Ovid, Virgil and Horace— and the elements of grammar and logic. He was, it is well known, a wild boy who poached rabbits, perhaps shot a deer, and had, rather sooner than he should have done, to marry a woman in the neighbourhood....Meanwhile, his extraordinarily gifted sister, let us suppose, remained at home. She was adventurous, as imaginative as agog to see the world as he was. But she was not sent to school. She had no chance of learning grammar and logic, let alone of reading Horace and Virgil. She picked up a book now and then, one of her brother's perhaps, and read a few pages. But her parents came in and told her to mend the stockings or mind the stew and not moon about with books and papers.

G.C. Beresford. Virginia Woolf. The youthful and beautiful Woolf before the terrors of an aggresive world took their toll on her. This is a far cry from the Woolf who threw herself into the Thames following the destruction of her Bloomsbury home.

This parable about the plight of a young woman who wants to be an author but has that desire rejected by a patriarchal society points to the strange reality that dominates any canonical reading of Western literature: half the members of the human race—women—were not permitted to tell their own stories in their own ways. Although one of the first major poets in the Western tradition, Sappho, was a woman, women were not allowed to evolve a notable tradition, let alone reclaim a lost one. But Woolf believed that the spirit of Shakespeare's smarter sister still lived in all women, and what was needed was both the determination to write and "five hundred pounds a year and a room of one's own." In other words, Woolf believed that literature could be transformed as an art if women were given the physical, economic, and social liberty to write.

In a treatise that she titled *A Room of One's Own*, Woolf announced that women had not only a right but also an obligation to express themselves. In urging women to take up the pen, Woolf outlined the possibilities of a new literature, one that would be created from the spirit that Freud called Eros, the desire to see society and the superego enriched through the life-sustaining vision of the female instincts toward the preservation and growth of the human species. Woolf urged her female audience to reject the limited horizons of the critics of the day, who argued against the great accomplishments that could come if women had the opportunity to write:

No, delightful as the pastime of measuring may be, it is the most futile of all occupations, and to submit to the decrees of measurers the most servile of attitudes. So long as you write

what you wish to write, that is all that matters; and whether it matters for ages or only for hours, nobody can say. But to sacrifice a hair of the head of your vision, a shade of its colour, in deference to some Headmaster with a silver pot in his hand or to some professor with a measuring-rod up his sleeve, is the most abject treachery, and the sacrifice of wealth and chastity which used to be said to be the greatest of human disasters, a mere flea-bite in comparison.

The new writing that would emerge, Woolf believed, would strengthen the overall scope of literature by providing not merely an echo of the old tradition but a new vision and a new voice, a means of expressing what she called "the accumulation of unrecorded life":

For women have sat indoors all these millions of years, so that by this time the very walls are permeated by their creative force, which has, indeed, so overcharged the capacity of bricks and mortar that it must needs harness itself to pens and brushes and business and politics. But this creative power differs greatly from the creative power of men....

It would be a thousand pities if women wrote like men, or lived like men, or looked like men, for if two sexes are quite inadequate, considering the vastness and variety of the world, how should we manage with one only? Ought not education to bring out and fortify the differences rather than the similarities?

Woolf felt that society needed a different voice. After all, only ten years prior to the composition of *A Room of One's Own*, European civilization (or the lack of it) had attempted mass annihilation in the war to end all wars. Woolf wondered aloud about the after-effects of that war:

When the guns fired in August 1914, did the faces of men and women show so plain in each other's eyes that romance was killed? Certainly it was a shock (to women in particular with their illusions about education, and so on) to see the faces of our rulers in the light of shell-fire. But lay the blame where one will, on whom one will, the illusion which inspired Tennyson and Christina Rossetti to sing so passionately about the coming of their loves is far rarer now than then. One has only to read, to look, to listen, to remember. But why say "blame"? Why, if it was an illusion, not praise the catastrophe, whatever it was, that destroyed illusion and put truth in its place?

War was an issue that she would study ten years after *A Room of One's Own*, on the eve of yet another world war, in *Three Guineas*, when Woolf suggested that Western society had been blind-sided by a symbolism that it continually failed to read. She became fasci-nated by the symbolism of military uniforms, by the secretive ways that a patriarchal society had encoded vital information about its goals in symbols that were mystifying to all but a few. What was needed to correct this destructive symbology, which had incited European nations to the First World War and had reinvented itself in the stylized symbolism of the Nazi movement, was the creation of intelligent and informed readers who would question both the written text and the text of life with critical discernment. What was also needed was a clarity in literature that would enable the imagination to cut through the nonsense of its own artistic processes. In other words, the purpose of literature should be to clarify what the imagination says and knows, not to discombobulate it through the complexities of the artistic self-indulgence that had marked the literature of the preceding century.

Although Woolf does not say so directly in *A Room of One's Own*, she perceived that culture and the Western imagination had somehow let everyone down. It was not just the fact that society was patriarchal but that literature had become an obscurant's game, a secret within a secret that was denied to half the human population. Woolf saw this as the problem with modern poetry:

But the living poets express a feeling that is actually being made and torn out of us at the moment. One does not recognize it in the first place; often for some reason one fears it; one watches it with keenness and compares it jealously and suspiciously with the old feeling that one knew. Hence the difficulty of modern poetry; and it is because of this difficulty that one cannot remember more than two consecutive lines of any good modern poet.

Poetry, to Woolf, was a male's game; fiction was for women because fiction "must stick to the facts, and the truer the facts, the better the fiction." This statement—which was built on the work of such exceptional writers as Katherine Mansfield (the only female writer whom Woolf envied), whose short stories were marvels of precision, perception, and execution—suggests that clarity of ideas, vision, and logic would go a long way toward correcting the exhausted and destructive patriarchy of literature that had almost ruined Western civilization. Had Freud and Woolf sat down together, they both might have concluded that the last redoubt of Eros—the life force of love and nurturing that allows the human passions and imagination to be expressed in creative and superego-building ways—was to be found through the rebirth of literature and the power of the artist to override the countdown to destruction with the simple reaffirmation of the humane values of "compassion, sacrifice and endurance." As Faulkner said, it is "the poet's, the writer's duty to write about these things."

18

WRITING OURSELVES
INTO EXISTENCE

Rainer Maria Rilke's *Letters to a Young Poet*
and James Joyce's *A Portrait of the Artist
as a Young Man* and *Ulysses*

I N November 1921, a young American philosopher from
Harvard, who had given up his studies to work as a bank
clerk in London's City district, left London with his wife
for a brief respite by the seaside. His nerves, he told his friends,
were bad. The sea air would do him good. As he sat on the front at
Margate, looking out on the English Channel, he composed the
first fifty lines of a poem that would change twentieth-century
literature. The stern young man struggled to write not only about
the failure of the civilization that had produced the Great War but
about the need within himself to find the connection, the golden
thread, that would make literary culture, for all its complexity and
absurdity, meaningful to him. At first, the task seemed daunting,
and he scribbled in pencil as he sat shivering in view of the sea wall,
"On Margate sands I can connect nothing with nothing." The brief
allusion to the negative universe of Shakespeare's *King Lear*
suggests that he saw the world around him as a kind of vacuum, a
place where the survivors huddled and questioned what they had
remaining at their disposal. But gradually the poem began to take
shape.

Another poet, another American, who had been dismissed from
the University of Pennsylvania for a supposed impropriety and who
had sought academic posts in every place from the University of
Toronto to Oxford before giving up the professorial world in favor
of the literary life, came to the bank clerk's rescue. In his editorial
hands, the fragments of an enormous cultural collage began to take
shape, and suddenly the traditions, the myths, the stories, and the

poetic rhythms of the past began to speak to a present that lay in ruins. The bank clerk, T.S. Eliot, realized just what he was doing, and together he and his American poet friend, Ezra Pound, completed their contribution to the rebuilding of our civilization and its sacred values and gave us *The Waste Land.*

As a poem, *The Waste Land* is a rare combination of epic and collage in which a host of voices echoes through the shards of Western society in the wake of a great war, trying to salvage some fragments of meaning from the cacophony before them and after them. The title of the poem suggests that post–First World War Europe had become a metaphorical desert of the spirit, similar to the Waste Forest of medieval romances such as *The Quest of the Holy Grail.* Somehow civilization, its culture, and particularly its literature had failed its practitioners, and barbarism had triumphed over humankind's natural inclinations toward order, sanity, and clear, coherent thinking. Yet for all the pessimism of Eliot's poem, it still contains the note of the heroic. The old idea that literature could teach and not merely delight, that it could inform the reader of moral choices that could be made for the betterment of society—the model that *The Aeneid* demonstrates so clearly—is part of what Eliot was attempting to create in *The Waste Land*, and although twentieth-century literature has consistently expressed a rejection of a moral purpose, the old Virgilian goals are still loud and clear. Throughout the voices in *The Waste Land*, there is a consistent, though sometimes muted, speaker, who looks on what he sees and comments on it with profound disappointment and sadness. This "witness" is part narrator but also part chorus. He both expresses concern over what he perceives and at the same time pulls the inter-cut scenes and statements together into a coherent vision. Near the conclusion of the final section of the poem, the commentator utters a famous pronouncement: "These fragments I have shored against my ruins." What Eliot's poem suggests is that the remnants of Western culture and civilization contain some of the elements necessary for a spiritual rebirth of society, and that regeneration and renewal lie in two important recognitions.

The first of these recognitions comes in the form of three words that Eliot borrows from the Hindu *Upanishads*: *Datta, Dayadhvam,* and *Damyata*, or, "Give, sympathize, and control." These terms suggest that what Western culture has lost is that generosity of both means and spirit that was so evident in *The Odyssey*, the ability to offer oneself like Galahad in *The Quest of the Holy Grail* or Aeneas in *The Aeneid*, and the necessary mental toughness of Saint Augustine to overcome the distractions of a world that plays between the extremes of the horrific and the frivolous. And when Saint Augustine makes a brief walk-on in the third section of the poem, what we see is not the strength of mind that overcame the Manichaean heresy but the burning desire and frail worldliness of a rhetorician who battled his own earthly needs. What is needed, Eliot seems to be saying, is a purpose, a goal, a grail, or a vision to drive society in a new quest toward the spiritual and intellectual renewal that would make the enormous sacrifice of the First World War worthwhile.

At the root of Eliot's thinking was Jessie Weston's *From Ritual to Romance*, a work that examined the symbolism and the archetypal events of medieval romance. Weston theorized that the quest story was an elaborate expression of fertility metaphors, where the chosen knight, the Galahad, was selected as a sacrifice whose martyrdom would raise the fallen kingdom of the Fisher King from the death, decay, and neglect into which it had fallen. Eliot's Waste Land was a labyrinth of voices, experiences, texts, and allusions that, like the Waste Forest of *The Quest of the Holy Grail*, needed constantly to be examined, interpreted, and understood. And, as in the Grail legend or the earlier journey epics on which the Grail story was based, the ultimate goal of all the tribulations and machinations was the reestablishment of a paradisal existence that had been lost to humankind.

The second of Eliot's two great recognitions in *The Waste Land* points directly to the role of the hero. In the miasma of voices and ideas that Eliot's poem presents, there is a conspicuous absence of a protagonist, a central individual who, in the epic tradition, would pull together all the disparate parties and, by physical strength, force of will, and spiritual purity, vanquish the forces of opposition and accomplish the impossible. The typical epic hero, the Aeneas or the Galahad, is someone who is able to put the concerns of his group and his purpose ahead of his own needs.

Eliot diverged from both Weston's thinking and the normal

pattern of medieval romance by suggesting that the new hero, the one who would restore the Waste Land to its spiritual and intellectual fruitfulness, would come from the mass of society itself. For this new hero—a voice that almost seems to emerge from the chorus-like everyman narrator who makes sporadic appearances in *The Waste Land*—the daily grind of urban existence would be his Knight School. In a universe shaped not so much by Christian values as by the mass-mediocratization prophesied by Alexis de Tocqueville in *Democracy in America*, the new hero is someone who has merely borne witness, a modern-day Tiresias who has "foresuffered all," and whose vatic vision now must turn inward upon itself. The new hero would be someone who, like Petrarch, would "turn an inward eye upon himself" and restore the fallen kingdom through his artistic vision. The quest would be for the vision with which one could not only express the needs to "give, sympathize, and control" but also teach others to seek the same clarity of thought, the same passion of pursuit, and the same point of destination on the "ever-retreating horizon" of the imagination. The new hero would be the artist, and Troynovant would be the minds of every reader.

The question was, however, how to create such a hero. There are two stories that seem to answer the question. The first story began on an autumn day in 1902. A young pupil and poet named Franz Xaver Kappus at the Military Academy of Wiener Neustadt sat beneath a large chestnut tree and read a book of poems, daydreaming about what the poetic life might be like. One of the professors, a chaplain named Horacek, walked up to the young student and seized the book from his hands, exclaiming, "So our pupil René Rilke has become a poet." Young Mr. Kappus seems to have been in awe of the thought that the poet whose works he was reading was alive and had also been a student of the priest's. Daring silence and indifference, the student wrote to the poet, and the poet wrote back, beginning an exchange of correspondence that lasted for several years.

In declining to offer the young poet any direct criticism on his poetry, Rainer Maria Rilke instead began a discussion of why a poet should write. Rather than throw words at an idea, Rilke instead opted to use moments from his own experience of life to advise the younger man on the path he should take with his own work:

> Things aren't all so tangible and sayable as people would usually
> have us believe; most experiences are unsayable, they happen in
> a space that no word has ever entered, and more unsayable than
> all other things are works of art, those mysterious existences,
> whose life endures beside our own, small, transitory life.

Rilke, at this point in his career, was struggling to articulate a kind of poetry that so far had been beyond the ability of writers to express. For him, the art of poetry was an "ever-retreating horizon" that he was determined to reach. His own personal quest for meaning emerges in his *Letters to a Young Poet*, the volume of correspondence that resulted from his extended exchange with Franz Kappus.

In 1902, as the conversation began, Rilke was ascending to the heights of his poetic career. He had traveled Europe extensively, had met Tolstoy, had served as secretary for the French sculptor Rodin, and was beginning to make a name for himself as a poet, an art he eventually took up as a religious vocation. He had not yet written his famous poem *The Panther*, that statement of desire and caged passion, but one can see in his advice to Kappus some of the yearning to resolve an unquenchable tension that is contained in *The Panther*:

> *His vision, from the constantly passing bars,*
> *has grown so weary that it cannot hold*
> *anything else. It seems to him there are*
> *a thousand bars; and behind the bars, no world.*
>
> *As he paces in cramped circles, over and over,*
> *the movement of his powerful soft strides*
> *is like a ritual dance around a center*
> *in which a mighty will stands paralyzed.*
>
> *Only at time, the curtain of the pupils*
> *lifts quietly —. An image enters in,*

rushes down through the tensed, arrested muscles,
plunges into the heart and is gone.

Almost two decades later, a mature Rilke would channel that same sense of passion and energy into his divinely meditative reflections on love, *The Duino Elegies*, where, in the *Fourth Elegy*, he lamented:

And you yourself, how could you know
what primordial time you stirred in your lover. What passions
welled up inside him from departed beings...

Oh gently, gently,
let him see you performing, with love, some confident daily task, —
lead him out close to the garden, give him what outweighs
the heaviest night....
Restrain him....

In one of his first letters to Kappus, Rilke offers a piece of advice that he would soon apply to his own works. It was the same advice that Dante had taken to heart in *La Vita Nuova* and that Sir Philip Sidney's muse had admonished him to follow in the sonnet sequence *Astrophel and Stella* ("'Fool', said my Muse to me, 'look in thy heart and write'"):

...write about what your everyday life offers you; describe your sorrows and desires; the thoughts that pass through your mind and your belief in some kind of beauty—describe all these with heartfelt, silent, humble sincerity and, when you express yourself, use the Things around you, the images from your dreams, and the objects that you remember. If your everyday life seems poor, don't blame *it*; blame yourself; admit to yourself that you are not enough of a poet to call forth its riches; because for the creator there is no poverty and no poor, indifferent place.

Rilke is recommending more than a kitchen-sink realism; he suggests something far more difficult, a heroic enterprise of celebrating the obvious and of recognizing the monumental scope that the simple actions of living embrace. When Kappus marveled at the fact that Rilke was in Rome, the elder poet responded, in a letter of October 29, 1903, that the places associated with the heroic, the tourist attractions that the past leaves behind, were no different from anywhere else:

No, there is not *more* beauty here than in other places, and all these objects, which have been marveled at by generation after generation, mended and restored by the hands of workmen, mean nothing, are nothing, and have no heart and no value; — but there is much beauty here because everywhere there is much beauty...and one slowly learns to recognize the very few Things in which something eternal endures that one can love and something solitary that one can gently take part in.

The artist, in Rilke's mind, was someone who could find poetry and the great themes anywhere, not merely in the places that tradition insisted had to be associated with art. There is, in Rilke's statement, a Whitmanesque recognition that each individual personality and each life contain an enormous amount of experience that is worthy of celebration. If Whitman had couched the American character in his poem *Song of Myself*, then Rilke was attempting to locate the artistic eye, the power of perception married with the strength of imagination, in the essence of everyday life. However hard it may have been for traditional literary minds to grasp this concept, it must be said that the great voices, not only of twentieth-century literature but of the literary continuum, always realize this. Yeats in his Salley Gardens beside the Garavagh River in Sligo, or Eliot on the seafront at Margate, or Robert Frost in his apple orchard in Massachusetts all acknowledge this. What they say to the reader is that experience itself, the daily act of living, is the stuff of which literature is made, and that great dreams can be dreamed anywhere, at any time, and by anyone. If there was one clear message sounded by poets in the twentieth century, from Fernando Pessoa in Portugal to Derek Walcott in St. Lucia, then surely this must be it.

What made the leap from the literary and the traditionally poetic all the harder to understand was a simple fact that all the great authors had acknowledged for centuries: the hardest thing to imagine is yourself. Rilke was striking at a key issue. What was more important as the substance of literature: the absurd outer boundaries of the imagination or the quiet and overlooked inner core of the self? Indeed, this question has been an enormous challenge for writers down through the ages. Teachers who assign creative assignments to grade-school classes are quick to observe that one should "write about something you know." Yet that maxim, "The hardest thing to imagine is yourself," a phrase coined by the contemporary Canadian poet David Wevill, seems to capture the essence of the struggle.

Rilke's answer to this question came straight out of the theories of John Locke. It was an answer that contained some elements of what triggered the Romantic movement, and an artist's response that would have sat well with Sigmund Freud. Rilke believed that all content originated in the writer's childhood:

> ...even if you found yourself in a prison, whose walls let in none of the world's sounds—wouldn't you still have your childhood, that jewel beyond all price, that treasure house of memories? Turn your attention to it. Try to raise up the sunken feelings of this enormous past; your personality will grow stronger, your solitude will expand and become a place where you can live in the twilight, where the noise of other people passes by, far in the distance.

The artist, Rilke seemed to believe, was someone who was able to perceive in his own experience the breadth and variety of life, and to celebrate that breadth and variety by recognizing the entire world as a place that is itself a work of art. To be an artist was to be able to live in both the inner and the outer world, and to communicate the relationship between the two to the reader:

> Think, dear Sir, of the world that you carry inside you, and call this thinking whatever you want to: a remembering of your own childhood or a yearning toward a future of your own—only be attentive to what is arising within you, and place that above everything you perceive around you. What is happening in your innermost self is worthy of your entire love; somehow you must

find a way to work at it, and not lose too much time or too much courage in clarifying your attitude toward people.

As was the case with the philosophy of the seventeenth-century British epistemologist Bishop Berkeley, artists, according to Rilke, carried the world inside them, and stored the experience of living in such a way that it could speak through their work with a profound sensitivity, energy, and eloquence. But to achieve this, the artist must become a solitary figure.

Rilke believed that the artist worked best in solitude. To be cut off, like many of Wordsworth's and Coleridge's characters in *Lyrical Ballads*, or to be alone on the top of a mountain with only one's thoughts, as was the case with Petrarch, allowed one to access something primordially important in one's personality and then listen intensely to what it had to say. Rilke's notion of solitariness is far different from that of Mary Shelley. For Rilke, the artist is not made an outcast but instead chooses the role of the observer, someone who stands back from the thread of life to understand in himself what it is that he sees in others, and to locate the exact expression that would convey the nature of the moment and the experience to others:

Only the individual who is solitary is placed under the deepest laws like a Thing, and when he walks out into the rising dawn or looks out into the event-filled evening and when he feels what is happening there, all situations drop from him as if from a dead man, though he stands in the midst of pure life.

Solitude, to Rilke, was not meant to provide a contemplative place for the sublime to fill with awe but to offer a means by which one could be closer to life. Solitude offered an imaginative and perceptual liberty through which one gained the insight and understanding necessary to all artistic endeavors. In other words, by moving away from things, by standing apart from life, the artist was actually closer to it:

It is like this everywhere; but that is no cause for anxiety or sadness; if there is nothing you can share with other people, try to be close to Things: *they* will not abandon you; and the nights are still there, and the winds that move through the trees and across many lands; everything in the world of Things and animals is still filled with happening, which you can take part in; and children are still the way you were as a child, sad and happy in just the same way—and if you think of your childhood, you once again live among them, among the solitary children, and the grownups are nothing, and their dignity has no value.

In what amounts to a corollary of Freud's notion that civilization is driven by the power of Eros, the life force that asks us both to preserve our species and to advance it, Rilke realizes that solitude is the individual's means of recognizing a kind of love that reveals the beauty and intricacy of the world:

> ...solitude, [is] a heightened and deepened kind of aloneness for the person who loves. Loving does not at first mean merging, surrendering, and uniting with another person (for what would a union be of two people who are unclarified, unfinished, and still incoherent—?), it is a high inducement for the individual to ripen, to become something in himself, to become world, to become world in himself for the sake of another person; it is a great, demanding claim on him, something that chooses him and calls him to vast distances. Only in this sense, as the task of working on themselves ("to harken and to hammer day and night"), may young people use the love that is given to them. Merging and surrendering and every kind of communion is not for them (who must still, for a long, long time, save and gather themselves); it is the ultimate, is perhaps that for which human lives are as yet barely large enough.

Rilke's paradox is that solitude puts one in touch with the world as well as with the experience of one's own extended narrative, the story of one's life and the inner thread that continuously winds out as we tell ourselves the story of ourselves. Life to a poet or a writer is the means by which those unbroken connections between one event and the next, and between the self and the world, are forged and reinforced on a daily basis. First and foremost the writer is an individual who is trying to connect himself to the world in order to understand his existence.

Like Saint Augustine in the *Confessions*, Rilke asks his young poet to examine the fabric of his own life, to seek the meaning of his own inner narrative from childhood right up to the living moment, in order to embrace the world around him and articulate a vision that can be passed on to others. The writer, the artist, in this sense, is a kind of guide for those supplicants in the communion of the superego, that restless, collective consensus of our most valued ideas.

The poet/writer is not so much a priest of culture as he is a theologian of it. He writes the liturgy rather than performing the mass. And it is the duty of the writer, as a contemporary of Rilke's—a young Irishman named James Joyce—claimed, to "forge in the smithy of my soul the uncreated conscience of my race." As Joyce saw it, the unquestioned and unchallenged life was a labyrinth, a place where we are apt to encounter and reencounter our worst nightmares. The poet/writer is someone who must go into the labyrinth armed only with a thread and answer the beast of Thanatos (that negative impulse toward death and destruction that Freud defined as the enemy of Eros) at the core of the puzzle. In *A Portrait of the Artist as a Young Man*, Joyce declared that the poet/writer was someone who would "recreate life out of life," and dedicate himself to the principles of personal freedom, self-awareness, and clarity of vision that enable artistic creation:

> He would create proudly out of the freedom and power of his soul, as the great artificer whose name he bore, a living thing, new and soaring and beautifully, impalpable, imperishable.

The artist, in Joyce's view, had within his power that means of shaping a nation, just as Aeneas had applied his focus and his sense of personal responsibility shaping the destiny and character of Rome. The purpose of life's journey for the poet/writer, in Joyce's eyes, was not only to "forge" that "uncreated conscience of the race" but to pursue the "ever-retreating horizon" of a vision of what might be possible in the human imagination, a concept that, in *Ulysses*, he called "the ineluctable modality." What Joyce meant is that once one is aware that things can be transformed and improved through the vision of the artist, then one cannot escape the possibility that things will be made better because of that vision. In this statement reside several millennia of Western thought and striving, the encapsulation of the notion that the imagination can always point the way to what is possible.

For Joyce, the experience of the artist led the way to that world of possibilities. In *A Portrait of the Artist as a Young Man*, he examined the ways in which an artist is created and educated by the world around him. Following on the model Saint Augustine established in the *Confessions*, Joyce created a *Bildungsroman*, a novel of the growth of a mind, around the emerging character of a young Irishman named Stephen Dedalus. Joyce's protagonist is named for the ancient artist of Classical mythology who constructed the labyrinth in which the Minotaur was caged by King Minos of Crete. After Daedalus completed the challenging task of constructing the labyrinth, Minos refused to let him and his son, Icarus, leave Crete, so fearful was the king of someone revealing the secrets of the labyrinth to the world. To escape Crete and Minos, Daedalus constructed wax wings for himself and his son. As the two were making good their escape, Icarus decided that he wanted a closer look at the sun. Despite prior warnings from his father, he flew higher and higher toward its heat and light until his wax wings melted and he fell into the sea and drowned. What seems to have fascinated Joyce and other twentieth-century writers who took up the motif of Daedalus and Icarus is the way in which the story serves as a metaphor for the subversive and defiant nature of the artist who faces the confines and restrictions of political oppression. W.H. Auden, in his poem *Musée des Beaux Arts*, examined a Renaissance painting titled *The Fall of Icarus* by Pieter Brueghel the Elder and concluded that, although artists and writers continuously accomplish great things, they are, more often than not, ignored by society:

> *In Brueghel's Icarus, for instance: how everything turns away*
> *Quite leisurely from the disaster; the ploughman may*
> *Have heard the splash, the foresaken cry,*
> *But for him it was not an important failure; the sun shone*
> *As it had to on the white legs disappearing into the green*

Water; and the expensive delicate ship that must have seen
Something amazing, a boy falling out of the sky,
Had somewhere to get to and sailed calmly on.

For Joyce, the indifferent world consisted of his native city of Dublin and his country of Ireland. Near the conclusion of *A Portrait of the Artist as a Young Man*, Stephen Dedalus defines what he thinks Ireland is when his friend Davin declares that being Irish should come before being a poet: "Do you know what Ireland is?" asked Stephen with cold violence. "Ireland is the old sow that eats her farrow." What confronts Stephen is the choice between being Irish or being an artist. He is trapped by his nationality, by his city, and by his own past, and the choice that he makes at the conclusion of the novel is between remaining and suffering in a spiritually and imaginatively stifling environment or "escaping the nets and snares" of his situation by metaphorically flying from that which would confine him. In the end, Stephen must decide whether he is going to follow the path that has been set for him by his society, his religion, and his family or whether he will pursue the truth that he must discover for himself, "what the heart is and what it feels."

Stephen realizes that he must reject all that has made him in order to discover a new consciousness and realize himself as an artist, a spokesperson for himself and his people. In a previously quoted speech and in a moment of rejection not unlike Satan's rejection of heaven and its order uttered in *Paradise Lost*, Stephen declares his intentions:

I will not serve that in which I no longer believe, whether it call itself my home, my fatherland, or my church: and I will try to express myself in some mode of life or art as freely as I can and as wholly as I can, using for my defence the only arms I allow myself to use—silence, exile, and cunning.

Stephen's declaration of arms, like the arming of Aeneas in the *nekusis* scene of *The Aeneid*, is the realization that he must become a kind of Odyssean character, and like the protagonist of *The Odyssey* allow his wits, and the weapons of his wits, "silence, exile, and cunning," to see him through the voyage of self-discovery on which he is about to embark. In other words, the artist is a hero who undertakes a voyage not so much to the homeland he has lost or to the homeland he wishes to reinvent but to the threshold of that realization where individuality and its vision triumph over all other things.

The deciding and defining moment for Stephen Dedalus, a moment of insight and revelation known as an *epiphany*, comes when he strolls along the Strand beach in Dublin. In a solitude that would have pleased Rilke, Stephen encounters a vision of wild, unleashed beauty that articulates the passion and freedom of the artist he longs to be:

> He was alone. He was unheeded, happy and near to the wild heart of life. He was alone and young and wilful and wild-hearted, alone amid the waste of wild air and brackish waters and the sea-harvest of shells and tangle and veiled grey sunlight and gayclad lightclad figures of children and girls and voices childish and girlish in the air.

What creates the apotheosis of Stephen's vision is his encounter with a young girl who

> ...stood before him in midstream, alone and still, gazing out to sea. She seemed like one whom magic had changed into the likeness of a strange and beautiful seabird. Her long slender bare legs were delicate as a crane's and pure save where an emerald trail of seaweed had fashioned itself as a sign upon the flesh. Her thighs, fuller and soft-hued as ivory, were bared almost to the hips, where the white fringes of her drawers were like feathering of soft white down. Her slate-blue skirts were kilted boldly about her waist and dovetailed behind her. Her bosom was as a bird's soft and slight, slight and soft as the breast of some dark-plumaged dove. But her long fair hair was girlish: and girlish, and touched with the wonder of mortal beauty, her face....
>
> Heavenly God! cried Stephen's soul, in an outburst of profane joy.

That moment of epiphany, the instant at which Stephen Dedalus appears to be freed from the confines and restraints of the world around him, is rich in the motifs of bird imagery, images that symbolically suggest flight, freedom, escape, and liberty. When his soul can no longer bear the exuberance and joy of his intellectual and spiritual liberation, he releases "an outburst of profane joy," a moment of what the twentieth-century Spanish poet Federico García Lorca called the *duende*. In his essay "The Theory and Function of the Duende," Lorca notes that the artist contains within him three distinct spirits: the good angel, who overrides the impulses that may seem contrary to social norms and expectations; the bad angel, whose thanetic impulses lead the artist to self-destruction; and the *duende*, who releases the truth of sublime moments of passion, pain, and exclamation through the voice of the artist. Lorca likens the shout of the flamenco singer, whose artifice and knowledge allow him to channel great expressions of power through his art, to the poet's expression of an epiphany. In the case of Stephen Dedalus, that shout on the Strand beach is the *duende*, the spirit of the artist, announcing its birth.

For all the passion and exuberance of that moment of release, an epiphany is a long time in the making, and it is the net sum of the life of the individual. Artists, Joyce would argue, are not merely born (as in the case of Michelangelo in Vasari's *The Lives of the Artists*), but are shaped and fired in the crucible of a society's constraints. In a Freudian sense, it would almost seem that the artist is the superego seeking out a means of renewing itself and extending the life of its society by questioning, challenging, and reinventing common beliefs and aesthetics just when society appears to be growing stale. Certainly, *A Portrait of the Artist as a Young Man* deals with the problems of living in a society that is constantly lowering its expectations and shortening its horizons.

Compositionally, *A Portrait of the Artist as a Young Man* predates Joyce's collection of short stories, *Dubliners*, which takes up the themes of confinement and escape, and examines various characters as they struggle with the challenges of their own intellectual, emotional, and spiritual paralyses. Each of the characters in *Dubliners* is part of a community of sufferers—all of the protagonists in the fifteen short stories that comprise the collection long for an escape of some kind from the mundane drabness of their lives, and all fifteen of the stories contain, in one form or another, the motif of the eucharist. Joyce originally intended to include a short story about a man who goes for an extended walk around the city of Dublin on a June day, and he wanted to title that story "Ulysses." He abandoned this notion, however, because he sensed the story lay outside the tight thematic concerns he was establishing in the rest of the collection. Instead, he saved the idea for a work that he began during the First World War, a work that would become the novel of all novels, *Ulysses*.

What Joyce needed to examine in his earliest work was the matter of his own life. In January 1904, he submitted to a small Irish literary magazine a biographical/analytical essay about the nature of being an artist, titled "A Portrait of the Artist as a Young Man." It was quickly rejected. But Joyce refused to drop the questions, the ideas, and even some of the passages that he had composed for the essay, and soon turned the discursive piece into his first novel, an effort he called *Stephen Hero*. After the book was rejected by numerous publishers, Joyce is said to have cast the manuscript onto the grate of his fireplace. The pages, the front and back ones charred, were rescued by his common-law wife, Nora Barnacle. *Stephen Hero* deals primarily with Joyce's experiences during his undergraduate days at University College, Dublin, how he learned the arguments of art and discourse, and the tribulations of his impoverished family. The development of the character of the artist, from childhood to adulthood, is missing from this early effort, however. After a period, Joyce was urged by Nora to rewrite the book, and he decided to follow Stephen Dedalus from the cradle to the moment when he leaves Ireland in pursuit of the intellectual union between Irish and continental culture.

But while *A Portrait* leaves out the artistic vision of what that "conscience of his race" might entail, Joyce completes the process in his following novel, *Ulysses*, where he revived the narrative of Stephen Dedalus for the opening three chapters. *Ulysses* shows a failed Stephen Dedalus, a dissipated and impoverished medical student who returned home too late for his mother's funeral and who exists as an intellectual outcast on the fringes of Dublin society. With *Ulysses*, Joyce turns for a model to Homer's *The Odyssey*. If *The Odyssey* contained a vision of the entire known world, the Mediterranean of the post–Trojan War era, then Joyce's *Ulysses* transforms Dublin into a metaphor for all the world, its experience and its expressions. In a grand *schema*, or structured arrangement of events, ideas, motifs, and themes, Joyce retells the story of *The Odyssey* (without Homer's digressions or use of the epic time frame) during the course of a single day, June 16, 1904. In the course of that day, Dedalus, the Telemachus figure of *Ulysses*, goes for an extended ramble. At the same time, a middle-aged Jewish man named Leopold Bloom, the Odysseus figure of the story, leaves his home to look after a number of personal and public matters. In the course of the day, Bloom crosses the Liffey seven times and circumnavigates Dublin before connecting with Dedalus, late that evening, at a prostitute's. Together, the metaphorical tandem of father and son make their way home. Meanwhile, Leopold's wife, Molly, has been at home all day, conducting a love affair and lying in bed. She is Joyce's equivalent of Penelope, who sat at home weaving and unweaving her tapestry for two decades in order to keep suitors at bay.

Each chapter of *Ulysses* coincides with an episode from *The Odyssey*—Odysseus' encounter with the Cyclops, for example, is transformed into Bloom's run-in with a one-eyed belligerent in Davie Byrne's pub off Grafton Street. Each of the chapters also coincides, in Joyce's grand schema, with an organ of the body, an

Jacques-Emile Blanche. Portrait of James Joyce. This is a portrait of the artist as the artist really was. Joyce's vision was an attempt to connect his culture to the larger continuum of European culture. The debate he waged paved the way for thinkers such as Joseph Campbell who perceived a universality to human ideas and imaginative experiences.

art, a color, a symbol, and a type of narrative structure. In short, what Joyce wanted to do was to create a work that would embody all fiction, that would show the net sum of literary knowledge as an organic union not only of narrative but of mind, body, and soul, almost to the point where the book takes on a life of its own. Joyce was well aware of what he had created. He remarked that it took ten years to write *Ulysses* and it should take ten years to read it.

Like the Homeric epic on which it is modeled, *Ulysses* obeys many of the conventions of epic poetry. Although it does not deal with a character of high birth whose actions shape the course of the world, Bloom's extended walkabout is a narrative that is meant to imply the entire known world. Bloom is an everyman figure, a bathetic man with tawdry, carnal tastes who masturbates on a beach while watching a young girl frolic in her bloomers as she revels in an equally bathetic fantasy, straight out of a housekeeping magazine, about what products she would use if she were married. Joyce had created a prototype of Leopold Bloom—a Hungarian Jew whose real name is Virag, the Hungarian word for flower—when he was writing *Dubliners*. The original story "Ulysses" would have been about a Jewish man named Hunter, a name that suggests the urgent seeking of the original Odysseus or the violent questing nature of a Theseus. But the transformation from Hunter or even Virag into Leopold Bloom is miraculous. His name, his habits, and his character suggest something earthy, alive, and growing, the force of Eros on two legs. Joyce recasts the stock everyman character from medieval literature into the flesh-and-blood realism of modern literature. What emerges is not an ideal picture but one that describes the heroism of the commonplace and the everyday.

Joyce inherited the notion that literature, especially imaginative literature in the Virgilian mode, should deal only with themes and events of a high or noble order, and that such works had to be expressed with an epic dignity and seriousness of language. However, *Ulysses* is far from this. It is one large joke in which Joyce plays with our expectations and knowledge of literature, its forms, themes, and expressions, beyond the point of irreverence. He wants to make us see that literature is not merely a matter of what we read but of how we read it, and to accomplish this, he changes narrative modes and themes just when we are becoming accustomed to them. Many readers remark that *Ulysses* is a tough read that seems to take forever. What makes it epic, though, is the fact that we are meant to slow our pace of assimilation down to a crawl and notice the depth and detail of the writing rather than merely experiencing the story for the narrative. In the end, the story works out as a comic structure. Stephen finds his metaphorical father; Leopold finds his metaphorical lost son; and both find their way home. Along the way, the book embraces everything from eating to sexual and toilet habits—a complete portrait of life and existence, but not necessarily one presented in conventional terms.

Many readers were shocked by what Joyce had written. Unable to find a publisher for the book among the leading trade houses of the day, which were wary of libel and anything that might possibly be construed as pornographic, Joyce eventually put the manuscript in the hands of a generous American bookseller in Paris named Sylvia Beach, who found a back-street publisher in Dijon willing to print the book and risk prosecution. Parts of the novel had already appeared in little magazines in the United States and Great Britain, and this advance publication of excerpts only served to awaken reaction against the book. All over the English-speaking world, post offices seized and burned copies of *Ulysses* on the grounds that it was immoral. Of course, it was not immoral; Joyce was, perhaps, one of the most moral writers of the twentieth century. Still, this was not a surprising reaction to a book that seemed, by the standard of the times, impossible to read; its implosiveness and its unexpected breadth confounded readers and made the work seem mysterious, if not entirely questionable. *Ulysses* became a pariah book in England, the United States, and Canada not because it depicted with candor and detail the natural bodily functions that each of us experiences on a daily basis but because readers did not know what to make of it.

In this way, it manifested a key problem that writers of the twentieth century have had to face: that readers not only need to be challenged by new ideas but also need to learn how to understand new ideas when they present themselves. *Ulysses*, of course, is now considered the standard against which all writers must measure themselves. But the reality, sad as it may be, is that the next James Joyce will have to fight the battle against censorship, ignorance, and cultural lethargy all over again, in order to keep the voice of the imagination alive and well.

No other work of literature comes close to attempting and attaining what Joyce's *Ulysses* accomplishes. Joyce said that *Ulysses* was meant to take all the knowledge of literature and cultural thought and contain it in a single day in the lives of three characters. What he realized was that the novel as a form of literature should show the reader the breadth and scope of an entire world. Both he and Rilke realized that writing is a form of courage. The blank page is more than merely an opportunity for the voice of the individual to express itself; it is the dark corridors of the labyrinth into which the hero must go if he is to overcome his fears and challenges. Rilke, perhaps, expressed it most clearly when he advised Franz Kappus how to arm himself as he embarked on his journey of expression and self-discovery:

> This is in the end the only kind of courage that is required of us: the courage to face the strangest, most unusual, most inexplicable experiences that can meet us.

What appears to lie at the root of the great narrative that flows throughout Western culture is the desire to understand the inexplicable, to answer the questions that constantly perplex the individual, and to respond to the challenges that are raised by the process of living. For Rilke, overcoming the fear of the inexplicable was the key purpose of writing:

> But the fear of the inexplicable has not only impoverished the reality of the individual; it has also narrowed the relationship between one human being and another, which has as it were been lifted out of the riverbed of infinite possibilities and set down in a fallow place on the bank, where nothing happens.

The purpose of literature may be as simple as our desire to work our way toward answers. The reason we cling to our stories with such passion and determination, telling and retelling them for centuries, may be that our stories fulfill a need in all of us to answer the unknown, to harness our imaginations in such a way that we preserve what is best about us. All we have to do is tell a story and ask that someone listen. Rilke realized that our ongoing stories, our myths, were really efforts on the part of humanity to make the unknown known, to look into the horizons of the imagination's *terra incognita* and find there a suitable and sustaining understanding worth the cost of the experience of living:

> How could we forget those ancient myths that stand at the beginning of all races, the myths about dragons that at the last moment are transformed into princesses? Perhaps all the dragons in our lives are princesses who are only waiting to see us act, just once, with beauty and courage. Perhaps everything that frightens us is, in its deepest essence, something helpless that wants our love.

If the vision of a single June day at the beginning of a long and arduous century can contain all the knowledge, all the ideas, and all the means of expression that we have at our disposal and roll it into one sustained instant of joy, exuberance, and intelligence, then perhaps our stories do amount to more than a maze of twists, turns, and titles.

So when the bank clerk with the bad nerves arrived in Margate just as the winter gales were beginning to blow on shore from the Channel, and the hissing shingle must have seemed like a chorus of naysayers, what he sought as he set words to paper was reassurance. The gray, cold sky must have seemed as bleak a prospect as the winds that blew against Odysseus' ship. Yet, like Odysseus struggling to reach home or Adam longing for the perfect world he had and lost, Eliot found that his vision, the desire to attain that defining place or understanding of oneself, was stronger than the challenges. What he was facing as he wrote *The Waste Land* was the doubt of his own existence, the uncertainty as to whether he could go on and articulate what made his place and time important and lastingly meaningful. What he did, in the end, was more than write a poem; he wrote himself into existence. Literature is, after all, the record of humanity's desire for affirmation. Eliot affirmed his voice and the role that his voice served in extending the continuum of literature, the desire to speak directly and honestly to the

443

future, and to create something beautiful and meaningful enough that later generations would know, understand, and be enriched by it. He added his thoughts and his perspectives to the ongoing chronicle of existence, just as every writer does, and by doing so, he wrote himself into that story and added his own few strands to the golden thread.

Writing for the writer is a means of taking control of the experience of the world and, after locating himself or herself there, shaping it in such a way that others can learn to redeem their own lives. Yet so many readers wonder, often in awe, where all this material comes from. How could Homer see in the story of a hapless navigator the mythic terrors of the unknown and the will to overcome them? How could those scribes in biblical times conceive of the grandeur of God and the power of creation and set it all in just a few lines? The answer is that it is all in our imaginations. Each of us possesses one. And each of us, either consciously or unconsciously, looks upon the fabric of our experiences as a narrative, a golden thread broken only by our deaths, that tells us where we have been, where we are going, and what we have to do to get there. There is the suggestion in all of this that the imagination is mapping our survival, that it is showing us the way toward the sanity and the "happily ever after" that all of us crave and struggle so hard to find. And if we listen hard enough and long enough, we will learn how the story ends.

ACKNOWLEDGMENTS

A VOTE of thanks is owed to the students of my course, Essential Texts: A Background to Literature, for their support and encouragement, and in particular to Fred Howe, Don Paterson, Ralph Bongard, Ralph Teoli, and Andrew Colombo for their feedback and suggestions. I offer a particular vote of thanks to the following individuals: to Valerie Jacobs whose transcriptions of my lectures were useful notes for this book; to Ira Bassen, Lynda Shorten and Greg Kelly, my producers at CBC This Morning; to Patricia Grant for her insights; to Elise Gervais, Dr. Mary Barrie, Lorraine Nishisato, John Rawle, Ann Kirkland, and Constance Brown Demb; to my fellow writers Michael Winter, Antonio D'Alfonso, M.T. Kelly, Austin Clarke, and Dr. John O'Meara for listening and responding, and for their good advice.

I owe special debts of gratitude to those whose feedback and belief in this project helped it to take shape: to my compatriots and sounding-boards Ray Robertson, Bea Gonzalez, Dana Gioia, David Wevill, Zulfikar Ghose, and Barry Callaghan; to Charlotte Shiu, Roy Nicol, and Nicole Langlois of HarperCollins for their grace under fire and for the outstanding professionalism they have shown; to the generous hearts of Molly Peacock and Michael Enright whose inspiration was a guide to me down the dark corridors; to my publisher, Iris Tupholme and my agent Bruce Westwood for the strength of their convictions and their unwavering belief in this book; to the brilliance of Janice Weaver who helped to unravel many of the knots in this thread and who did so much to help me through the labyrinth; and to my family, Homer Meyer, Margaret Meyer, Dr. Carolyn Meyer, Kerry Johnston, and Katie Meyer for their sacrifices and for being there.

SELECT BIBLIOGRAPHY

Abrams, M.H. et. al. *The Norton Anthology of English Literature, Major Authors Edition.* New York: W.W. Norton and Company Incorporated, 1975.

Alexander, Michael. Ed. and Trans. *The Earliest English Poems.* Harmondsworth: Penguin Books, 1975.

Aristotle. *Poetics* in *Classical Literary Criticism.* Trans. T.S. Dorsch. Harmondsworth: Penguin, 1975.

Auden, W.H. *Collected Poems.* Ed. Edward Mendelson. New York: Random House, 1976.

Augustine, Saint. *Confessions.* Trans. R.S. Pine-Coffin. Harmondsworth: Penguin, 1974.

Boethius. *The Consolation of Philosophy.* Trans. V.E. Watts. Harmondsworth: Penguin, 1976.

Brooke, Rupert. *The Collected Poems: With a Memoir by Edward Marsh.* London: Sidgwick and Jackson, 1979.

Boswell, James. *Life of Johnson.* Ed. R.W. Chapman and J.D. Fleeman. Oxford: Oxford UP, 1976.

Burke, Edmund. *A Philosophical Enquiry into the Origin of our Ideas of the Sublime and Beautiful.* Ed. Adam Phillips. Oxford: Oxford UP, 1998.

Capellanus, Andreas. *The Art of Courtly Love.* Trans. John Jay Parry. New York: Norton, 1969.

Chekhov, Anton. *Uncle Vanya. Plays.* Trans. Elisaveta Fen. Harmondsworth: Penguin, 1987.

Dante Alighieri. *The Comedy of Dante Alighieri the Florentine: Cantica I: Hell (L'Inferno).* Trans. Dorothy L. Sayers. Harmondsworth: Penguin, 1972.

———. *La Vita Nuova.* Trans. Barbara Reynolds. Harmondsworth: Penguin, 1975.

de Voragine, Jacobus. *The Golden Legend: Selections.* Ed. and Trans. Christopher Stace. Harmondsworth: Penguin Books, 1998.

Eliot, T.S. *Collected Poems, 1909–1962.* London: Faber and Faber Limited, 1974.

Faulkner, William. *The Portable Faulkner.* Ed. Malcolm Cowley. New York: Viking Press, 1967.

Freud, Sigmund. *Civilization and Its Discontents.* Trans. James Strachey. New York: Norton, 1962.

Homer. *The Odyssey.* Trans. E.V. Rieu. Harmondsworth: Penguin, 1973.

Johnson, Samuel. *The History of Rasselas: Prince of Abissinia.* Ed. D.J. Enright. Harmondsworth: Penguin, 1976.

Joyce, James. *A Portrait of the Artist as a Young Man.* Harmondsworth: Penguin, 1975.

———. *Ulysses.* Harmondsworth: Penguin, 1975.

Kipling, Rudyard. *The Definitive Editon of Rudyard Kipling's Verse.* London: Hodder and Stoughton, 1982.

Machiavelli, Niccolò. *The Prince.* Trans. George Bull. Harmondsworth: Penguin, 1973.

Marvell, Andrew. *The Complete Poems.* Ed. Elizabeth Story Donno. Harmondsworth: Penguin Books, 1981.

Milton, John. *Paradise Lost.* Ed. Merritt Y. Hughes. Indianapolis: Bobbs-Merrill, 1975.

Monmouth, Geoffrey of. *The History of the Kings of Britain.* Trans. Lewis Thorpe. Harmondsworth: Penguin, 1976.

More, Thomas. *Utopia.* Trans. Paul Turner. Harmondsworth: Penguin, 1973.

Ovid. *Metamorphoses.* Trans. Mary M. Innes. Harmondsworth: Penguin, 1976.

Petrarch. *Selections from the Canzoniere and Other Works.* Trans. Mark Musa. Oxford: Oxford UP, 1992.

The Quest of the Holy Grail. Trans. P.M. Matarasso. Harmondsworth: Penguin, 1976.

Rilke, Rainer Maria. *The Collected Poems of Rainer Maria Rilke.* Ed. and Trans. Stephen Mitchell. New York: Vintage Books, 1989.

————. *Letters to a Young Poet.* Trans. Stephen Mitchell. New York: Vintage, 1987.

Shakespeare, William. *The Complete Works. (The Complete Pelican Shakespeare).* Ed. Alfred Harbage. London: Allen Lane The Penguin Press, 1969.

Shakespeare, William. *King Lear.* Ed. Alfred Harbage. Harmondsworth: Penguin, 1986.

————. *The Sonnets.* Ed. Douglas Bush and Alfred Harbage. Baltimore: Penguin, 1970.

————. *The Tempest.* Ed. Northrop Frye. Harmondsworth: Penguin, 1980.

Shaw, Bernard. *Heartbreak House: A Fantasia in the Russian Manner on English Themes.* Ed. Dan H. Laurence. Harmondsworth: Penguin, 1964.

Shelley, Mary. *Frankenstein. Three Gothic Novels.* Ed. Peter Fairclough. Harmondsworth: Penguin, 1974.

Sir Gawain and the Green Knight. Trans. Brian Stone. Harmondsworth: Penguin, 1974.

Sophocles. *The Theban Plays.* Trans. E.F. Watling. Harmondsworth: Penguin, 1973.

Spenser, Edmund. *The Faerie Queene.* Ed. Thomas P. Roche, Jr. Harmondsworth: Penguin Books, 1978.

Stone, Brian. Ed. and Trans. *Medieval English Verse.* Harmondsworth: Penguin Books, 1973.

Swift, Jonathan. *Gulliver's Travels.* Ed. Maxwell Geismar. New York: Pocket Books, 1972.

Vasari, Giorgio. *The Lives of the Artists.* Trans. George Bull. Harmondsworth: Penguin, 1976.

Vaughan, Henry. *The Complete Poems.* Ed. Alan Rudrum. Harmondsworth: Penguin Books, 1976.

Virgil. *The Aeneid.* Trans. W.F. Jackson Knight. Harmondsworth: Penguin, 1977.

————. *The Pastoral Poems.* Trans. E.V. Rieu. Harmondsworth: Penguin, 1972.

Voltaire. *Candide or Optimism.* Ed. Norman L. Torrey. North-
   brook: AHM, 1946.

Walcott, Derek. *The Odyssey: A Stage Version.* New York: Farrar,
   Straus and Giroux, 1993.

Wilhelm, James J. Ed. and Trans. *Medieval Song: An Anthology of
   Hymns and Lyrics.* New York: E.P. Dutton and Company, 1971.

Woolf, Virginia. *A Room of One's Own.* London: Granada, 1985.

Yeats, W.B. *Collected Poems of W.B. Yeats.* London: Macmillan,
   1978.

The following works can be found in Abrams' *The Norton Anthology of English Literature, Major Authors Edition*:

Matthew Arnold's "Dover Beach"; William Blake's "Mock On,
   Mock On," "Songs of Innocence," and "The Tyger"; Thomas
   Hardy's "The Convergence of the Twain"; John Keats' "On
   First Looking into Chapman's Homer"; John Milton's "Lyci-
   das" and "When I Consider How My Light Is Spent"; Alfred,
   Lord Tennyson's "Ulysses"; and William Wordsworth's Pref-
   ace to the *Lyrical Ballads* and "Tintern Abbey."

The Wanderer and *The Seafarer* can be found in Alexander's *The
   Earliest English Poems.*

Adam lay yboundin and *I Singe of a Maiden* can be found in
   Stone's *Medieval English Verse.*

"Stabat Mater Dolorosa" can be found in Wilhelm's *Medieval
   Song.*

INDEX